Vietnamese

Vietnamese: An Essential Grammar is a concise and user-friendly reference guide to modern Vietnamese. It presents a fresh and accessible description of the language in short, readable sections.

Features include:

- Clear and up-to-date examples of modern usage.
- Special attention to those points which often cause problems to English-speaking learners.
- Vietnamese / English comparisons and contrasts highlighted throughout.

The final section covers pronunciation, providing an introduction to the syllable structure of Vietnamese, and highlighting common errors made by English-speaking learners. Accompanying audio tracks for this chapter are available at www.routledge.com/9781138210707.

Vietnamese: An Essential Grammar is ideal for learners involved in independent study and for students in schools, colleges, universities and adult classes of all types.

Binh Ngo is the Director of the Vietnamese Language Program in the Department of East Asian Languages and Civilizations at Harvard University, USA.

Routledge Essential Grammars

Essential Grammars describe clearly and succinctly the core rules of each language and are up-to-date and practical reference guides to the most important aspects of languages used by contemporary native speakers. They are designed for elementary to intermediate learners and present an accessible description of the language, focusing on the real patterns of use today.

Essential Grammars are a reference source for the learner and user of the language, irrespective of level, setting out the complexities of the language in short, readable sections that are clear and free from jargon.

Essential Grammars are ideal either for independent study or for students in schools, colleges, universities and adult classes of all types.

Essential Grammars are available for the following languages:

Norwegian
Urdu
Spanish
Czech
Serbian
Chinese
German
Hindi
Romanian
Swedish
Hungarian
Korean
Turkish
English
Danish
Latvian
Polish
Thai
Finnish
Modern Hebrew
Greek
Dutch
Catalan
North Sámi
Portuguese
Vietnamese

For more information about this series, please visit: www.routledge.com/Routledge-Essential-Grammars/book-series/SE0549

Vietnamese

An Essential Grammar

Binh Ngo

LONDON AND NEW YORK

First published 2021
by Routledge
2 Park Square, Milton Park, Abingdon, Oxon OX14 4RN

and by Routledge
52 Vanderbilt Avenue, New York, NY 10017

Routledge is an imprint of the Taylor & Francis Group, an informa business

© 2021 Binh Ngo

The right of Binh Ngo to be identified as author of this work has been asserted by him in accordance with sections 77 and 78 of the Copyright, Designs and Patents Act 1988.

All rights reserved. No part of this book may be reprinted or reproduced or utilised in any form or by any electronic, mechanical, or other means, now known or hereafter invented, including photocopying and recording, or in any information storage or retrieval system, without permission in writing from the publishers.

Trademark notice: Product or corporate names may be trademarks or registered trademarks, and are used only for identification and explanation without intent to infringe.

British Library Cataloguing-in-Publication Data
A catalogue record for this book is available from the British Library

Library of Congress Cataloging-in-Publication Data
Names: Ngo, Binh, author.
Title: Vietnamese : an essential grammar / Binh Ngo.
Description: Abingdon, Oxon ; New York, NY : Routledge, 2020. | Series: Routledge essential grammars | Includes bibliographical references and index.
Identifiers: LCCN 2020007686 (print) | LCCN 2020007687 (ebook) | ISBN 9781138210714 (hardback) | ISBN 9781138210707 (paperback) | ISBN 9781315454610 (ebook)
Subjects: LCSH: Vietnamese language—Grammar.
Classification: LCC PL4374 .N215 2020 (print) | LCC PL4374 (ebook) | DDC 495.9/225—dc23
LC record available at https://lccn.loc.gov/2020007686
LC ebook record available at https://lccn.loc.gov/2020007687

ISBN: 978-1-138-21071-4 (hbk)
ISBN: 978-1-138-21070-7 (pbk)
ISBN: 978-1-315-45461-0 (ebk)

Typeset in Times New Roman
by Apex CoVantage, LLC

Visit the eResources: www.routledge.com/9781138210707

 Printed in the United Kingdom
by Henry Ling Limited

Contents

Preface		**xxvi**
Introduction		**xxviii**
1	Vietnamese language	xxviii
2	How this book is organized	xxix
3	Symbols, abbreviations, contractions and typography	xxxi

Chapter I   Nouns, noun phrases and their components   I

1.1	Introduction to the Vietnamese nouns			1
1.2	Classification of nouns			2
	1.2.1	Common nouns vs. proper nouns		2
	1.2.2	Concrete nouns vs. abstract nouns		4
	1.2.3	Countable nouns vs. uncountable nouns		4
		1.2.3.1	Abstract nouns denoting concepts	4
		1.2.3.2	Mass nouns denoting material and substance	5
		1.2.3.3	Collective nouns denoting groups of people and sets of items	5
1.3	Noun phrases and their components			5
	1.3.1	Noun phrase #1: number + classifier + noun		5
		1.3.1.1	Numbers	5
			1.3.1.1.1 Cardinal numbers	5
			1.3.1.1.2 Ordinal numbers	8
			1.3.1.1.3 Decimals, fractions and percentage	8
			1.3.1.1.4 Addition, subtraction, multiplication and division	9

Contents

	1.3.1.1.5	*Twice, twice as much/ many . . . , three times* + comparative adjective in Vietnamese	10
	1.3.1.1.6	*Half* and *and a half* in Vietnamese	10
	1.3.1.1.7	Dates and clock time	11
	1.3.1.1.8	Approximations: *several, a few, some*; *few, little, many, much* in Vietnamese	16
	1.3.1.1.9	*More than, over, fewer than, under* and *nearly* used before a specified number or amount in Vietnamese	18
	1.3.1.1.10	*Pair* and *couple* in Vietnamese	19
1.3.1.2	Classifiers		20
	1.3.1.2.1	Classifiers for different types of nouns	20
	1.3.1.2.2	Constructions in which no classifier is used	24
1.3.2	Noun phrase #2: plural marker + classifier + noun		25
1.3.2.1	Plural markers		26
1.3.2.2	Determiners *every, each, all, entire, whole* in Vietnamese		27
	1.3.2.2.1	Cả	27
	1.3.2.2.2	Tất cả	28
	1.3.2.2.3	Mọi	28
	1.3.2.2.4	Mỗi	29
	1.3.2.2.5	Từng	30
	1.3.2.2.6	Toàn and toàn bộ	31
1.3.2.3	Đều emphasizing the plurality		31
1.3.3	Noun phrase #3: noun + attributive		32
1.3.3.1	Adjectives as attributives		32
	1.3.3.1.1	Positive, comparative and superlative of the adjectives	33
1.3.3.2	Adverbs of degree		35
1.3.3.3	Demonstrative adjectives as attributives		35
1.3.3.4	Question words gì and nào as attributives		36
1.3.3.5	Nouns as attributives		38

Contents

	1.3.3.5.1	Introduction of nouns functioning as attributives	38
	1.3.3.5.2	Use of của	39
	1.3.3.5.3	Possessive pronouns and personal pronouns	40
	1.3.3.5.4	Third personal pronouns	44
	1.3.3.5.5	Personal pronouns in the plural	45
	1.3.3.5.6	Other personal pronouns	45
	1.3.3.6	Verbs and verb phrases as attributives	46
1.4	Main functions of nouns and noun phrases		48
	1.4.1	Subject of a sentence	48
	1.4.2	Direct object of a verb	48
	1.4.3	Indirect object of a verb	48
	1.4.4	Subject predicative	49
	1.4.5	Object predicative	49
	1.4.6	Complement of a preposition	49
	1.4.7	Modifier of a noun as its attributive	49

Chapter 2 Verbs, verb phrases and their components **50**

2.1	Introduction to the Vietnamese verbs		50
2.2	Types of verbs		50
	2.2.1	Là and the English *to be*	51
	2.2.2	Có and the English *to have*	52
	2.2.3	Semantic groups of verbs	53
2.3	Verb phrase #1: tense / aspect marker + verb		53
	2.3.1	Tense markers	53
	2.3.2	Aspect markers	55
	2.3.2.1	Vừa / mới / vừa mới	55
	2.3.2.2	Sắp	56
	2.3.2.3	Chưa	56
	2.3.2.4	Vẫn / còn / vẫn còn	56
	2.3.2.5	Đang	57
	2.3.2.6	Vẫn and vẫn còn referring to persistence	57
	2.3.2.7	Rồi	58
	2.3.2.8	Xong	59
	2.3.2.9	Hết	60
	2.3.2.10	Hẳn	61
2.4	Verb phrase #2: verb + object		62

vii

Contents

	2.4.1	Verbs of giving		62
		2.4.1.1	Verb + indirect object + direct object	62
		2.4.1.2	Verb + direct object + cho + indirect object	63
		2.4.1.3	Verb + cho + indirect object + direct object	63
	2.4.2	Verbs of receiving		64
		2.4.2.1	Verb + direct object + của + indirect object	64
		2.4.2.2	Verb + của + indirect object + modified direct object	65
	2.4.3	Causative verbs		65
	2.4.4	Verbs of speaking, thinking and perceiving		68
		2.4.4.1	Verb + object	68
		2.4.4.2	$Verb_1$ + $verb_2$	69
		2.4.4.3	Verb + preposition + noun / pronoun	69
		2.4.4.4	Verb + clause	72
	2.4.5	Verbs of equating		72
2.5	Verb phrase #3: verb + adjective			73
	2.5.1	Adjective functioning as adverb of manner		73
	2.5.2	Positive, comparative and superlative of adjective modifying verb		74
	2.5.3	Bisyllabic adjectives modifying verb		74
	2.5.4	Adjectives following một cách		74
2.6	Verb phrase #4: adverb + verb, or verb + adverb			75
	2.6.1	Adverbs of degree		75
		2.6.1.1	Adverbs of degree modifying verbs of feelings	75
		2.6.1.2	Preference	76
		2.6.1.3	[Càng] ngày càng and mỗi lúc một	77
		2.6.1.4	Chỉ	78
	2.6.2	Adverbs of frequency		79
2.7	Verbs of motion			81
	2.7.1	Đi		81
		2.7.1.1	Đi + destination	81
		2.7.1.2	Đi + preposition + destination	81
	2.7.2	Other verbs of motion		82
	2.7.3	Verbs of motion and prepositions used with the geographical names of Vietnam		86
	2.7.4	Transitive verbs of motion with no direction		88
2.8	Verbs of appearance, existence and disappearance			89

	2.8.1	Có	89
	2.8.2	Còn	90
	2.8.3	Hết	90
	2.8.4	Mất	91
	2.8.5	Xuất hiện	92
	2.8.6	Xảy ra and diễn ra	92
	2.8.7	Biến mất	93
2.9	Verbs of reaching or bringing to a particular state or condition		93
2.10	Modal verbs		94
	2.10.1	Cần	94
	2.10.2	Có thể	95
	2.10.3	Dám	96
	2.10.4	Định	96
	2.10.5	Muốn	97
	2.10.6	Nên	97
	2.10.7	Phải	98
2.11	Imperatives		98
	2.11.1	Hãy	99
	2.11.2	Cứ	99
	2.11.3	Đi	100
	2.11.4	Nhé	100
	2.11.5	Mời	101
	2.11.6	Đã	102
	2.11.7	Đừng	102
	2.11.8	Không and không được	103
	2.11.9	Chớ	103
2.12	Verb constructions equivalent to the English passive voice		104
2.13	Main functions of verbs and verb phrases		105
	2.13.1	Predicate of a sentence	105
	2.13.2	Subject of a sentence	106
	2.13.3	Object of a verb	106
	2.13.4	Modifier of a noun as its attributive	106

Chapter 3 Adjectives, adjective phrases and their components — 107

3.1	Introduction to the Vietnamese adjectives		107
	3.1.1	Main distinction between a Vietnamese adjective and an English adjective	107

Contents

	3.1.2 Adjectives describing qualities and state of affairs	107
	3.1.3 Gradable and ungradable adjectives	108
3.2	Adjective phrases and their components	108
	3.2.1 Adjective phrase #1: adverb of degree + adjective	108
	3.2.2 Adjective phrase #2: adjective + adverb of degree	110
	3.2.2.1 Lắm vs. rất	110
	3.2.3 Adjective phrase #3: adjective + comparison marker	111
	3.2.3.1 Vietnamese construction for English *He is much older than me / than I am*	112
	3.2.3.2 Vietnamese construction for English *He is three years older than me / than I am. / He is three years my senior*	112
	3.2.3.3 Hơn as a full adjective	112
	3.2.3.4 Vietnamese constructions for English *less + adjective* and *the least + adjective*	112
	3.2.3.5 So với denoting the comparative of the adjective	113
	3.2.4 Adjective phrase #4: aspect / tense marker + adjective or: adjective + aspect / tense marker	113
	3.2.5 Adjective phrase #5: adjective + object or: adjective + preposition + object	114
	3.2.6 Adjective phrase #6: adjective + number + weight / length / height / temperature measures	115
	3.2.7 Adjective phrase #7: adjective + verb of motion	116
3.3	Main functions of adjectives and adjective phrases	116
	3.3.1 Modifier of a noun as its attributive	117
	3.3.2 Predicate of a sentence	117
	3.3.3 Modifier of a verb as an adverbial	117

Chapter 4   Word-formation   119

4.1	Introduction to the Vietnamese word	119
4.2	Main processes of forming new words in Vietnamese	119
	4.2.1 Compounding	120
	4.2.1.1 Co-ordinate compounds	120
	4.2.1.2 Subordinate compounds	121
	4.2.2 Affixation	124
	4.2.2.1 Prefixation	125
	4.2.2.2 Suffixation	128

4.2.3	Reduplication		130
	4.2.3.1	Whole resemblance	130
		4.2.3.1.1	Base word is completely repeated	130
		4.2.3.1.2	Tone changes	131
		4.2.3.1.3	Tone and final consonant change	131
	4.2.3.2	Partial resemblance	132
		4.2.3.2.1	Rhyme of reduplicated syllable changes	132
		4.2.3.2.2	Initial consonants change	132
	4.2.3.3	Trisyllabic reduplicatives	134
	4.2.3.4	Quadrisyllabic reduplicatives	134
	4.2.3.5	None of the syllables convey any meaning	135
	4.2.3.6	Reduplicatives containing -iếc	135
	4.2.3.7	Meanings of reduplicatives	135
		4.2.3.7.1	Nouns	135
		4.2.3.7.2	Adjectives	136
		4.2.3.7.3	Verbs	136
		4.2.3.7.4	Onomatopoeic words	137
4.2.4	Borrowing		137
	4.2.4.1	Loanwords from Chinese	137
		4.2.4.1.1	From second century BC to seventh century AD	137
		4.2.4.1.2	From seventh to seventeenth centuries	138
		4.2.4.1.3	From seventeenth century on	143
		4.2.4.1.4	Loanwords from the dialects of Chinese	144
		4.2.4.1.5	Chinese monosyllabic loanwords as components for word-formation	145
		4.2.4.1.6	Chinese quadrisyllabic template	145
	4.2.4.2	Loanwords from French	148
	4.2.4.3	Loanwords from English	150

Chapter 5   Sentences   152

5.1	Introduction to the Vietnamese sentences		152
	5.1.1	The constituents of a sentence	152
		5.1.1.1	Subject and predicate	152

Contents

	5.1.1.2	Object and object predicative	153
	5.1.1.3	Adverbials	153
		5.1.1.3.1 Adverbial of manner	154
		5.1.1.3.2 Adverbial of place	154
		5.1.1.3.3 Adverbial of time	155
		5.1.1.3.4 Adverbial of frequency	157
		5.1.1.3.5 Adverbial of degree	157
		5.1.1.3.6 Adverbial of cause	158
		5.1.1.3.7 Adverbial of purpose	159
		5.1.1.3.8 Adverbial of means	159
		5.1.1.3.9 Indefinite pronouns and adverbs	159
		5.1.1.3.10 Sentence adverbials	160
5.1.2	Classification of sentences		160
	5.1.2.1	Based on major purposes of communication	160
	5.1.2.2	Based on internal construction	160
	5.1.2.3	Positive and negative sentences	161
	5.1.2.4	Active and passive sentences	161
5.2	Declarative sentences		161
5.2.1	Positive declarative sentences		161
	5.2.1.1	Verbal predicate	161
	5.2.1.2	Adjectival predicate	162
	5.2.1.3	Nominal predicate	162
5.2.2	Negative declarative sentences		162
	5.2.2.1	Negative sentences with verbal predicate	162
	5.2.2.2	Negative sentences with adjectival predicate	164
	5.2.2.3	Negative sentences with nominal predicate	164
	5.2.2.4	Double negative with meaning of affirmation	164
5.3	Interrogative sentences		166
5.3.1	Interrogative sentences that do not contain questions word		166
	5.3.1.1	Construction có . . . không	166
	5.3.1.2	Construction có phải . . . không	166
	5.3.1.3	Replies that begin with *Yes*, *Yeah* or *No*	167
	5.3.1.4	Construction đã . . . chưa	167
	5.3.1.5	Construction . . . , phải không	168
	5.3.1.6	Construction có phải . . . không	168
	5.3.1.7	Construction . . . à	169
	5.3.1.8	Construction . . . chứ	170
	5.3.1.9	Construction . . . được không	170
	5.3.1.10	Construction . . . hay . . . meaning "or"	171
	5.3.1.11	Construction *either . . . or . . .* in Vietnamese	171

xii

5.3.2	Interrogative sentences containing question words		172
	5.3.2.1	Location	172
	5.3.2.2	Motion	172
	5.3.2.3	Time	173
	5.3.2.4	Cause	174
	5.3.2.5	Purpose	175
	5.3.2.6	Quantity	176
	5.3.2.7	*Who* and *whom* in Vietnamese	177
	5.3.2.8	*What* and *which* as question words in Vietnamese	177
	5.3.2.9	Plural marker những preceding question words ai, đâu, gì	179
5.3.3	Rhetorical questions		179

5.4 Exclamatory sentences   180

5.4.1	Quá, ôi	180
5.4.2	Thật	180
5.4.3	Thật là	180
5.4.4	Ơi là	181

5.5 Emphatic constructions   181

5.5.1	Emphatic positive declarative sentences with cũng		181
	5.5.1.1	Emphasized subject is denoted by the question word **ai** or the noun phrase **noun + nào**	181
	5.5.1.2	Emphasized object is expressed by the question word **ai** or the noun phrase **noun + gì / nào**	181
	5.1.1.3	Emphasized adverbials of place and time that are indicated by **ở đâu, bao giờ** or the noun phrase **noun + nào**	181
5.5.2	Emphatic positive declarative sentences with chẳng and chả following a question word		182
5.5.3	Emphatic positive declarative sentences with bất cứ / bất kì		182
5.5.4	Emphatic positive declarative sentences with có		183
5.5.5	Emphatic positive declarative sentences with có . . . mới . . .		183
5.5.6	Emphatic positive declarative sentences with mới showing emphasis on the adverbial of time		183
5.5.7	Emphatic positive declarative sentences with vừa / mới / vừa mới . . . đã . . .		184
5.5.8	Not only . . . but also . . . in Vietnamese		184
5.5.9	Emphatic có and những		185

5.5.10	Emphatic chính		186
	5.5.10.1	Subject	186
	5.5.10.2	Predicate with là	186
	5.5.10.3	Object	186
	5.5.10.4	Adverbials of cause and purpose	186
5.5.11	Emphatic ngay		187
5.5.12	Emphatic ngay cả		187
5.5.13	Emphatic chỉ ... là ...		187
5.5.14	Emphatic mãi		187
5.5.15	Emphatic tận		188
5.5.16	Emphatic quantity bao nhiêu là and toàn là		189
5.5.17	Emphatic negative declarative sentences		190
	5.5.17.1	Hề	190
	5.5.17.2	Specific construction "negation + verb + question word"	190
	5.5.17.3	English negative pronouns *none*, *no one*, *nobody*, *nothing*, *neither*, *nor* and negative adverbs *never*, *nowhere* in Vietnamese	191
5.5.18	Emphatic constructions "topic – comment"		193
	5.5.18.1	Subject as topic	193
	5.5.18.2	Subject as topic followed by a sentence	194
	5.5.18.3	Predicate as topic	194
	5.5.18.4	Object as topic	195
	5.5.18.5	Place and time as topic	195
5.6	Sentence particles		195
5.6.1	Initial particles		196
	5.6.1.1	À	196
	5.6.1.2	Ấy	196
	5.6.1.3	Dạ	196
	5.6.1.4	Mà	197
	5.6.1.5	Nào	197
	5.6.1.6	Ơi	197
	5.6.1.7	Thảo nào	198
	5.6.1.8	Thế à	198
	5.6.1.9	Thế thì	199
	5.6.1.10	Thì	199
	5.6.1.11	Thưa	199
5.6.2	Final particles		200
	5.6.2.1	Ạ	200
	5.6.2.2	Ấy	200
	5.6.2.3	Chứ	201

	5.6.2.4	Đây	201
	5.6.2.5	Đấy	201
	5.6.2.6	Hở	202
	5.6.2.7	Mà	202
	5.6.2.8	Này	203
	5.6.2.9	Nhỉ	203
	5.6.2.10	Rồi	203
	5.6.2.11	Thật	203
	5.6.2.12	Vậy	204

5.7 Compound sentences 204

5.7.1 Listing of two or more events with co-ordinating conjunction và meaning "and" 204

5.7.2 Contrasting two events with conjunctions nhưng or mà 205

5.7.3 Introducing a choice with conjunctions hoặc [là] or hay [là] 206

5.7.4 Contrasting two events by confirming one and negating another with không . . . mà . . . or . . . chứ không . . . 207

5.7.5 Expressing parallel increase or decrease with càng . . . càng . . . 207

5.7.6 Emphasizing a combination of two or more actions, events or features with vừa . . . vừa . . . 207

5.7.7 Emphasizing two items denoted by nouns with cả . . . và . . . 208

5.7.8 Emphasizing an added feature with đã . . . lại [còn] . . . [nữa] 208

5.8 Complex sentences 209

5.8.1 Nominal clauses 209

5.8.1.1 Subordinate declarative clauses 209

5.8.1.2 Subordinate interrogative clauses and the position of the question word in Vietnamese and English 210

5.8.2 Relative clauses 211

5.8.2.1 Conjunction mà 212

5.8.2.2 Nơi, khi and vì sao 212

5.8.3 Adverbial clauses 213

5.8.3.1 Place clauses 213

5.8.3.2 Temporal (or time) clauses 214

5.8.3.3 Conditional clauses 216

5.8.3.3.1 Nếu 216

5.8.3.3.2 Giả sử 218

Contents

5.8.3.3.3	Giá [như]	218
5.8.3.3.4	Mà	219
5.8.3.3.5	Hễ cứ . . . là / thì	219
5.8.3.3.6	Trừ phi	219
5.8.3.3.7	Kẻo	220
5.8.3.3.8	Muốn . . . phải	220
5.8.3.3.9	Nhỡ	221

5.8.3.4 Concessive clauses 221
5.8.3.5 Reason clauses 222
5.8.3.6 Result clauses 223
5.8.3.7 Purpose clauses 224

5.8.3.7.1	Để	224
5.8.3.7.2	Mà	224
5.8.3.7.3	Nhằm	224

5.8.3.8 Manner clauses 225
5.8.3.9 Proportion clauses 225
5.8.3.10 Similarity clauses with correlative
ai – người ấy, nào – ấy, đâu – đấy, thế
nào – thế ấy / sao – vậy 225
5.8.3.11 *W*-conditional clauses and *no matter*
in Vietnamese 226

5.8.3.11.1	Bất cứ / bất kì . . . cũng . . .	226
5.8.3.11.2	Dù . . . thì . . . cũng . . .	227
5.8.3.11.3	*No matter* in Vietnamese	227

Chapter 6 Problem words, phrases and constructions 229

6.1 Còn 229

6.1.1 As a full verb meaning "have something left;
there is / are left" 229

6.1.2 As an aspect marker denoting a continuing action
or state. **Còn** is equivalent to the English *still* 229

6.1.3 As an adverb of degree placed before an adjective
in the comparative to refer to a greater extent or
degree. **Còn** is similar to the English *even* or *still* 230

6.1.4 As a conjunction that serves to switch from one
subject to another one. **Còn** is similar to the
English *and* 230

6.2 Cũng and English *also, too, as well* and *either*
(in a negative statement) 230

xvi

6.3	Được			231
	6.3.1	As a full verb meaning "receive, get." The object should be something favorable		231
	6.3.2	As a full verb meaning "gain something necessary for further movement or development"		231
	6.3.3	As a full verb meaning "win a lawsuit; win a card game and get money"		231
	6.3.4	As a full verb used before a number to suggest that a number or an amount has been reched		231
	6.3.5	As a verb placed in front of another verb to convey the meaning "have the right or permission to do something"		232
	6.3.6	As a verb placed in front of another verb to denote an opportunity or a chance to do something		232
	6.3.7	As a verb inserted between another verb and the object or placed at the end of a statement with the meaning "be able to do something"		232
	6.3.8	As a verb placed before a transitive verb to refer to an action that is expressed by the passive voice in English		233
	6.3.9	As an adjective meaning "good, suitable"		233
	6.3.10	As an adverb used after a verb to emphasize the favorable feature of an event or action. The event or action itself is favorable from the speaker's perspective		233
	6.3.11	As an adverb used after a negation and in front of an adjective to reduce the unfavorable feature of an event. The event itself is unfavorable from the speaker's point of view		233
6.4	Lại			234
	6.4.1	As a full verb, **lại** conveys the meaning "come or go over, usually within a short distance" and is used chiefly in conversational Vietnamese		234
	6.4.2	**Lại** follows a verb		234
		6.4.2.1	To convey the sense of redoing something or performing an action again. In some cases, **lại** is similar to the English prefix *re-*	234
		6.4.2.2	To convey the sense of an action opposite of another action that was done before	234
		6.4.2.3	To convey the sense of an action directed towards one point	235

	6.4.2.4	To convey the sense of keeping something closed, locked or stopped; if the verb takes an object, the object is inserted between the verb and **lại**	235
6.4.3		**Lại** follows some adjectives to convey the meaning of reduction in size or amount	235
6.4.4		**Lại** serves as a conjuction to join two parts or a sentence to suggest that something is added to what has been spoken of before. Both parts should be either "favorable" or "unfavorable." **Đã** can be used before the first part to show emphasis on the addition. It is similar to the English *and moreover*	235
6.4.5		**Lại** is an adverb placed before a verb to imply that what happened or is happening is unfavorable. It is similar to the English *again*	236
6.4.6		**Lại** is an adverb placed after the question words of cause **tại sao** and **sao** to refer to the speaker's surprise	236
6.5	Mà		236
6.5.1		**Mà** serves as a conjunction	236
	6.5.1.1	To contrast two events, the second one of which is unexpected because of the first one	236
	6.5.1.2	To contrast two events. The first one is negated and the second one is confirmed	236
	6.5.1.3	To refer to a condition	237
	6.5.1.4	To refer to a purpose	237
	6.5.1.5	To show emphasis on the reason	237
	6.5.1.6	To be part of correlative conjunction **không những / không chỉ . . . mà còn . . .** and **không chỉ . . . mà cả . . .**	237
	6.5.1.7	To connect a subornative relative clause to the main clause as	237
	6.5.1.7.1	Relative pronoun	237
	6.5.1.7.2	Relative adverb of place	238
	6.5.1.7.3	Relative adverb of time	238
	6.5.1.8	To join two phrases of a sentence to convey the speaker's surprise or warning that something is unusual or bad may happen	238

	6.5.2		**Mà** serves as an emphatic particle	238
		6.5.2.1	As an initial particle, **mà** is fronted in a second statement with the meaning "moreover, besides" to introduce something new that is added to the idea conveyed in the previous statement	238
		6.5.2.2	As a final particle, **mà** is placed at the end of a statement to show emphasis on the fact that has already happened or is going on. The statement explains the reason for what has been mentioned	238
6.6	Mới			239
	6.6.1		As an adjective meaning "new"	239
	6.6.2		As an aspect marker meaning "just"	239
	6.6.3		As an aspect marker to put emphasis on the adverbial of time	239
	6.6.4		As a corellative aspect marker used with **đã**, **mới** shows emphasis on the quickness of the second action that took place right after the first action	239
	6.6.5		As a correlative word used with **có**, **mới** emphasizes the fulfillment of a requirement in order to perform an action	239
	6.6.6		As a correlative word used with **thôi** which is placed at the end of a statement, **mới** means "just, only" and refers to the past tense	239
	6.6.7		As an emphatic word placed before a number or a time to suggest that the number is too small or the time is too early; the word **có** can follow **mới** and precede the number for more emphasis	240
6.7	Phải			240
	6.7.1		As an adjective meaning "right": **tay <u>phải</u>** "right hand / arm;" **chân <u>phải</u>** "right leg / foot;" **phía bên [tay] <u>phải</u>** "on the right side;" **rẽ [tay] <u>phải</u>** "turn right;" etc.	240
	6.7.2		As a modal verb placed in front of another verb to express advice or an obligation	240
	6.7.3		As an adverb inserted between the main verb and the object to suggest that the subject runs into something unpleasant	240

6.8	Rồi		241
	6.8.1	As an aspect marker that refers to the completion of an action that began in the past. With this function, **rồi** is similar to the English *already*	241
	6.8.2	As an aspect marker that suggests that an event will be arriving in the future earlier than expected	241
	6.8.3	As a conjunction which denotes two actions occurring after one another. **Rồi** is similar to the English *and* or *and then*	241
	6.8.4	As a conjunction to join two parts of a sentence, the first of which serves as the reason or condition leading to the result in the second one. There is no equivalent in English	241
	6.8.5	As a final particle	241
6.9	Thì		242
	6.9.1	As a correlative conjunction, **thì** is used together with **nếu**, **giá**, **mà** and **hễ** in a complex sentence with a subordinate clause of condition. The subordinate clause precedes the main clause, and **thì** comes at the beginning of the main clause. In some instances, **thì** is equivalent to the English *then*	242
	6.9.2	As a correlative conjunction, **thì** is used together with **khi** or **trong khi** in a complex sentence with a subordinate clause of time. The subordinate clause precedes the main clause, and **thì** comes at the beginning of the main clause. With this function, **thì** does not have the English equivalent. The action is long-lasting in the subordinate clause and short in the main clause	242
	6.9.3	As an emphatic word used before the second action that took place right after the first one. This use of **thì** refers to the past tense	242
	6.9.4	As an emphatic word used after the question word of time that denotes the future tense. **Thì** shows emphasis on the speaker's expectation of an event that, in her / his opinion, should happen soon. **Thì** may also express the speaker's impatience. A parent may say to the child	242
	6.9.5	As an emphatic word used after the subject or the topic to introduce a comment on the subject or topic	243

6.10	English *and* and Vietnamese và	243	
6.11	English *good* and Vietnamese **tốt**	243	
	6.11.1 of high quality. Vietnamese uses **tốt** only in in some phrases	243	
	6.11.2 having or showing talent or skill. Vietnamese uses **giỏi**, not **tốt**	243	
	6.11.3 pleasant, enjoyable. Vietnamese uses different words depending on the nouns	244	
	6.11.4 convenient, suitable. Vietnamese used different words depending on the nouns	245	
	6.11.5 producing or promising to produce a favorable result	245	
	6.11.6 used to say how long something will continue or be valid, or something is still suitable to eat or drink. Vietnamese uses different expressions	245	
6.12	English *for* and Vietnamese cho	246	
	6.12.1 *For* as a conjunction meaning "because" is used in formal speech. *For* is fronted in a subordinate clause to refer to the reason why the preceding statement is true. It does not suggest why an action was performed, but just gives a piece of additional information which explains it. Vietnamese uses **vì** for this function	246	
	6.12.2 *For* as a preposition conveys many meanings. Only some of them correspond to the Vietnamese **cho**. The other ones are expressed by different words or phrases in Vietnamese.	246	
	6.12.2.1 indicating that something is intended to be given to someone or to belong to someone. Vietnamese uses **cho**	246	
	6.12.2.2 referring to an employee working for a company or a player of a particular team. Vietnamese uses **cho**	246	
	6.12.2.3 indicating that someone votes for someone. Vietnamese uses **cho**	247	
	6.12.2.4 referring to a place someone or something is going to or towards. Vietnamese uses different verbs of motion as prepositions or just the verb **đi**	247	
	6.12.2.5 indicating an amount of time or space. Vietnamese expresses this meaning in different ways	247	

		6.12.2.6	indicating the time an event is scheduled for. Vietnamese uses the preposition **vào** for a date and **vào lúc** for a clock time	247
		6.12.2.7	indicating the price or rate at which one pays. Vietnamese does not use any preposition	248
		6.12.2.8	showing the purpose of an object or action. Vietnamese uses **để**	248
		6.12.2.9	used to say what someone is (un)able to do. Vietnamese uses **đối với**	248
		6.12.2.10	used as a preposition of reason. Vietnamese chiefly uses **vì**	248
		6.12.2.11	There are several frequently used English phrases or constructions containing *for*, whose ideas Vietnamese conveys (1) with **cho** and (2) without **cho**	248
6.13	English *if* and Vietnamese **nếu**			249
	6.13.1	indicating the condition on which an action can or cannot be done. Vietnamese uses **nếu**		249
	6.13.2	indicating the concession, meaning "althogh, in spite of the fact that." *If* is often used with *even*. Vietnamese uses the construction **dù [cho] . . . thì . . . cũng [vẫn]**		250
	6.13.3	making a polite request or suggestion. Vietnamese does not have the equivalent construction and uses **được không** at the end of the question instead		250
	6.13.4	used in reported questions meaning "whether." Vietnamese uses the construction **có . . . không** for the present or future tense and **đã . . . chưa** for the past tense that encirles the predicate		250
6.14	English *so*			250
	6.14.1	Adverb *so* means		250
		6.14.1.1	to a degree that is suggested or stated. *So* is used before an adjective. Vietnamese uses **như thế** or **như vậy** after the adjective	250
		6.14.1.2	to a great degree; extremely. Vietnamese uses **rất, lắm, thật** or **vô cùng**	251
		6.14.1.3	in the same way. Vietnamese uses **cũng thế** or **cũng vậy**	251

- 6.14.2 Pronoun *so* refers to something that has just been stated or suggested. Vietnamese uses **như thế** or **như vậy** — 251
- 6.14.3 Conjunction *so* — 252
  - 6.14.3.1 meaning "therefore, for that reason." Vietnamese uses **vì vậy**, **vì thế**, **nên** or **cho nên** — 252
  - 6.14.3.2 used to state the purpose of the action mentioned in the previous statement. Vietnamese uses **để** — 252
  - 6.14.3.3 placed in front of a statement or a question to introduce them. Vietnamese uses **thế là** for the statement and **thế nào** for the question. **Thế là** is not followed by a comma, but **thế nào** is — 252
  - 6.14.3.4 used as an unpolite reply to a statement which is unimportant in the speaker's opinion. Vietnamese uses **thì đã sao [nào]** — 252
- 6.14.4 Adjective *so* functioning as the predicate with the meaning "true." Vietnamese uses different expressions — 253
- 6.15 English *that* — 253
  - 6.15.1 Demonstrative adjective *that, those* — 253
    - 6.15.1.1 used before a noun to indicate which person, thing or idea is being shown, pointed to or mentioned. Vietnamese uses **ấy** or **đó**, that are interchangeable, and **kia**. For the difference between **ấy / đó** and **kia**, please see 1.3.3.3. — 253
    - 6.15.1.2 used before *one* or *ones* to refer to the one that is far away or less familiar, compared to the one denoted by *this*. Vietnamese uses **kia** for *that* and **này** for *this* — 253
  - 6.15.2 Demonstrative pronoun *that* — 253
    - 6.15.2.1 used before the verb *to be* with the same meaning as in 6.14.1.1 — 253
    - 6.15.2.2 used after a verb or a preposition to refer to an action or event that has just been mentioned. Vietnamese uses **điều ấy / đó, việc ấy / đó, chuyện**

		ấy / đó or just thế / vậy after a verb and đó / đấy after a preposition	254
	6.15.3	Conjunction *that* connects a nominal declarative subordinate clause to the main clause. Vietnamese uses **rằng** or **là**	254
	6.15.4	Relative pronoun *that* connects a relative subordinate clause to the main clause. Vietnamese uses **mà** if *that* is not the subject of the subordinate clause	254
	6.15.5	Adverb of degree *that* placed in front of an adjective or another adverb, which is usually a quantifier, refers to the degree that is stated or suggested. Vietnamese uses **[đến] như thế**	255

Glossary of grammatical terms 256
Grammar index 266

Chapter 7 Pronunciation 273

7.1	Writing systems			273
7.2	Vietnamese alphabet			275
7.3	Structure of a Vietnamese syllable			276
	7.3.1	Tone		277
	7.3.2	Nuclear vowels		279
		7.3.2.1	Monophthong nuclear vowels	279
			7.3.2.1.1 Front vowels	279
			7.3.2.1.2 Central vowels	280
			7.3.2.1.3 Back vowels	282
		7.3.2.2	Diphthong nuclear vowels	283
	7.3.3	Initial consonants		284
		7.3.3.1	Initial consonants similar to English consonants	285
		7.3.3.2	Specific initial consonants	285
			7.3.3.2.1 Consonant [t] <t>	285
			7.3.3.2.2 Consonant [c] <ch>	285
			7.3.3.2.3 Consonant [ɲ] <nh>	286
			7.3.3.2.4 Consonant [k] <c>/<k>/<qu>	286
			7.3.3.2.5 Consonant [χ] <kh>	286
			7.3.3.2.6 Consonant [ɣ] <g>/<gh>	287
			7.3.3.2.7 Consonant [ŋ] <ng>/<ngh>	287
	7.3.4	Labialization		288
	7.3.5	Finals		289
		7.3.5.1	Semivowel finals	289
		7.3.5.2	Consonant finals	289

7.4	Difficulties of the Vietnamese sound system			293
	7.4.1	Tones		293
		7.4.1.1	Mid-level tone	293
		7.4.1.2	Mid-level tone in front of high-rising tone	293
		7.4.1.3	Vietnamese tones and English intonation	294
	7.4.2	Sounds		294
		7.4.2.1	Rounded and unrounded nuclear vowels	294
		7.4.2.2	Openness of the vowels	295

Glossary of phonetic terms   **296**
Bibliography   **301**

Preface

This book is the first work on practical Vietnamese grammar written in English. It offers a comprehensive account of present-day Vietnamese grammar and is addressed primarily to English-speaking learners of Vietnamese. Vietnamese, like any other language, is full of problems for the foreign learner. By comparing Vietnamese and English grammar, usage and pronunciation wherever the author finds it necessary, this work is unique in the sense of pointing out the linguistic difficulties which an English-speaking learner of Vietnamese may encounter. In addition to dealing with these problems whenever they come up in each chapter, this book contains a specific chapter titled *Problem words, phrases and constructions*, in which explanations for the tricky Vietnamese words, phrases and grammatical constructions compared with their English counterparts warn the learner of potential linguistic errors (s)he often makes due to the influence of English. The chapter *Pronunciation* also deals with the phonetic errors typical of English-speaking learners. The comparative analysis of the two languages is also helpful for Vietnamese learners of English. This book serves as a textbook as well as a reference work. The index shows both the section of a chapter and the page for the item which a user looks for.

This essential grammar of Vietnamese is intended for intermediate, advanced and advanced-high learners, as well as for instructors of Vietnamese. However, beginning learners can also use this book to study relatively simple points of Vietnamese grammar and phonetics.

In writing this book, I have drawn on my almost forty years of experience in teaching Vietnamese to non-native speakers and in doing research on Vietnamese linguistics and language pedagogy. From 1980 through 1991, I taught Vietnamese to Russian-speaking students at Moscow Lomonosov University, where I developed several textbooks. I have taught Vietnamese at Harvard University since 1992 and published a number of textbooks and courses for teaching Vietnamese to English-speaking students, as well as a course of American English for Vietnamese speakers. My research works include numerous papers on Vietnamese linguistics, contrastive analysis and foreign language teaching methodology delivered at international conferences, and articles on the Vietnamese language published in Vietnam's major newspapers, journals and magazines.

My deep gratitude is expressed to the Department of East Asian Languages and Civilizations at Harvard University for its strong encouragement and support for my teaching and research work. I am grateful to my colleagues in our department of East Asian Languages and Civilizations Zhao Jie (赵洁) for her checking the meanings and sequence of components of several Chinese bisyllabic loanwords in the chapter *Word-formation* of this book, and James Chan (陳忠) for his help with the Cantonese loanwords in the same chapter. My sincere appreciation is due to Mr. Tony Di Bartolo and Mr. Kevin McGowan of the Harvard Media Production Center for their excellent production of the audio files for Chapter 7 of this book. I would like to say sincere thanks to Ms. Naia Poyer of the Department of East Asian Languages and Civilizations at Harvard for recording the English part of the audio files.

Introduction

1 Vietnamese language

Vietnamese is the official language of Vietnam. It is spoken by more than ninety million people in Vietnam and about four million overseas Vietnamese. The language belongs to the subfamily of Mon-Khmer languages in the Austroasiatic family of languages.

Vietnamese has a vast variety of dialects that can be divided roughly into four main groups: northern dialect, north-central dialect, south-central dialect and southern dialect. The dialectal differences are reflected chiefly in the vocabulary and phonetic system. There are very few differences concerning grammatical constructions. In spite of the dialectal differences, Vietnamese people in all regions of the country have no difficulty understanding one another.

The version of the northern dialect spoken in the capital city of Hanoi is the oldest dialect of the language. It represents the phonetic system more fully than the other dialects. Its vocabulary is regarded as the standard vocabulary that is used in the media, books and education.

The second most significant dialect is the dialect spoken in Saigon (Ho Chi Minh City), the biggest city of the country and the most important political, economic and cultural center in southern Vietnam.

This book introduces standard Vietnamese based on the Hanoi dialect. However, in some cases, the equivalents from the Saigon dialect are also provided.

Vietnamese is a tone language, in which changes in the tone of syllables indicate different meanings. Each syllable has a particular tone. The Hanoi dialect has six tones, which are discussed in Chapter 7.

Vietnamese is a member of the group of isolating languages which have no inflectional endings. All the words are invariable, and the grammatical relationships are shown by auxiliary words and word order.

Many words in everyday vocabulary are monosyllabic (consisting of one syllable) or bisyllabic (consisting of two syllables). The number of polysyllabic words consisting of more than two syllables is rather small. In addition to the vocabulary of Mon-Khmer origin, Vietnamese has a large number of Chinese loanwords. The number of loanwords borrowed from French and English is much smaller. The loanwords are discussed in the chapter Word-formation.

For a very long period Chinese characters were used in Vietnam for official documents of the royal court, as well as for poetry, literature and education. Modern Vietnamese employs the romanized writing system, which was devised in the early seventeenth century and officially became the national writing system in the early twentieth century. The writing systems of the language are discussed in Chapter 7.

2 How this book is organized

The book is divided into seven chapters as follows:

Chapter 1: Nouns, nouns phrases and their components

This chapter discusses noun as a word class, as well as other word classes which function as components of noun phrases, such as numerals along with how addition, subtraction, multiple and division, dates and clock time are expressed in Vietnamese; classifiers as they are conventionally called; determiners; adjectives, including demonstrative adjectives, serving as attributives in noun phrases; personal pronouns; kinship terms used as personal pronouns. The chapter concludes with a summary of main syntactical functions of nouns and noun phrases.

Chapter 2: Verbs, verb phrases and their components

Verbs as a word class, as well as its grammatical categories such as tense, aspect, voice; modal verbs and imperatives; semantic groups of verbs and other word classes functioning as components of verb phrases are dealt here. The chapter concludes with a summary of main syntactical functions of verbs and verb phrases.

Chapter 3: Adjectives, adjective phrases and their components

This chapter introduces adjectives as a word class and its grammatical and semantic categories such as comparison, degree; other word classes functioning as components of adjective phrases. The chapter concludes with a summary of main syntactical functions of adjectives and adjective phrases.

Introduction

Since the other word classes in most cases function as parts of the noun phrases, verb phrases and adjective phrases, they are discussed within these phrases. If learners or instructors look for a clear explanation of the use of a word belonging to the other word classes, including pronouns, numbers, quantifiers, classifiers, adverbs, prepositions, conjunctions, determiners, they should look them up in the comprehensive grammar index.

Chapter 4: Word-formation

This chapter discusses the ways new words are formed from the vocabulary existing in the language, as well as loanwords in Vietnamese. Reduplication is one of the most difficult areas of vocabulary for non-native speakers. The part of reduplication provides the main information of how reduplicatives are formed, their meanings and how they function in speech. The Chinese loanwords are discussed in-depth, both from the historical and from the structural and semantic standpoints. Some examples of French and English loanwords are also given.

Chapter 5: Sentences

The previous four chapters focus on the structural units, which are words and phrases. This chapter deals with logical aspects of communication whose main unit is sentence. Some specific communicative features of Vietnamese sentences such as emphatic construction "topic – comment" are also discussed.

Chapter 6: Problem words, phrases and constructions

This chapter makes a contrastive analysis of Vietnamese and English both at the level of structural units and at the level of usage. The comparison of Vietnamese and English words, phrases and sentences helps learners of Vietnamese avoid the grammatical and usage errors typical of English speakers.

Chapter 7: Pronunciation

This chapter introduces the Vietnamese phonetic system based on the syllable structure. Each sound is described in detail and the character or combination of characters that represents the sound is discussed. Contrastive analysis is also made here to point out the pronunciation difficulties which English-speaking learners of Vietnamese encounter due to the influence of their native language. The Romanized writing system and spelling rules are introduced in this chapter. Some inconsistencies of the writing system and spelling rules are discussed as well.

Most of the examples given in this grammar to illustrate grammatical explanations are taken from authentic sources such as modern Vietnamese literature and contemporary Vietnamese newspapers and magazines published in Vietnam, as well as conversations of educated native speakers. Those examples have been collected by the author of this grammar for teaching and research purposes. In several cases, made-up examples are used to point out the difference between two grammatical constructions or to clearly indicate the contrast of two or more phrases and sentences.

The glossary of grammatical terms at the end of the grammar part and the glossary of phonetic terms at the end of the pronunciation part provide explanations for the technical terms used in this book.

At the end of the grammar part of the book, there is a detailed index which gives both the section numbers and the pages for ease of reference.

3 Symbols, abbreviations, contractions and typography

Grammar part

Bold face is used for Vietnamese words, phrases and sentences, or a grammatical construction.

Italics indicate the English equivalent of a Vietnamese grammatical construction.

[ ] square brackets enclose the optional words and components of a grammatical construction. For instance, **Chợ ấy [đã] rẻ lại [còn] gần [nữa]. Chợ ấy đã rẻ lại còn gần nữa.** is the full construction, where the components **đã, còn** and **gần** are optional. That is, the sentence **Chợ ấy rẻ lại gần.** is also correct.

[ ] square brackets in chapter *Word-formation* are used for Chinese pinyin of a Chinese character or word.

* asterisk indicates incorrect usage. For example, the sentence ***Chợ ấy rẻ lại xa.** is impossible.

/ slash denotes that either of the two or more words is possible, or the two or more words are interchangeable. For instance: **hai nghìn / ngàn** means **nghìn / ngàn** are interchangeable; **hai nghìn** and **hai ngàn** convey the same meaning of "two thousand."

" " double quotation marks are used for English translation of meanings of Vietnamese words or phrases. However, a Vietnamese phrase or sentence as an example for a grammatical construction is in bold face and is followed by the English translation without quotation marks.

\ reversed slash is placed between a traditional Chinese character and its simplified form. For instance: 個\个 means 個 is the traditional character, and 个 is the simplified one.

Ø this symbol is used when a component of a construction or a system is absent.

lit. means literal(ly)

< means "derived from." For example, **tây** < 西 means **tây** was borrowed from the Chinese 西.

+ plus sign is used to indicate the components of a phrase or a grammatical construction and their sequence. For instance, **number + classifier + noun** refers to the construction of a noun phrase, in which a number precedes a classifier, and the classifier is followed by a noun.

Phonetic part

[ ] square brackets refer to the sound, and in some cases, the phonetic transcription. For example, **[d]** refers to the sound **d** as **day** in English.

/ / two slashes enclose a phoneme. For instance: /d/ indicates the phoneme **d**, to which the sound **[d]** corresponds.

< > angle brackets enclose an alphabet letter or character which represents a sound and, in some cases, a phoneme. For example, **<đ>** indicates character **đ**, which represents the sound **[d]** and the phoneme /d/.

Chapter 1

Nouns, noun phrases and their components

1.1 Introduction to the Vietnamese nouns

A noun performs two main syntactic functions in a sentence: either as the subject or the object. The following features make nouns in Vietnamese different from nouns in many European languages.

1.1.1. The form of a noun is invariable. It does not change no matter what function in a sentence it performs:

Sinh viên này học ở trường Đại học Quốc gia Hà Nội. Tôi quen sinh viên này. This student studies at Hanoi National University. I know this student.

In the first sentence, the noun **sinh viên** is the subject of the sentence. In the second one, it is the object of the verb **quen**. Compare the same sentence in Russian and German, where the noun *student* changes its forms:

Russian: Этот <u>студент</u> учится в Ханойском Государственном университете. Я знаю этого <u>студента</u>.
German: Dieser <u>Student</u> studiert an der Hanoi Staatsuniversität. Ich bin mit diesem <u>Studenten</u> bekannt.

1.1.2. A noun in Vietnamese does not refer either to the plural or the singular, whereas in many European languages a particular form of a noun always refers either to the singular or the plural:

singular	plural
a student	student**s** (English)
un étudiant	des étudiant**s** (French)
ein Student	die Student**en** (German; nominative and accusative)
студент	студент**ы** (Russian; nominative)

1 Nouns, noun phrases and their components

The noun **sinh viên** would follow the number **một** "one" to denote "a student" or **các** and **những** to denote the plural "students." In some contexts, **sinh viên** may refer to the plural without any marker. The use of the plural markers **các** and **những** and the use of nouns without these markers to denote the plural will be discussed in 1.3.2.1.

1.1.3. In a number of European languages, gender is a grammatical category, which is characteristic of many word-classes, including nouns. The grammatical gender is a feature of any noun in those languages. The contrast of the grammatical gender maybe "masculine vs. feminine" as in French, or "masculine vs. feminine vs. neuter" as in German and Russian. For instance, the inanimate noun denoting the concept of a house or a building can have different grammatical genders in those languages:

> French: la maison (feminine), le bâtiment (masculine).
> German: das Haus (neuter), die Wohnung (feminine), das Gebäude (neuter), der Bau (masculine).
> Russian: дом (masculine), квартира (feminine), здание (neuter).

In these European languages, an animate noun has specific morphological means to refer to both the grammatical gender and the natural gender. For instance, the animate noun "student" can be in:

> French: un étudiant (masculine) vs. une étudiant**e** (feminine).
> German: ein Student (masculine) vs. eine Studen**tin** (feminine).
> Russian: студент (masculine) vs. студент**ка** (feminine).

The grammatical gender is not a feature of nouns in Vietnamese. The animate noun **sinh viên** refers either to a female or a male student.

1.2 Classification of nouns

Based on the meanings and the way nouns are used, nouns in Vietnamese fall into the following groups.

1.2.1 Common nouns vs. proper nouns

Common nouns refer to general concepts. Proper nouns name specific people, places, institutions etc.

The first letter of a proper noun is capitalized: **Tuấn** (personal given name), **Nhổn** (place). If the name contains two or more syllables, the first letter of each syllable is capitalized; there is no hyphen between the syllables: **Hoàn Kiếm** (the name of a lake), **Hà Nội** (the name of Vietnam's capital city), **Nam Định** (the name of a province and the city that is its provincial center).

A Vietnamese personal name usually consists of three part. The family name (**họ**) comes first; it is followed by a middle name (**tên đệm** or **tên lót**) and the given name comes last. The first letter of each part is capitalized, and there is no hyphen between the parts. For example, **Phạm Ngọc Tuấn**, **Nguyễn Thu Hương**.

A personal name may have only two parts, which are the family name and the given name: **Phạm Tuấn**, **Nguyễn Hương**. It may have more than three parts: **Phạm Trần Ngọc Tuấn**, **Nguyễn Thị Thu Hương**.

In many cases, a given name may indicate the gender of the person. **Tuấn** is usually a male name, while **Hương** is a female name. Of course, there are occasionally women named **Tuấn** and there are men named **Hương**. Ther is a number of names which can be given to both women and men, such as **Anh**, **Bính**, **Cầm**, **Diệu**.

The number of given names is much larger than the number of family names. **Nguyễn** is the most common family name in Vietnam. The other common family names are **Bùi**, **Đào**, **Đặng**, **Đinh**, **Đoàn**, **Đỗ**, **Hà**, **Hoàng**, **Lê**, **Ngô**, **Phạm**, **Phan**, **Trần**, **Trịnh**, **Vũ**. The family names do not have meaning. Most family names have corresponding Chinese characters, which in Chinese do not have meanings either. The given names in most cases have meanings as their corresponding Chinese characters (Chinese loanwords will be discussed in Chapter 4: Word-formation, 4.6. Borrowing).

Unlike European and Chinese family names, Vietnamese family names are not used for addressing. Vietnamese uses full names consisting of family name, middle name and given name, or just personal given names instead. Compare:

Vietnamese	English
Ông Phạm Ngọc Tuấn or **Ông Tuấn**	Mr. Johnson
Bà Nguyễn Thu Hương or **Bà Hương**	Mrs. Smith
Cô Trịnh Nguyệt Cầm or **Cô Cầm**	Ms. Collins
Giáo sư Trần Duy Hiền or **Giáo sư Hiền**	Prof. Clark
Bác sĩ Đoàn Tiến or **Bác sĩ Tiến**	Dr. Peterson

A geographical name in Vietnamese always follows the status noun, while a geographical name in English can either precede the status name or follow it and the preposition *of*. The status noun in Vietnamese is not capitalizes. For example,

Classification of nouns

1
Nouns, noun phrases and their components

New York City or *the City of New York* vs. **thành phố Hà Nội**, *Washington State* or *the State of Washington* vs. **tỉnh Đồng Nai**.

The sequence of wording of postal addresses is similar to English. Very often the word **người nhận** meaning "recipient," which is equivalent to the English "to" comes first. There is no zip code in Vietnam.

Vietnamese	English
Người nhận: ông Phạm Ngọc Tuấn	To: Mr. Robert Johnson
125 phố (street) **Đinh Tiên Hoàng**	78 Washington Street
quận (district) **Hoàn Kiếm**	San Diego, CA 92119
Hà Nội	

The sender's address is written on the back of the envelope, and the word **người gửi** meaning "sender" sometimes is added. The sequence is the same as with the recipient's address.

1.2.2 Concrete nouns vs. abstract nouns

Common nouns may be concrete or abstract. Concrete nouns refer to physical objects and substances, whereas abstract nouns indicate qualities, feelings or events (see 1.2.3.1.).

Concrete nouns fall into two groups, which are countable (or count) nouns and mass nouns (see 1.2.3.2.). The feature of a noun being countable or uncountable is crucial to the grammatical constructions for nouns and noun phrases. It is dealt in detail later.

1.2.3 Countable nouns vs. uncountable nouns

Proper nouns are uncountable. Common nouns can be either countable or uncountable. Countable nouns refer to concrete entities that are perceptible and tangible. However, in order to count a concrete entity which is denoted by a countable noun, some grammatical rules should be followed. The rules are discussed in 1.3.2.

Uncountable nouns cannot be used immediately after a number. They fall into the following three groups.

1.2.3.1 Abstract nouns denoting concepts

khoa học "science," **văn hoá** "culture," **triết học** "philosophy," **hội hoạ** "painting," **âm nhạc** "music," **tri thức** "knowledge," **toán học** "mathematics," **chính**

trị "politics." When an abstract noun is used after a number, another noun, which is called a "classifier," should be used: **một nền âm nhạc dân tộc độc đáo** "a unique national music;" **nền** is the classifier used for abstract nouns. For more on classifiers, see 1.3.1.7.1.

1.2.3.2 Mass nouns denoting material and substance

gỗ "wood, timber," **sắt** "iron," **không khí** "air," **tre** "bamboo," **muối** "salt," **đường** "sugar." Material nouns are not used immediately after a number. There should be another noun inserted between the number and the material noun: **một tấm gỗ** "a plank," **hai cây tre** "two bamboo trees," **ba cân muối** "three kilograms of salt," **bốn thìa đường** "four spoons of sugar."

1.2.3.3 Collective nouns denoting groups of people and sets of items

cha mẹ "parents," **bàn ghế** "furniture," **sách vở** "books," **giáo viên** "teachers," **chim chóc** "birds." Some collective nouns can be used as countable nouns that are used right after a number: **ba giáo viên** "three teachers."

1.3 Noun phrases and their components

A noun phrase is a phrase whose head word is a noun. Bases on the components of a noun phrase, there are three major types of noun phrases in Vietnamese.

1.3.1 Noun phrase #1: <u>number + classifier + noun</u>

ba quyển sách "three books," **bốn ngôi nhà** "four houses." **Sách** "book" and **nhà** "house" are nouns; **ba** "three" and **bốn** "four" are numbers, **quyển** and **ngôi** are classifiers, which are inserted between the numbers and the nouns. Phrases *__ba nhà__ and *__bốn sách__ are grammatically incorrect.

See 1.3.1.2. for further details of this type of noun phrase.

This part discusses two components of this type of noun phrases: numbers and classifiers.

1.3.1.1 Numbers

1.3.1.1.1 CARDINAL NUMBERS

The basic set of the numbers in Vietnamese consists of the following numbers: **không** "zero," **một** "one," **hai** "two," **ba** "three," **bốn** "four," **năm** "five," **sáu** "six," **bảy / bẩy** "seven," **tám** "eight," **chín** "nine," **mười** "ten," **trăm** "hundred," **nghìn / ngàn** "thousand," **triệu** "million," **tỉ** "billion."

The Chinese loanword **vạn** meaning "ten thousand" is obsolete in Vietnamese. However, it is commonly used in such set expressions as **hàng vạn** "tens of thousands of," **hàng nghìn hàng vạn** "thousands and tens of thousands of": **hàng vạn người đổ về khu trung tâm thành phố trong đêm Giao thừa.** Tens of thousands of people come to the downtown area of the city on the New Year's Eve.

See the note at the end of 1.3.1.1.1. for more about the English *dozens of, hundreds of, thousands of, millions of* in Vietnamese.

Note: The first version of spelling for number "seven" **bảy** is used everywhere in Vietnam, while the second one **bẩy** is typical of the Hanoi dialect; accordingly, natives of Hanoi pronounce this word with a less open vowel. Vietnamese has the following commonly used pairs of this kind: **bày / bầy** "(to) display, show," **cày / cầy** "(to) plow," **cạy / cậy** "(to) pry," **chày / chầy** "pestle," **chảy / chẩy** "(to) flow," **dày / dầy** "thick," **dãy / dẫy** "row, line," **dạy / dậy** "(to) teach," **gảy / gẩy** "(to) pluck (the strings of a musical instrument)," **gãy / gẫy** "broken," **giàu / giầu** "rich, wealthy," **giày / giầy** "shoes," **lạy / lậy** "pray," **màu / mầu** "color," **nãy / nẫy** "a moment ago," **nhàu / nhầu** "wrinkled," **nhảy / nhẩy** "(to) jump," **nhạy / nhậy** "sensitive," **phảy / phẩy** "comma," **tàu / tầu** "train, ship," **tày / tầy** "having a blunt point," **thày / thầy** "(male) teacher."

Numbers from 11 to 19 have the numbers from **một** to **chín** added to **mười**, except for number "fifteen," where **năm** changes to **lăm**: **mười một** "eleven," **mười hai** "twelve," **mười ba** "thirteen," **mười bốn** "fourteen," **mười lăm** "fifteen," **mười sáu** "sixteen", . . . , **mười chín** "nineteen."

Numbers 20, 30, 40, 50, 60, 70, 80 and 90 have **mươi** (with the mid-level tone) added to **hai, ba, . . . , chín**: **hai mươi** "twenty," **ba mươi** "thirty," . . . , **chín mươi** "ninety."

Numbers 21, 31, 41, 51, 61, 71, 81 and 91 have **mốt** (with high-rising tone) added to **hai mươi, ba mươi, . . . , chín mươi**: **hai mươi mốt** "twenty-one," **ba mươi mốt** "thirty-one", . . . , **chín mươi mốt** "ninety-one."

Note: Vietnamese spelled-out numbers do not contain any hyphen.

Numbers 24, 34, 44, 54, 64, 74, 84 and 94 have two versions: **hai mươi bốn** or **hai mươi tư** "twenty-four," **ba mươi bốn** or **ba mươi tư** "thirty-four," . . . , **chín mươi bốn** or **chín mươi tư** "ninety-four." The numbers with **bốn** are used everywhere; the numbers with **tư** are used in the Hanoi dialect only.

Numbers 25, 35, 45, 55, 65, 75, 85 and 95 have two versions: **hai mươi lăm** or **hai mươi nhăm** "twenty-five," **ba mươi lăm** or **ba mươi nhăm** "thirty-five", . . . , **chín mươi lăm** or **chín mươi nhăm** "ninety-five." The numbers with **lăm** are used everywhere; the numbers with **nhăm** are used in the Hanoi dialect only.

The numbers **hai, ba, sáu, bảy / bẩy, tám** and **chín** do not change and are added to the numbers with **mươi**: **hai mươi hai** "twenty-two," **ba mươi ba** "thirty-three," **bốn mươi sáu** "forty-six," **năm mươi bảy / bẩy** "fifty-seven," **sáu mươi tám** "sixty-eight," **chín mươi chín** "ninety-nine."

Note: In colloquial Vietnamese, the numbers from 21 to 29 and from 31 to 39 have a phonetic change: **hai mươi** and **ba mươi** are shortened to become **hăm** and **băm**. For example, **hăm hai** "twenty-two," **băm lăm / nhăm** "thirty-five."

The word **chục** "dozen" is used in colloquial Vietnamese for number **mười** "ten" in round numbers only: **hai mươi** "twenty" can be **hai chục**, **năm mươi** "fifty" can be **năm chục**, but **hai mươi mốt** cannot be *hai chục mốt. **Chục** is commonly used for money: **hai mươi nghìn / ngàn đồng** can be **hai chục nghìn / ngàn đồng**. Very often, both **nghìn / ngàn** and **đồng** are understood. In that case, **hai chục** means "twenty thousand dong."

When **chục** is used to count a small number of things, especially in the market, it conveys different meanings in different regions of Vietnam. **Một chục xoài** in Hanoi means "ten mangoes," in Saigon means "twelve mangoes" and in some areas of the Mekong Delta may denote "fourteen mangoes."

Numbers 100, 200, 300, 400, 500, 600, 700, 800 and 900 have the word **trăm** added to **một, hai, . . . , chín**: **một trăm** "one hundred," **hai trăm** "two hundred," **chín trăm** "nine hundred." So, "one hundred and twenty-four" is **một trăm hai mươi bốn** or **một trăm hai mươi tư**, "two hundred and fifty-five" is **hai trăm năm mươi lăm** or **hai trăm năm mươi nhăm**, etc.

If the ten level is skipped, the word **linh** or **lẻ** is used: "one hundred and one" is **một trăm linh một** or **một trăm lẻ một**, "nine hundred and five" is **chín trăm linh năm** or **chín trăm lẻ năm**. The Hanoi dialect used to have only **linh**, but nowadays, people in Hanoi use both **linh** and **lẻ**, whereas the central and southern dialects use only **lẻ**.

Note: The word **và** meaning "and" is not used for numbers in Vietnamese. Compare: three hundred <u>and</u> forty-five (345) is **ba trăm bốn mươi lăm / nhăm**.

Numbers 1 000, 2 000, 3 000, 4 000, 5 000, 6 000, 7 000, 8 000 and 9 000 have the word **nghìn** or **ngàn** added to **một, hai, . . . , chín**: **một nghìn** or **một ngàn** "one thousand," **hai nghìn** or **hai ngàn** "two thousand," **chín nghìn** or **chín ngàn** "nine thousand." The Hanoi dialect used to have only **nghìn**, but nowadays, people in Hanoi use both **nghìn** and **ngàn**, whereas the central and southern dialects use only **ngàn**. So, "one thousand two hundred and thirty-four" (1,234) is **một nghìn hai trăm ba mươi bốn** or **một ngàn hai trăm ba mươi tư**. When the hundred level is skipped, the phrase **không trăm** is used. "One thousand and thirty-four" (1,034) is **một nghìn / ngàn không trăm ba mươi bốn / tư**. In colloquial Vietnamese, **không trăm** may be left out: **một nghìn / ngàn ba mươi bốn / tư**.

Noun phrases and their components

Note: Vietnamese does not use a comma to separate thousands. A space or a dot is used instead. For instance, **1 234** or **1.234** "one thousand two hundred thirty-four." The comma is used for decimals (see 1.3.1.1.3).

The words **triệu** and **tỉ** are used in the same way, as **trăm** and **nghìn / ngàn**. Here are some examples:

> 57,406,725 in English is **57 406 725** or **57.406.725** in Vietnamese, which is spelled out as **năm mươi bảy / bảy triệu bốn trăm linh / lẻ sáu nghìn bảy / bảy trăm hai mươi lăm / nhăm**.
> 408,764,529,003 in English is **408 764 529 003** or **408.764.529.003** in Vietnamese, which is spelled out as **bốn trăm linh / lẻ tám tỉ bảy / bảy trăm sáu mươi bốn / tư triệu năm trăm hai mươi chín nghìn / ngàn [không trăm] linh ba**.

Note: In order to convey the meanings of the English *dozens of, hundreds of, thousands of, millions of,* Vietnamese puts **hàng** in front of **chục, trăm, nghìn, triệu**:

> **Quán cà phê này bán <u>hàng chục</u> loại cà phê.** This coffee shop sells dozens of kinds of coffee.
> **<u>Hàng nghìn</u> người đến đưa tang nhà thơ.** Thousands of people attended the poet's funeral.

The Chinese loanword **vạn** meaning "ten thousand" is rarely used for an exact number in modern Vietnamese, but is commonly used with the meaning "tens of thousands of."

1.3.1.1.2 ORDINAL NUMBERS

Ordinal numbers add the word **thứ** before the cardinal numbers: **thứ hai, thứ ba, thứ năm, thứ sáu, thứ bảy / bẩy, thứ tám, thứ chín, thứ mười, thứ mười một** etc. There are two exceptions: the ordinal "first" is **thứ nhất**, not *thứ một; the ordinal number "fourth" is **thứ tư**, not *thứ bốn.

Note: **thứ nhì** meaning "second" is to some extent obsolete and is used in contemporary Vietnamese to denote the second place in a race or competition only.

1.3.1.1.3 DECIMALS, FRACTIONS AND PERCENTAGE

Decimals are indicated by a comma, which is pronounced as **phảy** or **phẩy**: 10.8 in English is **10,8** in Vietnamese, which is spelled out as **mười phảy / phẩy tám**.

When the comma is followed by a zero, **không** should be used instead of **linh**. 10.08 in English is **10,08** in Vietnamese, which is spelled out as **mười phảy / phẩy không tám**.

Fractions are formed by inserting the word **phần** between two cardinal numbers: 3/5 is **ba phần năm**, 9/10 is **chín phần mười**. 1/2 is **một phần hai** or **một nửa**. **Một phần hai** is used in sciences, while **một nửa** is used when there is no need to indicate a precise number. For more about **nửa**, see 1.3.1.1.5.

Percentage is formed by adding **phần trăm** to the end of a number: 27% is **hai mươi bảy / bảy phần trăm**; 1.5% in English is 1,5% in Vietnamese, which is spelled out as **một phảy / phẩy năm phần trăm**; 0.4% in English is 0,4% in Vietnamese, which is spelled out as **không phảy / phẩy bốn phần trăm**. In English, we can leave out "zero" and say "point four percent." In Vietnamese, **không** should be used.

1.3.1.1.4 ADDITION, SUBTRACTION, MULTIPLICATION AND DIVISION

The prepositions which the verbs **cộng** "add," **trừ** "subtract," **nhân** "multiply" and **chia** "divide" take should be memorized in order to use these verbs correctly, because their use is different from the English equivalents.

The verbs **cộng** and **nhân** take the preposition **với**. The word **là** meaning "is" or the word **bằng** meaning "be equal" is used before the result.

Mười lăm cộng với ba mươi mốt là / bằng bốn mươi sáu. Fifteen added to thirty-one is forty-six.

Mười lăm nhân với ba mươi mốt là / bằng bốn trăm sáu mươi lăm / nhăm. Fifteen multiplied by thirty-one is four hundred and sixty-five.

The verb **trừ** takes the preposition **đi**, which sometimes is understood. The word **còn** meaning "(to) remain" is used before the result. Note that the word order is different from English.

Mười lăm trừ [đi] ba mươi mốt còn âm mười sáu. Thirty-one subtracted from fifteen is minus sixteen.

The verb **chia** takes the preposition **cho**. **Bằng** is used before the result.

Mười lăm chia cho ba mươi bằng không phẩy năm. Fifteen divided by thirty is zero point five.

Note: The word **âm** meaning "minus" is used in math and physics. The opposite word is **dương** "plus." They are used for temperatures as well. For instance, −15°C is spelled out as **âm mười lăm độ C**. Vietnam, as the vast majority of countries in the world, uses the Celsius scale for temperatures.

Noun phrases and their components

1 Nouns, noun phrases and their components

1.3.1.1.5 TWICE, TWICE AS MUCH / MANY ..., THREE TIMES + COMPARATIVE ADJECTIVE IN VIETNAMESE

Gấp is placed after an adjective as in (1) and (2), or a phrase referring to an amount as in (3) and (4), and in front of a number to convey this meaning. Note that with the meaning "twice" **gấp đôi** is used instead of *gấp hai:

(1) **Lương chị ấy cao gấp đôi lương anh ấy.** Her salary is twice greater than his.
(2) **Căn nhà mới lớn / to / rộng gấp ba căn nhà cũ.** The new house is three times as large as the old one.
(3) **Anh ấy phải lớn tuổi gấp đôi cô ấy.** He must be twice her age.
(4) **Chị ấy kiếm được nhiều tiền gấp đôi anh ấy.** She earns twice as much money as he does.

The word **lần** meaning "time" can be added after the number more than **gấp đôi** "twice":

(2a) **Căn nhà mới lớn / to / rộng gấp ba lần căn nhà cũ.**

One more example with **lần**:

My test has nine errors, three times as many as his. **Bài kiểm tra của tôi có chín lỗi, nhiều gấp ba lần bài của anh ấy.**

1.3.1.1.6 HALF AND AND A HALF IN VIETNAMESE

Nửa and **rưởi** (with the low-falling-rising tone) both mean "half," but they are not interchangeable. **Nửa** always precedes a noun: **nửa tháng** "half a month." **Rưởi** is used in conversational Vietnamese to denote a half of the number it follows. **Rưởi** follows only a number ending in **trăm**, **nghìn / ngàn** or **triệu**: **một trăm rưởi** "one hundred and fifty" (150), **hai nghìn / ngàn rưởi** "two thousand five hundred" (2,500), **ba triệu rưởi** "three million five hundred thousand" (3,500,000).[1]

Rưỡi (with the high-rising-broken tone) mean "and a half" and follows a noun, which in turn follows a number: **một tháng rưỡi** "a month and a half," **hai năm rưỡi** "two years and a half." In the phrase **một rưỡi** meaning 1:30 AM or 1:30 PM, the noun **giờ** "o'clock; hour" is understood (see 1.3.1.1.6.9.).

The English *half* can function as an adverb with the meaning "to an extent that is equal or nearly equal to half of something." The Vietnamese **nửa** also performs this function, but **một** should be added in front of **nửa**:

Chai nước đã vơi đi một nửa. The bottle of water is half empty.

1.3.1.1.7 DATES AND CLOCK TIME

1.3.1.1.7.1 YEARS

Năm meaning "year" precedes the word **nay** (with the mid-level tone) to refer to "this year": **năm nay**; precedes the word **ngoái** to refer to "last year": **năm ngoái**; and follows the word **sang** to refer to "next year": **sang năm**. In the southern dialect, "next year" is **năm tới**.

Note: **năm** meaning "year" and **năm** meaning "five" are homonyms:

Năm năm rồi không gặp. "I haven't seen you for five years."

1.3.1.1.7.2 SEASONS

Mùa "season" is placed before the names of the seasons of the year: **mùa xuân** "spring," **mùa hè** "summer," **mùa thu** "autumn, fall" and **mùa đông** "winter."

When listing the seasons of the year, Vietnamese people use this sequence from spring to winter. The word **mùa hạ** meaning "summer" is occasionally used in literature and poetry instead of **mùa hè**.

Note: the Vietnamese equivalent of "the fall semester / term" is **học kì một**, and "the spring semester" is **học kì hai**. Vietnamese does not use the names of the seasons for the periods of instruction in schools into which an academic year is divided.

1.3.1.1.7.3 MONTHS

Tháng meaning "month" precedes the word **này** to refer to "this month": **tháng này**; the word **trước** to refer to "last month": **tháng trước**; and the word **sau** to refer to "next month": **tháng sau**. In the southern dialect "next month" is **tháng tới**.

Vietnamese uses the cardinal numbers after the word **tháng** to denote the twelve months of the year, with some exceptions.

January is **tháng một**. Vietnamese has another word for January: **tháng giêng**, which is interchangeable with **tháng một**. However, when people talk about a date of January by the lunar calendar, they use only **tháng giêng**: **ngày mười hai tháng giêng âm lịch** "the twelfth of January by the lunar calendar." **Lịch** means "calendar," **âm lịch** means "lunar calendar," **dương lịch** means "solar calendar."

February is **tháng hai**, March is **tháng ba**. April is **tháng tư**, not *tháng bốn. May is **tháng năm**, June is **tháng sáu**, July is **tháng bảy / bẩy**, August is **tháng tám**, September is **tháng chín**, October is **tháng mười**.

1 Nouns, noun phrases and their components

November is **tháng mười một**. However, some people say **tháng một** for November of the lunar calendar: **ngày mười hai tháng một âm lịch** "the twelfth of November by the lunar calendar."

December is **tháng mười hai**. Vietnamese has another word for December: **tháng chạp**, which is interchangeable with **tháng mười hai**. However, when people talk about a date of December by the lunar calendar, they use only **tháng chạp**: **ngày mười hai tháng chạp âm lịch** "the twelfth of December by the lunar calendar."

The word **mùng / mồng** is added before the number to denote a date from the first day through the tenth day of each month: **ngày mùng / mồng một tháng chạp âm lịch** "the first of December by the lunar calendar."

The question "What date is today?" can be either **Hôm nay ngày mùng / mồng mấy?** or **Hôm nay ngày bao nhiêu?** The question with **mấy** is used for the dates from the first day through the tenth day of the month, whereas the question with **bao nhiêu** refers to the dates from the eleventh and higher:

Q: **Hôm nay ngày mùng / mồng mấy?**
A: **Hôm nay ngày mùng / mồng ba tháng tư.** Today is the 3rd of April.

Q: **Hôm nay ngày bao nhiêu?**
A: **Hôm nay ngày mười ba tháng tư.** Today is the 13th of April.

Note 1: Names of the months of the year are not capitalized in Vietnamese.

Note 2: Sometimes the numbers are written instead of the words: **tháng 2** instead of **tháng hai**, **tháng 4** instead of **tháng tư**. Although Vietnamese people write **tháng 4**, they spell out **tháng tư**, not ***tháng bốn**.

| 1.3.1.1.7.4 | WEEKS |

Tuần meaning "week" precedes the word **này** to refer to "this week": **tuần này**; the word **trước** to refer to "last week": **tuần trước**; and the word **sau** to refer to "next week": **tuần sau**. In the southern dialect "next week" is **tuần tới**.

| 1.3.1.1.7.5 | DAYS |

Vietnamese has two words with the meaning "day," which are **ngày** and **hôm**. They are not interchangeable in most cases: **hôm nay** "today," **hôm qua** "yesterday," **hôm kia** "the day before yesterday," **ngày mai** "tomorrow," **ngày kia** "the day after tomorrow." In the southern dialect, "the day after tomorrow" is **ngày mốt**.

| 1.3.1.1.7.6 | DAYS OF THE WEEK |

Vietnamese uses the ordinal numbers to denote the days of the week. There are two exceptions: Suday is **chủ nhật** and Wednesday is **thứ tư**. The other days of the week are **thứ hai** "Monday," **thứ ba** "Tuesday," **thứ năm** "Thursday," **thứ sáu** "Friday," **thứ bảy / bẩy** "Saturday."

The question "What day is today?" is **Hôm nay thứ mấy?** Vietnamese has two words meaning "how many?", which are **mấy** and **bao nhiêu**, but only **mấy** is used in this case. The question *__Hôm nay thứ bao nhiêu?__ is incorrect. The difference between **mấy** and **bao nhiêu** will be discussed in Chapter 5. Sentences. 5.3.2.6. Questions with **mấy** and **bao nhiêu**.

Note 1: Names of the days of the week are not capitalized in Vietnamese.

Note 2: Very often the numbers are written instead of the words: **thứ 2** instead of **thứ hai**, **thứ 5** instead of **thứ năm**. "Wednesday" is **thứ 4**, that is spelled out as **thứ tư**, not *__thứ bốn__.

1.3.1.1.7.7 DATES OF A MONTH AND A YEAR

Vietnamese goes from the date to the month to the year, which is the only possible word order: **ngày mùng / mồng một tháng năm năm hai nghìn không trăm hai mươi** "the 1st of May 2020." Dates are written in numbers in three ways: 1/ **ngày 01 tháng 5 năm 2020**; 2/ **01-5-2020**; 3/ **01/5/2020**.

1.3.1.1.7.8 DIVISION OF THE DAY TIME

The day is divided into the following periods of time, which can be different from English in terms of the clock time:

sáng "morning" from 4 AM to 11 AM
trưa "noon and early afternoon" from 11 AM to 2 PM
chiều "afternoon and early evening" from 2 PM to 6 PM
tối "evening" from 6 PM to 11 PM
đêm "night" from 11 PM to 4 AM

Note: The division of a day based on the clock time is approximate, because some people may say **bốn giờ đêm** instead of **bốn giờ sáng**, especially in northern Vietnam, where in the winter it is still dark at 4 AM.

The word **buổi** meaning "time period" is added before **sáng, trưa, chiều** and **tối** to refer to the according periods of time: **buổi sáng, buổi trưa, buổi chiều, buổi tối**.

The word **ban** also meaning "time period" is added before **ngày** and **đêm** to refer to the daytime: **ban ngày**, and the nighttime: **ban đêm**.

Note: The demonstrative adjectives **này** and **nay** meaning "this" are not interchangeable. Their tones should be memorized.

1 Nouns, noun phrases and their components

Này (with the low-falling tone) is used in the following words: **tuần này** "this week," **tháng này** "this month," **thập niên này** "this decade," **thế kỉ này** "this century."

Nay (with the mid-level tone) is used in the following words: **hôm nay** "today," **năm nay** "this year."

Nay is also added to the periods of time of the day: **sáng nay** "this morning," **trưa nay** "this noon or early afternoon," **chiều nay** "this afternoon or early evening," **tối nay** "this evening or tonight," **đêm nay** "tonight."

Qua and **mai** are added to the nouns **sáng**, **trưa**, **chiều**, **tối** and **đêm** to denote yesterday's and tomorrow's periods of time: **sáng qua, trưa qua, chiều qua, tối qua, đêm qua; sáng mai, trưa mai, chiều mai, tối mai, đêm mai.**

Năm này is possible, but the phrase conveys the meaning "in the same year in the past or in the future" and is used to refer to an action, which took or will take place in the same year as the other action: **Tôi tốt nghiệp đại học năm hai nghìn linh năm. Cũng vào năm này bạn tôi lấy chồng.** "I graduated from college in 2005. My friend got married in the same year."

On the other hand, **ngày nay**, **tuần nay** and **tháng nay** are possible, but they also convey the meanings very different from **hôm nay**, **tuần này** and **tháng này** respectively. **Ngày nay** means "at the present time" referring to a long period of time related to the present. **Tuần nay** and **tháng nay** are used in a particular grammatical construction to denote an action that began in the past and is going on at the moment of speaking: **Anh ấy học thi suốt cả tuần nay.** "He has been studying for the exams for the entire week." For more on this construction, see Chapter 2. Verbs. 2.3. Tense and aspect markers.

1.3.1.1.7.9 CLOCK TIME

To indicate the clock time, Vietnamese uses **giờ** "hour," **phút** "minute" and **giây** "second." For instance, "five o'clock ten minutes thirty seconds" is **5 giờ 10 phút 30 giây**. Vietnamese rarely writes the clock time in words; it uses numbers instead.

Here are some useful expressions for telling the clock time.

5 giờ đúng or **đúng 5 giờ** "5 o'clock sharp." When used with a period of time of the day, only the latter word order is possible: **đúng 5 giờ chiều**, not the former one *****5 giờ chiều đúng**.

The clock time between the 1st minute and the 29th minute of an hour is **5 giờ 10 phút, 5 giờ 28 phút**, etc. The word **phút** is optional after the numbers which end in 0 or 5: **5 giờ 10**. It is mandatory after the other numbers: *****5 giờ 28** is incorrect.

The clock time between the 31st minute and the 59th minute can be said in the same way: **5 giờ 45 [phút]**. In conversational Vietnamese, the word **kém** is used with the meaning "to," "of" or "before": **6 giờ kém 15 [phút]** "quarter to / of / before 6." Vietnamese does not have the word equivalent to the English "quarter."

"Half" is **rưỡi** (see 1.3.1.3): **5 giờ 30** or **5 giờ rưỡi** "5:30" or "half past five." In conversational Vietnamese, the word **giờ** may be dropped when used befor **rưỡi**: **5 rưỡi**.

The question "What time is it?" is a set expression in Vietnamese **Bây giờ mấy giờ rồi?** The word **bây giờ** means "now," and **rồi** is a tense marker (see Chapter 2. Verbs. 2.3. Tense and aspect markers). Only **mấy** is used in this question. The answer to this question usually leaves **bây giờ** and **rồi** out: **5 [giờ] rưỡi**.

Vietnam does not have the AM and PM system. People add the periods of time of the day to the clock time instead: **7 giờ sáng, 4 [giờ] rưỡi chiều, 12 giờ đêm**. Very often, military time, which is 24-hour clock, is used in official settings. For instance, **4 [giờ] rưỡi chiều** is **16 giờ 30, 12 giờ đêm** is **24 giờ**. Sometimes the letter **h** that stands for the French word "heure" with the meaning of "hour" is used instead of **giờ**: **16h30**.

The noun for "clock" and "watch" is **đồng hồ**, which is used with the verb **chạy** in the expressions **đồng hồ chạy đúng** "the clock / watch runs correctly;" **đồng hồ chạy chậm** "the clock / watch runs slow;" **đồng hồ chạy nhanh** "the clock / watch runs fast;" and **đồng hồ đứng / chết** "the clock / watch has stopped / is dead."

The noun **giờ** conveys two meanings: 1/ "o'clock": **5 giờ 15 [phút]** "5:15;" 2/ "hour": **5 giờ 15 phút** "five hours and fifteen minutes." In this phrase, **phút** cannot be left out. For intance:

Máy bay bay từ Hà Nội đến Tokyo mất 5 giờ 15 phút. It takes five hours and fifteen minutes to fly from Hà Nội to Tokyo.

Note 1: Vietnamese has another word with the meaning "hour," which is **tiếng**. We can say: **Máy bay bay từ Hà Nội đến Tokyo mất 5 tiếng 15 phút**. The sentence with **giờ** is formal, while the sentence with **tiếng** is neutral.

That being said, the sentence (1) **Ngày mai bộ môn chúng ta họp từ một giờ đến một giờ rưỡi** conveys two meanings:

1 Tomorrow our department will have a meeting from 1:00 PM to 1:30 PM.
2 Tomorrow our department meeting will last from an hour to an hour and a half.

Noun phrases and their components

With the second meaning, the sentence sounds very formal. It would be less formal if **giờ** is replaced with **tiếng**:

(2) **Ngày mai chúng ta họp từ một <u>tiếng</u> đến một <u>tiếng</u> rưỡi.**

However, the ambiguity of (1) can be avoided if the second **giờ** is left out because **một rưỡi** conveys only one meaning, that is "one thirty" as in (3):

(3) **Ngày mai chúng ta họp từ một giờ đến một rưỡi.** Tomorrow we will have a meeting from 1:00 PM to 1:30 PM.

Note 2: Vietnamese has another word which is also spelled **tiếng** with the meaning of "language." **Tiếng** "hour" and **tiếng** "language" are homonyms. However, there is no ambiguity when **tiếng** is used after a number, because the phrase **hai tiếng** conveys only the meaning "two hours." The phrase "two languages" in Vietnamese has the classifier **thứ** inserted between the number and the noun: **hai thứ tiếng**. For more on classifiers, see 1.3.1.7.

1.3.1.1.7.10   TIME IN VIETNAMESE

Vietnamese has two words with the meaning "time (duration in which events succeed one another or which is necessary for something)," that are **thời gian** and **thì giờ**. Like the English noun *time*, they are uncountable nouns. **Thời gian** is a general term for "time," while **thì giờ** denotes the amount of time that is needed for doing something. That said, **thời gian** can replace **thì giờ**, but not vice versa: **Anh ấy không đủ thời gian / thì giờ làm việc này.** "He didn't have enough time to do this." **Chị ấy tốt nghiệp đại học trong thời gian chiến tranh.** "She graduated from college during the war [time]." **Thì giờ** is impossible in the second sentence.

1.3.1.1.8   APPROXIMATIONS: *SEVERAL, A FEW, SOME; FEW, LITTLE, MANY, MUCH* IN VIETNAMESE

The term "quantifier" which refers to how much or how many we are talking about is used for these words in this work. Like numbers, all the Vietnamese quantifiers function as components of a noun phrase, in which they precede the noun: **mấy quyển sách, vài quyển sách, ít sách, nhiều sách**. However, in this type of noun phrases, some of them take a classifier before the noun, the others do not. We will discuss their use in detail after the classifiers are introduced in 1.3.1.2.

Some of the quantifiers can be components of a verb phrase, the others cannot. For more on verbs, see Chapter 2: Verbs.

| 1.3.1.1.8.1 | QUANTIFIER + CLASSIFIER + NOUN |

Mấy and **vài** convey the meaning "a few, several, some." **Mấy** can be used in any style, while **vài** is characteristic of conversational Vietnamese. **Một vài**, **vài ba**, **dăm** and **dăm ba** all are used in colloquial Vietnamese. **Một vài** indicates a number between two and three; **vài** and **vài ba** refer to a number between two and four; **dăm** and **dăm ba** indicate a number between three and five. All these quantifiers are treated as numbers. That means, they should be followed by a classifier when used before a countable noun which usually takes a classifier. There is a number of countable nouns which do not take a classifier (see 1.3.1.7.). Here are some examples for these quantifiers:

mấy / vài / một vài / vài ba / dăm / dăm ba (quantifier) **quyển** (classifier) **sách** (noun) "several / a few books"
mấy / vài / một vài / vài ba / dăm / dăm ba (quantifier) **cái** (classifier) **áo** (noun) "several / a few shirts"
mấy / vài / một vài / vài ba / dăm / dăm ba (quantifier) **ngôi** (classifier) **nhà** (noun) "several / a few houses"

Mươi (with the mid-level tone) refers to a number around ten and functions in the same way:

mươi quyển sách "about ten books," **mươi cái áo** "about ten shirts."

| 1.3.1.1.8.2 | QUANTIFIER + NOUN |

Một số means "a number of" and is used before countable nouns. Unlike a number or a quantifier in 1.3.1.1.8.1., **một số** is placed right before a countable noun without a classifier: **một số sách**. **Một số** can be used before some collective nouns as well: **một số bàn ghế**, **một số sách vở**, whereas a number and the previously mentioned quantifiers cannot. **Hai bàn ghế** or **vài sách vở** is incorrect.

Một ít means "a few, some" when used before a countable noun: **một ít sách** "a few books;" before a collective noun like **sách vở**: **một ít sách vở** "a few books." **Một ít** with the meaning "a little" can be used before uncountalbe nouns which denote material and substance: **một ít đường** "a little sugar," **một ít bánh mì** "some bread." The other quantifiers cannot be used with these nouns. We cannot say **vài đường** or **dăm ba bánh mì**.

Nhiều corresponds to the English *many* or *much*, and **ít** corresponds to *few* or *little*. However, the ways in which the Vietnamese **nhiều** and **ít** and the English *many, much, few* and *little* are used are different.

Nhiều and **ít** are used before countable nouns; in this case they are equivalent to *many* and *few* respectively. Note that, when a countable noun which usually takes a classifier is used after **nhiều** and **ít**, it does not take any classifier: **nhiều** ∅ **sách** "many books," **ít** ∅ **sách** "few books."

Nhiều and **ít** are used before uncountable nouns as well. In this case they are equivalent to the English *much* and *little* respectively:

> **Chúng tôi có nhiều thời gian / thì giờ.** We have a lot of time.
> **Chị ấy có ít thời gian / thì giờ đọc sách.** She has little time for reading.

Like the English *much* and *little*, **nhiều** and **ít** can function as adverbs of manner or degree. With this function, they follow a verb:

> **Trong thời gian ôn thi, sinh viên học rất nhiều.** When preparing for the final exams, students study pretty much.
> **Đêm qua tôi ngủ ít lắm.** I slept very little last night.

1.3.1.1.9 MORE THAN, OVER, FEWER THAN, UNDER AND NEARLY USED BEFORE A SPECIFIED NUMBER OR AMOUNT IN VIETNAMESE

Hơn is placed in front of a number to denote a number which is more than that number:

> **Công ti có hơn 2.000 nhân viên.** The company has more than 2,000 employees.
> **Tôi chờ ông ấy hơn nửa tiếng rồi.** I've been waiting for him for over half an hour.
> **Hơn một năm nay chúng tôi không gặp nhau.** We haven't seen each other in over a year.

When *more than* follows the negation, Vietnamese used **không quá**:

> **Chỉ được chọn không quá hai thứ.** Choose no / not more than two things.

When *over* is used for someone's age, **trên** should be used instead of **hơn**:

> **Bệnh này rất phổ biến đối với đàn ông trên 70 tuổi.** The illness is most common in men over 70.

Both **hơn** and **trên** are used for prices:

> **Căn hộ này giá hơn / trên bốn tỉ đồng.** This apartment costs over four billion dong.

The opposite meanings of **hơn** and **trên** are expressed by **chưa đến / chưa tới** "fewer than" and **dưới** "under":

Công ti có chưa đến / chưa tới 200 nhân viên. The company has fewer than 200 employees.

Chúng tôi chỉ phải chờ chị ấy chưa đến / chưa tới 15 phút. We only waited for her under fifteen minutes.

When speaking of someone's age, **dưới** is used:

Trẻ em dưới 10 tuổi vào xem không mất tiền. Admission is free for children under (the age of) ten.

Both **chưa đến / chưa tới** and **dưới** are used for prices:

Căn hộ này giá chưa đến / chưa tới / dưới hai tỉ đồng. This apartment costs under two billion dong.

Gần that is equivalent to the English *nearly* is used to refer to a number only a little fewer than the mentioned number:

Ông ấy giảng dậy ở trường này gần ba mươi năm. He taught at this school for nearly thirty years.

Gần hai trăm nhà khoa học tham dự hội thảo. Nearly two hundred scientists attended the conference.

1.3.1.1.10 PAIR AND COUPLE IN VIETNAMESE

Vietnamese also has two nouns for *pair* and *couple*, which are **đôi** and **cặp**. However, their use differs from the English use of *pair* and *couple* in some instances.

Đôi: **một đôi giầy / giày** "a pair of shoes;" **hai đôi tất** "two pairs of socks;" **ba đôi găng** "three pairs of gloves;" **một đôi đũa** "a pair of chopsticks;" **một đôi chim bồ câu** "a pair of doves;" **đôi bàn tay** "a pair of hands;" **đôi bàn chân** "a pair of feet."

Cặp: **một cặp kính** "a pair of glasses."

Both **đôi** and **cặp** are used with the following nouns: **đôi / cặp vợ chồng** "a couple (two people who are married);" **đôi / cặp mắt** "a pair of eyes;" **đôi / cặp môi** "the lips (of a person)."

Some nouns are used after the noun *pair* and preposition *of* in English, but their Vietnamese counterparts are used right after the classifier: "a pair of trousers / pants" is **một cái quần**, "a pair of scissors" is **một cái kéo**; and vice versa: unlike the Vietnamese **đôi / cặp môi** and **đôi vai**, the English nouns "lips" and "shoulders" are not used after the nouns *pair* and *couple*.

1 Nouns, noun phrases and their components

1.3.1.2 Classifiers

Vietnamese has a group of *nouns* which we conventionally call *classifiers*. They are placed between a number and a countable noun in this type of noun phrase (number + classifier + noun), between a plural marker and a noun in the second type of noun phrase (plural marker + classifier + noun) and in some constructions of the third type of noun phrase (noun + attributive). Classifiers refer to a variety of semantic classes of nouns. The lexical meanings of some nouns serving as classifiers are vague, for instance, **cái, chiếc**. The others convey lexical meanings, but when used before a particular class of nouns, their own lexical meanings may blur or disappear altogether. For example, **con** lit. means "child," but when it is used before a class of nouns denoting animals, there is no semantic relation between "a child" and "an animal."

The Vietnamese classifiers and the Chinese measure words (量詞 \ 量词) have something in common. Both are *nouns* placed before countable nouns and refer to a particular class of nouns. In both languages, some classifiers or measure words convey very abstact meanings (compare: Vietnamese **cái** and Chinese *gè* 個 \ 个), whereas most of Vietnamese classifiers and Chinese measure words have certain lexical meanings but do not maintain them when they refer to particular classes of nouns. However, in many grammatical constructions, the use of classifiers in Vietnamese is very different from the use of measure words in Chinese, which is not discussed in this work.

If classifiers are regarded as nouns with blurred lexical meanings, noun phrase #1 **number + classifier + noun** would become **number + noun$_1$ + noun$_2$**

In the latter construction, where the term *classifier* is not used, the first noun (noun$_1$), which is the classifier in the traditional grammar and the meaning of which is vague, is considered the head word of the noun phrase and is modified by a noun whose meaning is more concrete (noun$_2$). This kind of word order is typical of Vietnamese syntax where in most cases the modifying word follows the modified word. This work introduces classifiers in the traditional way for learners' convenience.

1.3.1.2.1 CLASSIFIERS FOR DIFFERENT TYPES OF NOUNS

The following classifiers are most commonly used in Vietnamese.

Cái and **chiếc** are interchangeable when they are used before a large number of nouns indicating inanimate objects. For example, **cái / chiếc áo** "a shirt," **cái / chiếc xe** "a vehicle."

Only **chiếc** can be used before a noun that refers to an individual item in a set of two or more items: **chiếc đũa** "a chopstick from a set of two chopsticks,"

chiếc giày / giày "a shoe from a set of two shoes." In these phrases, **chiếc** cannot be replaced with **cái**. On the other hand, only **cái** can be placed before a noun, which may follow another classifier, to convey some emphasis or connotation. For example, **Cái quả bưởi này to quá!** "How big this grapefruit is!" Only **cái** can be used before a verb and an adjective to turn them into nouns. For instance, **cái bắt tay** "a handshake" (**bắt tay** means "shake someone's hand"), **cái đẹp** "the beauty" (**đẹp** means "[to be] beautiful").

In colloquial Vietnamese, **cái** is used in front of a female name to refer to a third person. For instance, **cái Lan, cái Hồng**. This usage is not the noun phrase that is being discussed here.

Bản lit. means "copy, document" is used for documents, copies, musical works: **bản án** "a court ruling," **ba bản co pi / ba bản phô tô** "three (xeroxed) copies," **bản Tuyên ngôn Độc lập** "The Declaration of Independence," **bản giao hưởng** "a symphony."

Bộ lit. means "a set" and is used for sets of things: **bộ bàn ghế** "a set of furniture," **bộ quần áo** "a suit," **bộ cốc chén** "a set of cups." **Bộ** is used for some cultural items as well: **một bộ phim hay** "a good movie," **một bộ sách học tiếng Anh** "a set of English textbooks."

Note: **Bộ** is used before the noun **mặt** "(human) face," and the phrase should be followed by an attributive: **một bộ mặt hớn hở** "a smiling face," **một bộ mặt giận dữ** "an indignant face." **Bộ mặt** is also used with the figurative meaning: **Bộ mặt của thành phố đã thay đổi nhiều trong thời gian gần đây.** "The face of the city has recently changed a lot."

Bức is used for letters, pictures and paintings: **một bức ảnh** "a photo," **hai bức tranh** "two paintings," **ba bức thư** "three letters;" as well as for some things which function as dividers: **một bức tường** "a wall," **một bức vách** "a wall," **hai bức mành mành** "two bamboo curtains."

Căn is used for small houses, apartments and rooms: **một căn nhà** "a (small) house," **hai căn hộ** "two apartments," **ba căn phòng** "three rooms." **Căn** can also be used before the word **bệnh**, which lit. means "disease, illness." **Căn bệnh** also conveys the figurative meaning as "disease" in English: **Nghiện rượu là một căn bệnh của xã hội.** "Alcoholism is a disease of our society."

Cặp is used for items which come in sets of two. See 1.3.1.6.

Cây lit. meaning "a tree" is used before nouns which refer to fruits to denote a tree with a particular kind of fruits: **một cây xoài** "a mango tree," **hai cây na** "two custard apple trees," **mười cây chuối** "ten banana trees." **Cây** is also used before the names of trees to refer to a particular kind of trees: **hai cây tre** "two bamboo trees," **năm cây bạch dương** "five birches."

1
Nouns, noun phrases and their components

Con lit. meaning "child" is used for animals, fish, birds: **hai con mèo** "two cats," **ba con chó** "three dogs," **bốn con cá chép** "four carp," **năm con chim sẻ** "five sparrows." **Con** is also used for a number of nouns as set expressions: **con thuyền** "a boat," **con đò** "a ferry boat," **con sông** "a river," **con mắt** "an eye," **con dao** "a knife," **con đường** "a road," **con tem** "a postage stamp," **con số** "a number, a digit, a figure," **con thoi** "a shuttle," **con người** "a human being."

Cơn lit. meaning "fit, bout" is used for the following nouns: **cơn mưa** "rain," **cơn gió** "wind," **cơn bão** "storm, tornado," **cơn sốt** "fever," **cơn giận** "anger."

Củ lit. meaning "bulb, tuber" is used for nouns which denote roots as food: **củ hành** "onion," **củ tỏi** "garlic," **củ khoai** "(sweet) potato," **củ sắn** "manioc, cassava," **củ cà-rốt** "carrot," **củ gừng** "ginger," **củ su hào** "kohlrabi," **củ lạc** "peanut."

Cuộc is used for events in which a number of people participate: **cuộc cách mạng** "revolution," **cuộc chiến tranh** "war," **cuộc mít tinh** "rally" and for some other nouns: **cuộc đời** "life." **Cuộc** also functions as a prefix to turn a verb or static verb into a noun: **cuộc sống** "life," **cuộc họp** "meeting," **cuộc vui** "amusement." For more on the prefix **cuộc**, see 4.2.2.1.

Cuốn lit. meaning "(to) roll" is used for nouns which denotes books: **một cuốn sách** "a book," **hai cuốn từ điển** "two dictionaries," **ba cuốn tiểu thuyết** "three novels," **một cuốn vở** "a notebook," **một cuốn sổ** "a small notebook."

Đám lit. meaning "patch, mass; crowd" is used for the following nouns: **đám cỏ** "grass," **đám mây** "cloud," **đám đông** "crowd," **đám ma** "funeral," **đám tang** "funeral, funeral procession." **Đám** is also used to turn some verbs into nouns: **đám cháy** "fire," **đám cưới** "wedding."

Hòn is used for round things: **hòn đá** "a stone," **hòn gạch** "a brick," **hòn sỏi** "gravel," **hòn bi** "a small metal ball, a marble," **hòn ngọc** "a pearl, a gem." **Hòn** is also used for islands and mountains: **hòn đảo** "an island," **hòn núi** "a mountain."

Khẩu is used for weapons: **khẩu súng** "a gun," **khẩu tiểu liên** "an assault rifle," **khẩu cối** "a mortar," **khẩu đại bác** "a cannon."

Kiện is used for luggage, parcels, goods: **ba kiện hành lí** "three pieces of luggage," **năm kiện hàng** "five pieces of goods."

Lá is used for thin and flat items: **lá cờ** "a flag," **lá phiếu** "a vote (the piece of paper used to make one's vote)," **lá đơn** "an application." **Lá** is used for letters and is interchangeable with **bức**: **lá thư / bức thư** "a letter."

Món lit. meaning "dish (food cooked as a meal)" is used for the following nouns: **món đồ trang sức** "a piece of jewelry," **món hàng** "an item of merchandize," **món nợ** "a debt," **món quà** "a gift, present," **món tiền** "an amount of money."

Note: the phrase **món hàng** in contemporary Vietnamese chiefly conveys the figurative meaning "an unusual or valuable thing (purchased or received)." For instance, **món hàng độc đáo** "a unique thing," **món hàng quí giá** "an invaluable thing."

Nền lit. meaning "floor, background" is used for some abstract nouns: **nền khoa học** "science," **nền văn hoá** "culture," **nền âm nhạc** "music," **nền kinh tế** "economy," **nền văn học** "literature."

Ngôi is used for buildings in general: **ba ngôi nhà** "three houses," and for some other nouns: **ngôi đình** "a community hall," **ngôi mộ** "a tomb," **ngôi sao** "a star."

Người lit. meaning "human being" can be used for nouns denoting professions and occupations when an emphasis on the people's characteristics is made: **một người thầy thuốc tận tâm** "a dedicated physician," **một người giáo viên gương mẫu** "an exemplary teacher," **một người lính dũng cảm** "a brave soldier."

Pho is used for statues: **pho tượng** "a statue."

Quả lit. means "fruit" and is used before the nouns which denote a particular kind of fruit: **một quả dừa** "a coconut," **hai quả dứa** "two pineapples," **ba quả dưa hấu** "three watermelons," **bốn quả thanh long** "four dragon fruits."

Quyển is similar to **cuốn** and is used in the northern dialect, where **quyển** and **cuốn** are interchangeable. The southern dialect uses only **cuốn** for books.

Tấm is used for long thin flat items: **tấm vải** "a piece of fabric," **tấm thảm** "a rug," **tấm ván** "a plank, a board." When used for photos, **tấm** and **bức** are interchangeable: **tấm ảnh / bức ảnh**. **Tấm** is used with some abstract nouns to denote positive feelings: **tấm lòng vàng** "good-heartedness," **tấm thịnh tình** "hospitality."

Tên meaning "name" is used as a term with negative connotations for people: **tên lính** "an enemy soldier," **tên địch** "an enemy soldier," **tên cướp** "a robber."

Thanh is used for things that have a long shape: **thanh gỗ** "a piece of wood," **thanh tre** "a piece of bamboo," **thanh sắt** "a piece of iron," **thanh gươm / kiếm** "a sword," **thanh sô-cô-la** "a chocolate bar."

Thứ lit. meaning "rank, sort, kind" is used for languages: **ba thứ tiếng** "three languages" (see Note 2 about the homonyms **tiếng** in 1.3.1.4.9.).

Toà is used for tall buildings: **hai toà nhà** "two tall buildings." **Toà** is used for some other nouns denoting large buildings as well: **toà lâu đài** "a palace," **toà thành** "a citadel."

Tờ lit. meaning "a sheet of paper" is used for newspapers, magazines and other items printed on paper: **một tờ báo** "a newspaper," **hai tờ tạp chí** "two magazines," **ba tờ rơi** "three flyers," **bốn tờ quảng cáo** "four flyers," **tờ khai** "a form (to be filled out)," **tờ truyền đơn** "a leaflet."

1
Nouns, noun phrases and their components

Trái is used for fruits in the Saigon dialect: **một trái thơm** "a pineapple," **hai trái thanh long** "two dragon fruits," **ba trái chôm chôm** "three rambutans."

Vị borrowed from Chinese (位) is used before some nouns denoting people, positions or professions to show respect for those people: **vị tổng thống** "a president," **vị chủ tịch** "a chairperson," **vị tướng** "a general," **vị giáo sư** "a professor."

Viên is two homonyms in Vietnamese which are Chinese loanwords. They correspond to two Chinese characters. The first one in Chinese lit. means "member" (員 \ 员), and the second one means "round" (圓 \ 圆). Both are used in Vietnamese as classifiers.

Viên$_1$ meaning "member" is used for several nouns denoting positions, ranks and occupations. The phrases containing **viên** may convey some negative connotation; for instance, they may show disrespect: **viên thư kí** "a secretary," **viên thẩm phán** "a judge." **Viên** with the meaning "member" is used as a suffix for word-formation. For more on the suffix **viên** see 4.2.2.2.

Viên$_2$ meaning "something round" is used for nouns which refer to round items: **viên thuốc** "a pill, tablet," **viên đạn** "a bullet." **Viên** and **hòn** are interchangeable in some phrases: **viên gạch / hòn gạch** "a brick," **viên bi / hòn bi** "a small metal ball, a marble," **viên ngọc / hòn ngọc** "a pearl, a gem."

Vở lit. means "note book" and is used for plays: **vở kịch** "a drama," **vở ca kịch / ô pê ra** "an opera," **vở vũ kịch / ba lê** "a ballet," **vở chèo** "a play for northern traditional theater," **vở tuồng** "a play for central traditional theater," **vở cải lương** "a play for southern traditional theater."

1.3.1.2.2 CONSTRUCTIONS IN WHICH NO CLASSIFIER IS USED

1.3.1.2.2.1 NOUNS REFERRING TO FUNCTIONS OF BUILDINGS

Classifiers **ngôi** and **toà** are used for buildings, **căn** for small houses and rooms. However, if a noun refers to the function of a building or a room, no classifier is used: **một bệnh viện** "a hospital," not *một toà bệnh viện; **một thư viện** "a library," not *một ngôi thư viện; **hai phòng học** "two classrooms," not *hai căn phòng học; **ba phòng khám tư** "three private clinics," not *ba căn phòng khám tư.

1.3.1.2.2.2 NOUNS DENOTING PEOPLE AND THEIR OCCUPATIONS

Generally speaking, nouns which denoting people and their occupations do not take classifiers, unless there is a need to place emphasis on their characteristics or to convey some connotation, as in the cases of the previously mentioned **người** and **viên**: **một kĩ sư** (vs. **một người kĩ sư** or **một viên kĩ sư**) "an engineer," **hai kiến trúc sư** (vs. **hai người kiến trúc sư**) "two architects", **ba ca sĩ** (vs. **ba người ca sĩ**) "three singers."

| 1.3.1.2.2.3 | SOME QUANTIFIERS

The quantifiers **mấy, vài, dăm, một vài, vài ba** and **dăm ba** meaning "several, a few" are treated as numbers, which are followed by classifiers: **mấy / vài / dăm / một vài / vài ba / dăm ba tờ báo** "several newspapers." However, when a countable noun follows **nhiều, ít** and **một số**, no classifier is used: **nhiều Ø sách, ít Ø sách, một số Ø sách**.

<u>Note</u>: In some cases, the use of a classifier in Vietnamese corresponds to the use of the English definite article *the*. When no classifier is used in front of a noun, the noun denotes the indefinite reference. When a classifier precedes a noun, the phrase may suggest the definite reference. Compare:

Tôi Ø cần từ điển mới. I need *a* new dictionary. Or: I need new dictionaries.
Tôi cần <u>quyển</u> từ điển mới. I need *the* new dictionary.

| 1.3.2 | *Noun phrase #2:* <u>plural marker + classifier + noun</u>

For instance, **những quyển sách (này)** "(these) books," **các cô sinh viên (ấy)** "(those) (female) students." **Sách** and **sinh viên** are nouns, **những** and **các** are plural markers, **quyển** is the classifiers for books; the noun **sinh viên** meaning people does not take a classifier (see 1.3.1.2.2.2.). **Này** and **ấy** are demonstrative adjectives, which are discussed in 1.3.3.4.

Unlike European languages, a Vietnamese noun does not have inflections to indicate number (see 1.1.2.). A noun in Vietnamese does not have a suffix to denote the plural of the nouns for people unlike the Chinese "們 \ 们." In order to indicate the plurality, Vietnamese uses the plural markers **các** or **những**, depending on the meaning of the sentence, or does not use any word to convey the meaning of plurality if the plurality is clear from the context. Compare:

	singular	plural
Chinese	學生 \ 学生	學生們 \ 学生们
Vietnamese	**học sinh**	**các học sinh**
		or: **những học sinh**
		or: **học sinh**

This part discusses the plural markers and the determiners which are placed before the noun to refer to the plurality as a component of this type of noun phrases.

1.3.2.1 Plural markers

When common nouns appear out of a context, they refer either to the singular or to the plural:

nhà "a house" or "houses"
sách "a book" or "books"
sinh viên "a student" or "students"

The notion of plurarity is conveyed either by **các** or by **những**, which are not interchangeable in the vast majority of cases. **Các** implies that all the items of a set or all the people of a group are involved, while **những** indicates only a certain number of items of a set or a certain number of people of a group which have already been spoken of, or are clear from the context. That being said, **những** cannot be used if there is no context which suggests that only a certain number of items or people are referred to. Compare:

(1) **Tuần trước, chúng tôi đi thăm <u>các</u> thành phố lớn ở đồng bằng sông Cửu Long**. Last week, we visited the large cities in the Mekong River Delta.
(2) **Tuần trước, chúng tôi đi thăm <u>những</u> thành phố lớn ở đồng bằng sông Cửu Long có trường đại học**. Last week, we visited the large cities in the Mekong River Delta that have universities.

(1) implies that this group of people visited all the large cities in the Mekong River Delta, whereas (2) refers only to those large cities where there are universities. Probably, this group of people is interested in learning about higher education in the Mekong River Delta. The phrase **có trường đại học** separates a certain number of large cities from the large cities in general.

Note 1: In many cases, a plural marker is not used if the context makes the plurality clear. For instance, in the sentence **Các sinh viên về nghỉ hè rồi.** "(All) the students have left (their college) for summer vacation.", the plural marker **các** can be dropped with no change in meaning, and the sentence sounds more normal, especially in spoken Vietnamese: **Sinh viên về nghỉ hè rồi**.

Further examples for nouns referring to the plurality without a plural marker:

Nhà trong khu này đắt lắm. <u>Houses</u> in this neighborhood are expensive.
Kĩ sư đang cố gắng tìm giải pháp cho vấn đề kĩ thuật ấy. <u>Engineers</u> are trying to figure out a solution to that technology problem.

Note 2: When a number more than one precedes the noun, the plural marker is not used, unlike English where the plural marker should be used to refer to a number more than one. Compare: **một ngôi nhà** "a house" vs. **hai ngôi nhà** "two hous<u>es</u>;" **một quyển sách** "a book" vs. **ba quyển sách** "three book<u>s</u>."

<u>Note 3</u>: Only **các** is used to form the second and third personal pronouns in the plural (see 1.3.3.7.).

<u>Note 4</u>: Only **những** is used before the noun **người**: **những người giáo viên này** "these teachers," **những người Mĩ kia** "those Americans." **Các người** conveys only the meaning "you (in the plural)" and is used in conversational Vietnamese to express the speaker's negative feelings towards the people (s)he is talking to:

> **Tôi đã nói với các người nhiều lần rồi mà các người không nghe tôi.** I have told you many times but you didn't want to listen to me.

1.3.2.2 Determiners *every, each, all, entire, whole* in Vietnamese

These determiners refer to the plurality or the entirety of something. Vietnamese uses a number of determiners which function differently and in most cases are not interchangeable.

1.3.2.2.1 CẢ

Cả conveys two meanings: "all" and "even."

Cả with the meaning "all" is placed before a noun which refers to a group of people or a set of items and implies that all the people or items are involved:

> **Cả gia đình anh ấy đang đi nghỉ.** All his family is on vacation.

With this function, **cả** and **tất cả** are interchangeable: **Tất cả gia đình anh ấy đang đi nghỉ.**

Cả and **tất cả** are also interchangeable when used before a noun which refers to something as a whole:

> **Chúng tôi ăn hết cả / tất cả cái bánh.** We have eaten all of the cake.

Cả is placed before a noun which denotes a period of time: **cả ngày, cả đêm, cả tuần, cả tháng** etc. With this meaning, **cả** cannot be replaced with **tất cả**:

> **Hôm qua mưa cả ngày.** It was raining the entire day yesterday.

Only **cả** is possible in this sentence.

1 Nouns, noun phrases and their components

Cả also conveys the emphatic meaning "even." With this meaning, **cả** is placed before the word or the phrase on which the emphasis is shown:

> **Trước đây, Việt Nam phải nhập khẩu cả gạo.** Before, Vietnam had to import even rice.

In this sentence, the noun **gạo** functioning as the object of the verb **nhập khẩu** is emphasized. The phrase **cả gạo** can be placed at the beginning of the sentence, and **cũng** meaning "also, as well" follows the subject and precedes the verb:

> **Trước đây, <u>cả gạo</u> Việt Nam <u>cũng</u> phải nhập khẩu.**

One more example:

> **Cửa hàng này mở cửa cả chủ nhật.** This store is open even on Sundays. Or: **<u>Cả chủ nhật</u> cửa hàng này <u>cũng</u> mở cửa.**

In this sentence, the emphasis is put on the time expression **chủ nhật** "on Sundays."

1.3.2.2.2 TẤT CẢ

Tất cả, in addition to the function discussed in 1.3.2.2.1., is placed before a noun in the plural which implies people or items considered individually:

> **Tất cả các ngọn đèn trong phòng được bật sáng.** All the lights in the room are on.
> **Tất cả các bác sĩ ở bệnh viện này nói được tiếng Anh.** All the doctors at this hospital can speak English.

With this meaning, **tất cả** cannot be replaced with **cả**. In spoken Vietnamese, the plural marker **các** can be left out: **Tất cả đèn trong phòng được bật sáng. Tất cả bác sĩ ở bệnh viện này nói được tiếng Anh**.

Tất cả may be used before a personal pronoun in plural:

> **Tất cả chúng tôi sẽ đến họp.** We all will be attending the meeting.

1.3.2.2.3 MỌI

Mọi conveys two meanings, with each of which it functions very differently.

1.3.2.2.3.1. With the meaning "all, every," **mọi** is used before a countable noun without the plural marker:

> **Cô ấy hiểu biết về mọi lĩnh vực.** She is knowledgeable in all the areas.

With this meaning, **mọi** can be replaced with **tất cả**. However, **tất cả** should be followed by the plural marker, while **mọi** is placed right in front of the noun:

> **Cô ấy hiểu biết về tất cả <u>các</u> lĩnh vực.**

Tất cả and **mọi** can be used together, which precedes a countable noun without the plural marker **các** to put more emphasis on the object which follows **tất cả mọi**:

> **Cô ấy hiểu biết về <u>tất cả mọi</u> lĩnh vực.**

Mọi is used in such set expressions, as **mọi người** "everybody," **mọi nơi mọi lúc** "everywhere and anytime." **Mọi** in these expressions can follow **tất cả** with more emphasis: **tất cả mọi người, tất cả mọi nơi mọi lúc**.

1.3.2.2.3.2. **Mọi** with the meaning "every" can be used with nouns denoting time to express the idea of an action that occurred in the past but does not continue at the moment of speaking. This construction contains the word **nhưng** "but, however" to convey the meaning of contrast. With this meaning, **mọi** is placed right before the noun without the plural marker:

> **Mọi năm tháng mười một thời tiết ở Hà Nội bắt đầu lạnh rồi, nhưng năm nay giữa tháng 11 mà nhiệt độ vẫn lên đến trên ba mươi độ C.** Every year the weather in Hanoi in November began to get cold, but this year temperature in mid-November is still in the low 30s Celsius.

1.3.2.2.4 MỖI

Mỗi and **mọi** at first glance may sound close to each other. In fact, they are pronounced differently and are not interchangeable at all.

Mỗi conveys different meanings and with each of those meanings functions differently. **Mỗi** meaning "each" is placed before a countable noun without the plural marker, and the sentence should contain a phrase which refers to a number or an amount of something. The sentence denotes a specific quantity of

I Nouns, noun phrases and their components

something which belongs to each individual member of the same class. For example:

> **Anh ấy cố gắng thu xếp thời gian tập thể thao mỗi tuần bốn buổi.**
> He tries to arrange his time so that he can work out four times a week.

In this sentence, the quantity phrase **bốn buổi** "four times" is mandaroty for using **mỗi**.

> **Mời các bạn ngồi mỗi bàn bốn người.** Please sit down, four at each table.

In this sentence, **bốn người** is the necessary quantity phrase.

Note: With this meaning, the **mỗi** phrase precedes the quantity phrase. The word order is opposite in English. Compare: **mỗi tuần bốn buổi** vs. "four times a week," **mỗi bàn bốn người** vs. "four (people) at each table."

Mỗi is used together with the number **một** "one" to emphasize the small number of something, and the number is only *one*, in contrast with what is expected:

> **Cả buổi sáng tôi chỉ làm được mỗi một việc là dọn dẹp căn phòng của anh ấy.** It took me the entire morning to do just one thing, which was to clean his room.

In this sentence, the speaker expected to do more things on that morning, but (s)he was able only to clean the room.

Mỗi can be used before a noun which denotes time, and the phrase is followed by **một** and an adjective which modifies the verb:

> **Mưa mỗi lúc một to.** It is raining harder and harder.

In this sentence, **lúc** means "moment," **to** is the adjective which modifiers the verb **mưa**. For more on this construction, see 2.6.1.3.

1.3.2.2.5 TỪNG

Từng also means "every," but emphasizes the idea that each individual person in a group performs an action, or each individual item in a set is the object of an action. **Từng** is placed before the noun, which often is followed by the word **một** to place more emphasis on the individual. No plural marker is used between **từng** and the noun:

> **Sau khi viết xong bài, chị ấy kiểm tra từng câu một.** After finishing writing the paper, she checked every single sentence in the paper.

In this sentence, the noun **câu** is the object of the action **kiểm tra**.

> **Từng người một đến bắt tay chúc mừng cô ấy.** Each person came up to her to shake her hand and congratulate her.

In this sentence, each person in this group of people performs the action of coming up to the woman to shake her hand and congratulate her.

1.3.2.2.6 TOÀN AND TOÀN BỘ

Toàn coveys the same meaning as **cả** and **tất cả** when used before a noun which refers to a group of people or a set of items, but **toàn** is chiefly used in formal Vietnamese:

> **cả trường = tất cả trường = toàn trường** "all (students of) the school"
> **nội dung cả bài = nội dung tất cả bài = nội dung toàn bài** "the main idea(s) of the entire paper"
> **cả thành phố = tất cả thành phố = toàn thành phố** "all (the people in) the town"

Toàn bộ conveying the similar meaning is used before a bisyllabic (two-syllable) noun which refers to something as a whole: **toàn bộ cuộc đời** "all the life, one's whole life," **toàn bộ vấn đề** "the whole issue," **toàn bộ lãnh thổ** "the entire territory."

1.3.2.3 Đều emphasizing the plurality

The word **đều**, whose original meaning is "equal," is used after the subject and in front of the predicate to emphasize the plurality in the sense that the action is performed by all the people of a group; or the quality is related to all the items of a set. **Đều** places emphasis on the plurality of the fronted part of the sentence, which can be:

1 The subject of the sentence:

> **Mọi người đều biết chuyện gì đã xảy ra.** Everybody is aware of what has happened.

In this sentence, the emphasis is on "everybody."

2 The object of an action; the object is placed at the beginning of the sentence:

> **Những người ấy tôi đều quen.** I know all of those people.

In this sentence, the emphasis is on "all of those people."

3   The adverbials of place and time which come at the beginning of the sentence:

>   **Ở trong này và ở ngoài kia đều lạnh**. It is cold both here and out there.

In this sentence, the emphasis is on "here and out there."

>   **Năm ngoái và năm nay vùng này đều ít mưa**. (Both) last year and this year this region has not had enough rain.

In this sentence, the emphasis is on "last year and this year."

Note: If both the subject and the object, or both the subject and the place or time are in the plural, what comes first in the sentence is emphasized:

>   **Khách đều đã đi thăm các di tích lịch sử trong thành phố**. All the guests have visited the historic sites of the city. (The emphasis is on the subject **khách** "guests.")
>   **Các di tích lịch sử trong thành phố khách đều đã đi thăm**. The guests have already visited all the historic sites of the city. (The emphasis is on the object **các di tích lịch sử** "historic sites.")
>   **Chúng tôi đều bận vào tối nay và tối mai**. We all are busy tonight and tomorrow night. (The emphasis is on the subject **chúng tôi** "we.")
>   **Tối nay và tối mai chúng tôi đều bận**. We are busy both tonight and tomorrow night. (The emphasis is on the time **tối nay và tối mai** "tonight and tomorrow night.")

1.3.3 | Noun phrase #3: *noun + attributive*

Attributive is a word or a phrase which modifies the head of a noun phrase. Attributive can be 1/ an adjective; 2/ question words **gì** and **nào**; 3/ a noun or pronoun; 4/ a verb or verb phrase. This part discusses the major word classes which function as attributives in this type of noun phrase.

1.3.3.1 | Adjectives as attributives

When an adjective modifies a noun in a noun phrase, it follows the noun. Compare the word order in Vietnamese and English:

>   **sách mới** (lit. book new) "new book"
>   **nhà lớn** (lit. house big) "big house"
>   **ba cái áo trắng** (lit. three classifier shirt white) "three white shirts"

| 1.3.3.1.1 | POSITIVE, COMPARATIVE AND SUPERLATIVE OF THE ADJECTIVES

When modifying the noun, an adjective can be used in the positive, comparative or superlative:

(1) **Tôi cần một quyển từ điển mới như quyển này.** I need a dictionary as new as this one.
(2) **Tôi cần một quyển từ điển mới hơn quyển này.** I need a dictionary newer than this one.
(3) **Tôi cần quyển từ điển mới nhất.** I need the newest dictionary.

In the nouns phrases **một quyển từ điển mới như quyển này** (1), **một quyển từ điển mới hơn quyển này** (2) and **quyển từ điển mới nhất** (3), the adjective **mới** is used in the positive (**mới như quyển này** "as new as this one"), the comparative (**mới hơn quyển này** "newer than this one") and the superlative (**mới nhất** "the newest"). In these cases, the adjective is the head word of the adjective phrase, and the entire adjective phrase in turn modifies the noun functioning as an attributive. For more on adjective phrases, see 3.2.

| 1.3.3.1.1.1 | POSITIVE OF THE ADJECTIVE

An adjective forms its positive by putting **như** or **bằng** between the adjective and the second noun as in (1). The second classifier **quyển** is mandaroty in the positive. The difference between **như** and **bằng** is that **như** conveys a general meaning of positive comparison, whereas **bằng** refers to a quality or quantity which can be mesured:

Họ muốn mua một ngôi nhà lớn như ngôi nhà này. They want to buy a house which would be as big as this one.

In this sentence, the two houses are compared in a general sense.

Họ muốn mua một ngôi nhà lớn bằng ngôi nhà này. They want to buy a house which would be as big as this one.

In this sentence, the speaker implies the size of the two houses.

The negation **không** is placed before the adjective:

Họ muốn mua một ngôi nhà không lớn như / bằng ngôi nhà này. They want to buy a house which would not be as big as this one.

1.3.3.1.1.2 COMPARATIVE OF THE ADJECTIVE

An adjective forms its comparative by adding **hơn**. The second noun is optional in the comparative:

> **Họ muốn mua một ngôi nhà lớn hơn ngôi nhà này.** They want to buy a house which would be bigger than this one.

Or:

> **Họ muốn mua một ngôi nhà lớn hơn.** They want to buy a bigger house.

The negation **không** is placed before the adjective, and the second noun is mandatory:

> **Họ muốn mua một ngôi nhà không lớn hơn ngôi nhà này.** They want to buy a house which would not be bigger than this one.

It is not possible to say: ***Họ muốn mua một ngôi nhà không lớn hơn.**

1.3.3.1.1.3 SUPERLATIVE OF THE ADJECTIVE

An adjective adds **nhất** to form its superlative:

> **Họ muốn mua ngôi nhà lớn nhất.** They want to buy the biggest house.

The word **hơn cả** can be used instead of **nhất** in formal Vietnamese:

> **Các nhà nghiên cứu ở trung tâm này đã tìm ra giải pháp tốt hơn cả.** The researchers at this center have found the best solution.

1.3.3.1.1.4 SECOND + SUPERLATIVE ADJECTIVE + NOUN + NEXT TO / AFTER + NOUN IN VIETNAMESE

> **Hà Nội là thành phố lớn thứ hai ở Việt Nam sau Sài Gòn.** Hà Nội is the second largest city in Vietnam next to / after Sài Gòn.
> **Huế là thành phố đông dân thứ hai ở miền Trung sau Đà Nẵng.** Huế is the second most densely populated city in central Vietnam next to / after Đà Nẵng.

For more on adjectives functioning as the predicate of the sentence, see 5.2.1.2. Adjectival predicate.

1.3.3.2 Adverbs of degree

An adjective which modifies the noun in a noun phrase can be in turn modified by an adverb of degree. The adjective and adverb form an adjective phrase. Some adverbs of dergree are placed before the adjective, while others are placed after the adjective.

In a noun phrase, **rất** meaning "very" is placed after the noun and before the adjective: **một ngôi nhà rất đẹp** "a very beautiful house," **một bản nhạc rất hay** "a very good musical work."

Lắm denotes a higher degree of quality than **rất** and is placed after the adjective: **một ngôi nhà đẹp lắm** "a really beautiful house," **một bản nhạc hay lắm** "a really good musical work."

Khá denotes a lower degree of quality than **rất** and is placed before the adjective: **một ngôi nhà khá đẹp** "a fairly beautiful house," **một bản nhạc khá hay** "a fairly good musical work."

In these phrases, **khá** is used with "favorable" adjectives. **Khá** can be used before with "unfavorable" adjectives as well: **một chiếc xe khá đắt** "a rather expensive car (or motorbike)."

Hơi meaning "rather" is used before "unfavorable" adjectives only: **một chiếc xe hơi đắt** "a rather expensive car (or motorbike)."

Đủ means "enough" and is placed after the adjective: **một quyển từ điển đủ lớn (để đọc báo)** "a dictionary big enough (to read newspapers)."

Tương đối lit. means "relatively" and is placed before the adjective: **sức khoẻ tương đối tốt** "fairly good health," **bài thi tương đối khó** "a relatively difficult exam."

1.3.3.3 Demonstrative adjectives as attributives

Standard Vietnamese has four demonstrative adjectives: **này, kia, ấy, đó**.

The demonstrative adjective **này** corresponds to **đây**, which functions as the demonstrative pronoun. **Ấy** corresponds to **đấy**, which functions as the demonstrative pronoun. **Kia** and **đó** function both as demonstrative adjectives and demonstrative pronouns, depending on the grammatical construction and their positions in a sentence. See 5.2.1.3. for the demonstrative pronouns and their functions.

Này meaning "this" refers to a person or an item which is close to the speaker and the person(s) (s)he is talking to: **kĩ sư này** "this engineer," **cái áo này** "this shirt." It may denote an item which has been spoken of most recently: **bộ phim này** "this movie." In this phrase, the speaker has already mentioned the movie beofore.

Ấy meaning "that" indicates a person or an item which is far away from the speaker, but close to the person(s) the speaker is talking with: **kĩ sư ấy** "that engineer," **cái áo ấy** "that shirt," **bộ phim ấy** "that movie."

Đó conveys the same meaning as **ấy** and they are interchangeable in the northern dialect. Only **đó** is used in the southern dialect.

Kia meaning "that" denotes a person or an item which is far away from both the speaker and the person(s) (s)he is talking to. Usually both the speaker and the person(s) (s)he is talking to can see that person or item and the speaker may be pointing to it: **cô sinh viên kia** "that (female) student," **quyển từ điển kia** "that dictionary." Without a context, **bộ phim kia** as an abstract thing would not make sense.

When the person or the item has already mentioned, the noun denoting it can be omitted: **cái này** "this one," **quyển kia** "that one," **những tờ ấy** "those ones." The implied noun can be recovered from the context: **cái [áo] này** "this shirt," **quyển [từ điển] kia** "that dictionary," **những tờ [tạp chí] ấy** "those magazines."

Note 1: When the noun is modified by an adjective and a demonstrative, the word order is as follows: classifier + noun + adjective + demonstrative: **cái áo đỏ này** "this red shirt," **quyển từ điển mới kia** "that new dictionary." Note that the word order of the English noun phrase is opposite.

Note 2: The meaning changes if the word order changes: **quyển từ điển mới kia** is a noun phrase and means "that new dictionary," whereas **Quyển từ điển kia mới** is a complete sentence and means "That dictionary is new." For more on adjectives functioning as the predicate of the sentence, see 5.2.1.2. Adjectival predicate.

Note 3: In the recent years the demonstrative pronoun **đấy** in the Hanoi dialect is used with the function of the demonstrative adjective **ấy**. For instance, **kĩ sư đấy**, **cái áo đấy**, **bộ phim đấy**. This non-standard usage is acceptable only in colloquial speech.

1.3.3.4 Question words gì and nào as attributives

Gì is the equivalent of the English "what," and **nào** is the equivalent of "which." They function as attributives in this type of noun phrase. In Vietnamese, **gì** and **nào** follow a noun to modify it, whereas "what" and "which" in English precede the noun: **sách gì?** "what kind of books?", **quyển sách nào?** "which book?"

Since **gì** is used to ask a general question about a person or a thing, a classifier is not used, whereas a classifier should be used befor the noun which is followed by **nào**, if the noun takes a classifier:

(1) Q: **Bà ấy là bác sĩ gì?** A doctor in what area is she?
(2) A: **Bà ấy là bác sĩ mắt.** She is an ophtalmologist.

(3) Q: **Bác sĩ nào hẹn khám cho anh?** Which doctor made the appointment to see (examine) you?
(4) A: **Bác sĩ Thu hẹn khám cho tôi.** *Doctor Thu made the appointment to see (examine) me.*

Because the noun **bác sĩ** "doctor, physician" does not take a classifier (see 1.3.1.7.2.2.), no classifier is used in the noun phrase **bác sĩ nào** (3).

(5) Q: **Chị tìm tạp chí gì?** *What kind of a journal are you looking for?*
(6) A: **Tôi tìm tạp chí lịch sử.** *I am looking for journals on history.*
(7) Q: **Chị tìm tờ tạp chí nào?** *Which journal are you looking for?*
(8) A: **Tôi tìm tờ tạp chí số ra tháng 11 năm 2017.** *I am looking for the issue of the journal which came out in November 2017.*

In (5), the question refers to the general information about a kind of journals, therefore no classifier is used before the noun **tạp chí**. In (7), **nào** refers to a particular issue of the journal. The classifier **tờ** is used before the noun **tạp chí**.

Note 1: Only **nào** is placed after the noun **nước** "country," **gì** is not used in this case. A question about a person's nationality and the reply to it should be:

Q: **Chị là người nước nào?** *Where (what country) are you from?*
A: **Tôi là người Nhật.** *I am Japanese / from Japan.*

Nước is used only in the question before the question word **nào** and is not used in the reply. The sentence *****Tôi là người nước Nhật.** is incorrect.

Note 2: Both **gì** and **nào** are possible after the noun **tiếng** "language." They maintain the difference between **gì** and **nào**:

(1) Q: **Học kì này cậu học tiếng gì?** *What language are you taking this semester?*
(2) A: **Mình định học tiếng Tây Ban Nha.** *I am planning to take Spanish.*
(3) Q: **Học kì này cậu học tiếng nào?** *Which language are you taking this semester?*
(4) A: **Mình định học tiếng Tây Ban Nha.** *I am planning to take Spanish.*

In (1) **gì** is used because the speaker is asking a general question about a foreign language the person in (2) is going to take this semester. In (3) **nào** is used because the foreign languages their school offers this semester have been mentioned before, and the person in (4) is going to choose one of them.

I Nouns, noun phrases and their components

Tiếng should be used both in the question and in the reply. For more on the use of **người** and **tiếng**, see 1.3.3.5.1.

1.3.3.5 Nouns as attributives

1.3.3.5.1 INTRODUCTION OF NOUNS FUNCTIONING AS ATTRIBUTIVES

A noun can function as an attributive of a noun phrase and is called nominal attributive. With this function, the nominal attributive <u>follows</u> the noun, which is the head of the noun phrase. Note the opposite word order in English, where a nominal attributive <u>precedes</u> the noun when modifying it: **một đôi giầy da** (lit. one pair shoe leather) "a pair of leather shoes," **da** is nominal attributive; **một quyển từ điển Việt-Anh** (lit. one classifier dictionary Vietnam England) "a Vietnamese-English dictionary" (lit. **Việt** means "Vietnam," **Anh** means "England"), **Việt-Anh** is nominal attributive; **người Pháp** (lit. person / people France) "a French person," **Pháp** is nominal attributive; **tiếng Nhật** (lit. language Japan) "Japanese language," **Nhật** is nominal attributive.

Note 1: In English, an adjective which is derived from the name of a country can be used to refer to the nationality and the language spoken in the country:

She is [an] American. She speaks English.

Because Vietnamese does not have a grammatical means to form an adjective from a noun like American < America and English < England, the name of a country only refers to the country: **Việt Nam** "Vietnam," **Mĩ** "America, the USA," **Anh** "England, the UK," **Pháp** "France," **Nhật [Bản]** "Japan" etc.

In order to form a noun for the nationality, **người** "person or people" is used before the name of the country: **người Việt [Nam]** "Vietnamese person / people," **người Mĩ** "American person / people," **người Anh** "English person / people," **người Pháp** "French person / people," **người Nhật [Bản]** "Japanese person / people." **Nhật Bản** is the full name of Japan. However, Vietnamese usually leaves out **Bản** in spoken Vietnamese and uses only **Nhật** instead.

In order to form a noun for the language spoken in a country, the noun **tiếng** "language" is placed before the name of the country: **tiếng Việt** "Vietnamese language," **tiếng Anh** "English language," **tiếng Pháp** "French language," **tiếng Nhật** "Japanese language."

That being said, the sentences **She is [an] American. She speaks English**. in Vietnamese are **Chị ấy là người Mĩ. Chị ấy nói tiếng Anh**. The sentences ***Chị ấy là Mĩ. Chị ấy nói Anh**. are not possible.

Note 1: There is a slight difference between **người Việt Nam** and **người Việt**. The former refers to the Vietnamese nationality of a person, while the latter denotes the Vietnamese origin of a person. **Hàn Quốc** is the Vietnamese name of South Korea. Only **người Hàn Quốc** is used for "South Korean person / people." *__Người Hàn__ is not possible, unless used in a historical context. Only **người Trung Quốc** is correct. *__Người Trung__ is not possible. The term **người Hoa** usually refers to the overseas Chinese. Both **người Nhật** and **người Nhật Bản** are used, but the former is more common in everyday Vietnamese.

Note 2: As for languages, only **tiếng Việt** is used, *__tiếng Việt Nam__ is incorrect, and the same with **tiếng Nhật** for the Japanese language. However, either **tiếng Trung Quốc** or **tiếng Trung** or **tiếng Hoa** is used for the Chinese language (Mandarin). Both **tiếng Hàn** and **tiếng Triều Tiên** are used for the Korean language, but the former is more common in contemporary Vietnamese. **Triều Tiên** is the name of the entire peninsula.

Noun phrases and their components

1.3.3.5.2 USE OF CỦA

The noun which modifies the head of the noun phrase follows the head and refers to the possession: **nhà bạn tôi** "my friend's house," **phòng bác sĩ Loan** "Doctor Loan's office." In general, in order to indicate the possession, Vietnamese uses the word **của**, which lit. means "property." **Của** can be added to these two sentences with no change in their meanings: **nhà của bạn tôi**, **phòng của bác sĩ Loan**. In this grammatical construction, **của** functions as a preposition, which is equivalent to the English "of" or the possessive case: **the car (or motorbike) of my friend**, or **my friend's car (or motorbike)**; **the office of Doctor Loan**, or **Doctor Loan's office**. For more on **của** as a verbal predicate, see the note in 5.2.1.3.

The preposition **của**, however, is mandatory in the following cases:

1) If the head of the noun phrase is modified by other words: **ngôi nhà mới của bạn tôi** "my friend's new house." In this phrase, the noun **nhà** is modified by the classifier **ngôi** and the adjective **mới**. The phrase *__ngôi nhà mới bạn tôi__ is incorrect. Another example: **tiểu thuyết *Chiến tranh và hoà bình* của Lev Tolstoi** "Novel *War and Peace* by Leo Tolstoy." The title *Chiến tranh và hoà bình* modifies the noun **tiểu thuyết**, therefore **của** cannot be omitted.

2) If the head of the noun phrase contains a verb as its component: **câu trả lời của anh ấy** "his answer." In this phrase, the noun **câu trả lời** meaning "answer" contains the component **trả lời**, which is a verb. If the preposition

I Nouns, noun phrases and their components

của is left out, the meaning changes: **câu trả lời anh ấy** means "the answer to his question." Another example: in the sentence **Bài kiểm tra của bạn tôi có nhiều lỗi** "My friend's quiz has quite a few mistakes (my friend made quite a few mistakes in his quiz)", the noun **bài kiểm tra** contains the component **kiểm tra**, which is a verb with the meaning "to test." If **của** is dropped, the sentence **Bài kiểm tra bạn tôi có nhiều lỗi** means "The quiz designed to test my friend contains quite a few typos."

3) If the head of the noun phrase is a kinship term, **của** is not used: **bà tôi** "my grandmother," **chú chị ấy** "her uncle." However, **của** should be used to avoid ambiguity: **bà Hiền** means "Mrs. / Ms. Hiền," whereas **bà của Hiền** means "Hiền's grandmother;" **chú Vinh** means "uncle Vinh," while **chú của Vinh** means "Vinh's uncle."

Possessive pronouns and personal pronouns in Vietnamese will be discussed in depth below.

1.3.3.5.3 POSSESSIVE PRONOUNS AND PERSONAL PRONOUNS

English has the following possessive adjectives and possessive pronouns which correspond to the personal pronouns: my, mine ↔ I; our, ours ↔ we; your, yours ↔ you; his ↔ he; her, hers ↔ she; its ↔ it; their, theirs ↔ they. Vietnamese uses **của** before a personal pronoun to turn it into a possessive pronoun.

Note: In many instances, English uses a possessive pronoun whereas Vietnamese does not. For example, the English sentence *He defended his doctoral dissertation last year* should be **Anh ấy bảo vệ luận án tiến sĩ năm ngoái**. The sentence ***Anh ấy bảo vệ luận án tiến sĩ của anh ấy / của mình năm ngoái** would not make sense because he could not defend someone else's dissertation.

Strictly speaking, Vietnamese has only the following personal pronouns:

	Singular	Plural
First Person	**tôi, mình**	**chúng tôi, chúng ta, ta, chúng mình, mình**
Second Person	∅	∅
Third Person	**nó**	**họ, chúng nó**

There is no second personal pronouns which function only as personal pronouns.[2] Vietnamese uses kinship terms as first, second and third personal pronouns. There are some differences between the kinship terms in the northern and southern dialects. The charts here list the kinship terms in the two dialects separately for comparison.

Noun phrases and their components

The kinship terms in the northern dialect are as follows (the symbol + stands for "married to"):

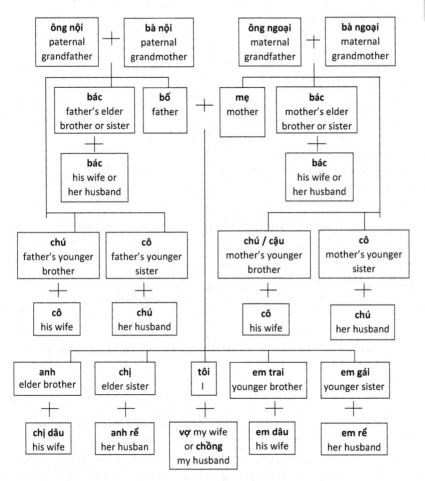

In the northern dialect the kindship terms are differentiated by the hierarchy of the relatives.

The kinship terms in the southern dialect are as follows:

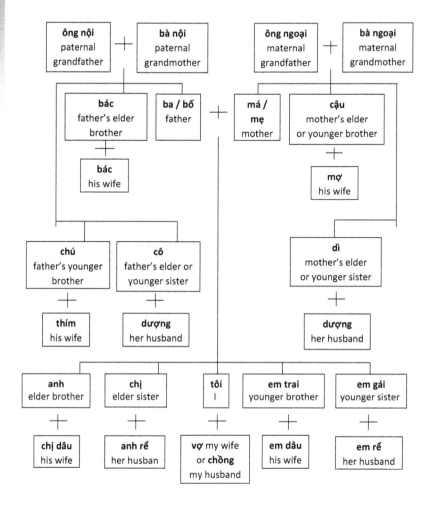

In the southern dialect the kinship terms are differentiated by 1) whether they are on the paternal or maternal side; 2) whether they are related by bloood or by marriage; 3) whether it is a male or a female relative. However, there are two exceptions in the southern system of kinship terms: 1) **dượng** is either father's sister's husband or mother's sister's husband (the principle paternal side vs. maternal side is not relevant); 2) **bác** is either father's elder brother or father's elder brother's wife (the principle related by blood vs. related by marrige and the principle male vs. female are not relevant).

There are several kinship terms which are commonly used but not included in the charts.

Cụ means "great-grandparent" in standard Vietnamese, which is equivalent to **cố** in central and southern Vietnam.

Cha means "father" and is used in formal Vietnamese. Some families in Vietnam use this term instead of **bố** or **ba**. Since **cha** is rather formal, the compound **cha mẹ** is often used for the relations between the generations instead of **bố mẹ**: **cha mẹ và con cái** "parent-child" or "parents-children;" **cha mẹ và giáo viên** "parent-teacher."

Cháu refer to two generations. It means "nephew" or "niece," and also means "grandchild."

The English term "cousin" is expressed by the kinship terms which precede the word **họ**: **anh họ, chị họ, em họ. Họ** can follow a kinship term denoting the older generation, for instance, **chú họ** "father's male cousin;" and the younger generation, for instance, **cháu họ** "cousin's son or daughter."

The English term "in-law" corresponds to different terms in Vietnamese. The in-laws of the same generation are **anh rể** "husband of one's elder sister," **em rể** "husband of one's younger sister," **chị dâu** "wife of one's elder brother" and **em dâu** "wife of one's younger brother." **Bố chồng** is one's husband's father, **mẹ chồng** is one's husband's mother, **bố vợ** is one's wife's father, **mẹ vợ** is one's wife's mother.

Note: The gender of some kinship terms is unclear. In that case, the words **trai** "male" and **gái** "female" are added. For instance, **em trai** "younger brother," **em gái** "younger sister," **con trai** "son," **con gái** "daughter."

Many of the kinship terms can be used as personal pronouns.

Anh is used to address a young male person. **Chị** is used to address a young female person. An older person may use **cô** to address a young female person.

Bác is used to address an older person of both genders. **Ông** and **bà** are used for an older male and female person respectively, but in very formal Vietnamese.

Em and **cháu** are used for addressing children.

Tôi meaning "I, me" is the first personal pronoun used in the most formal and polite situations.

Mình is also the first personal pronoun used for more friendly relations.

Mình also serves as a reflexive pronoun, which corresponds to the English reflexive pronouns ending in *-self*. For instance:

> **Anh ấy chỉ có thể trách <u>mình</u> chứ không thể trách người khác.**
> He can blame himself rather than the others.
> **Bà ấy không thích nói về <u>mình</u>.** She doesn't like to talk about herself.

Noun phrases and their components

1
Nouns, noun phrases and their components

The choice of a kinship term as a second personal pronoun usually depends on 1/ the age of the persons involved in a conversation; 2/ their social positions; and 3/ their relations. In most cases, a non-native speaker should go ahead and ask the person(s) he / she is interacting with what term can be appropriate in a particular situation.

Note 1: The kinship terms used by the members of a family can be either "I" or "you":

Father: **Con muốn sáng mai bố đánh thức con dậy lúc mấy giờ?**
What time do you want me to wake you up tomorrow morning?
Son / daughter: **Sáng mai bố đánh thức con dậy lúc sáu giờ nhé.**
Please wake me up at 6 AM.

In the father's question, **con** is "you," **bố** is "I, me." In the son's / daughter's response, **bố** is "you," **con** is "I, me."

Note 2: Very often Vietnamese use one's name as a second personal pronoun in a friendly context. For instance, person A is an older woman than person B; person B's name is **Hiền**.

A: **Hiền có giúp chị được việc này không?** Could you help me with this?
B: **Vâng, em giúp chị được.** Yes, I could.

In A's question, **Hiền** is "you," **chị** is "I, me." In B's response, **em** is "I, me," **chị** is "you."

Note 3: The two persons in this conversation are using friendly personal pronouns to address each other and to refer to themselves. They cannot go back to the formal pronouns, such as **chị** and **tôi**, unless they are no longer in friendly relations. In other words, they can go from a more formal term to a more familiar term, but not the other way.

Note 4: In Vietnamese schools, a female teacher is addressed by her students as **cô**, and a male teacher is addressed as **thày / thầy**. At elementary, middle and high schools, a teacher uses **em** to address a student. A female teacher refers to herself as **cô**, and a male teacher refers to himself as **thày / thầy**. At a college or university, a faculty member addresses a female student as **chị** and a male student as **anh**. A faculty member uses **tôi** to refer to herself / himself.

| 1.3.3.5.4 | THIRD PERSONAL PRONOUNS |

Third personal pronouns are formed by adding **ấy** to a kinship term: **bà** "grandmother; you" → **bà ấy** "she;" **ông** "grandfather; you" → **ông ấy** "he;" **chị** "elder sister; you" → **chị ấy** "she;" **cô** "aunt; you" → **cô ấy** "she;" **anh** "elder brother; you" → **anh ấy** "he;" **bác** "uncle or aunt; you" → **bác ấy** "(s)he;" **cụ** "great-grandfather / great-grandmother; you" → **cụ ấy** "(s)he;" etc.

The pronoun **nó** "(s)he," "it" may be used for both people and things. When **nó** refers to an adult person, it sounds familiar. As a rule, **nó** cannot be used for an older person or a person for whom one is supposed to express respect.

Even when **nó** is used for a child, it is still familiar. In a polite context, an adult person would not be use **nó** for the child of the person (s)he is talking to. "**Cháu**" is the appropriate term. However, the child's parent can use **nó**:

A: **Cháu học thế nào?** How is your child doing in school? (lit. "How does (s)he study?")
B: **Nó học cũng được.** (S)he is doing OK.

Nó can be used for any animal and inanimate object as well.

| 1.3.3.5.5 | PERSONAL PRONOUNS IN THE PLURAL |

Both **chúng tôi** and **chúng ta** mean "we." The exclusive **chúng tôi** excludes the person(s) a group of people is talking to, while the inclusive **chúng ta** includes the person(s) a group of people is talking to. **Chúng mình** can be either exclusive or inclusive depending on the context.

Chúng em meaning "we" is used by students to refer to themselves when they speak with their teacher.

The second personal pronouns in the plural are formed by adding **các** to the kinship terms: **bà → các bà; ông → các ông; chị → các chị; anh → các anh; cậu → các cậu; em → các em; cháu → các cháu** and so on.

The third personal pronouns in the plural are formed by adding **các** to the singular third pronouns: **bà ấy → các bà ấy; ông ấy → các ông ấy; chị ấy → các chị ấy; anh ấy → các anh ấy; cậu ấy → các cậu ấy; em ấy → các em ấy; cháu ấy → các cháu ấy** and so on.

The plural third pronoun **họ** sounds cold and distant, which is used when the speaker does not want to show any emotions. It is why this term is not used for members of a family. For instance, children never call their parents **họ**.

The plural third pronoun **chúng nó** is very familiar and is used for children or by young people when they speak of their peers.

| 1.3.3.5.6 | OTHER PERSONAL PRONOUNS |

In addition to the personal pronouns introduced earlier, there are several other terms functioning as the personal pronouns.

Noun phrases and their components

1
Nouns, noun phrases and their components

Bạn lit. meaning "friend" is widely used as a second personal pronoun in the singular when a neutral language is needed, for instance, in a questionnaire, a survey or an announcement. This term is rarely used as a singular second pronoun in a conversation between two people.

The plural second pronoun **các bạn** is commonly used in formal speech, as well as in conversational Vietnamese.

Người ta refers to third persons in general excluding the participants in the current conversation. It is to some degree similar to the English *people*, the French *on* or the German *man*:

> **Đừng làm thế, người ta cười cho.** Don't do that. *People* would find you to be foolish.
> **Anh ấy không cần biết người ta nghĩ gì về anh ấy.** He doesn't care what *people* think of him.

The first singular pronoun **tớ** is mostly used by young people in a very friendly relaxed setting. The second personal pronoun used with **tớ** is **cậu**, if the other speaker is a male, or **đằng ấy**, if the other speaker is either a male or a female:

> **Cậu / Đằng ấy làm giúp tớ việc này nhé?** "Would you mind doing this for me, please?"

Tao as a first singular personal pronoun is extremely familiar and is chiefly used by young people. Otherwise, it may convey a very negative connotation. Generally speaking, a non-native speaker should not use **tao** to refer to herself or himself when interacting with Vietnamese.

The second singular personal pronoun used in a pair with **tao** is **mày**. **Mày** is used for both a female or a male speaker:

> **Mày làm giúp tao việc này nhé?** Would you mind doing this for me, please?

Hắn is used as a third personal pronoun for a male. This term chiefly conveys a negative connotation.

Y is another third personal pronoun, which, like **hắn**, conveys a negative connotation, but is used for both genders.

1.3.3.6 Verbs and verb phrases as attributives

In Vietnamese a verb can easily come after a noun to modify it. The noun and the verb or verb phrase form a noun phrase. For instance, **nhà để xe** is composed of the noun **nhà** "house," which is the head of the phrase, the verb **để** "(to) park" and the noun **xe** "car" or "motorbike." Many of such units are perceived by native speakers as whole words, which are equivalent to whole words in European languages. In this case, **nhà để xe** corresponds to the English and French *garage*, the German *Garage*, the Russian *гараж*, and to the loanword **ga ra** used in spoken Vietnamese (see 4.2.4.2. for French loanwords).

Some grammarians regard them as compound nouns, which will be discussed in 4.1., while others analyze them as three separate words, which modify each other and first form a verb phrase, and then form a noun phrase. The noun **xe** modifies the verb **để** as its direct object. The verb phrase **để xe** meaning "park a motorbike or a car" modifies the noun **nhà** to form the noun phrase **nhà để xe**, which would be translated word for word into English as *a house to park motorbikes / cars*, or *a house where motorbikes / cars are parked*. The subordinate relation between **nhà**, **để** and **xe** in the noun phrase **nhà để xe** can be illustrated as follows:

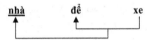

The head of the noun phrase is underscored, and the arrows show the direction from the modifier to the modified.

An extended verb phrase just follows a noun to modify it as its attributive in Vietnamese, whereas European languages need a verb infinitive or a subordinate clause to express the same ideas:

(1) **Bà ấy mở một cửa hàng bán hàng tạp hoá và văn phòng phẩm.** She opened a shop to sell dry goods and office supplies. Or: She opened a shop that sells dry goods and office supplies.

(2) **Họ sống trong một ngôi nhà nhỏ nằm ngay trên bờ hồ.** They live in a small house that lies right on the (bank of the) lake.

In (1) the nous **hàng tạp hoá** and **văn phòng phẩm** modify the verb **bán** as its direct objects; the verb phrase **bán hàng tạp hoá và văn phòng phẩm** modifies the noun **cửa hàng**:

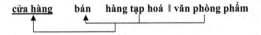

In (2) the verb phrase **nằm ngay trên bờ hồ** modifies the noun **nhà**, which has already been modified by the number **một**, the classifier **ngôi** and the adjective **nhỏ**. The noun phrase **một ngôi nhà nhỏ nằm ngay trên bờ hồ**

consists of severel levels of subordinate relations, which can be shown as follows:

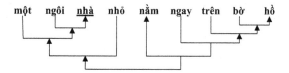

In 1.3.1.2., we discussed the subordinate relationship between the abstract noun **ngôi** and the concrete noun **nhà**, in which **nhà** modifies **ngôi**. In that case, the arrow has a different direction:

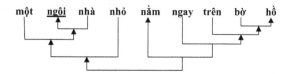

1.4 Main functions of nouns and noun phrases

In the following pair of examples, the first sentence contains a noun, the second one has a noun phrase.

1.4.1 Subject of a sentence

Sinh viên đang chuẩn bị thi. Students are studying for their final exams.

Sinh viên lớp này sẽ thi vào ngày mai. The students of this class are taking their final tomorrow.

1.4.2 Direct object of a verb

Nhà máy này sản xuất **ô tô**. This factory manufactures cars.

Nhà máy này sản xuất **ô tô vừa chạy bằng xăng vừa chạy bằng điện**. This factory manufactures hybrid cars that run on both gas and electricity.

1.4.3 Indirect object of a verb

Tôi tặng **bạn** một quyển sách về lịch sử Việt Nam hiện đại. I gave my friend(s) a book (as a gift) on modern Vietnamese history.

Tôi tặng **những người bạn mới** một quyển sách về lịch sử Việt Nam hiện đại. I gave my new friends a book (as a gift) on modern Vietnamese history.

| **1.4.4** | *Subject predicative* |

A noun or noun phrase following the verb **là** functions as the predicate of a sentence:

>Main functions of nouns and noun phrases

Bố anh ấy <u>là kĩ sư</u>. His father is an engineer.
Bố anh ấy <u>là kĩ sư chuyên về tin học</u>. His father is a computer science engineer (lit. an engineer spezializing in computer science.)

| **1.4.5** | *Object predicative* |

Họ coi anh ấy là <u>bạn</u>. They regard him as a friend.
Họ coi anh ấy là <u>một người bạn tốt đáng tin cậy</u>. They regard him as a good reliable friend.

For more on objective predicative, see 2.4.5.

| **1.4.6** | *Complement of a preposition* |

Chị ấy đi Việt Nam công tác vào <u>mùa hè</u>. She is going to Vietnam on a business trip in the summer.
Chị ấy đi Việt Nam công tác vào <u>mùa hè sang năm</u>. She is going to Vietnam on a business trip in the summer of next year.

| **1.4.7** | *Modifier of a noun as its attributive* |

Giáo sư Thành là chủ nhiệm <u>khoa</u>. Professor Thành is the Dean of the Faculty.
Giáo sư Thành là chủ nhiệm <u>khoa Việt Nam học Đại học Khoa học xã hội và nhân văn</u>. Professor Thành is the Dean of the Faculty of Vietnamese studies at the University of Social Sciences and Humanities.

Notes

1 The numbers in this paragraph are written in English, with a comma separating thousands.
2 The term **mày** as a second singular personal pronoun is discussed later.

Chapter 2

Verbs, verb phrases and their components

2.1 Introduction to the Vietnamese verbs

The main syntactic function of a verb in European languages is to form the predicate of a sentence. In some languages, including Vietnamese, not only verbs but adjectives aslo perform this syntactic function. This work does not use the terms *dynamic verbs* and *static* (or *state*, or *stative*) *verbs* for Vietnamese. The majority of verbs denote an action, which are dynamic verbs, whereas some verbs indicate state of affairs, and they may be called *static verbs*. On the other hand, most adjectives describe the qualities or characteristics of a noun, but some adjectives can express the state of affairs of the subject as well. Such adjectives can also be referred to as *static verbs* (as in Chinese). The terms *verb* and *adjective* are used in this work in the traditional sense. This chapter is discussing verbs in Vietnamese. Adjectives will be discussed in the next chapter.

The following features make Vietnamese verbs different from verbs in many European languages.

2.1.1. The form of a verb is invariable. It does not conjugate for personal pronouns, tenses, gender or number.

2.1.2. The tense is usually indicated by the time expression in a sentence, or is clear from the context. There are a number of words which may refer to a particular tense. Some of them are used for emphasis of a tense. The other words function as aspect markers.

2.2 Types of verbs

Verbs in Vietnamese can be divided into three major types: verb **là** "be," verb **có** "have" and all other verbs, which include different semantic groups of verbs such as causative verbs, vebs of motion, modal verbs, verbs of speaking, etc.

2.2.1 | Là and the English to be

The English *to be* functions as (a) an auxiliary verb (aa) to form the continuous tenses of the verb (He *is working* on his book. I *was reading* when he called me.); (ab) to form the passive voice (The house *is being painted*. I *was told* that the conference *will be held* next month.); (ac) to give an order or to tell someone about a rule (The payment of the bill *is* to be received by or on the due date.); (ad) to show what should happen (Those students *are* to graduate from college this spring.).

The English *to be* also functions as (b) a verb (ba) to link a noun to the subject (They *are* students at this school.); (bb) to link an adjective to the subject to show the subject's quality or state (The new documentary about the Vietnam war *is* very *powerful*. We *were* so *hungry* when we came home from the swimming pool.); (bc) to link a possessive pronoun to the subject to show the possession (This book *is hers*.); (bd) used after *there* to show that something exists (*There is* a lot of snow out there.).

The English *to be* can function as (c) a full verb when preceding an adverb of place or time (*Where is* she? She *is* still *on the way to her office*. The party *was on Saturday night*.)

The function of the Vietnamese verb **là** corresponds only to (ba) of the English *to be*. All the other functions of the English *to be* are expressed by different words or grammatical constructions in Vietnamese. As a rule of thumb, **là** is used before a noun, which is part of the nominal predicate, but is not used before an adjectival predicate. Compare:

English: My friend *is* a teacher.
Vietnamese: **Bạn tôi là giáo viên**.

English: My friend *is* young.
Vietnamese: **Bạn tôi ø trẻ**.

For more on adjectival predicates, see 5.2.1.2.

Note 1: In formal Vietnamese, when the emphasis is shown on the quality denoted by an adjective which functions as the predicate, the verb **là** can be placed in front of the adjective as an intensifier for the emphasis, not as the predicate. Compare the following sentences:

(1) **Vấn đề này quan trọng.** This issue is important.
(2) **Tất cả chúng tôi đều thấy rằng vấn đề này là quan trọng.** We all realized that this issue is important indeed.

2
Verbs, verb phrases and their components

In (1) there is no emphasis. In (2) the emphasis is placed on the adjective **quan trọng**, and the verb **là** is used as an intensifier for the emphatic statement.

See 5.2.2.3. and 5.3.1.2. for the negations and questions containing the verb **là** as the predicate.

Note 2: When a noun which follows **là** as the nominal predicate indicates professions and occupations, **là** and the verb **làm** are interchangeable:

> **Bà ấy là / làm giáo viên ở trường này từ hơn hai mươi năm nay.**
> She has been a teacher at this school for more than twenty years.

Note 3: **Là** may be used as the predicate in existence sentences, which is equivalent to the English *there is / there are*. See 5.1.1.3.2. for detail.

2.2.2 *Có and the English* to have

When functioning as (a) full verbs, both the Vietnamese **có** and the English *to have* indicate possession in its broadest sense: **có tiền** "have money," **có nhà** "have a house," **có xe** "have a car," **có thì giờ** "have time," **có việc làm** "have a job," **có nhiều việc phải làm** "have a lot of things to do," **có hẹn** "have an appointment," **có giờ lên lớp** "have a class meeting."

A big difference between the Vietnamese full verb **có** and the English *to have* is that **có** can begin a sentence of existence while *to have* cannot perform this function. The English introductory *there* is used in the phrases *there is* and *there are* instead. Compare:

> **Có người đang cần gặp chị.** *There is* a person / *are* people who need to talk to you.
> **Chẳng có ai muốn giúp họ cả.** *There is* nobody willing to help them.

See 5.1.1.3.2. and 5.1.1.3.3. for detail about **có** and *there is / there are* in the existence sentences which contain adverbs of place and time.

Both **có** and *to have* are used (b) to form idiomatic expressions. In some expressions, **có** is equivalent *to have*: **có kinh nghiệm** "have experience," **có hai con** "have two children," **có bạn gái / bạn trai** "have a girlfriend / boyfriend," **có hậu** (1) "have a happy ending" (**Bộ phim kết thúc có hậu** = The movie has a happy ending); (see **có hậu** (2) in the following paragraph); **có hậu quả nghiêm trọng** "have serious consequences," **có tình** "have warm, kindly feelings," **có ý kiến khác nhau về một vấn đề** "have differents opinions on a matter."

However, the idiomatic expresssions with **có** in Vietnamese are equivalent to *to be + adjectives* in English in most cases: **có của / có của ăn của để** "be wealthy," **có chửa / có mang / có bầu** "be pregnant," **có da có thịt** "not be skinny," **có gia đình** "be married," **có chồng** "be married (speaking of a woman)," **có vợ** "be married (speaking of a man)," **có hạn** "be limited," **có hậu** (2) "be thoughtful and grateful," **có hiếu** "be filial," **có học** "be well-educated," **có ích** "be helpful or useful," **có lí** "be reasonable," **có tuổi** "be middle-aged."

A number of words in Vietnamese that contain **có** are perceieved by native speakers as whole words. **Có** has completely lost its original meaning in such words as **có khi** "probably" (**Bây giờ mới đi có khi muộn** = We're not leaving until now and, probably, we'll be late); **có mặt** "be present," **có thể** "can, be able."

Both **có** and *to have* function (c) as auxiliary verbs. The functions they perform are very different in the two languages.

Có is used along with **không** in a question construction:

Chị có quen anh ấy không? Do you know him?

For more on this question construction, see 5.3.1.1.

Có can be used before a full verb for emphasis:

Tôi có quen anh ấy. I do know him.

For more on the emphatic **có**, see 5.5.2.

The English *to have* is used as an auxiliary verb to form the perfect tense: *to have written, to have been writing.*

Verb phrase #1: tense / aspect marker + verb

2.2.3 Semantic groups of verbs

Vietnamese verbs belong to different semantic groups such as verbs of speaking and thinking, verbs of feeling, verbs of giving and receiving, causative verbs, verbs of motion, modal verbs. Verbs of each group share some grammatical characteristics and are used in specific grammatical constructions, which are discussed as verb phrases that follow.

2.3 Verb phrase #1: tense / aspect marker + verb

2.3.1 Tense markers

Tense is a grammatical category of verbs in European languages which refers to the time of situation. Different forms of a verb signal the change of its internal

2
Verbs, verb phrases and their components

structure and refer to different tenses. Compare the present and past tenses in English and German: *(he) goes* vs. *went*; *(er) geht* vs. *ging*. The forms of a verb in Russian indicate either the present vs. the past: *(он) идёт* vs. *шёл*, or the past vs. the future: *(он) пошёл* vs. *пойдём*. The forms of a verb in French may indicate all the three tenses, which are present, past and future: *(il) va* vs. *allait* vs. *ira*.

Since the form of a Vietnamese verb is invariable, tense is not a grammatical category of the Vietnamese verb. In general, when a sentence contains a time expression, or the time is clear from the context, a tense marker is not used:

(1) **Họ đến Hà Nội vào đêm qua.** They arrived in Hà Nội last night.
(2) **Hôm nay họ đi thăm một số di tích lịch sử của thủ đô.** Today they are visiting some historic sites of the capital city.
(3) **Tối mai họ bay vào Sài Gòn.** They will be flying down to Sài Gòn tomorrow night.

The time expressions **đêm qua** "last night" in (1), **hôm nay** "today" in (2) and **tối mai** "tomorrow night" in (3) make the tense clear in each sentence.

There are three tense markers in Vietnamese, which are used to emphasize a particular time in which an action takes place. They are **đã**, **đang** and **sẽ**. These tense markers can be placed in front of the main verbs of the three sentences shown to put emphasis on whether an action took place in the past, or is still going on at the present, or will take place in the future. For instance, the tense markers can be added to the three sentences as follows:

(1a) **Họ đã đến Hà Nội vào đêm qua.**
(2a) **Hôm nay họ đang đi thăm một số di tích lịch sử của thủ đô.**
(3a) **Tối mai họ sẽ bay vào Sài Gòn.**

See 2.3.2.5. for the use of **đang** as an aspect marker.

The marker **sẽ** can be used before a verb phrase to show emphasis on the speaker's determination to carry out an action in the future:

Trước thứ tư tuần sau tôi sẽ làm xong việc này cho chị. I will certainly have done this job for you by next Wednesday.

Note: The negations **không** is placed after the tense markers **đã**, **đang** and **sẽ**:

Anh ấy đã không làm như chúng tôi yêu cầu. He did not do it the way we wanted him to do.

Nó đang không có việc gì làm, có thể giao việc này cho nó. He has nothing to do at this point. We can assign him the job.

Tối mai họ sẽ không bay vào Sài Gòn mà đi Nha Trang. They are not going to fly down to Sài Gòn tomorrow night. They will go to Nha Trang instead.

> Verb phrase #1: tense / aspect marker + verb

2.3.2 Aspect markers

Aspect is a grammatical category of verbs in European languages which typically indicates the duration, repetition, beginning or completion of the action or state denoted by the verb. English has two aspects: progressive (or continuous) and perfect. For instance, *is / was / will be doing* vs. *has / had done*. Russian has two aspects, which are imperfect and perfect. For example, *буду читать* vs. *прочту*, *читала / читал* vs. *прочла / прочёл*.

Vietnamese has a number of words which are used together with the main verb of a sentence to indicate the notion of the recent past or immediate future, the duration or persistence of an action, or its completion. They take very different positions in a sentence.

2.3.2.1 Vừa / mới / vừa mới

Vừa / mới / vừa mới are interchangeable and placed right in front of the verb to represent the action which has been completed only in the recent past. They are translated into English as "just":

Chúng tôi vừa / mới / vừa mới thi. We have just taken the final exam(s).

A time expression which refers to a particular moment in the recent past can be added to the sentence:

Chúng tôi vừa / mới / vừa mới thi sáng nay. We have just taken the final exam(s) this morning.

The English translation is made just to illustrate the meaning of the recent past in Vietnamese. The time expression (this morning) is not used in this type of English sentence containing *just*.

See 5.5.6. for **mới** showing emphasis on the adverbials of time.

2.3.2.2 Sắp

Sắp is placed in front of the main verb to denote an action which will take place in the immediate future. **Sắp** is equivalent to the English phrases *be going to* or *be about to*:

> **Chúng tôi sắp thi.** We are going to take the final exam(s). / We are about to take the final exam(s).

The question *Are you going / about to take the final exam(s)?* would contain the negation **chưa** in Vietnamese, which comes at the end of the question:

> **Các bạn sắp thi chưa?**

Sắp is not used with **không** in a negative statement. The idea *We are not going / about to take the final exam(s).* would be expressed in Vietnamese as follows:

> **Chúng tôi chưa thi.**

A time expression can be added to the negative statement:

> **Tuần này chúng tôi chưa thi.** We are not going / about to take the final exam(s) this week.

2.3.2.3 Chưa

The negation **chưa** is placed in front of the main verb to represent an uncompleted action in the past, present or future. **Chưa** is usually translated into English as "not yet":

> **Tuần trước chị ấy chưa đi công tác về.** Last week she still had not returned from the business trip.
> **Anh ấy chưa định đi.** He is not planning to go yet.
> **Tuần sau tôi chưa đi.** Next week I still will not have gone.

See 5.3.1.4. for the details of the questions and replies containing **chưa**.

2.3.2.4 Vẫn / còn / vẫn còn

Vẫn / còn / vẫn còn are interchangeable and placed in front of the main verb to denote an action which began in the past and is still going on at the moment of speaking. They are similar to the English *still*:

Bà ấy vẫn / còn / vẫn còn giảng dậy ở trường này. She is *still* teaching at this school.

Verb phrase #1: tense / aspect marker + verb

2.3.2.5 Đang

Đang performs a two-fold function. On the one hand, as a tense marker it refers to the present time in which an action is taking place. On the other hand, it indicates the duration of an action which is still going on. In this case, **đang** serves as an aspect marker. It can come after **vẫn / còn / vẫn còn** to put more emphasis on the duration of the action:

Bà ấy vẫn / còn / vẫn còn đang giảng dậy ở trường này.

Đang can be placed before **còn** as well:

Bà ấy đang còn giảng dậy ở trường này.

The aspect function of **đang** is clearer in the sentences that refer to the past or future tense. The meaning of present tense completely disappears:

Vào tháng năm năm ngoái, người ta vẫn còn đang xây dựng con đường cao tốc này. Last May they were still constructing this highway.
Tháng năm sang năm anh ấy vẫn đang còn học đại học, chưa tốt nghiệp. Next May he will still be a student, will have not yet graduated.

Đang as an aspect marker is very commonly used for the relation of past and future events in the temporal clauses. See 5.8.3.2.

2.3.2.6 Vẫn and vẫn còn referring to persistence

Vẫn and **vẫn còn** are also used to refer to the persistence of an action which is going on longer than expected or desirable:

Trời vẫn [còn] mưa. It is still (persistently) raining.
Sắp đến giờ đi rồi mà anh ấy vẫn [còn] ngủ. We are leaving soon, but he is still asleep.

Còn alone cannot be used for this feature of the action. However, in conversational Vietnmamese, **hãy còn** is used with this meaning for an action that can be observed at the moment of speaking. The second sentence may be said this way:

Sắp đến giờ đi rồi mà anh ấy hãy còn ngủ.

Hãy with this function should not be mixed up with the imperative **hãy** (see 2.11. for the imperative **hãy**).

Because **vẫn** indicates the persistence of an action, it is used in the clause of concession. For more on the concessive clause, see 5.8.3.4.

2.3.2.7 Rồi

Rồi meaning "already" comes at the end of a sentence to denote a completed action:

> **Tôi nói chuyện với anh ấy về vấn đề này rồi.** I have already talked to him on this matter.

Đã can be added in front of the verb to emphasize the completion:

> **Tôi đã nói chuyện với anh ấy về vấn đề này rồi.**

Rồi also comes at the end of a sentence to refer to an action which began in the past and is continuing in the present. Compare sentences (1) and (2), (3) and (4):

> (1) **Chúng tôi chờ anh ấy nửa tiếng.** We waited for him (for) half an hour.
> (2) **Chúng tôi chờ anh ấy nửa tiếng rồi.** We have been waiting for him (for) half an hour.
> (3) **Cô ấy làm việc ở công ti này ba năm.** She worked for this company (for) three years.
> (4) **Cô ấy làm việc ở công ti này ba năm rồi.** She has been working for this company (for) three years.

The meaning of (4) can be conveyed by the construction **từ + amount of time + nay**:

> (4a) **Cô ấy làm việc ở công ti này từ ba năm nay.**

If the time point is mentioned, in this case that is the year, the construction **từ + X year + đến nay** expresses the same meaning:

> (4b) **Cô ấy làm việc ở công ti này từ năm 2020 đến nay.** She has been working for this company since the year of 2020.

The construction **từ + amount of time + nay** is not used for the clock time. It is impossible to say *__Chúng tôi chờ anh ấy từ nửa tiếng nay__. However, if the time point is mentioned, the construction **từ + X giờ + đến giờ** can be used to convey the same meaning of (2):

> (2a) **Chúng tôi chờ anh ấy từ bảy giờ đến giờ. (Bây giờ là bảy rưỡi.)**
> We have been waiting for him since 7 o'clock. (Now it is seven and a half.)

Rồi can be placed at the end of a statement containing **vừa, mới** and **vừa mới** to put more emphasis on the recent past. In this case, **rồi** does not convey the meaning of an action that is going on at the moment of speaking:

> **Họ <u>vừa mới</u> đến <u>rồi</u>.** They have just arrived.
> **Buổi họp <u>vừa mới</u> kết thúc <u>rồi</u>.** The meeting was just over.

Verb phrase #1: <u>tense / aspect marker + verb</u>

2.3.2.8 Xong

Xong meaning "finished, done" is placed after a verb to express an action which reached an end:

> **Họ làm <u>xong</u>.** They have / are finished / done.

If the verb takes an object, **xong** is either inserted between the verb and the object, or placed at the end of the sentence:

> **Họ làm <u>xong</u> việc ấy. = Họ làm việc ấy <u>xong</u>.** They have finished / done that work.

However, if the object is expressed by a long phrase, **xong** should be inserted between the verb and the object:

> **Họ làm <u>xong</u> việc mà chúng tôi giao cho họ.** They have finished / done the job that we assigned (to) them.

It would be incorrect to say: ***Họ làm việc mà chúng tôi giao cho họ <u>xong</u>**.

Xong may be used in combination with some other aspect and tense markers to put more emphasis on the completion:

> **Họ <u>đã</u> làm <u>xong</u> việc ấy <u>rồi</u>.**
> **Họ <u>vừa / mới / vừa</u> mới làm <u>xong</u> việc ấy <u>rồi</u>.**

The negation **chưa** meaning "not yet" is placed in front of the verb to denote that the action has not been completed yet:

> **Họ <u>chưa</u> làm xong việc ấy.** They have not yet finished the job.

2.3.2.9 Hết

Hết meaning "end" performs three functions.

1 It is placed <u>in front of some verbs or adjectives</u> to denote a state which is no longer continuing. **Rồi** usually comes at the end of the sentence:

> **Trời <u>hết</u> nắng <u>rồi</u>.** The sun is no longer shining.
> **Bà ấy <u>hết</u> lo về chuyện ấy <u>rồi</u>.** She is no longer worried about it.

The negative statement containing **hết** uses **chưa**, not **không**:

> **Trời <u>chưa</u> hết nắng.** The sun is still shining.
> **Bà ấy <u>chưa</u> hết lo về chuyện ấy.** She is still worried about it.

2 It is placed <u>after a verb and before its object</u> to indicate an amount or quantity of something which is used up when an action is completed:

> **Ông ấy đọc <u>hết</u> tờ báo.** He [has finished] read the whole newspaper.
> **Họ làm <u>hết</u> việc mới về.** They did not leave until finishing all the things (they were supposed to do).

The negative statement containing **hết** with this function can use either **chưa** or **không**, but the two negations convey different meanings.

> **Ông ấy <u>chưa</u> đọc <u>hết</u> tờ báo.** He has not yet finished reading the whole newspaper.

The negative statement with **chưa** implies that he will continue reading the newspaper until finishing it.

> **Ông ấy <u>không</u> đọc <u>hết</u> tờ báo.** He did not finish reading the newspaper.

The statement with **không** emphasizes his inability to finish reading the whole newspaper, because he was so tired and fell asleep while reading, or the newspaper had many boring articles, etc.

The difference between **hết** and **xong** is that **hết** emphasizes the amount which has been finished up when the action is completed, while **xong** refers to the process of an action which is completed. **Xong** can either be placed between the verb and its object or come at the end of the sentence:

> **Họ làm <u>xong</u> việc. = Họ làm việc <u>xong</u>.** They have finished the job.

Hết should be inserted between the verb and its object:

> **Họ làm <u>hết</u> việc.** They have finished all the things to do.

It would be impossible to say *__Họ làm việc <u>hết</u>__.

3 It is placed after several verbs to refer to an action performed by the subject in the <u>plurality</u>, which is similar to the English *all*. The action was done in the past and its result remains evident at the moment of speaking. Very often, it is used together with **rồi**:

> **Khách về <u>hết</u> <u>rồi</u>.** The guests have all left. / All [of] the guests have left.
> **Báo cáo viên đến <u>hết</u> <u>rồi</u>. Có thể bắt đầu cuộc họp.** The presenters have all arrived. / All [of] the presenters have arrived. Let's start our meeting.
> **Báo hôm nay bán <u>hết</u> <u>rồi</u>.** All [of] today's newspapers have been sold out.

Verb phrase #1: <u>tense / aspect marker + verb</u>

2.3.2.10 Hẳn

Hẳn follows a verb to show emphasis on the completion of an action and the result of the completed action is evident at the moment of speaking:

> **Năm ngoái bà ấy bị ốm khá nặng nhưng bây giờ khỏi <u>hẳn</u>.** She got sick pretty seriously last year but has fully recovered now.
> **Mưa đã tạnh <u>hẳn</u> chưa?** Has the rain completely stopped?

If the verb takes an object, **hẳn** is inserted between the verb and the object:

> **Tôi bận quá nên quên <u>hẳn</u> cuộc hẹn.** I was so busy that I completely forgot about the appointment.

Very often, **đã** and **rồi** can be added to put more emphasis on the completion in a positive statement. **Đã** comes in front of the verb, **rồi** follows **hẳn**. The first sentence can be extended this way:

> **Năm ngoái bà ấy bị ốm khá nặng nhưng bây giờ <u>đã</u> khỏi <u>hẳn</u> <u>rồi</u>.**

Hẳn is commonly used in the phrases "adjective + verb of motion" (see 3.2.7. for more details about this type of adjective phrases). **Hẳn** goes between the adjective and the verb of motion:

> **Trời tối <u>hẳn</u> đi.** It has gotten completely dark.
> **Căn phòng không có bàn ghế trông rộng <u>hẳn</u> ra.** The room with no furniture looks really large.

2.4 Verb phrase #2: verb + object

As in English, the direct object follows the verb in Vietnamese: **đọc sách** "read a book," **nói tiếng Anh** "speak English," **làm nhà** "build a house," **mua thực phẩm** "buy food."

A verb can have more than one object. The direct object is immediately affected by the action denoted by the verb. The indirect object is less affected by the action. The word order of the verb phrase and the use of a preposition, if the verb takes a preposition, are more complicated in both English and Vietnamese:

> I gave my friend a book. **Tôi cho bạn tôi một quyển sách.**
> I gave the book to my friend. **Tôi cho bạn tôi quyển sách (ấy).**
> I sent him a letter. / I sent a letter to him. **Tôi gửi thư cho anh ấy.**
> I sent him a detailed letter on this issue. **Tôi gửi cho anh ấy một bức thư chi tiết về việc này.**

Different semantic groups of verbs which have different grammatical constructions are discussed below.

2.4.1 Verbs of giving

This semantic group of verbs conveys the general meaning of giving, which includes **bán** "sell," **biếu** "present with a gift," **cấp** "provide," **cho** "give," **chuyển** "pass, forward," **đưa** "pass," **gửi** "send," **giao** "assign," **mua** "buy," **nộp** "hand in, submit," **nhường** "cede, yield," **tặng** "give something as a gift," **trả** "return, give back," **viết** "write," etc.

There are three grammatical constructions for this group of verbs.

2.4.1.1 Verb + indirect object + direct object

The verbs **cho, tặng, trả** and **biếu** use this construction:

> **Anh ấy cho tôi sách.** He gave me a book / books.
> **Anh ấy biếu tôi sách.** He gave a book / books (as a gift). (formal)
> **Anh ấy tặng tôi sách.** He gave me a book / books (as a gift).
> **Anh ấy trả tôi sách.** He returned the book / books to me. / He gave the book / books back to me.

2.4.1.2 Verb + direct object + cho + indirect object

In this construction, the preposition **cho**, which is mandatory, is inserted between the direct and the indirect objects. The verbs **bán, cấp, chuyển, đưa, gửi, giao, mua, nộp, nhường, viết** belong to this construction:

> **Họ gửi thư <u>cho</u> chúng tôi.** They sent us a letter. / They sent a letter to us.
> **Chị ấy mua vé xem phim <u>cho</u> cả lớp.** She bought movie tickets for all the class.
> **Thứ hai tuần sau chúng tôi phải nộp bài <u>cho</u> cô giáo.** We should hand in the paper to the (female) teacher next Monday.
> **Bà trưởng phòng giao việc này <u>cho</u> anh ấy.** The (female) head of the office has assigned this job to him.
> **Anh ấy nhường đường <u>cho</u> chúng tôi.** He yielded the way to us.

2.4.1.3 Verb + cho + indirect object + direct object

The verbs of the previous group (2.4.1.2.) can be used with a different word order, in which the preposition **cho** is inserted between the verb and the indirect object, and the direct object follows the indirect object, especially when the direct object is expressed by a long phrase. For example:

> (1) **Họ gửi <u>cho</u> chúng tôi một bức thư chi tiết về vấn đề chúng tôi bàn trong cuộc họp tuần trước.** They have sent us a detailed letter on the issue that we discussed at the meeting last week.
> (2) **Giám đốc công ti giao <u>cho</u> anh ấy việc khó nhất là tìm ra lỗi của phần mềm này.** The director of the company has assigned (to) him the hardest job, which is to find out the error(s) of the software.

In (1) and in (2), the emphasis is on the direct objects **bức thư chi tiết** . . . and **việc khó nhất** . . . , while the word order in the contstruction of 2.4.1.2. shows emphasis on the indirect object:

> (1a) **Họ gửi một bức thư chi tiết về vấn đề chúng tôi bàn trong cuộc họp tuần trước <u>cho</u> chúng tôi.**
> (2a) **Giám đốc công ti giao việc khó nhất là tìm ra lỗi của phần mềm này <u>cho</u> anh ấy.**

In (1a) and (2a), the emphasis is on the indirect objects **chúng tôi** and **anh ấy**.

Verb phrase #2: <u>verb + object</u>

2.4.2 Verbs of receiving

The verbs of this semantic group convey the general sense of taking or receiving. They are **ăn cắp** "steal," **ăn trộm** "burgle, burglarize," **cướp** "rob," **chiếm** "seize, capture, occupy," **lấy** "take, gain possession of something," **lấy cắp** "steal," **lấy trộm** "burgle, burglarize," **mượn** "borrow," **nhận được** "receive," **vay** "borrow," etc.

2.4.2.1 Verb + direct object + của + indirect object

Hôm qua tôi nhận được một cú điện thoại của anh ấy. I received a phone call from him yesterday.
Họ vay tiền của ngân hàng để mua nhà. They have borrowed money from the bank to buy a house.
Bây giờ sinh viên ít khi mượn sách của thư viện vì có thể đọc trên mạng. Nowadays students rarely borrow books from the library because they can read them online.
Kẻ trộm lấy bức tranh của bảo tàng cách đây mấy năm. Thieves took the painting from the museum a few years ago.
Nó lấy ví của tôi! He took my wallet!
Chúng nó cướp đồ nữ trang của bà ấy. They robbed her of her jewels.

The preposition **của** may be left out when the verbs are **vay** and **mượn**:

Họ vay tiền Ø ngân hàng ...
... sinh viên mượn sách Ø thư viện ...

Note: Vietnamese does not have the verb which is equivalent to the English verb *to lend*. In order to express the meaning of lending something to someone, Vietnamese uses the verb **cho** before the verbs **mượn** and **vay**: **cho mượn** "lend," **cho vay** "lend money." These verbs belong to the previous group of verbs of giving, but the grammatical construction is a bit different:

cho + indirect object + mượn / vay + direct object

Bạn tôi hay cho tôi mượn sách báo tiếng Việt. My friend often lends me books and newspapers in Vietnamese. / My friend often lends books and newspapers in Vietnamese to me.
Ngân hàng không cho họ vay tiền. The bank did not lend them the money. / The bank did not lend the money to them.

2.4.2.2 Verb + của + indirect object + modified direct object

Verb phrase #2: verb + object

If the direct object is modified by other words or a phrase, it is placed after the indirect object; in this case the preposition **của** immediately follows the verb:

> **Họ vay <u>của</u> ngân hàng một số tiền rất lớn để mua nhà.** They have borrowed a large amount of money from the bank to buy a house.
> **Chúng nó cướp <u>của</u> bà ấy mấy món đồ nữ trang đắt tiền.** They robbed her of some of her expensive jewels.

<u>Note 1</u>: The preposition *from* is used in English whereas the Vietnamese verbs take the preposition **của**. **Từ** is incorrect: *****Họ vay tiền <u>từ</u> ngân hàng.**

<u>Note 2</u>: The Vietnamese verb **lấy** and the English verb *to take* are equivalent to each other only with a few of the many meanings they convey. In most cases, other Vietnamese verbs are used for the phrases where the English *to take* is used:

> It looks like rain. You had better *take* an umbrella with you. **Trời trông như sắp mưa. Chị nên <u>mang</u> theo ô.**
> This bus *takes* you to downtown. **Xe buýt tuyến này sẽ <u>đưa</u> anh vào trung tâm thành phố.**
> It would *take* him at least two days to fix your computer. **Anh ấy chữa máy vi tính của anh chắc <u>mất</u> ít nhất hai ngày.**
> I *take* the bus to work. **Tôi <u>đi</u> xe buýt đi làm [việc]. / Tôi đi làm [việc] bằng xe buýt.**
> Do you *take* credit cards? **Cửa hàng có <u>nhận</u> thẻ tín dụng [để thanh toán] không?**
> His daughter started *taking* ballet lessons when she was five years old. **Con gái anh ấy bắt đầu <u>tập</u> ba-lê từ năm lên 5 tuổi.**
> I am *taking* five classes this semester. **Học kì này tôi <u>học</u> 5 môn.**
> Students will have already *taken* all the final exams by mid-May. **Sinh viên sẽ <u>thi</u> xong tất cả các môn vào giữa tháng 5.**
> I will *take* two days off next week. **Tuần sau tôi sẽ <u>nghỉ</u> 2 ngày.**

Lấy cannot be used in these sentences.

2.4.3 *Causative verbs*

The verbs of this semantic group express causation. They denote the action which causes the direct object to perform its own action. The full construction of this subgroup is as follows:

verb$_1$ + direct object + verb$_2$

2 Verbs, verb phrases and their components

Verb₁ denotes the action taken by the subject which causes the direct object to take its own action denoted by **verb₂**. The direct object is usually a person.

The main verbs (verb₁) of this subgroup are **bảo** "tell someone to do something," **bắt** "force, make someone do something," **cấm** "prohibit," **cho** "let someone do something," **cho phép** "allow," **dạy / dậy** "teach," **đề nghị** "suggest," **để** "let someone do something," **giúp / giúp đỡ** "help," **khuyên** "advise," **khuyến khích** "encourage," **mời** "invite," **nhờ** "ask someone to do something," **ra lệnh** "command," **sai** "order," **thuyết phục** "persuade," **xin** "ask someone to do something," **yêu cầu** "request."

Họ <u>bảo</u> tôi chờ họ ở đây lúc bẩy giờ sáng. They told me to meet them here at 7 AM.

Họ <u>bắt</u> tôi chờ gần một tiếng đồng hồ. They made me wait for nearly an hour.

Nhà trường <u>cấm</u> học sinh hút thuốc lá trong trường. The school prohibits students from smoking on the campus.

Bà ấy <u>cho phép</u> chúng tôi dùng xe của bà ấy trong khi bà ấy đi công tác. She allowed us to drive her car when she was on the business trip.

Bố anh ấy <u>dậy</u> anh ấy bơi khi anh ấy còn rất bé. His father taught him how to swimm when he was very little.

Chị ấy <u>giúp</u> chúng tôi hoàn thành công việc đúng thời hạn. She helped us complete the work on time.

Bố mẹ anh ấy đã <u>thuyết phục</u> được anh ấy trở lại trường học tiếp. His parents have persuaded him to go back to college.

This group also contains the verb **làm [cho]** "make someone do something":

Anh ấy kể một câu chuyện tiếu lâm <u>làm [cho]</u> chúng tôi cười chảy cả nước mắt. He told a joke which made us laugh until we cried.

The verb **làm [cho]** can also denote an action which causes someone to change her / his physical or emotional state. The grammatical construction is as follows:

verb + direct object + adjective

Tin mới nhận được <u>làm [cho]</u> bà ấy rất vui. The news made her happy.

Câu anh nói <u>làm [cho]</u> ông ấy giận lắm. What you said made him very angry.

The direct object of the verb **làm [cho]** may be an event in nature:

> **Ở Sài Gòn, những cơn mưa vào buổi chiều tối làm [cho] thời tiết mát mẻ.** In Sài Gòn, the rains in the late afternoon and evening make the weather cooler.

Verb phrase #2: verb + object

Note 1: The verb **cấm** can take the negative phrase **không được** that is inserted between the direct object and the verb$_2$:

> **Nhà trường cấm học sinh không được hút thuốc lá trong trường.** The school prohibits students from smoking on the campus.

This sentence shows more emphasis on the prohibition than the sentence

> **Nhà trường cấm học sinh hút thuốc lá trong trường.**

Note 2: The verb **dạy / dậy** can take a noun in the place of verb$_2$. With this usage, the verb belongs to the group of verbs of giving (see 2.4.1.1.).

> **Giáo sư Smith dạy / dậy chúng tôi môn lịch sử Việt Nam.** Professor Smith taught us a course on Vietnamese history.

Note 3: The verb **khuyên** can take the modal verb **nên**, which means "should." **Nên** is placed after the direct object and in front of the verb$_2$:

> **Tôi khuyên anh nên xin lỗi ông ấy.** I would advise you to apologize to him.

Note 4: The verb **ra lệnh** takes the preposition **cho** that comes in front of the direct object:

> **Có tiếng còi báo hoả hoạn. Thủ trưởng ra lệnh cho chúng tôi ra khỏi khu nhà ngay lập tức.** The fire alarm went off, and the boss commanded us to leave the building immediately.

Note 5: The English verb *to ask* conveys many meanings (we are not going to discuss here the English phrasal verbs *to ask after*, *to ask around* and *to ask for*). Vietnamese uses different verbs to express those meanings.

The Vietnamese verb **hỏi** corresponds only to the English *to ask a question*:

> **Tôi có thể hỏi anh một câu được không?** May I *ask* you a question?
> **Chúng ta phải hỏi anh ấy tại sao anh ấy không đến họp.** We should *ask* him why he didn't come to the meeting.

67

2 Verbs, verb phrases and their components

To ask [someone] for something would be **xin [ai] cái gì**:

> **Tôi muốn <u>xin</u> cô phục vụ một cốc nước đá.** I would like to *ask* the waitress for a glass of ice water.

To ask someone to do something would be **bảo, nhờ, đề nghị** or **yêu cầu**, depending on whether it is a polite request or a very strong request, whether it is a formal or informal situation:

> **Chị ấy <u>bảo</u> tôi đừng nói chuyện này với bất cứ ai.** She *asked* me not to say anything about it to anyone. (rather informal)
> **Tôi muốn <u>nhờ</u> anh giúp tôi làm việc này.** I would like to *ask* you to help me with this. (polite, rather formal)
> **Bà giám đốc <u>đề nghị</u> chúng tôi hoàn thành việc này trong ngày hôm nay.** The director has *asked* us to complete this work today. (formal)
> **Bà giám đốc <u>yêu cầu</u> chúng tôi hoàn thành việc này trong ngày hôm nay.** The director has *asked* us to complete this work today. (formal and strong)

To ask someone to / over in the sense of *inviting someone to go somewhere or do something* would be **mời**:

> **Cô ấy chỉ <u>mời</u> vài người bạn đến ăn sinh nhật.** She *has* asked just a few friends to her birthday party.
> **Anh ấy <u>mời</u> tôi đi ăn tối.** He *asked* me over for dinner.

See 5.8.3.3.1. for the construction *to ask if / whether or not*.

2.4.4 Verbs of speaking, thinking and perceiving

The main verbs of this group are **cảm thấy** "feel, believe," **cho rằng / là** "believe, guess," **giải thích** "explain," **hiểu** "understand," **hỏi** "ask a question," **hứa** "promise," **kể** "tell," **lo** "worry," **nghe** "listen," **nghĩ** "think," **nhắc** "remind," **nhìn** "look at," **nhớ** "remember, miss," **nói** "say, speak, tell," **nói chuyện** "converse," **quên** "forget," **sợ** "fear, be scared," **thấy** "see," **tin** "believe," **trả lời** "reply, answer," **tưởng** "think, believe," **xem** "watch."

The verbs of this group are used in different constructions.

2.4.4.1 Verb + object

The object is a noun or pronoun. For instance, **cảm thấy đói** "feel hunger / hungry," **hiểu tiếng Việt** "understand Vietnamese," **kể truyện cổ tích** "tell a fairy tale," **nghe nhạc** "listen to music," **nhìn mấy bông hoa cắm trong lọ** "look at the flowers in the vase," **nhớ nhiều từ** "remember a lot of vocaburary," **nhớ nhà** "miss one's family, be homesick," **nói tiếng Anh** "speak English," **quên nhiều từ** "forget a lot of vocabulary," **sợ chó** "be afraid of dogs," **thấy ngôi nhà từ đằng xa** "see a house far away," **tin những gì họ nói** "believe what they have said," **trả lời thư** "reply to a letter," **xem ti vi** "watch TV."

Verb phrase #2: verb + object

2.4.4.2 Verb₁ + verb₂

The verbs **cảm thấy, nhớ** (with the meaning of remembering), **quên** and **sợ** can take another verb phrase:

> **Chúng tôi <u>cảm thấy</u> có lỗi trong chuyện ấy.** We have the feeling of being guilty about it.
> **Tối mai <u>nhớ</u> ra sân bay đón anh ấy lúc tám giờ nhé.** Please remember to go to the airport to pick him up tomorrow night at eight o'clock.
> **Họ <u>sợ</u> không đến được đúng giờ vì đường rất đông xe.** They feared not to be able to arrive on time because the traffic was very heavy.
> **Tôi <u>quên</u> ghi lại số điện thoại của chị ấy nên bây giờ không gọi điện cho chị ấy được.** I forgot to put down her phone number, so I cannot call her now.

The verb **quên** can take the negation **không** or **chưa** before the second verb, and the meaning remains unchanged:

> **Tôi <u>quên</u> đặt vé đi xem kịch. = Tôi <u>quên chưa</u> đặt vé đi xem kịch.** I have forgotten to book the tickets for the play.

The verb **nhắc** belongs to this semantic group, but takes the construction **verb₁ + direct object + verb₂**; the direct object is a person:

> **Anh ấy <u>nhắc</u> chúng tôi đúng 6 giờ sáng mai phải có mặt ở đây để lên đường.** He reminded us to be here tomorrow exactly at 6 AM for departure.

2.4.4.3 Verb + preposition + noun / pronoun

Some verbs of this group take different prepositions. We will look at each of the prepositions.

2 Verbs, verb phrases and their components

The verbs **kể, nói, nhắc, hát** and **giải thích** take the construction:

verb + cho + indirect object + direct object + về

Tôi kể cho các bạn một câu chuyện về chuyến đi thăm đồng bằng sông Cửu Long. I told my friends a sroty about the trip to the Mekong Delta.

Very often, in this construction the verb **nghe** "listen" is inserted between the indirect object and direct object; the meaning remains the same: . . . **kể cho các bạn nghe một câu chuyện về chuyến đi thăm đồng bằng sông Cửu Long.**

The construction **verb + cho + indirect object + nghe + direct object** is used for some other verbs as well: **nói, hát, giải thích**:

Chị ấy hát cho cả lớp nghe một ca khúc tiền chiến. She sang a prewar song to everybody in the class.
Giáo sư Dũng giải thích cho chúng tôi nghe [về] những đặc điểm của chương trình máy tính mới này. Professor Dũng explained to us the specific features of the new software.

The verbs **nói, nghĩ** and **nhớ** take different prepositions depending on the meanings they convey.

The preposition **về** is used for speaking of the content of something, usually in detail: **nói về lịch sử Việt Nam thế kỉ 17** "speak of Vietnamese history in the seventeenth century;" **nghĩ về chuyến đi sắp tới** "think about the upcoming trip;" **nhớ về những khó khăn khi còn đi học** "remember the hardships when being a student."

The preposition **đến** conveys the meaning that someone or something is just mentioned in a conversation, not spoken of in detail: **nói đến một nhân vật lịch sử** "mention a famous figure in the history;" **nghĩ đến những người thân** "think about one's relatives;" **nhớ đến câu chuyện sáng nay** "think (recall) of the incident that occurred this morning."

The verb **tin**, in addition to the direct object (see 2.4.4.1.), also takes the preposition **ở** before the nouns denoting people:

Chúng tôi tin ở anh ấy. We believe in him.

It takes the preposition **vào** before the nouns denoting something abstract:

Hiện giờ đang rất khó khăn nhưng họ tin vào tương lai. There are currently a lot of hardships, but they believe in the future (that will be much better).

The Vietnamese prepositions **ở** and **vào** here are equivalent to the English *in*, that the verb *to believe* takes.

The verb **hứa** combines two constructions in 2.4.4.2. and 2.4.4.3., taking the preposition **với**:

> verb₁ + **với** + indirect object + verb₂
>
> **Anh ấy <u>hứa</u> với chúng tôi sẽ không bao giờ làm như thế nữa.** He promised us not to do that anymore.

Verb phrase #2: <u>verb + object</u>

Note 1: The Vietnamese verbs equivalent to the English *to listen* and *to hear* should not be mixed up, although they all contain **nghe**.

The English *to listen* is **nghe** in Vietnamese: **nghe nhạc** "listen to music," "**nghe tin thời sự trên ti vi** "listen to / watch the news on TV," **nghe giáo sư giảng** "listen to the professor's lecture."

The English *to hear* with the meaning "to know that a sound is being made, using one's ears" is **nghe thấy**:

> **Tôi <u>nghe thấy</u> có ai đó đang gõ cửa.** I can hear someone knocking on the door.
> **Chị có <u>nghe thấy</u> tiếng ồn ngoài phố không?** Do you hear the noise from the street?

The English *to hear* with the meaning "be told or find out a piece of information" is **nghe nói**, **thấy nói** or **nghe thấy nói**. These three verbs are interchangeable:

> **Tôi <u>nghe nói / thấy nói / nghe thấy nói</u> cháu thi đỗ vào Đại học Bách khoa.** I heard that your child has passed the entrance exams to be admitted to the University of Technology.
> **Anh có <u>nghe nói / thấy nói / nghe thấy nói</u> về tai nạn nghiêm trọng xẩy ra hôm qua ở ngã tư này không?** Did you hear about the nasty accident that happened at this intersection yesterday?

Note 2: The English verbs *to speak*, *to talk*, *to tell* and *to say* correspond to the Vietnamese verbs **nói** and **nói chuyện**, which are not interchangeable.

To speak a language is **nói**: **nói tiếng Anh** "speak English," **nói nhiều thứ tiếng** "speak many languages."

To speak to / with someone, to talk to / with someone is **nói chuyện với**: **nói chuyện với giáo sư** "speak to / with the professor," **nói chuyện với bạn** "talk to / with one's friends."

2 Verbs, verb phrases and their components

To tell someone something and *to say something to someone* are **nói với**:

Tôi muốn nói với các anh các chị một vấn đề quan trọng. I would like to tell you something important.

2.4.4.4 Verb + clause

Most of the verbs of this semantic group can take a noun clause. The English *that* is the conjunction **rằng** which is used in formal Vietnamese; and **là**, which is used in less formal speech. In many cases the conjuction **rằng** or **là** is understood:

Anh ấy nói với chúng tôi [rằng] anh ấy sắp đi Việt Nam. He told us that he is going to leave for Vietnam.

Chúng tôi nghe nói / thấy nói / nghe thấy nói [là] hôm qua nhiều máy tính ở một số nước bị tin tặc tấn công. We heard that many computers in a number of countries were hacked by cyber criminals yesterday.

Cổ động viên tin [rằng] đội của họ sẽ thắng trận chung kết. The fans believed that their team would win the final game.

Note: The verb **tưởng** implies "something turns out in a different way than it was thought of" always precedes a noun clause. The conjunction **rằng** or **là** is often left out:

Tôi tưởng bà ấy là giáo sư trường này. (Thực ra bà ấy chỉ giảng dậy ở đây một học kì.) I thought she is a professor at this college. (It turns out that she is teaching here just for one semester.)

2.4.5 Verbs of equating

Ther are a number of verbs which take two objects of an equation, and the word **là** is inserted between the two objects. In some grammars, the second object is called *object predicative*. The main verbs of this group are **gọi** and **coi**.

verb + object$_1$ + là + object$_2$

Người Mĩ gọi cái thùng xe là *trunk*, còn người Anh thì gọi là *boot*. Americans call an enclosed space in the back of a car *trunk*, and Britons call it a *boot*.

Người Nam gọi quả dứa là trái thơm. In Vietnam, southerners call a pineapple *trái thơm*.

Chúng tôi <u>coi</u> anh ấy <u>là</u> một chuyên gia giỏi trong lĩnh vực này. We regard him as a good expert in this area.

Tôi không còn <u>coi</u> anh ấy <u>là</u> một người bạn nữa. I do not count him as my friend anymore.

Some verbs denoting appointment, designation or election, such as **bầu, cử, chỉ định**, take the same construction, but **làm** is used instead of **là**:

Giảng viên và công nhân viên <u>bầu</u> ông ấy <u>làm</u> Hiệu trưởng trường Đại học Khoa học xã hội và nhân văn. The faculty and staff at the university have elected him (as) the Chancellor of the University of Social Sciences and Humanities.

Chính phủ <u>cử</u> bà ấy <u>làm</u> Bộ trưởng Bộ Giáo dục và đào tạo. The Government appointed her (as) Minister of Education and Training.

<u>Note</u>: The word **mình** "oneself" can function as the object of a verb. It replaces the pronoun or noun that is the subject of a sentence. For example:

Chúng tôi không coi <u>mình</u> thuộc thế hệ trẻ nữa. We do not consider ourselves as people of the young generation (lit. We do not consider ourselves belonging to the young generation).

Anh ấy chỉ nghĩ đến <u>mình</u> thôi. He only thinks of himself.

For details of using **mình** as a personal pronoun, see 1.3.3.5.3.

2.5 Verb phrase #3: <u>verb + adjective</u>

2.5.1 *Adjective functioning as adverb of manner*

In Vietnamese, an adjective follows a verb to modify it, performing the function of the adverb of manner. For instance, **học giỏi** "study well," **múa đẹp** "dance beautifully," **hiểu rõ** "understand clearly," **đi nhanh** "walk fast," **làm chậm** "work or do something slowly," **nói hay** "speak well."

When the verb takes an object, the adjective usually comes after the object. For example, **học toán giỏi** "study math well," **múa ba-lê đẹp** "dance ballet beautifully," **hiểu vấn đề rõ** "understand the issue clearly," **làm bài tập về nhà chậm** "do homework slowly."

Some of these adjectives functioning as adverbs of manner can be placed between the verb and the object. For example, **học giỏi toán**, **hiểu rõ vấn đề**.

2.5.2 Positive, comparative and superlative of adjective modifying verb

The adjective which follows a verb performing the function of the adverb of manner can take the positive, comparative and superlative forms of comparison (see 1.3.3.1.1.): **học cũng giỏi như bạn mình** "study as well as one's friend," **đi nhanh hơn** "walk faster," **nói hay nhất so với những thuyết trình viên khác** "speak the best of the speakers."

2.5.3 Bisyllabic adjectives modifying verb

Many bisyllabic adjectives can either follow a bisyllabic verb or precede it to maitain the phonetic symmetry: **tham gia tích cực** = **tích cực tham gia** "participate actively," **thuyết trình say sưa** = **say sưa thuyết trình** "talk enthusiastically."

> Anh ấy <u>tham gia tích cực</u> / <u>tích cực tham gia</u> mọi hoạt động của hội sinh viên. He participates actively in all the activities of the student association.
>
> Giáo sư <u>thuyết trình say sưa</u> / <u>say sưa thuyết trình</u> về văn học Việt Nam cuối thế kỉ 18 đầu thế kỉ 19. The professor is talking enthusiastically about Vietnamese literature in the late 18th in the early 19th centuries.

In most cases, bisyllabic adjectives are either of Chinese origin (**tích cực** < 積極 \ 积极) or reduplicatives (**say sưa**). When placed in front of the verb, the bisyllabic adjective shows emphasis on the quality of the action.

2.5.4 Adjectives following một cách

In formal Vietnamese, a verb can precede an adjective phrase which contains **một cách** and a bisyllabic adjective, or a reduplicative adjective. This adjective phrase also serves as the adverb of manner. To some extent, this kind of adjective phrase is equivalent to the English *in a . . . way* or *in a . . . manner*: **tiếp đón một cách thân tình** "to receive warmly," **chào hỏi một cách niềm nở** "to greet in a friendly way," **nhìn một cách nghi ngờ** "to look in a suspicious way," **mời một cách lịch sự** "to invite in a polite manner," **nói một cách nhẹ nhàng và điềm tĩnh** "to speak in a gentle and calm manner."

Note: The adjective which is used after **một cách** shoult be a bisyllabic adjective. A monosyllabic (one-syllable) adjective cannot follow **một cách**. The reason is Vietnamese tends to maintain the phonetic symmetry in a phrase (see 2.5.3.). This rule applies to any phrase. Here are some examples for noun phrases:

> **Áo sạch** "a clean shirt;" the noun **áo** is a monosyllabic noun, which precedes the monosyllabic adjective **sạch**.

Áo quần sạch sẽ "clean clothes;" the compound noun **áo quần** meaning "clothes" is a bisyllabic noun, which precedes the reduplicative adjective **sạch sẽ**.

Trời mát "cool weather;" the noun **trời** is a monosyllabic noun, which precedes the monosyllabic adjective **mát**.

Thời tiết mát mẻ "cool weather;" the noun **thời tiết** is a bisyllabic noun, which precedes the reduplicative adjective **mát mẻ**.

> Verb phrase #4: adverb + verb, or verb + adverb

2.6 Verb phrase #4: adverb + verb, or verb + adverb

Since the adverbs of place and time very often perform the functions of the adverbials of place and time in a sentence, they will be discussed in 5.1.1.3.2. and 5.1.1.3.3. Here we are looking only at the adverbs of degree and adverbs of frequency.

2.6.1 Adverbs of degree

2.6.1.1 Adverbs of degree modifying verbs of feelings

In general, an adverb of degree modifies an adjective or another adverb (see 1.3.3.2.). However, an adverb of degree may be placed before or after a verb to modify it. The meaning of the verb usually implies the dergee by itself, for example, the verbs of feelings and emotions such as **thích** "like," **yêu** "love," **ghét** "dislike, hate," **sợ** "be afraid," **nhớ** "miss," **khâm phục** "admire," **kính trọng** "respect," **ngưỡng mộ** "deeply admire," **coi thường** "look down on," **ngạc nhiên** "be surprised," etc.

<u>rất</u> thích nhạc cổ điển "like classical music very much"
yêu súc vật <u>lắm</u> "love animals so much"
nhớ nhà <u>quá</u> "miss one's family so much"
<u>rất</u> ngưỡng mộ nhà văn ấy "deeply admire that author"
<u>hết sức</u> ngạc nhiên khi nghe tin ấy "be so surprised at the news"

Note 1: Unlike the English phrase *very much* used with the verbs of feelings, the word **nhiều** should not be used with this function:

We admire him <u>very much</u>. = **Chúng tôi <u>rất</u> ngưỡng mộ ông ấy.**

The sentence *****Chúng tôi ngưỡng mộ ông ấy <u>rất nhiều</u>.** is influenced by the English usage and should be considered non-standard. Another example:

They miss you <u>very much</u>. = **Họ <u>rất</u> nhớ chị.** Or: **Họ nhớ chị <u>lắm</u>.**

*** Họ nhớ chị <u>rất nhiều</u>.** Or: ***Họ nhớ chị <u>nhiều lắm</u>.** is non-standard.

Note 2: The verbs of feelings and emotions can take the marker of the adjective superlative **nhất** meaning "[the] best" or "[the] most." Note the possible word orders: "**verb + object + nhất**" that is similar to the English word order, and "**verb + nhất + object**":

A: **Trong số những chiếc áo này, chị thích chiếc nào nhất / chị thích nhất chiếc nào?** Which of these shirts do you like [the] best / most?
B: **Tôi thích chiếc áo xanh lá cây nhất. / Tôi thích nhất chiếc áo xanh lá cây.** I like the green one [the] best / most.

2.6.1.2 Preference

The idea of preference is usually expressed by the verb of feeling **thích** "like" and the modal verb **muốn** "want, like" together with the word of comparison **hơn**. The most commonly used constructions are:

subject + thích + noun₁ / verb₁ + hơn + noun₂ / verb₂
or:
subject + muốn + verb₁ + hơn + verb₂

This construction is similar to the English phrases *to prefer something to something* and *would rather . . . than . . .* For example:

(1) **Tôi thích quyển từ điển này hơn quyển kia.** I prefer this dictionary to that one.
(2) **Bạn tôi thích trời lạnh hơn trời nóng.** My friend prefers cold weather to hot [weather]. / My friend would rather have cold weather than hot [weather].
(3) **Anh ấy thích tập thể thao hơn xem thể thao trên ti vi.** He prefers doing sports to watching sports on TV. / He would rather do sports than watch sports on TV.
(4) **Hè này chúng tôi muốn đi du lịch sang châu Âu hơn sang châu Á.** This summer we would prefer traveling to Europe than to Asia. / This summer we would rather travel to Europe than to Asia. / This summer we would like to travel to Europe better than to Asia.

Là can be added in front of the second verb for emphasis. Sentences (3) and (4) may be as follows:

(3a) **Anh ấy thích tập thể thao hơn là xem thể thao trên ti vi.**
(4a) **Hè này chúng tôi muốn đi du lịch sang châu Âu hơn là sang châu Á.**

Vietnamese uses the emphatic conjunction **thà** to convey the idea that both options are bad, but the second one is unacceptable, so one would rather accept the first one. **Thà** is used in two constructions:

subject + thà + verb₁ + chứ không + verb₂
or:
subject + thà + verb₁ + còn hơn + verb₂

Verb phrase #4: adverb + verb, or verb + adverb

Chúng ta <u>thà</u> làm việc cả thứ bảy chủ nhật này cho xong <u>chứ không</u> làm việc đến đêm khuya trong tuần sau. / Chúng ta <u>thà</u> làm việc cả thứ bảy chủ nhật này cho xong <u>còn hơn</u> làm việc đến đêm khuya trong tuần sau. We would work on this weekend to complete the job rather than work until late at night next week.

Thà muộn còn hơn là không bao giờ. Better late than never. (This proverb in Vietnamese does not use **chứ không**.)

2.6.1.3 [Càng] ngày càng and mỗi lúc một

There are several adverbs of degree which are usually inserted between the verb and the adjective in the construction **verb + adjective**. They cannot modify a verb without an adjective, which functions as the adverb of manner. These adverbs of degree are **[càng] ngày càng** "more and more, increasingly," **mỗi lúc một** "more and more, increasingly," **mỗi ngày một** "more and more every day," **mỗi năm một** "more and more every year," **mỗi tuổi một** "more and more every year (speaking of a person's age)," etc.:

Ông ấy đi <u>mỗi lúc một</u> nhanh. Or: **Ông ấy đi <u>[càng] ngày càng</u> nhanh.** He walked / is walking faster and faster.
Nền kinh tế phát triển <u>[càng] ngày càng</u> mạnh. The economy developed more and more rapidly.
Cháu bé <u>mỗi tuổi một</u> thêm hiểu biết. The child is becoming more and more knowledgeable (every year).
Diễn giả thuyết trình <u>mỗi lúc một</u> say sưa. The speaker is talking more and more enthusiastically.

Note: The two phrases **[càng] ngày càng** and **mỗi lúc một** share the meaning "more and more, increasingly." **Mỗi lúc một** puts more emphasis on the change which takes place during a short period of time and is usually can be seen:

Mưa <u>ngày càng</u> to. It is raining harder and harder.

Mưa mỗi lúc một to. It is raining harder and harder. (The speaker can see the rain that is becoming heavier and heavier at the moment of speaking.)

Mỗi lúc một is not used for a change that takes place in a longer period of time. We cannot say ***Nền kinh tế phát triển mỗi lúc một mạnh.**

2.6.1.4 Chỉ

The word **chỉ** meaning "only, just" can be treated as an adverb of degree. The English *only* and *just* can be placed in different positions in a sentence depending on the meaning they convey:

(1) She is taking *only / just* four courses this semester. (not more than four) **Học kì này chị ấy chỉ học bốn môn [thôi].**
(2) He *only / just* lent me the book. (He did not give it to me for good.) **Anh ấy chỉ cho tôi 'mượn quyển sách [thôi].**
(3) He lent the book *only / just* to me (or: to me *only*.) (not to anyone else) **Anh ấy chỉ cho 'tôi mượn quyển sách [thôi].**

The rule of thumb is **chỉ** is always placed in front of a verb (or an adjective which functions as the predicate). **Thôi,** that adds more emphasis to the restriction, is optional and comes at the end of the sentence. Because **chỉ** always precedes a verb, in some cases the speaker needs to stress the word to which **chỉ** applies to make it clear, as in (2) and (3), **mượn** and **tôi** are stressed respectively. We will look at two more examples, where the English *just* is placed in different positions of a sentence and changes the meaning, whereas a particular word is stressed in Vietnamese:

(4) *Just* read this page. (implies "not to translate") **Chỉ 'đọc trang này thôi.**
(5) Read *just* this page. (implies "no need to read other pages") **Chỉ đọc trang 'này thôi.**

Sometimes Vietnamese adds other words to make everything clear instead of stressing a particular word. For instance, in (3) **một mình** can be added in front of **tôi**:

Anh ấy chỉ cho một mình tôi mượn quyển sách này thôi.

In (4) the extended sentence would be:

Chỉ đọc trang này thôi, đừng dịch.

In (5) the extended sentence would be:

> **Chỉ đọc <u>một</u> trang này thôi.**

<u>Note</u>: When the English *only* refers to a person's age, **mới** is used instead of **chỉ**:

> **Cô ấy <u>mới</u> 16 tuổi đã được vào học đại học.** She was *only* 16 years old when she was admitted to college.

Verb phrase #4: adverb + verb, or verb + adverb

2.6.2 Adverbs of frequency

The basic adverbs of frequency are **luôn** "always," **luôn luôn** "always, at all times," **thường** "often, frequently," **thường xuyên** "regularly," **hay** "often," **thỉnh thoảng** "sometimes, occasionally," **đôi khi** "occasionally," **ít khi** "rarely," **một / hai / ba lần** "once, twice, three times," **hiếm khi** "seldom," **không bao giờ** "never," **chưa bao giờ** "have never yet." The position of an adverb of frequency is after the subject and in front of the verb. Here are some examples:

> **Anh ấy <u>luôn</u> đến đúng giờ.** He always comes on time.
> **Chúng tôi <u>thường</u> gặp nhau vào sáng thứ bảy để chơi quần vợt.** We often get together to play tennis Saturday mornings.
> **Lớp chúng tôi <u>thường xuyên</u> làm bài kiểm tra.** Our class regularly takes quizzes.
> **Họ <u>hay</u> đến ăn ở nhà hàng này.** They often come to have a meal at this restaurant.
> **Ông ấy <u>thỉnh thoảng</u> ghé thư viện mượn sách.** He occasionally comes by the library to borrow books.
> **Dạo này anh ấy <u>ít khi</u> đến thăm chúng tôi.** Nowadays he rarely comes to see us.
> **Tôi <u>chưa bao giờ</u> đi Sapa cả.** I have never been to Sapa.

<u>Note 1</u>: Among the previously mentioned adverbs of frequency, only **hay** takes the negation **không**, which comes in front of the adverb itself:

> **Bây giờ họ <u>không hay</u> đến ăn ở nhà hàng này nữa.** Now they don't often come to have a meal at this restaurant.

The other adverbs of frequency cannot be used with the negation **không**. The adverbs **không bao giờ** and **chưa bao giờ** themselves express negation.

2 Verbs, verb phrases and their components

The English *not always* would be **không phải bao giờ cũng** or **không phải lúc nào cũng**:

> Things will *not always* go as planned. **Mọi việc <u>không phải bao giờ</u> / <u>không phải lúc nào</u> cũng diễn ra như đã định trước.**

Note 2: The adverbs **thỉnh thoảng, đôi khi, ít khi** and **hiếm khi** can be placed at the beginning of a sentence:

> **<u>Thỉnh thoảng</u> ông ấy ghé thư viện mượn sách.**
> **<u>Ít khi</u> anh ấy đến thăm chúng tôi.**

Note 3: There are three homonyms **hay**.

1/ **hay** is an adverb of frequency meaning "often," which always precedes a verb:

> **Ngã tư này <u>hay</u> xẩy ra tai nạn giao thông.** Traffic accidents often occur at this intersection.

The English adverb *often* can be placed in different positions of a sentence, whereas the Vietnamese **hay** always precedes the verb phrase. Compare:

> My friend travels more *often* than I do. **Bạn tôi <u>hay</u> đi du lịch hơn tôi.**
> They go out to dinner fairly *often*. **Họ rất <u>hay</u> đi ăn nhà hàng.**
> *Often*, they stay up late to watch TV. **Họ <u>hay</u> thức khuya xem ti vi.**

2/ **hay** is an adjective meaning "good, interesting," which functions (1) as an attributive in a noun phrase; (2) as an adverb of manner in a verb phrase; (3) as the predicate of a sentence:

> (1) **Đấy là một bài dân ca <u>hay</u>.** That is a good folksong. (attributive in the noun phrase **một bài dân ca hay**, in which the noun **dân ca** is the head of the phrase)
> (2) **Cô ấy hát dân ca rất <u>hay</u>.** She sings folksongs beautifully. (adverb of manner in the verb phrase **hát dân ca rất hay**, in which the verb **hát** is the head of the phrase)
> (3) **Bài dân ca này rất <u>hay</u>.** This folksong is really good. (the predicate of the sentence)

3/ **hay** serves as a conjunction with the meaning "or." It can be used either in a statement or in a question:

> **Có thể đi từ Hà Nội vào Sài Gòn bằng máy bay <u>hay</u> tầu hoả.** You can go from Hà Nội down to Sài Gòn by airplane or by train.

Tuần sau chúng ta đi vào Sài Gòn bằng máy bay <u>hay</u> tầu hoả? Will we take the airplane or the train to go down to Sài Gòn next week?

For more on using **hay** in questions, see 5.3.1.10.

2.7 Verbs of motion

The verbs of motion can denote either just motion or both motion and direction. They can be used intransitively or transitively. The motion itself implies one of the two points: the departure point and the destination, or both of them. We will look at the verbs of motion in Vietnamese from these perspectives.

2.7.1 Đi

The basic intransitive verb of motion is **đi** "go, travel." This verb may be used either with a preposition or with no preposition. When used as the main verb of the sentence, it indicates no direction. It may follow another verb of motion to describe the direction.

2.7.1.1 Đi + destination

This construction with no preposition is used when the destination is the geographical names for cities, countries or continents. For instance, **đi Hà Nội** "go / travel to Hà Nội," **đi Nha Trang** "go / travel to Nha Trang," **đi Paris** "go / travel to Paris," **đi Anh** "go / travel to England," **đi châu Phi** "go / travel to Africa."

2.7.1.2 Đi + preposition + destination

When the destination is denoted by a noun which refers to a particular place, but smaller than a town, **đi** takes a preposition, which usually is a verb of motion expressing a particular direction. For instance, **đi đến nhà bạn** "go to a friend's house;" **đi vào nhà** "enter a house;" **đi xuống nhà** "go downstairs;" **đi lên nhà** "go up to a higher part of the house;" **đi sang / qua nhà hàng xóm** "go over to a neighbor's house;" **đi lại nhà người bà con** "come over to see a relative."

There are some idiomatic expressions in which **đi** does not take a preposition before a noun which denotes a particular small place:

đi chợ "go shopping" (to buy food)
đi cửa hàng cửa hiệu "go shopping"
đi siêu thị "go shopping"
đi bệnh viện "go to the hospital" (to be examined by a doctor)

đi bưu điện "go to the post office"
đi nhà hàng "go out to eat"
đi thư viện "go to the library"

The destination for **đi** can be expressed by some demonstrative pronouns that function as adverbs of place: **đây** "here," **đấy** "there," **đó** "there." They are treated as the previously mentioned nouns:

đi + preposition + **đây / đấy / đó**

In this case, the verbs of motion referring to particular directions function as the prepositions:

đi + **ra / vào / lên / xuống / sang / qua / đến / tới / về / lại** + **đây / đấy / đó**

The verbs of motion denoting particular directions will be discussed in depth in 2.7.2.

Some other intransitive verbs of motion with no direction such as **chạy** "run," **bay** "fly," **nhảy / nhẩy** "jump," **chuyển** "move, transfer" are used in the same way like **đi**.

2.7.2 Other verbs of motion

The main intransitive verbs of motion referring to particular directions are **ra** "go or come out," **vào** "go or come in," **lên** "go or come up," **xuống** "go or come down," **sang** "go or come over," **qua** "go or come over," **đến / tới** "arrive," **về** "go or come back," **lại** "come over, come by, stop by," **đi** "go away."

The verb **đi** alone usually does not refer to a particular direction. However, when following another intransitive verb of motion with no direction, **đi** indicates the direction away from the speaker. In this case, the pair **đi – đến** and **đi – lại** are equivalent to the pair of verbs which denote the direction away from the speaker and towards the speaker in other languages, like the English *to go – to come*, the German *gehen – kommen*, the French *aller – venir*, the Chinese 去 – 來 \ 来:

Anh ấy <u>đến</u> / <u>lại</u> chỗ tôi đúng lúc tôi phải <u>đi</u>. He came over to see me at the moment when I had to leave.

<u>Note 1</u>: The Hanoi dialect uses both **đến** and **tới**. The Saigon dialect uses only **tới**.

Note 2: These verbs of motion with a particular direction may follow **đi** with the meaning "go," but **đi** can be understood:

Chị ấy [đi] sang nhà hàng xóm rồi. She has gone over to see a neighbor.

Đang đèn đỏ, không [đi] qua đường được. You may not cross the street right now due to the red light.

The other intransitive verbs with no direction cannot be ommitted:

Chị ấy chạy sang nhà hàng xóm rồi. She has run over to see a neighbor.

Đang đèn đỏ, đừng chạy qua đường. Nguy hiểm lắm. Please do not run across the street against the red light right now. It is very dangerous.

In Vietnamese, the direction is described from either the speaker's or the subject's (of the motion) point of view:

Anh ấy đến đây hôm qua. He arrived [here] yesterday.

The verb **đến** denotes the movement towards the speaker.

Anh ấy đi ra ngoài vườn. He went out to the garden.

The speaker may be inside the house, and the person spoken of is moving to the garden outside of the house. Or, the speaker is absent from the context, and the person denoted by **anh ấy** is moving from the inside (of the house) towards the garden. This point should be taken into account when you express the idea of such an English sentence:

My friends went *to* the fourth floor to dance.

In Vietnamese, if the speaker is on a floor lower than the fourth one, it would be:

Các bạn tôi [đi] lên tầng bốn khiêu vũ.

If the speaker is on the fifth floor or higher, it would be:

Các bạn tôi [đi] xuống tầng bốn khiêu vũ.

The prepositions of location are used in the same way. For instance, the English preposition *on* in the sentence *My friends are dancing on the fourth floor*.

Verbs of motion

corresponds to two different prepositions in Vietnamese, depending on the speaker's location. If they are dancing on a floor higher than the floor where the speaker is, it would be:

Các bạn tôi đang khiêu vũ <u>trên</u> tầng bốn.

If they are dancing on a floor lower than the floor where the speaker is, it would be:

Các bạn tôi đang khiêu vũ <u>dưới</u> tầng bốn.

The verbs of motion **lên**, **xuống**, **ra** and **vào** can be used together with the prepositions of location **trên** (1), **dưới** (2), **trong** (3) and **ngoài** (4) respectively. The verb **đi** is optional:

(1) **Các bạn tôi [đi] <u>lên trên</u> tầng bốn khiêu vũ.**
(2) **Các bạn tôi [đi] <u>xuống dưới</u> tầng bốn khiêu vũ.**
(3) **Họ đang [đi] <u>vào trong</u> nhà.** They are entering the house. / They are coming in to the house.
(4) **Họ đang [đi] <u>ra ngoài</u> phố.** They are coming out to the street.

<u>Note 1</u>: When these four verbs of motion are used together with the prepositions of location, and the locations *here* and *there* are mentioned, the <u>demonstrative adjectives</u>, not the adverbs of place, are used:

[đi] + lên trên / xuống dưới / vào trong / ra ngoài + này / ấy / đó / kia

Compare: **đi + lên / xuống / vào / ra + đây / đấy / đó** (see 2.7.1.2.)

<u>Note 2</u>: The verb **về** lit. means "go back, come back, return." The use of this verb, however, is a bit complicated.

Về alone means "be back":

Chị ấy đã về. She is back (at home or in the place she left some time ago).

When following **đi**, the meaning of **đi về** depends on the context. For example:

Chị ấy đi về rồi. She is gone (she has left her office).
Chúng mình đến giờ đi về rồi. It is time for us to leave.

If the departure point is mentioned, the word order is as follows:

1) **subject + ở + location + về**

   Chị ấy ở Việt Nam về tuần trước. She returned *from* Vietnam last week.

2) **subject + đi + location + về**

   Chị ấy đi Việt Nam về tuần trước. She returned *from* Vietnam last week.

The two sentences convey the same meaning. Strictly speaking, the preposition **từ** is not used with the meaning "from" in this case. However, under the influence of some European languages, the sentence **Chị ấy từ Việt Nam về tuần trước.** is becoming more common in contemporary Vietnamese.

However, if the person is returning from Vietnam but is not be back in the USA yet because she is making a stop in another place on the way from Vietnam back to the USA, we would say:

Chị ấy từ Việt Nam về tuần trước nhưng chưa về đến nơi vì còn dừng lại Berlin mấy ngày. She left Vietnam last week but is not back (at home) yet because she is having a stay in Berlin for a couple of days.

Note 3: The prepositions for areas of water such as **ao** "pond," **hồ** "lake," **sông** "river," **biển** "sea, ocean" and **nước** "water" may be very different in English and Vietnamese. In general, **trên** can be used for the English *on* when a location on land next to the area of water is referred to. For example:

The hotel is located *on* the lake / river / ocean. **Khách sạn nằm trên hồ / sông / biển.**

When there is a need to make it clear that the hotel lies on the shores of the lake / river / ocean, not as a floating hotel, Vietnamese would add **bờ** "shores" in front of the areas of water:

Khách sạn nằm trên bờ hồ / sông / biển. The hotel is located on the [shores of the] lake / river / ocean.

2 Verbs, verb phrases and their components

The idea of "in the water" is expressed by **dưới** in Vietnamese:

> There is a wide variety of tropical fish *in* the lake. **Dưới hồ có nhiều loài cá vùng nhiệt đới.**

Accordingly, the verb of motion which denotes the movement into the water is **xuống**: to jump *in[to]* the river = **nhảy / nhẩy xuống sông**. The verb of motion to express the movement out of the water to the shore is **lên**: to jump *out of* the water [to the shore] = **nhảy / nhẩy lên bờ**.

Note 4: When the verb **ra** precedes a location, it conveys the meaning "the subject is going out of a place and heading to another one":

> **Chủ nhật chúng tôi thường đi ra ngoại thành.** We usually go out to the suburbs of the city on Sundays.

The sentence implies that the subject **chúng tôi** is getting out of the city and going to its suburbs.

> **Ông ấy ra thành phố buôn bán.** He went out to the city to do business.

The sentence implies that the subject **ông ấy** lived in the countryside but has left his village for the city to do business.

In order to express the idea of "leaving a place," **ra** takes the preposition **khỏi**:

> **Họ ra khỏi thành phố khi trời còn chưa sáng.** They left (got out of) the town when it was still dark.

See 5.2.2.4. for the use of **khỏi** as a notional verb.

There are several idiomatic expressions containing the verb **ra** with the meaning "to go to a place":

> **ra chợ** "go to market"
> **ra siêu thị** "go to the supermarket"
> **ra ga** "go to the railroad station"
> **ra sân bay** "go to the airport"

2.7.3 Verbs of motion and prepositions used with the geographical names of Vietnam

2.7.3.1. The rule of thumb is, if you are in Vietnam and move from the north to the south, the verb **[đi] vào** is used. If you move from the south to the north, **[đi] ra** is used. For instance, if the speaker is in Hà Nội, she / he would say:

Ngày mai tôi [đi] <u>vào</u> Sài Gòn công tác một tuần. Tomorrow I am going *down to* Sài Gòn on a business trip for a week.

If the speaker is in Sài Gòn, she / he would say:

Ngày mai tôi [đi] <u>ra</u> Hà Nội công tác một tuần. Tomorrow I am going *up to* Hà Nội for a business trip for a week.

Accordingly, the prepositions **trong** and **ngoài** are used for locations:

Công ti chúng tôi có văn phòng đại diện <u>trong</u> Sài Gòn. Our company has a representative office in Sài Gòn.
Công ti chúng tôi có văn phòng đại diện <u>ngoài</u> Hà Nội. Our company has a representative office in Hà Nội.

If you move from a place in the lowlands to a place in the mountains, the verb **[đi] lên** is used, and the verb **[đi] xuống** is used for the opposite direction. For instance, **từ Hà Nội [đi] lên Sapa** "go / travel from Hà Nội *up to* Sapa;" **từ Sài Gòn [đi] lên Đà Lạt** "go / travel from Sài Gòn *up to* Đà Lạt;" **từ Sapa [đi] xuống Hà Nội** "go / travel from Sapa *down to* Hà Nội."

Note 1: The verbs **vào** and **ra**, and, accordingly, the prepositions **trong** and **ngoài**, are used only for the Vietnamese geographical names for the historical reasons. As for the geographical names in other countries, the verbs **lên** and **xuống**, and, accordingly, the prepositions **trên** and **dưới** are used. For example, if the speaker is in New York, she / he would say in Vietnamese:

Tôi sắp <u>đi xuống</u> Houston thăm người bạn. I am going to travel *down to* Houston to visit my friend.

Or, if the speaker is in Marseille, she / he would say:

Tôi có nhiều bà con <u>trên</u> Paris. I have many relatives in Paris.

Note 2: The word **ở** functioning as a preposition of location is "neutral" because it refers to any location. It can be used in front of the prepositions **trong**, **ngoài**, **trên** and **dưới**:

Công ti chúng tôi có văn phòng đại diện <u>ở</u> <u>trong</u> Sài Gòn.
Công ti chúng tôi có văn phòng đại diện <u>ở</u> <u>ngoài</u> Hà Nội.

2
Verbs, verb phrases and their components

When a learner of Vietnamese is not sure which preposition should be chosen for a particular location in Vietnam, **ở** is the safest one to use:

Công ti chúng tôi có văn phòng đại diện <u>ở</u> Sài Gòn.
Công ti chúng tôi có văn phòng đại diện <u>ở</u> Hà Nội.

In these two sentences, the location of the speaker can be anywhere in the world.

2.7.3.2. Some idiomatic expressions for relatively short distances which are different from the verbs of motion discussed in 2.7.3.1.

If you are in Hà Nội and are going to travel to Hải Phòng or Nam Định, you would say [đi] <u>xuống</u> Hải Phòng and [đi] <u>xuống</u> Nam Định.

If you are in Sài Gòn and you are going to travel to Vũng Tàu (on the ocean), you would say [đi] <u>ra</u> Vũng Tàu.

If you are in Sài Gòn and are going to travel to Cần Thơ or Cà Mau in the Mekong Delta, or to the Mekong Delta itself, you would say [đi] <u>xuống</u> Cần Thơ, [đi] <u>xuống</u> Cà Mau or [đi] <u>xuống</u> Đồng bằng sông Cửu Long.

Accordingly, the preposition of location **dưới** is used for Hải Phòng and Nam Định if the speaker is in Hà Nội; if the speaker is in Sài Gòn, the preposition **ngoài** is used for Vũng Tàu, and **dưới** is used for the locations in the Mekong Delta.

However, if you are traveling for a longer distance, for instance, from Hà Nội to the Mekong Delta, you would say [đi] <u>vào</u> Đồng bằng sông Cửu Long.

2.7.4 Transitive verbs of motion with no direction

The basic transitive verbs of motion with no direction are **chuyển** "move, forward, transfer," **mang** "carry," **xách** "carry with the handle of the object," **đưa** "take, bring, pass," **đem** "take, bring."

These verbs take the preposition denoted by verbs of motion which refer to particular directions. In addition to the previously discussed verbs of motion, the verb **đi** can be used after a transitive verb of motion to denote a movement away from the speaker. The construction looks like:

subject + transitive verb + object + verb of motion as preposition + destination

Chiều nay tôi sẽ [lái xe] <u>đưa</u> các anh <u>ra</u> sân bay. I will drive you to the airport this afternoon.

Chị làm ơn <u>chuyển</u> những thứ giấy tờ này <u>vào</u> văn phòng của công ti trong Sài Gòn. Please forward these documents to the office of the company in Sài Gòn.

The destination may be understood:

> **Anh làm ơn <u>mang</u> đống đồ đạc này <u>đi</u> cho tôi.** Please take this stuff away (out of my room) for me.

2.8 Verbs of appearance, existence and disappearance

The main verbs of this semantic group are **có** "have," **còn** "have something left," **hết** "have no more; run out; end," **mất** "lose; pass away," **xuất hiện** "appear," **xảy / xảy ra** "happen, occur," **diễn ra** "happen, occur, take place," **biến mất** "disappear."

These verbs are used with different grammatical constructions. We will look at each of them.

2.8.1 Có

Có takes a direct object meaning the possession:

> **subject + có + object**
>
> **có tiền** "have money," **có nhà** "have a property," **có thì giờ / thời gian** "have time," etc.

When **có** precedes the words **nhiều** "much, many" and **ít** "few, little," **có** may be left out in informal speech:

> **Bà ấy [<u>có</u>] <u>nhiều</u> thì giờ rỗi lắm, còn tôi thì [<u>có</u>] rất <u>ít</u> thì giờ.** She has a lot of free time. As for me, I have very little time.

Note: the phrase **có nhà** conveys two meanings "have a house or property" or "be at home" depending on the context.

Có is also used with no subject, which is similar to the English construction *there is* and *there are*.

> **[location] + có + object**
>
> **Ngoài vườn <u>có</u> nhiều thứ hoa.** There is a variety of flowers in the garden out there.

The phrase **ngoài vườn** is the location, which comes first in this construction. The location may be left out, as in the following sentence:

> **<u>Có</u> người hỏi chị.** Someone is asking for you. / There is someone asking for you.

2.8.2 Còn

Còn can function as a full verb (see 2.3.2.4. for **còn** as an aspect marker) with the meaning "still have, have something left."

subject + còn + object

Chúng tôi còn hai bài thi nữa. We still have two final exams.
Chúng ta còn 15 phút nữa là có thể về được rồi. We have fifteen minutes left before we can go home.

Còn can be used without a subject. In this case, **còn** is similar to the English *to remain*. It suggests that an amount of time remains until something happens, or a distance remains for someone to go in order to reach a destination:

Chỉ còn 5 phút nữa là trận đấu kết thúc. Only five minutes *still remain* in the game.
Còn ba cây [số] nữa mới đến. [We] will not get there until we go for three more kilometers.

2.8.3 Hết

Hết meaning "have nothing left, run out of" is the opposite of **còn**. (See 2.3.2.9. for **hết** as an aspect marker.)

subject + hết + object

Chúng ta hết thời gian rồi. We have run out of time. / Our time is up.
Họ hết tiền rồi cho nên hè năm nay không đi du lịch ở đâu cả. They have no money left, so they are not going to travel anywhere this summer.

Hết can be used without a subject:

Sắp hết học kì một rồi. The first (fall) semester will be over soon.

Strictly speaking, there is an inversion in this type of sentences. **Học kì một** "the first (fall) semester" is the subject; **hết** is an intransitive verb meaning "end, be over." In more formal speech, the verb **kết thúc** meaning "finish" is used instead of **hết** with no inversion, and the meaning remains the same:

Học kì một sắp kết thúc rồi.

2.8.4 Mất

Verbs of appearance, existence and disappearance

Mất as a transitive verb means "lose," and as an intransitive verb means "die, past away." It can be used to denote that it takes an amount of time to do something. We will look at the use of each of them.

2.8.4.1. **Mất** as a transitive verb is used before an object:

subject + mất + object

(1) **Họ mới mất nhiều tiền lắm.** They have just lost a lot of money.
(2) **Nó mất việc tháng trước.** He lost his job last month.
(3) **Cả thành phố đang mất điện.** The power outage has left the entire town in the dark. (lit.: The entire town has lost electricity.)

Because this meaning refers to a negative result, very often **bị** is placed in front of **mất** to emphasize the negative connotation:

(1a) **Họ mới bị mất nhiều tiền lắm.**
(2a) **Nó bị mất việc tháng trước.**
(3a) **Cả thành phố đang bị mất điện.**

Mất is used in many idiomatic expressions such as **mất bình tĩnh** "lose temper;" **mất cắp** "have something stolen;" **mất kiên nhẫn** "lose patience;" **mất mùa** "have a bad harvest;" **mất ngủ** "suffer from insomnia;" **mất trộm** "have something stolen by a burglar or burglars, be burglarized;" etc. All these idiomatic expressions can have **bị** in front of **mất** to put more emphasis on the negative result.

2.8.4.2. **Mất** as an intransitive verb means "pass away" and is used in formal and polite speech. For example:

Bà ấy mất năm ngoái. She passed away last year.

2.8.4.3. **Mất** is used after a verb phrase and before an amount of time to denote a particular amount of time needed to do something, which is similar to the English phrase *it takes someone a certain amount of time to do something*:

Anh ấy chữa máy vi tính của tôi mất ba ngày. It took him three days to fix my computer.
Chúng tôi hành trình xuyên Việt mất hai tuần. Our trans-Vietnam trip took two weeks.

2.8.5 Xuất hiện

Xuất hiện is an intransitive verb meaning "appear, show up":

> **Chương trình ti vi này <u>xuất hiện</u> cách đây không lâu.** This TV show has appeared recently.
>
> **Anh ấy <u>xuất hiện</u> ngoài cửa và xin lỗi chúng tôi vì đã bắt chúng tôi phải chờ lâu.** He showed up at the door and appologized to us for keeping us waiting for a long time.

When a location is mentioned, and the subject is usually a natural event, the adverbial of location may come first in the construction:

location + xuất hiện + subject

> **Trên bầu trời <u>xuất hiện</u> một đám mây đen rất lớn.** A very big dark cloud appeared in the sky.
>
> **Dưới sông <u>xuất hiện</u> một chiếc thuyền buồm.** A sailboat appeared on the river.

2.8.6 Xảy ra and diễn ra

Xảy ra and **diễn ra** mean "happen, occur, take place" and are used with one of the following constructions:

(1) **Subject + xảy ra / diễn ra + time / location**
(2) **Time / location + xảy ra / diễn ra + subject**

> (1) **Tai nạn giao thông <u>xảy ra</u> hôm qua ở đầu đường đằng kia.** The traffic accident happened at the corner over there yesterday.
>
> (2) **Hôm qua ở đầu đường đằng kia <u>xảy ra</u> tai nạn giao thông.** The traffic accident happened at the corner over there yesterday.

In (1) the time and location are emphasized. In (2) the emphasis is put on the subject.

Xảy ra and **diễn ra** are in most cases not interchangeable. **Diễn ra** is used to talk about events that are planned ahead of time:

> **Buổi hoà nhạc sẽ <u>diễn ra</u> tại công viên trung tâm thành phố vào chiều mai.** The concert is scheduled to occur at Central Park of the city tomorrow evening.

Xảy ra refers to something unpleasant or dangerous that happens unexpectedly:

> **Tuần trước ở vùng này <u>xảy ra</u> một cơn bão tuyết dữ dội.** This region was hit by a severe blizzard last week.

The English phrase *to happen to* is **xảy ra với** or **xảy đến với**:

> **Hôm qua trên đường tôi đi làm có một chuyện tức cười <u>xảy ra</u> / <u>xảy đến với</u> tôi.** A funny thing happened to me when I was on my way to work yesterday.

2.8.7　Biến mất

Biến mất means "disappear." Like the English *to disappear*, **biến mất** conveys two meanings: (1) to become impossible to see or find; (2) to stop existing. With the first meaning, **biến mất** usually takes the preposition **khỏi**:

> (1) **Anh kĩ sư <u>biến mất</u> <u>khỏi</u> công ti. Lâu rồi không gặp anh ấy.** The engineer has disappeared from the company. We have not seen him for a while.
> (2) **Một số loài cá <u>biến mất</u> sau thảm hoạ về môi trường.** A number of species of fish have disappeared since the environment disaster.

2.9　Verbs of reaching or bringing to a particular state or condition

The basic verbs of this semantic group are **trở thành** "become," **trở nên** "become," **biến thành** "become" and **biến ... thành** "turn something into something." Although all of them suggest the idea of changing, they are used in different ways and are not interchangeable.

Trở thành and **biến thành** are intransitive and followed by a noun. **Trở thành** refers to the result of a long process:

> **Sau mấy năm cùng học trung học, họ <u>trở thành</u> bạn thân.** They became close friends after [the years they spent together at] high school.
> **Cô ấy sẽ <u>trở thành</u> một vận động viên xuất sắc.** She will become a great athlete.

Biến thành is used to emphasize a sudden change:

> **Sau cơn mưa to kéo dài ba tiếng liền, một số đường phố trong thành phố <u>biến thành</u> những con sông nhỏ.** After the heavy

rain that lasted for three hours, some streets in the city became small rivers.

Trở nên is intransitive and is followed by an adjective or a verb denoting a state or condition:

>**Vào mùa đông, ngày <u>trở nên</u> ngắn hơn, còn đêm thì <u>trở nên</u> dài hơn.** In the winter, day is getting shorter, and night is getting longer.
>**Anh ấy <u>trở nên</u> quen dần với công việc mới của mình.** He is step by step becoming accustomed to his new duties.
>**Nghe xong câu chuyện, ông ấy <u>trở nên</u> tức giận.** He got angry after hearing the story.

The transitive verb **biến . . . thành** takes two objects: **subject + biến + object$_1$ + thành + object$_2$**

The second object refers to the resul of the change:

>**Nhà máy sản xuất ô tô đã <u>biến</u> thị trấn nhỏ này <u>thành</u> một trung tâm công nghiệp sầm uất.** The automobile factory turned this small town into a busy industrial center.

2.10 Modal verbs

Modal verbs denote possibility, permission, advice or willingness. The basic modal verbs in Vietnamese are **cần, có thể, dám, định, muốn, nên, phải**. All of them are used before another verb to form the predicate of a sentence, except for **cần**, which can function as the main verb of a sentence as well. We will discuss each of them.

2.10.1 Cần

Cần is equivalent to the English *need*.

1 It is used in front of another verb.

>**Anh <u>cần</u> nghỉ ngơi trước chuyến bay xa sang Việt Nam.** You need to have some rest before your long flight to Vietnam.
>**Chúng ta <u>cần</u> bàn về vấn đề này.** We need to discuss this issue.
>**Chị <u>không cần</u> mang theo ô đâu. Hôm nay trời nhiều mây nhưng không mưa.** You need not carry an umbrella with you. It is overcast today but is not going to rain.

2 It takes an object as a transitive verb.

   Tôi <u>cần</u> một quyển từ điển Việt-Anh. I need a Vietnamese-English dictionary.

   Chúng tôi đang rất <u>cần</u> sự giúp đỡ của chị. We badly need your help now.

2.10.2 Có thể

Có thể means "can," may," "be able" and suggests

1/ a possibility.

   Ngày mai <u>có thể</u> mưa. It may be raining tomorrow.
   Họ <u>có thể</u> không đến kịp vào tối nay. They may / might not [be able to] arrive on time tonight.

2/ an ability

   Tôi <u>có thể</u> chữa máy vi tính cho anh. I can fix your computer.
   Bạn tôi <u>có thể</u> bơi năm cây số liền không nghỉ. My friend can / is able to swim for five kilometers without having a stop.

3/ a permission

   Làm xong việc này, các anh <u>có thể</u> về được rồi. You can leave after having this job done.
   Tối thứ bẩy các cháu <u>có thể</u> thức khuya hơn một tí. Saturday night children can stay up a bit late.

Note 1: The negative form of **có thể** is **không thể** or **chưa thể** depending on the tense. *__Không có thể__ and __chưa có thể__ are incorrect in standard Vietnamese. However, **không có thể** and **chưa có thể** are common in colloquial speech of the Saigon dialect.

   Tôi nghe tin nhắn anh ấy để lại trong di động mấy lần nhưng <u>không thể</u> hiểu anh ấy định nói gì. I listened to his message left on my cell phone a couple of times but coundn't understand what he wanted to say.
   Tuần sau tôi <u>chưa thể</u> làm xong việc này được. I will not yet be able to finish this job by next week.

Note 2: The question construction **subject + có thể +verb phrase + [được] không** is a good way of introducing a polite request:

   Các anh các chị có thể chờ tôi mấy phút [được] không? Could[n't] you wait for me a few minutes, please?

2.10.3 Dám

Dám is similar to the English modal verb *dare*. It is chiefly used in negative statements and questions:

> Tôi <u>không dám</u> ngắt lời họ khi họ đang nói chuyện với nhau. I did not dare / dared not interrupt them when they were talking to each other.
>
> Thấy ông ấy giận quá, chúng tôi <u>không dám</u> nói gì nữa. We realized that he got really angry so we did not dare / dared not say anything.
>
> Cậu <u>có dám</u> hỏi năm nay cô ấy bao nhiêu <u>không</u>? Do you dare / dare you ask how old she is?

<u>Note 1</u>: The English ordinary verb *dare* with the meaning "challenge" is **thách** or **đố** in Vietnamese:

TEACHER: **Sao em lại trèo cây trong sân trường?** Why did you climb the tree in the school yard?
STUDENT: **Thưa thầy, một bạn <u>thách</u> / <u>đố</u> em.** Another boy dared me (to climb it), sir.

<u>Note 2</u>: **Không dám** is a very polite and formal way to acknowledge someone's thanks:

A: **Cám ơn bà đã giúp đỡ tôi nhiều.** Thank you very much for being so helpful to me.
B: **Không dám.** You're welcome. / It was my pleasure.

2.10.4 Định

Định used as a modal verb means "plan to do something" or "intend to do something":

> Tuần này được nghỉ bốn ngày liền, chúng tôi <u>định</u> đi lên Sapa. We are going to have four consecutive days off this week, so we are planning to travel up to Sapa.
>
> Anh ấy <u>không định</u> mua xe ô tô vì ở thành phố này giao thông công cộng rất tốt. He is not planning to buy a car because the public transportation is really good in this town.

2.10.5 Muốn

Muốn as a modal verb conveys two meanings.

(1) want to, would like to

> **Tôi <u>muốn</u> nhờ anh dịch bài này ra tiếng Việt cho tôi.** I would like to ask you to translate this article into Vietnamese for me.
> **Có ai đó <u>muốn</u> gặp anh.** Someone wants / would like to speak with you.

(2) **Muốn** suggests that a change into a different state or condition is imminent; with this meaning **muốn** is usually preceded by **như**.

> **Trời <u>như</u> <u>muốn</u> mưa.** It appears / seems to begin raining soon.
> **Tôi thấy người <u>như</u> <u>muốn</u> ốm.** I have the feeling that I am going to get sick.

<u>Note</u>: Unlike the English *to want* or *would like*, that can take a direct object to express what you want, **muốn** cannot take a direct object. It should be followed by another verb:

> I *want / would like a drink*. **Tôi <u>muốn</u> <u>uống</u> nước.** Or: **Tôi <u>muốn</u> <u>uống</u> cái gì đó.**

However, it can take a direct object if the direct object is the subject of another action:

> **Tôi <u>muốn</u> anh làm việc này cho tôi.** I want you to do this for me.
> **Chúng tôi <u>muốn</u> cháu thi vào trường y.** We would like our daughter / son to take the entrance exams to medical school.

2.10.6 Nên

Nên as a modal verb is used to give advice or to say what you think is right for someone to do:

> **Cậu <u>nên</u> bỏ thuốc lá.** You really should / ought to give up smoking.
> **Các anh các chị chuyên về Việt Nam học <u>nên</u> xem bộ phim *Người Mĩ trầm lặng*. Hay lắm!** You major / specialize in Vietnamese studies, you should / ought to see movie *The Quiet American*. It's a great movie.

Note: Since **nên** refers to advice, the verb **khuyên** meaning "advise" is very often used together with the modal verb **nên**, which follows the object:

> **Tôi khuyên anh nên bỏ thuốc lá.** I would advise you to give up smoking.

2.10.7 Phải

Phải as a modal verbs is used to express

1/ someone's obligation or duty:

> **Học sinh ngày nào cũng phải làm bài tập về nhà.** Students should do homework every day.

2/ an obligation imposed by the speaker:

> **Các anh các chị phải đọc bài báo này chuẩn bị cho buổi thảo luận ngày mai.** You should read this article to prepare for tomorrow's discussion.

3/ an external obligation:

> **Không còn xe buýt nữa nên chúng tôi phải đi bộ về nhà.** There were no more buses, so we had to walk home.

4/ advice; **phải** is similar to **nên** but advice sounds stronger:

> **Bác sĩ bảo tôi phải bỏ thuốc lá.** My doctor told me to give up smoking. Or: My doctor said I must give up smoking.

Note: **Cần** as a modal verb and **phải** may be used together to emphasize the necessity. Compare with **cần** in 2.10.1. (1):

> **Anh cần nghỉ ngơi trước chuyến bay xa sang Việt Nam.** You need to have some rest before your long flight to Vietnam.
> **Anh cần phải nghỉ ngơi trước chuyến bay xa sang Việt Nam.** You must have some rest before your long flight to Vietnam.

2.11 Imperatives

Vietnamese has many ways of expressing commands, requests, suggestions and invitations. Second person imperatives are the most commonly used in any language. The main difference between Vietnamese and English second person imperatives is that the subject *you* is very often mentioned in an imperative sentence in Vietnamese whereas it is understood in English. Compare:

Chị / Anh / Bác . . . làm ơn đóng cửa sổ lại. Please close the window.

In informal English, however, the person addressed can be expressed by a noun placed at the end of the imperative sentence. The noun in most cases is a personal name. For instance:

Be quiet, Kate.

In Vietnamese, the second personal pronouns, including personal names, are placed at the beginning of the imperative sentence. The Vietnamese equivalent command would be:

Khanh [ơi], khē chứ. Be quiet, Khanh.

The choice of the right way of conveying commands, requests, suggestions and invitations depends on 1/ whether the situation is formal or informal; 2/ whether the speaker wants to express a command, a request, a suggestion or an invitation.

The Vietnamese imperative particles are placed in different positions of imperative sentences. It is very important to remember the position of a particular imperative particle.

2.11.1 Hãy

Hãy is placed in front of a verb phrase to express a strong and formal command or request, which the speaker is quite certain will be obeyed:

Hãy cẩn thận. Be careful.

A second personal pronoun can be placed before **hãy**:

Chị / Anh / Bác / Các anh các chị . . . hãy cẩn thận.
Hãy nhớ lấy những gì tôi sắp nói với các anh các chị. Bear in mind what I am going to tell you.

2.11.2 Cứ

Cứ is placed before a verb phrase to encourage someone to do something without hesitation or interruption. If a second personal pronoun is mentioned, **cứ** is inserted between the personal pronoun and the verb:

Nếu có chuyện gì, anh cứ gọi điện cho tôi. Please do not hesitate to give me a call if something comes up.

Chị cứ nói, tôi đang ghi đây. Please keep speaking. I am writing down what you are saying.

2.11.3 Đi

Đi is placed at the end of an imperative sentence to suggest starting an action. It is similar to the English expression *go ahead and do something*:

Đi ngủ đi. Go to sleep.
Các bác ăn đi, đừng chờ tôi. Please go ahead and start eating. Don't wait for me.
Các em làm bài tập này đi. Please go ahead and do this drill.

Note: Very often **cứ** and **đi** are used in combination to put emphasis on the encouragement to the other person(s) to start or keep doing something:

Chị cứ nói đi, tôi đang ghi đây. Please start / keep speaking. I am writing down what you are saying.

2.11.4 Nhé

Nhé is placed at the end of the imperative sentence to convey

1/ a mild suggestion or an invitation; the speaker may expect the other person's / persons' agreement:

Các bác ở lại xơi cơm với chúng tôi nhé. Please stay and have lunch / dinner with us, OK? Or: Would you stay and have lunch / dinner with us?
Cậu uống bia nhé. Would you like a beer?
Chúng mình đi xem phim nhé. Let's go to see a movie, OK?

Nhé can be combined with **cứ** to make the encouragement milder and more friendly:

Các bạn cứ nghỉ nhé. Please keep resting, OK?

All the three imperative particles **cứ**, **đi** and **nhé** can be used together in one imperative sentence as well:

Các bạn cứ nghỉ đi nhé. Please go ahead and take a rest, OK? Or: Please keep resting, OK?

2/ a mild request that may contain a nuance of warning:

Tôi cho anh mượn sách nhưng đọc xong anh phải trả tôi ngay nhé. I can lend you the book but you should return it to me right after you finish reading it, OK?

Chị phải gửi xe máy nhé, kẻo bị mất cắp đấy. You should park your motorbike in a monitored parking lot, otherwise it would be stolen.

2.11.5 Mời

Mời, which lit. means "invite," is placed right before a second personal pronoun to suggest a polite invitation to do something. It is similar to the English *please*:

Mời chị vào đây. Please come in.
Mời các bạn lên xe. Please get on the car.

Note 1: **Mời** conveying a polite suggestion or invitation should be followed by a second personal pronoun. Otherwise, the imperative statement may sound unfriendly or impolite. Compare:

Mời chị vào đây. Please come in.
Mời Ø vào. Come in.

Note 2: If the subject precedes **mời**, **mời** functions as a full verb to suggest a true invitation:

Chúng tôi mời anh chị tối thứ bẩy này đi ăn với chúng tôi. We would like to invite you to have dinner with us this Saturday night.

Note 3: In northern Vietnam, before starting to have a meal, people who are sitting at the same table would say to one another something like the following expressions to show good manners:

A child to her / his parents: **Con mời bố mẹ xơi cơm.**
A host to a guest: **Mời bác / anh / chị . . . xơi cơm.**

In a friendlier and more relaxed situation, one would say:

Mời cả nhà. Everybody, go ahear and eat.
Mời các bạn. Go ahead and eat, guys.

These expressions are used in a way similar to *enjoy your meal* in English, *bon appétit* in French, *guten Appetit* in German, *приятного аппетита* in Russian, 慢慢兒吃 \ 慢慢儿吃, 好好吃飯 \ 好好吃饭 or 吃好 in Chinese.

2.11.6 Đã

Đã comes at the end of a suggestion to imply that the action mentioned in the suggestion should be done before another action can begin. **Đã** is similar to the English *first* placed and the end of a statement with the implication *and then* something happens:

(1) **Uống chén nước đã**. Let's have a cup of tea first. Or: Have a cup of tea first.
(2) **Chờ tạnh mưa đã rồi đi**. Let's wait until the rain stops, and then we'll go / you can go.

In (1) **đã** is used at the end of the sentence, and the second action is understood, whereas in (2) the second action is explicitly mentioned, and **rồi** follows **đã**. **Rồi** is mandatory here. If it is a piece of advice, **hãy** can be placed after **rồi** to show more emphasis on the speaker's insistence:

(2a) **Chờ tạnh mưa đã rồi hãy đi**.

In colloquial Vietnamese, **hẵng** can be used instead of **hãy**:

(2b) **Chờ tạnh mưa đã rồi hẵng đi**.

2.11.7 Đừng

Đừng is placed at the beginning of a negative imperative sentence in front of the verb to convey the negation to the imperative sentence. It is equivalent to the English *do not / don't*:

Đừng vội. Mình còn nhiều thì giờ. Do not / Don't hurry. We have plenty of time.
Đừng nói chuyện ấy với ai. Do not / Don't tell it to anybody.
Đừng đi đến đấy vào ban đêm. Nguy hiểm lắm. Do not / don't go there at night. It may be very dangerous out there (that place is not safe).

Có can follow **đừng** and precede the verb phrase to put more emphasis on the negative imperative:

Đừng có đi đến đấy vào ban đêm. Nguy hiểm lắm.

In colloquial Vietnamese, **mà** follows **đừng có** to make a warning sound stronger:

> **Đừng** <u>có</u> <u>mà</u> **đi đến đấy vào ban đêm. Nguy hiểm lắm.** I would like to warn you not to go there at night. It may be very dangerous out there.

In friendly relaxed situations, **nhé** can be added to the end of the negative imperative sentence to make the request not to do something milder:

> **Đừng nói chuyện ấy với ai <u>nhé</u>.** Don't tell it to anybody, OK?

2.11.8 Không and không được

Prohibitions may be expressed by using **không được** before the verb phrase:

> **<u>Không được</u> làm ồn.** Don't make noise.
> **<u>Không được</u> hút thuốc ở đây.** Don't smoke here. (Smoking is prohibited here.)

In written instructions or on signs in public places, just **không** is used in front of the verb phrase to refer to prohibitions:

> **<u>Không</u> cắt hoặc làm hỏng dây điện.** Do not cut or damage the power cord.
> **<u>Không</u> làm ồn.** Do not make noise.
> **<u>Không</u> hút thuốc ở đây.** Do not smoke here.

2.11.9 Chớ

Advice given to someone not to do something is expressed by **chớ**, which is followed by a verb phrase:

> **<u>Chớ</u> làm như thế.** Don't do that.
> **<u>Chớ</u> dại mà tin nó.** Don't be foolish to believe him. (It would be foolish of you to fall for his trick.)

Có may be inserted between **chớ** and the verb phrase to express emphasis on the advice not to do something:

> **<u>Chớ</u> <u>có</u> làm như thế.**
> **<u>Chớ</u> <u>có</u> dại mà tin nó.**

Compared with **đừng** (see 2.11.7.), the use of **chớ** is restricted only to offering advice. When both **đừng** and **chớ** convey advice not to do something, **chớ** sounds stronger.

2.12 Verb constructions equivalent to the English passive voice

Many grammarians do not recognize the passive voice as a grammatical category in Vietnamese. However, influenced by European languages, first of all by French, Vietnamese has for a long time made use of several constructions to convey the meanings of the passive voice. And yet, it is important to note that the passive voice is much more common in English than in Vietnamese. In many instances, the passive voice is normal in English, whereas the active voice is preferred in Vietnamese.

As in European languages, only transitive verbs can be used in the passive voice constructions in Vietnamese. In the active voice, the subject performs an action, and the object is "acted upon." In the passive voice, the grammatical subject no longer performs the action, but is acted upon. The performer of the action, that is also called *agent*, becomes the grammatical object. The word order of the Vietnamese passive voice differs from English:

gramm. subj. (= logical obj.) + được / bị / do + gramm. obj. (= logical subj.) + verb

Được, bị and **do** are called passive voice markers. **Được** is used to talk about an action that is favorable from the speaker's perspective (1), whereas **bị** refers to an unfavorable action (2). The full construction is expressed as follows:

(1) **Một số học sinh được ban giám hiệu nhà trường khen thưởng.** Some students were praised and awarded by the school administration.
(2) **Một số học sinh khác bị ban giám hiệu nhà trường kỉ luật.** Several other students were disciplined by the school administration.

The agent (grammatical object) is not mentioned if its identification is irrelevant. The agent **ban giám hiệu nhà trường** in these sentences can be omitted:

(1a) **Một số học sinh được khen thưởng.** Some students were praised and awarded.
(2a) **Một số học sinh khác bị kỉ luật.** Several other students were disciplined.

Do is neutral in the sense of favorableness or unfavorableness and is used to emphasize the performer of the action. In a sentence with **do**, the agent is mandaroty:

> **Chiếc xe này <u>do</u> nhà máy Ford ở Việt Nam sản xuất.** This car was manufactured by a Ford factory in Vietnam.

The agent **nhà máy Ford ở Việt Nam** cannot be left out.

> **Quyển tiểu thuyết này <u>do</u> một nhà văn nổi tiếng dịch ra tiếng Việt.** This novel was translated into Vietnamese by a well-known author.

The agent **một nhà văn nổi tiếng** is necessary for the sentence to be complete.

<u>Note</u>: In some cases, the passive voice marker **bởi** is used along with **được** or **bị**. In such sentences, the verb usually expresses a habitual action or common occurrence, and the agent is not a person or people. The word order is a bit different:

> **gramm. subj. (= logical obj.) + được / bị / + verb + bởi + gramm. obj. (= logical subj.)**

Here are some examples:

> **Ngôi làng yên tĩnh <u>được</u> bao bọc <u>bởi</u> những thửa ruộng mầu mỡ và những vườn cây ăn quả xum xuê.** The peaceful village is surrounded by the lush rice paddies and exuberant orchards.
> **Họ <u>bị</u> ràng buộc <u>bởi</u> những tập quán cũ.** They are bound by old traditions.

If the agent is people, **bởi** cannot be used. Such a sentence as *__Quyển tiểu thuyết này <u>được</u> dịch ra tiếng Việt <u>bởi</u> một nhà văn nổi tiếng.__ is incorrect in standard Vietnamese. **Do** or **được** should be used instead: **Quyển tiểu thuyết này <u>do</u> / <u>được</u> một nhà văn nổi tiếng dịch ra tiếng Việt.**

2.13 Main functions of verbs and verb phrases

In the following pair of examples, the first sentence contains a verb, the second one has a verb phrase.

2.13.1 Predicate of a sentence

> **Ông ấy <u>đang làm việc</u>.** He is working.

Ông ấy <u>đang làm việc với đoàn đại biểu Quốc hội</u>. He is meeting with a delegation of the National Assembly.

2.13.2 Subject of a sentence

<u>Đi</u> cũng là học một cái gì đó. Traveling is also a way of learning something.
<u>Tiếp xúc với người bản ngữ</u> là một trong những cách học ngoại ngữ tốt nhất. To interact / Interacting with native speakers is one of the best ways to learn a foreign language.

<u>Note</u>: In English, a verb can also serve as the subject of a sentence, but the verb should be either a to-infinitive (*to interact*) or a gerund (*interacting*).

2.13.3 Object of a verb

Nó chỉ thích <u>chơi</u> thôi. He likes just hanging out.
Ông ấy rất thích <u>nghe nhạc cổ điển</u>. He likes listening / to listen to classical music.

2.13.4 Modifier of a noun as its attributive

Sinh viên được rèn luyện kĩ năng <u>viết</u>. Students are trained to improve their writing skills.
Sinh viên được rèn luyện kĩ năng <u>viết báo cáo nghiên cứu khoa học</u>. Students are trained to improve their skill at writing reports on research work.

Note

1 **Nhau** is the reciprocal in Vietnamese, which is equivalent to English *one another* or *each other*.

Chapter 3

Adjectives, adjective phrases and their components

3.1 Introduction to the Vietnamese adjectives

3.1.1 Main distinction between a Vietnamese adjective and an English adjective

The main distinction between a Vietnamese adjective and an English adjective is that an adjective in Vietnamese can function as the predicate of a sentence by itself, while an adjective in English follows a verb such as *to be, to become, to seem*, etc., to function as a predicative. Compare:

(1) **Kĩ sư Hùng giỏi**. Engineer Hùng *is good*.

The adjective **giỏi** alone functions as the predicate of the sentence. The adjective *good* functions as the predicative and along with the verb *is* forms the predicate of the sentence.

3.1.2 Adjectives describing qualities and state of affairs

As in many other languages, most Vietnamese adjectives describe the qualities or characteristics of a noun. However, some adjectives can express the state of affairs of the subject as well. Compare:

(2) **Kĩ sư Hùng đang chữa máy vi tính**. Engineer Hùng is fixing a computer.
(3) **Kĩ sư Hùng đang nghỉ**. Engineer Hùng is having a rest.
(4) **Kĩ sư Hùng tuần này đang ốm**. Engineer Hùng is sick this week.
(5) **Kĩ sư Hùng khoẻ rồi**. Engineer Hùng has already recovered.

In (1) the adjective **giỏi** "be good (at something)" describes the characteristics of the noun phrase **kĩ sư Hùng**, which is the subject of the sentence. In (2) the verb phrase **đang chữa** "be fixing" refers to an action performed by the subject. In (3)

3
Adjectives, adjective phrases and their components

the verb phrase **đang nghỉ** "be having a rest" indicates the physical state in which the subject is at the moment of speaking. In (4) the adjective phrase **đang ốm** "be currently sick" also denotes the physical state in which the subject is. In (5) the adjective phrase **khoẻ rồi** "have recovered" is used to refer to a change in the state in which the subject is.

3.1.3 Gradable and ungradable adjectives

As in other languages, Vietnamese adjectives may be *gradable* or *ungradable*. Gradable adjectives allow intensification and comparison. All the three adjectives in the above mentioned sentences (1), (4) and (5) are gradable:

> **rất giỏi** "very good;" the adverb of degree **rất** is the intensifier, which is placed in front of the adjective **giỏi** to modify it;
> **ốm quá** "really sick;" the adverb of degree **quá** is the intensifier, which follows the adjective **ốm** to mofidy it;
> **khoẻ hơn** "hearthier;" the adjective **hơn** follows the adjective **khoẻ** to refer to a higher degree of the characteristics indicated by the adjective **khoẻ**.

Ungradable adjectives do not allow intensification or comparison. The adjectives such as **chung** "common," **riêng** "separate," **tư** "private," **tư nhân** "private," **độc thân** "single," **quốc doanh** "state-owned, state-run" are ungradable adjectives in Vietnamese.

3.2 Adjective phrases and their components

An adjective phrase is a phrase whose head word is an adjective. Bases on the components of an adjective phrase, their meanings and positions, there are three major types of adejctive phrases in Vietnamese.

3.2.1 Adjective phrase #1: *adverb of degree + adjective*

Here are the main adverbs of degree that come in front of an adjective to modify it: **rất** "very," **khá** "rather, pretty," **hơi** "rather, a little bit," **đủ** "enough," **tương đối** "relatively," **hết sức** "extrmely":

> **rất mát** "very cool," **khá lạnh** "rather cold, pretty cold," **hơi nóng** "a little bit hot," **tương đối ấm** "relatively warm, pretty warm," **hết sức chăm chỉ** "extremely diligent."

Note 1: The English adverb *enough* follows an adjective, whereas the Vietnamese adverb **đủ** precedes it:

Is the tea *strong enough*? **Trà đã <u>đủ đặc</u> chưa?**
He is *old enough* to make his own decisions. **Anh ấy <u>đủ khôn lớn</u> để tự quyết định nhiều vấn đề.**

Note 2: The adverb of degree **hơi** is used to refer to unfavorable characteristics or qualities from the speaker's perspective, or in the common sense. We can say **hơi nóng** "a little bit hot" but we would not say *****hơi tốt** "a little bit good." The other adverbs of degree which come in front of an adjective can be used to denote either favorable or unfavorable characteristics or qualities.

Note 3: The English phrase *a little [bit]* conveys several meanings, which are denoted by different words or phrases in Vietnamese.

When meaning "a small amount," *a little [bit]* corresponds to **một ít**, **một chút** or **một tí**, which are placed after verbs and before nouns:

Could you give me *a little bit* milk for my coffee, please? **Chị làm ơn cho tôi xin <u>một tí</u> sữa để cho vào cà phê.**
I told him *a little bit* about my recent Europe trip. **Tôi kể cho anh ấy nghe <u>một ít</u> về chuyến đi châu Âu vừa rồi.**
They speak *a little bit* Japanese. **Họ nói <u>một ít</u> tiếng Nhật.**

When meaning "to a small degree," *a little [bit]* is denoted by **hơi**, which is placed before an adjective and some verbs:

The weather is *a little bit* cold today. **Trời hôm nay <u>hơi</u> lạnh.**
I was *a little bit* disappointed with my mid-term test results. **Tôi <u>hơi</u> buồn vì kết quả bài kiểm tra giữa học kì [không được tốt lắm].**

Note 4: The adjectives **ấm** "warm," **nóng** "hot," **mát** "cool," **lạnh** "cold" are used to describe the weather and temperature. The adjectives **ấm** and **mát** refer to pleasant feelings and cannot be used with **hơi**. Such phrases as *****hơi ấm** and *****hơi mát** are incorrect.

Note 5: The bisyllabic adjective **hết sức** "extremely" precedes bisyllabic adjectives in formal Vietnamese: **hết sức khẩn trương** "extremely quick," **hết sức thận trọng** "extremely careful," **hết sức nghiêm trọng** "extremely serious." It cannot be used with monosyllabic adjectives.

Adjective phrases and their components

3.2.2 Adjective phrase #2: *adjective + adverb of degree*

The basic adverb of degree which follows an adjective to modify it is **lắm**, that means "very:" **tốt lắm** "very good," **đẹp lắm** "very pretty," **tồi lắm** "very poor (speaking of the quality of something)." Another adverb of degree that comes after the adjective is **thế** (see 3.2.2.2.).

3.2.2.1 Lắm vs. rất

On the scale of degree, **lắm** suggests a higher point than **rất**. The negation **không** does not precede **rất** and **lắm**. In order to convey the meaning "not very" Vietnamese uses **không** in front of the adjective, not in front of these adverbs of degree. **Rất không + adjective** and **không + adjective + lắm** convey different meanings. Compare:

Positive statements

Quyển từ điển này rất tốt. This dictionary is very good.
Quyển từ điển này tốt lắm. This dictionary is really good.

Negative statements

Quyển từ điển này rất không tốt. This dictionary is not good at all. Or: This dictionary is really bad.
Quyển từ điển này không tốt lắm. This dictionary is not very good.

The sentence ***Quyển từ điển này không rất tốt**. is incorrect.

Note: There are two adverbs of degree that can either precede or follow an adjective and convey different meanings depending on their positions. They are **quá** and **thật**.

Quá means "really, excessively" when following an adjective; it is chiefly used in exclamatory statements:

Trời hôm nay nóng quá. The weather is so hot today. Or: How hot the weather is today.

When preceding an adjective, **quá** means "too; to a higher degree than is allowed":

Trời hôm nay quá nóng, không thể tập chạy ngoài trời. The weather is too hot today. It is impossible to practice running outside.

Thật lit. means "true, real." When placed in front of an adjective, **thật** implies "to the full, to the greatest possible extent." It is very often used after a verb, and the phrase **thật + adjective** modifies the verb:

> **Buổi họp tối qua <u>thật căng thẳng</u>**. Last night's meeting was so tense. (The phrase **thật căng thẳng** functions as the predicate of the sentence.)
> **Chúng ta phải <u>đi thật nhanh</u> để kịp chuyến xe buýt.** We should walk as quickly as possible to catch the bus. (The phrase **thật nhanh** modifies the verb **đi** as an adverbial of manner.)

Thật follows an adjective to convey the meaning "truly, really":

> **Bộ phim <u>hay thật</u>.** The movie is truly great. (The phrase **hay thật** functions as the predicate of the sententce.)
> **Chị ấy <u>đánh bóng bàn giỏi thật</u>**. She plays ping-pong really well. (The phrase **giỏi thật** modifies the verb phrase **đánh bóng bàn** as an adverbial of manner.)

Thật can be stressed to turn these statements into exclamations:

> **Bộ phim hay 'thật!** How good the movie is!
> **Chị ấy đánh bóng bàn giỏi 'thật!** How well she plays ping-pong!

The construction **adjective + thật là + the same adjective** is used to put more emphasis on the quality of the subject or the action in the same exclamations; **thật** remains stressed:

> **Bộ phim <u>hay 'thật là hay</u>! Chị ấy đánh bóng bàn <u>giỏi 'thật là giỏi</u>!**

3.2.2.2. **Thế** follows an adjective, and the phrase comes at the end of a statement to denote a high degree of a quality, and in some cases it may refer to the speaker's surprise as well. It is similar to the English *so* placed before an adjective:

> **Sao trông anh mệt mỏi thế?** Why do you look so exhausted?
> **Trong phòng lạnh thế.** It's so cold in the room.

In the Saigon dialect, **vậy** is used instead of **thế** with this function.

3.2.3 | Adjective phrase #3: *adjective + comparison marker*

We discussed the comparison and superlative of the adjectives in 1.3.3.1.1. Here are a few more points which may cause problems for English-speaking learners of Vietnamese.

> Adjective phrases and their components

3
Adjectives, adjective phrases and their components

3.2.3.1 Vietnamese construction for English *He is much older than me / than I am*

The Vietnamese construction for such English sentences as *He is much older than me / than I am.* is **subject + adjective + hơn + object of comparison + nhiều**:

Anh ấy lớn tuổi hơn tôi nhiều.

3.2.3.2 Vietnamese construction for English *He is three years older than me / than I am. / He is three years my senior*

The idea of the English sentences *He is three years older than me / than I am. / He is three years my senior.* is:

Anh ấy [lớn] hơn tôi ba tuổi.

3.2.3.3 Hơn as a full adjective

Hơn by itself can function as a full adjective which implies a comparison in the sense of "better." Very often, what two people or things are compared in is clear only from the context:

Nó học hơn tôi. He studies better than me / than I do.

In this sentence, the adjective **giỏi** "good" is understood. The full sentence would be **Nó học giỏi hơn tôi.**

In the sentence in 3.2.3.2., the adjective **lớn** may be omitted, and the meaning of the sentence is clear from the context, in which the age of two people is spoken of:

Anh ấy hơn tôi ba tuổi.

3.2.3.4 Vietnamese constructions for English *less + adjective* and *the least + adjective*

The English *less* placed before an adjective is expressed by the construction **không + adjective + như / bằng + object of comparison**:

I found this movie *less interesting* than the other one we saw last time.
Tôi thấy bộ phim này không hay như / bằng bộ phim chúng ta xem lần trước.

The English *the least* placed before an adjective is mainly expressed by the antonym of the adjective in the superlative in Vietnamese:

Adjective phrases and their components

He is *the least tall* of my teammates. **Anh ấy <u>thấp nhất</u> trong số các bạn cùng đội với tôi.**

Compare *tall* and **thấp** "short." Another example:

This plan is *the least bad* choice. **Phương án này là sự lựa chọn <u>tốt nhất</u>.**

Compare *bad* and **tốt** "good."

3.2.3.5 So với denoting the comparative of the adjective

The comparative of the adjective that functions as the predicate of the sentence can be expressed with **so với**. The construction with **so với** is characteristic of formal Vietnamese:

A + comparative + so với B
or:
So với B, A + comparative

Mùa hè năm nay nóng hơn so với mùa hè năm ngoái. / So với mùa hè năm ngoái, mùa hè năm nay nóng hơn. This summer is hotter compared to the last one.
Đồng bằng sông Cửu Long lớn hơn nhiều so với đồng bằng sông Hồng. / So với đồng bằng sông Hồng, đồng bằng sông Cửu Long lớn hơn nhiều. The Mekong Delta is much larger compared to the Red River Delta.

3.2.4 *Adjective phrase #4: <u>aspect / tense marker + adjective</u> or: <u>adjective + aspect / tense marker</u>*

A large number of gradable adjectives can be used with an aspect or tense marker. The aspect and tense markers maintain their meanings:

Trời <u>đang lạnh</u> bỗng nhiên ấm hẳn lên. All of a sudden, the cold weather has turned so warm.
Họ làm được thế là <u>tốt rồi</u>. What they have done is already good.

3.2.5 Adjective phrase #5: <u>adjective + object</u> or: <u>adjective + preposition + object</u>

An adjective may take an object: **giỏi toán** "be good at math," **khá ngoại ngữ** "be good *at* foreign languages," **gần thư viện** "close *to* / near the library," **xa thành phố** "be far *away from* the city," **đông người** "full *of* people, crowded," **vắng khách** "have few customers," **giầu khoáng sản** "rich *in* natural resorces."

Note: The English adjectives *good, close, far, full* and *rich* require prepositions before a noun, while **giỏi, khá, gần, xa, đông** and **giầu** take direct objects.

An adjective may be modified by a prepositional phrase:

Vùng Bắc Ninh <u>nổi tiếng về dân ca quan họ</u>. The area of Bắc Ninh is famous for its quan họ folksongs.

Note: Vietnamese has many adjectives in which an adjective is followed by a noun (adjective + noun). They are not adjective phrases but rather "idiomatic" adjectives because their meanings are not the sum of the meanings of their components. They are not noun phrases either, because the adjective precedes the noun, whereas in noun phrases an adjective functioning as attributive follows a noun (see 1.3.3.1.). Many of these "idiomatic" adjectives contain a noun referring to a part of body. Most of them are either bisyllabic or quadrisyllabic. The number of trisyllabic adjectives is rather small. Some examples:

bisyllabic

cao tay "sagacious, shrewd" (lit. high + hand)
cao tầng "high-rise" (lit. high + story, floor)
khéo tay "dexterous" (lit. skillful + hand)
mát tay "deft" (lit. fresh + hand)
nặng tai "hard of hearing" (lit. heavy + ear)
nhẹ dạ "light-minded" (lit. light + womb, heart)
nóng tính "bad-tempered" (lit. hot + nature)
sáng trăng "moonlit" (lit. bright + moon)
to gan "bold" (lit. big + liver)
to mồm "vocal, vociferous" (lit. big + mouth)
yếu tim "easy to be scared" (lit. weak + heart)

trisyllabic

sạch nước cản "rather good in chess; eye-catching (of a young woman)" (lit. clean + move (in chess) + check, block)
yếu bóng vía "easy to be scared" (lit. weak + spirit)

quadrisyllabic

cứng đầu cứng cổ "stubborn, pig-headed" (lit. hard + head + hard + neck)
nhanh chân nhanh tay "spry" (lit. quick + leg + quick + hand)
thấp cổ bé họng "underprivileged and unable to protect oneself" (lit. short + neck + small + throat)
xanh vỏ đỏ lòng "having a heart contrary to appearances" (lit. green + peel + red + heart)

3.2.6 Adjective phrase #6: _adjective + number + weight / length / height / temperature measures_

Note the different word order in Vietnamese and English:

Bể bơi kích thước Thế vận hội <u>dài năm mươi mét</u>. An Olympic size swimming pool is _fifty meter(s) long_.
Anh ấy <u>cao một mét bẩy mươi hai</u>. He is _one meter seventy-two tall_.

Note 1: The Vietnamese adjective **nặng** is used for weight measuring while English uses the verb _to weigh_:

Quả bưởi này <u>nặng hai cân</u>. This grapefruit _weighs two kilo(gram)s_.

Note 2: The Vietnamese adjective **rộng** "wide, broad" is used for the area of a place whereas English denotes the area by different expressions:

Căn phòng này <u>rộng hai mươi mét vuông</u>. The _area of this room is twenty square meters._ / This room _is twenty square meters in area._ / This room _has an area of twenty square meters._

Note 3: The Vietnamese adjectives **nóng** "hot" and **lạnh** "cold" are used for temperature measuring when the temperature is very high or very low. The English adjectives _hot_ and _cold_ are not used for this function:

Hôm nay Hà Nội <u>nóng 35 độ C</u>. It is 35 degrees Celsius in Hanoi today.
Tuần sau Boston <u>lạnh âm 2 độ F</u>. It will be two degrees Fahrenheit below zero in Boston next week.

When the temperature is normal for the time of the year, **nóng** or **lạnh** is not used:

Hôm nay 25 độ. It's 25 degrees today.

3 Adjectives, adjective phrases and their components

3.2.7 Adjective phrase #7: *adjective + verb of motion*

Four verbs of motion **ra**, **lên**, **đi** and **lại** (see 2.7. for the details about the verbs of motion) follow some adjectives to denote a change in the quality or characteristics of the subject. In most cases, **ra** and **lên** suggest an improvement or enlargement; **đi** and **lại** refer to a reduction or decline.

Note that only certain adjectives can take a verb of motion to refer to the change. Some adjectives can take two of them. It is a good idea to memorize the phrases as idiomatic ones:

> **đẹp ra / đẹp lên** to become more beautiful vs. **xấu đi** to worsen; become less beautiful
> **dài ra** to become longer vs. **ngắn đi / ngắn lại** to become shorter
> **nặng lên** to become heavier vs. **nhẹ đi** to become lighter (weight)
> **to ra / to lên** to become bigger vs. **nhỏ đi / nhỏ lại** to become smaller
> **cao lên** to become taller vs. **thấp đi** to become shorter
> **sáng ra** to become brighter (light) vs. **tối đi** to become darker
> **nóng lên** to become hotter vs. **lạnh đi** to become colder
> **ấm lên** to become warmer vs. **mát đi, dịu đi / dịu lại** to become cooler
> **khoẻ ra / khoẻ lên** to become healthier or stronger; to recover vs. **ốm đi** someone's health becomes worse; **yếu đi** to become weaker
> **béo ra** to gain weight, become heavier vs. **gầy đi** to become thinner
> **nhiều lên** to have more vs. **ít đi** to have less or fewer

Here are some examples:

> **Sau khi đi nghỉ ngoài biển về, trông ông ấy <u>khoẻ ra</u>.** He looks healthier after vacationing on the sea.
> **Mấy tháng không gặp cháu, tôi thấy cháu <u>cao</u> hẳn <u>lên</u>.** I haven't seen him (a child) for a few months. He is much taller now.
> **Mùa đông mới có năm giờ mà trời <u>tối đi</u> nhiều.** It is only five o'clock PM, but it is getting quickly dark in winter.
> **Trên đường đi, chúng tôi nói chuyện rất vui nên có cảm giác quãng đường như <u>ngắn lại</u>.** We had a very nice conversation when traveling so we had the feeling that the distance became shorter.

3.3 Main functions of adjectives and adjective phrases

In the following pair of examples, the first sentence contains an adjective, the second one has an adjective phrase.

Main functions of adjectives and adjective phrases

3.3.1 Modifier of a noun as its attributive

Tôi đã có dịp gặp nhạc sĩ <u>nổi tiếng</u> ấy. I have got a chance to meet that famous composer.

Note the opposite word order in Vietnamese and English: **nhạc sĩ nổi tiếng ấy** vs. that famous composer.

Tôi đã có dịp gặp nhạc sĩ <u>nổi tiếng vì các ca khúc phản chiến</u>. I have got a chance to meet the composer famour for his anti-war songs.

3.3.2 Predicate of a sentence

Mùa đông năm nay <u>lạnh</u>. The winter is cold this year.
Mùa đông năm nay <u>lạnh hơn mùa đông năm ngoái nhiều</u>. This year the winter is much colder than last year.
Mùa đông năm nay <u>lạnh nhất</u>. This year's winter is the coldest.

The predicate expressed by the superlative of an adjective may come first in a sentence to perform the function of topic in a topic – comment sentence, especially in a sentence with an adverbial of place and time. The comment which is in most cases a noun phrase follows the verb **là**, which cannot be used before an adjective as the predicate in a subject – predicate sentence. For example:

Trong năm năm vừa qua, <u>lạnh nhất</u> <u>là</u> mùa đông năm nay. Over the last five years, this year's winter is the coldest.
Ở Hà Nội, <u>đẹp nhất</u> <u>là</u> kiến trúc khu Ba Đình. In Hanoi, the architecture in Ba Đình area is the most beautiful.

See 5.5.18.3. for more details about the predicate as topic in topic – comment sentences.

3.3.3 Modifier of a verb as an adverbial

Họ đang làm việc <u>khẩn trương</u>. They are currently working hard.
Họ đang làm việc <u>hết sức khẩn trương</u> để kịp hoàn thành công việc trước cuối tháng này. They are currently working extremely hard in order to complete the work by the end of this month.

<u>Note 1</u>: In English, in many cases the suffix -ly is added to an adjective to form an adverb: bad manners → behaved badly. In some cases, the adjective and the adverb have the same form: fast runner → running fast; slow runner → running

3 Adjectives, adjective phrases and their components

slow / slowly. In Vietnamese, since a word does not change its form, the adjective can function as an adverb to modify a verb.

Note 2: The meaning of some adjectives may change depending on the functions the adjectives perform in a sentence. For instance, the adjective **khác** means "another" when modifiyng a noun as its attributive in a noun phrase:

> **Cho tôi đổi quyển từ điển này lấy một quyển khác.** I would like to exchange this dictionary for another one.

In this sentence, **khác** modifies the noun **từ điển** in the phrase **quyển [từ điển] khác**, and the whole phrase is the second object of the verb **đổi** + object$_1$ + **lấy** + object$_2$.

When functioning as the predicate of a sentence, **khác** conveys the meaning "differ from, be different from" and takes a direct object:

> **Khí hậu Hà Nội rất khác khí hậu Sài Gòn.** The climate in Hanoi differs greatly from the climate in Saigon. / The climate in Hanoi is very different from the climate in Saigon.

Khác is the predicate of this sentence, and **khí hậu** is its object. Only functioning as the predicate, **khác** can take the verb of motion **đi** to imply a change:

> **Mấy năm vừa qua, anh ấy khác đi nhiều.** He has significantly changed in the recent years.

Chapter 4

Word-formation

This chapter deals with the processes of forming new words from existing words and with the words borrowed from other languages.

4.1 Introduction to the Vietnamese word

Vietnamese belongs to the type of *isolating* languages, whose words are invariable. Unlike the *inflecting* languages, whose words change their internal structure by using inflectional endings to display grammatical relationships, Vietnamese expresses grammatical relationships between the words in a sentence by using auxiliary words and word order. French, German, Russian and, to some extent, English are inflecting languages. Vietnamese, Chinese and many southeast Asian languages are isolating languages.

In Vietnamese, each syllable in most instances corresponds to a word. There are monosyllabic (one-syllable), bisyllabic (two-syllable), trisyllabic (three-syllable) and quadrisyllabic (four-syllable) words. Mono- and bisyllabic words make up the vast majority of Vietnamese vocabulary.

4.2 Main processes of forming new words in Vietnamese

This work discusses four processes of word-formation in Vietnamese: compounding, affixation, reduplication and borrowing. Many linguists do not recognize affixation as a method of creating new words in Vietnamese, because they regard the so-called affixes as independent words and, as a result, the way those words are combined with other words to create new words is compounding. Those words, however, are treated in this work as affixes to help foreign learners of Vietnamese associate this process with affixation in European languages.

4.2.1 Compounding

Compounding is the process of making new words in which a new word is created by putting together two or more base words. The new word is called a *compound*. For instance, (1) the compound noun **nhà cửa**, which means "houses," consists of two nouns: **nhà** "house" + **cửa** "door"; (2) the compound noun **nhà ăn**, which means "dining hall," is composed of the noun **nhà** + the verb **ăn** "eat;" (3) the compound verb **ăn uống**, which means "eat (speaking of eating in general)," contains two verbs **ăn** + **uống** "drink;" (4) the compound adjective **trong sáng**, which means "clear, free from what obscures," is made from two adjectives **trong** "clear" + **sáng** "light, bright;" (5) the compound adjective **trong veo**, which means "very clear," consists of the adjective **trong** and the emphatic element **veo**, which alone does not have its own lexical meaning and is used for emphasizing the quality of being clear only. Compounds can be nouns as (1) and (2), verbs as (3), adjectives as (4) and (5).

4.2.1.1 Co-ordinate compounds

The relationship between the components of a compound may be *co-ordinate* in the sense that they have the same grammatical status and belong to the same word class. Compounds (1), (3) and (4) are examples of co-ordinate compounds. Both **nhà** and **cửa** are nouns, both **ăn** and **uống** are verbs, both **trong** and **sáng** are ajectives. The components of each compound have the equal grammatical status between themselves.

In most instances, co-ordinate compound nouns refer to a general kind of things: **nhà cửa** is "houses in general." One of the most important grammatical features of compound nouns is that they are uncountable. The noun phrase **một ngôi nhà** "a house" is normal, but we cannot say *****một ngôi nhà cửa**. On the other hand, a construction company that builds houses is called **công ti xây dựng nhà cửa**. We would not say *****công ti xây dựng nhà**.

Co-ordinate compound verbs and adjectives denote more abstract notions than each verb or adjective forming the compounds. For example, the compound **ăn uống** means "consume food and drinks in general." One cannot say *****Anh chờ tôi đi ăn uống đã rồi tôi đi với anh**. in the sense "Please wait for me. I will eat something and then will come with you." If the verb **uống** is left out, the sentence sounds normal: **Anh chờ tôi đi ăn đã rồi tôi đi với anh**. because the idea of the latter sentence refers to a one-time event, whereas the compound verb **ăn uống** suggests a general idea of eating. On the other hand, the noun phrase **chế độ ăn uống** meaning "diet" is normal since the compound verb **ăn uống** suggests a regimen of eating and drinking in general.

The compound adjective **trong sáng** means "free from what obscures" and very often is used in the figurative sense. We cannot say *****Nước sông ở khúc này trong sáng**. implying "The water in this section of the river is clear." The correct sentence should be **Nước sông ở khúc này trong**. The phrase **văn phong trong sáng** meaning "a clear and beautiful style of writing" is normal because the compound adjective **trong sáng** conveys a figurative meaning.

However, in order to maintain the *phonetic symmetry* of a phrase, Vietnamese tends to use a bisyllabic compound if the other component of the phrase is also a bisyllabic word (see 4.2.4.1.6. for quadrisyllabic template). Compare: the word **dọn nhà** meaning "move to another place, change one's residence" has two monosyllabic components **dọn** "clean up" and **nhà** "house." The verb phrase **dọn dẹp nhà cửa**, which refers to the cleanup in a particular house, is composed of two bisyllabic words: the compound verb **dọn dẹp** and the compound noun **nhà cửa**. We would not say *****dọn dẹp nhà**.

The adjective **trong sáng** may be used after a bisyllabic noun to convey a literal meaning as well. Compare the following two phrases which convey the same meaning: **trời trong** "a clear sky" and **bầu trời trong sáng** "a clear sky." The noun **bầu** serves as the classifier for skies, and the phrase **bầu trời** contains two syllables, therefore the bisyllabic compound adjective is used with the literal meaning.

In some co-ordinate compounds, the meaning of the second component is unclear due to historical reasons, but they follow the same rules of usage for compounds. A few examples for compound nouns, in which the sign (?) follows the component whose lexical meaning is vague: **bếp núc** (?) "kitchens," **chợ búa** (?) "markets," **đường sá** (?) "roads, roadways," **gà qué** (?) "poultry," **phố xá** (?) "streets," **thuốc men** (?) "medicines, medications," **xe cộ** (?) "vehicles," etc.

4.2.1.2 Subordinate compounds

The relationship between the components of a compound is *subordinate* when one component grammatically depends on the other one and semantically modifies it. The compound noun (2) **nhà ăn** and the compound adjective (5) **trong veo** in 4.2.1. are subordinate compounds.

4.2.1.2.1. In (2), the noun **nhà** lit. meaning "house" serves as the base word and refers to a broad notion of a place where a certain kind of activities is performed. In this case, the activity of eating is denoted by the verb **ăn** "eat," which modifies the noun **nhà** and narrows the notion of a place to a particular place for eating. That being said, the compound noun **nhà ăn** conveys a narrower meaning than the base noun **nhà**. In other words, the base noun **nhà** refers to the general class of entities to which the compound **nhà ăn** belongs.

4 Word-formation

The base noun defines the word class of the compound. The components of this compound belong to different word classes: **nhà** is a noun, **ăn** is a verb. The components of a subordinate compound may belong to the same word class, as in **nhà máy**, where the noun **máy** meaning "machine" modifies the base noun **nhà**, and the compound noun **nhà máy** means "factory, plant." Some more examples for compound nouns that contain the base noun **nhà**:

nhà bạt "a big tent"
nhà bếp "kitchen"
nhà chùa "Buddhist temple"
nhà để xe "garage"
nhà hàng "restaurant"
nhà hát "opera house"
nhà hộ sinh "maternity (a section of a hospital)"
nhà khách "guest house"
nhà thờ "church"
nhà trọ "hostel"
nhà tu "convent, monastery"
nhà tù "prison, jail"

Examples of the same type of subordinate compound nouns for the base noun **xe** "vehicle":

xe ba gác "delivery cart"
xe buýt "bus"
xe cấp cứu "ambulance"
xe cứu hoả "fire truck"
xe đạp "bicycle"
xe đẩy "stroller"
xe điện "street car"
xe lửa "train"
xe máy "motorbike"
xe ngựa "horse carriage"
xe trượt tuyết "sleigh or sled"
xe xích-lô "pedicap"

Examples of the same type of subordinate compound verbs for the base verb **làm** "do, make":

làm bàn "score"
làm bếp "cook"
làm bộ "be haughty"

làm chủ "own"
làm cỏ "weed"
làm dáng "coquet"
làm duyên "coquet"
làm gương "set the example"
làm khách "be too formal or polite"
làm lành "make up with someone"
làm ơn "do a favor"
làm quen "make acquaintance"
làm ruộng "be a farmer"
làm thuê "be hired to do a job for wages"

Examples of the same type of subordinate compound adjectives for the base adjective **khó** "hard, difficult":

khó bảo "be disobedient, stubborn"
khó chịu "be unbearable or displeased"
khó coi "be unacceptable"
khó hiểu "be hard to understand"
khó nghe "be hard to accept"
khó nghĩ "be hard to decide"
khó ở "be under the weather"
khó thương "be untolerable"
khó tính "be hard to please"

Note: The boundary between a compound and a phrase is not always clear-cut. **Nhà để xe** "garage" can be defined as a whole word, which is a subordinate compound noun, or as a noun phrase, where the verb phrase **để xe** modifies the noun **nhà**, as it was noted in 1.3.3.6. The same happens to **xe cấp cứu** "ambulance," **xe cứu hoả** "fire truck" and **xe trượt tuyết** "sleigh," in which the verbs **cấp cứu** "provide emergency medical care," **cứu hoả** "extinguish fire" and **trượt tuyết** "ski" may be considered modifiers of the noun **xe**.

4.2.1.2.2. Compound (5) **trong veo** belongs to the second type of the subordinate compounds. The adjective **trong** lit. meaning "clear" serves as the base word and refers to a broad notion of being clear. The component **veo** does not carry any lexical meaning by itself, but adds some shade of meaning to the base adjective **trong** and intensifies the notion of being clear. The compound adjective **trong veo** means "very clear." The component **vắt** in the compound adjective **trong vắt** is treated in the same way. The component **suốt** in **trong suốt**, however, conveys its own lexical meaning "throughout" and intensifies the notion of being clear by adding the nuance of being so clear that one can see throughout. Thus, the subordinate compound adjectives **trong veo**, **trong vắt**, **trong suốt** and the reduplicative **trong trẻo** add some shades of meaning to the base adjective **trong**. For more on reduplicatives, see 4.5.

Further examples of the same type of subordinate compound adjectives for the base adjective **trắng** "white":

> **trắng bệch** "be pale white"
> **trắng bóc** "very white"
> **trắng bong** "very white"
> **trắng dã** "be unpleasantly white (speaking of eyes)"
> **trắng hếu** "be unpleasantly white (speaking of skin)"
> **trắng lốp** "be white (speaking of many white things placed next to each other)"
> **trắng muốt** "be crystally white"
> **trắng nhờn** "be unpleasantly white (speaking of teeth)"
> **trắng nõn** "be pleasantly white"
> **trắng phau** "be very white"
> **trắng tinh** "be pure white"
> **trắng trẻo** (reduplicative) "be pleasantly white (speaking of complexion)"
> **trắng xoá** "be dazzling white"

Examples of the same type of subordinate compound adjectives for the base adjective **đen** "black":

> **đen đúa** (reduplicative) "be unpleasantly black"
> **đen đủi** (reduplicative) "be out of luck"
> **đen kịt** "be all black"
> **đen nhánh** "be shining black"
> **đen nhẻm** "be black (speaking of complextion)"
> **đen sì** "be all black"
> **đen thui** "be all black"
> **đen trũi** "be all black"

4.2.2 Affixation

Affixation is the process of making new words in which a derivational component called an *affix* is added to a word. This process is typical of many European languages. For instance, in the English adjective *bearable*, the suffix *-able* is attached to the verb *to bear*, which occurs as a word by itself, to form the adjective *bearable*. The prefix *un-* in turn is attached to the adjective *bearalbe* to form the adjective *unbearable*. An affix can be attached to a part of word as well. For example, the word *legal* consists of the root *leg* meaning "law," which does not exist in English as a word by itself, and the suffix *-al*, which appears elsewhere.

In Vietnamese, affixes can occur as separate words by themselves with their own lexical meanings. It is the reason why some grammarians regard the so-called affixation as part of the subordinate compounds that were discussed in 4.2.1.2. This work introduces affixation as a process of word-formation to help English-speaking learners of Vietnamese since it is similar to the affixation in English.

Main processes of forming new words in Vietnamese

4.2.2.1 Prefixation

Prefixation is the way of making new words when a derivational component called *prefix* is placed in front of a word. Here are some words which serve as prefixes commonly used in Vietnamese.

The word **nhà**, borrowed from Chinese (家), comes before another word to form nouns with the meaning of people connected with a particular occupation or activity. This prefix is a homonym of the Vietnamese noun **nhà** "house" and is similar to the English suffixes *-er, -or* or *-ist*. Some examples:

nhà + báo "newspaper" → **nhà báo** "journalist, reporter"
nhà + giáo, which is part of the word **giáo dục** "educate," → **nhà giáo** "educator, teacher"
nhà + khoa học "science" → **nhà khoa học** "scientist"
nhà + kinh tế "economy, economics" → **nhà kinh tế** "economist"
nhà + nho "Confucianism" → **nhà nho** "Confucianist"
nhà + nông "farming, agriculture" → **nhà nông** "farmer"
nhà + sử học "history" → **nhà sử học** "historian"
nhà + tư tưởng "idea, thought" → **nhà tư tưởng** "philosopher"
nhà + vật lí "physics" → **nhà vật lí** "physicist"

The word **sự**, which is a Chinese borrowing (事) with the meaning "thing," is placed before a verb or an adjective to turn the verb or adjective into a noun:

sự + có mặt "be present" → **sự có mặt** "presence"
sự + chuẩn bị "prepare" → **sự chuẩn bị** "preparation"
sự + giàu có "be rich, wealthy" → **sự giàu có** "richness, wealthiness"
sự + phát triển "develop" → **sự phát triển** "development"
sự + sống "(to) live" → **sự sống** "life"
sự + thay đổi "(to) change" → **sự thay đổi** "change"
sự + trong sáng "be clear" → **sự trong sáng** "clarity"
sự + vắng mặt "be absent" → **sự vắng mặt** "absence"
sự + ủng hộ "(to) support" → **sự ủng hộ** "support"

4
Word-formation

The word **việc** meaning "thing, job, work" is placed in front of a verb to turn it into a noun. The noun with **việc** conveys a less abstract meaning than the nouns containing the prefix **sự**:

việc + chuẩn bị "prepare" → **việc chuẩn bị** "preparation(s)"
việc + học tập "(to) study" → **việc học tập** "study / studies"
việc + phát triển "develop" → **việc phát triển** "development"
việc + tiếp xúc "interact, communicate" → **việc tiếp xúc** "interaction, communication"
việc + tổ chức "organize" → **việc tổ chức** "organization"

The word **cuộc** meaning "activity" comes in front of a verb, an adjective or a noun to turn the verb or adjective into a noun with the meaning of an activity or event, in which a number of people participate:

cuộc + điều tra "investigate" → **cuộc điều tra** "an investigation"
cuộc + họp "have a meeting" → **cuộc họp** "a meeting"
cuộc + mít tinh "demonstration, rally" → **cuộc mít tinh** "a rally"
cuộc + nói chuyện "talk, speak, converse" → **cuộc nói chuyện** "a talk"
cuộc + sống "(to) live" → **cuộc sống** "life"
cuộc + vui "be happy; have fun" → **cuộc vui** "amusement, entertainment"

Note: All the three nouns **cuộc đời**, **cuộc sống** and **sự sống** convey the meaning "life." However, they are not interchangeable in most instances. **Sự sống** is the most abstract and refers to the general condition that distinguishes organisms from inorganic objects: **sự sống trên trái đất** "life on the earth." **Cuộc sống** denotes a period of life of a person or a group of people with the implication of the quality of life: **cuộc sống đầy đủ** "a wealthy and happy life;" **cuộc sống khó khăn** "a hard life;" **cuộc sống đang được cải thiện** "life is improving." **Cuộc đời** usually suggests a period of time when a person is alive: **cuộc đời của một nghệ sĩ nổi tiếng** "a well-known artist's life."

The word **buổi** is placed in front of the nouns to denote different parts of the day: **buổi sáng** "morning," **buổi trưa** "shortly before noon and early afternoon," **buổi chiều** "late afternoon and early evening," **buổi tối** "everning" (see 1.3.1.4.8.). It is also used before a number of verbs and nouns to form nouns which refer to activities, social events, sessions or performances:

buổi + biểu diễn "perform" → **buổi biểu diễn** "a performance as a social event"
buổi + học "(to) study" → **buổi học** "a class meeting"
buổi + họp "have a meeting" → **buổi họp** "a meeting"

> buổi + hoà nhạc "give a concert, perform musical works" → **buổi hoà nhạc** "a concert"
> buổi + khiêu vũ "(to) dance" → **buổi khiêu vũ** "a dance as a social event"
> buổi + liên hoan "(to) party" → **buổi liên hoan** "a party"
> buổi + nói chuyện "speak, converse" → **buổi nói chuyện** "a meeting for someone's speech"
> buổi + tập "(to) practice (music and sports)" → **buổi tập** "a practice session"
> buổi + thảo luận "discuss" → **buổi thảo luận** "a discussion as an event"
> buổi + trình diễn "perform, make a presentation" → **buổi trình diễn** "a performance, presentation"

The word **chủ nghĩa**, which is a Chinese borrowing (主義 \ 主义) and equivalent to the English suffix *-ism* of Greek origin, comes before a noun or an adjective to form nouns that refer to doctrines, political beliefs and systems of ideas:

> chủ nghĩa + ấn tượng "impression" → **chủ nghĩa ấn tượng** "impressionism"
> chủ nghĩa + cá nhân "individual" → **chủ nghĩa cá nhân** "individualism"
> chủ nghĩa + cổ điển "classical" → **chủ nghĩa cổ điển** "classicism"
> chủ nghĩa + cộng sản "communism" (a theory based on holding all property in common) → **chủ nghĩa cộng sản** "communism" (a political doctrine based on Marxism)
> chủ nghĩa + cơ hội "opportunity" → **chủ nghĩa cơ hội** "opportunism"
> chủ nghĩa + dân tộc "nation" → **chủ nghĩa dân tộc** "nationalism"
> chủ nghĩa + hiện thực "reality" → **chủ nghĩa hiện thực** "realism"
> chủ nghĩa + lãng mạn "romantic" → **chủ nghĩa lãng mạn** "romanticism"
> chủ nghĩa + quốc tế "international" → **chủ nghĩa quốc tế** "internationalism"
> chủ nghĩa + xã hội "society" → **chủ nghĩa xã hội** "socialism"

The word **tính**, which is a Chinese borrowing (性) with the meaning "character, characteristics," is placed in front of a noun or an adjective to form abstract nouns that denote the characteristics or features of a concept. **Tính** is to some degree similar to the English suffixes *-ity* and *-ness*:

> tính + bất biến "invariable" → **tính bất biến** "invariability"
> tính + cơ động "mobile" → **tính cơ động** "mobility"
> tính + cụ thể "concrete" → **tính cụ thể** "concreteness"

Main processes of forming new words in Vietnamese

tính + khả thi "feasible" → **tính khả thi** "feasibility"
tính + kiên nhẫn "patient" → **tính kiên nhẫn** "patience"
tính + sư phạm "pedagogy, teachers' training" → **tính sư phạm** "characteristics of teachers' training"
tính + thực tiễn "practical" → **tính thực tiễn** "practicality"
tính + trong sáng "clear" → **tính trong sáng** "clarity"
tính + trừu tượng "abstract" → **tính trừu tượng** "abstractness"

The word **trưởng**, which is a Chinese borrowing (長 \ 长) with the meaning "chief, head, leader," comes in front of a noun to form nouns that denote the head of a group or organization:

trưởng + ban "section" → **trưởng ban** "head of a section"
trưởng + đoàn "group, delegation" → **trưởng đoàn** "head of a group or delegation"
trưởng + phòng "office" → **trưởng phòng** "head of an office"

4.2.2.2 Suffixation

Suffixation is the way of making new words when a derivational component called *suffix* follows a word. Here are some words which serve as commonly used suffixes.

The word **học**, which is a Chinese borrowing (學 \ 学) with the meaning "to study," comes after a noun to form nouns that indicate an area of knowledge or a field of scientific study. **Học** is equivalent to the English suffix *-logy* of Greek origin, or to the word *studies*:

hoá "become" + **học** → **hoá học** "chemistry"
kinh tế "economy" + **học** → **kinh tế học** "economics"
lịch sử "history" + **học** → **sử học** "history as a field of study" (the component **lịch** is dropped)
sinh vật "living thing" + **học** → **sinh [vật] học** "biology"
toán "calculate" + **học** → **toán học** "mathematics"
văn "literal work" + **học** → **văn học** "literature"
xã hội "society" + **học** → **xã hội học** "sociology"
Hán "Han dynasty, Han Chinese" + **học** → **Hán học** "Chinese studies, Sinology"
Việt Nam + **học** → **Việt Nam học** "Vietnamese studies"

The same word **trưởng** comes after a noun to form nouns that denote the head of a group or organization:

bộ "ministry, department" + **trưởng** → **bộ trưởng** "minister, secretary of a department"

cửa hàng "department store" + **trưởng** → **cửa hàng trưởng** "manager of a department store"

đại đội "company (military unit)" + **trưởng** → **đại đội trưởng** "head of a company"

đội "team" + **trưởng** → **đội trưởng** "captain of a team"

đơn vị "unit" + **trưởng** → **đơn vị trưởng** "head of a group"

hiệu "school" (a Chinese borrowing 校 with the meaning "school") + **trưởng** → **hiệu trưởng** "principal, chancellor, president (of a university)" (the word was borrowed as a whole word from Chinese 校長 \ 校长; see 4.2.4.1. for more about Chinese loanwords).

kế toán "accounting" + **trưởng** → **kế toán trưởng** "head of an accounting section"

tiểu đoàn "batalion" + **trưởng** → **tiểu đoàn trưởng** "head of a batalion"

Note: The word **trưởng** comes both in front of a noun (see 4.4.1.), which is the Vietnamese word order, and after a noun, which is the Chinese word order. The Chinese word order is more common in Vietnamese.

The word **viên**, which is a Chinese borrowing (員 \ 员) with the meaning "member," comes after a noun to form nouns that denote members of a group or organization:

đảng "party" + **viên** → **đảng viên** "party member".

đoàn "group, delegation, Vietnam's youth organization" + **viên** → **đoàn viên** "member of a group, delegation or youth organization".

hội "association" + **viên** → **hội viên** "member of an association".

The word **hoá**, which is a Chinese borrowing (化) with the meaning of changing or transforming, comes after a noun or adjective to form verbs with the meaning of causing to conform or transform to a different state. **Hoá** is equivalent to the English suffix *-ize*:

công nghiệp "industry" + **hoá** → **công nghiệp hoá** "industrialize".

cơ khí "mechanics" + **hoá** → **cơ khí hoá** "mechanize".

hệ thống "system" + **hoá** → **hệ thống hoá** "systemize".

hiện đại "modern" + **hoá** → **hiện đại hoá** "modernize".

tự động "automatic" + **hoá** → **tự động hoá** "automatize, automate".

Main processes of forming new words in Vietnamese

4 Word-formation

4.2.3 Reduplication

Reduplication is the process of making new words in which two or more syllables of a new word contain phonetic resemblance to each other. Vietnamese is extremely rich in reduplicatives. Foreign learners of Vietnamese should try to memorize commonly used reduplicatives. This section discusses reduplicatives in the sense of how a reduplicative is formed and how the meaning of a reduplicative changes in comparison with the meaning of the base word.

The phonetic resemblance of the syllables of a reduplicative may be whole or partial. A whole resemblance occurs when the syllables of a reduplicative precisely repeat each other:

> **chiều** "evening" → **chiều chiều** "evenings;" **lắc** "(to) shake" → **lắc lắc** "shake repetedely;" **đen** "black" → **đen đen** "to some degree black."

The syllables of a reduplicative have a partial resemblance when only a part of the base word is repeted:

> **lắc** → **lắc lư** "swing" (the initial consonant [l] is repeated); **rối** "be tangled" → **bối rối** "be puzzled, confused" (the rhyme [ối] is repeated).

4.2.3.1 Whole resemblance

4.2.3.1.1 BASE WORD IS COMPLETELY REPEATED

The base word is completely repeated. These reduplicatives can be nouns, adjectives or verbs.

Noun reduplicatives covey the meaning of the plural:

> **đêm** "night" → **đêm đêm** "every night"
> **đời** "life" → **đời đời** "forever"
> **ngày** "day" → **ngày ngày** "every day"
> **người** "human being" → **người người** "every one"
> **sáng** "morning" → **sáng sáng** "every morning"
> **tối** "evening" → **tối tối** "every evening"

Adjective reduplicatives denote a lesser degree of the quality expressed by the monosyllable adjectives. The meanings of some of them are similar to the meanings of the English adjectives which end in -*ish*:

> **đỏ** "red" → **đỏ đỏ** "reddish"
> **gầy** "thin, skinny" → **gầy gầy** "slender"
> **nhanh** "quick" → **nhanh nhanh** "somewhat quick"

trắng "white" → **trắng trắng** "whitish"
tròn "round" → **tròn tròn** "roundish"
vàng "yellow" → **vàng vàng** "yellowish"
xanh "green, blue" → **xanh xanh** "greenish" or "bluish"

Verb reduplicatives suggest actions that are continuously repeated with less intensity than the actions expressed by the monosyllable verbs: **cười** "laugh" → **cười cười** "laugh for a while without a loud burst of sound," **đập** "(to) hit" → **đập đập** "hit lightly several times," **khuấy** "(to) stir" → **khuấy khuấy** "stir continuously," **vỗ** "(to) tap" → **vỗ vỗ** "tap lightly several times," **vội** "(to) hurry" → **vội vội** "hurry a bit."

4.2.3.1.2 TONE CHANGES

The whole phonetic resemblance of syllables may be slightly changed when the reduplicated syllable changes the tone compared to the tone of the base word.

Very often, the reduplicated syllable comes before the base word. If the base word has the high-rising tone (**thanh sắc**), the reduplicated syllable has the mid-level tone (**thanh ngang**): **ấm** "warm" → **âm ấm** "to some degree warm," **khá** "good" → **kha khá** "rather good," **trắng** "white" → **trăng trắng** "whitish."

If the base word has the low-falling-broken tone (**thanh nặng**), the reduplicated syllable has the low-falling tone (**thanh huyền**): **chậm** "slow" → **chầm chậm** "a bit slow," **lạnh** "cold" → **lành lạnh** "a bit cold," **nặng** "heavy" → **nằng nặng** "a bit heavy," **sợ** "be scared" → **sờ sợ** "be a little bit scared."

If the base word has the low-falling-rising tone (**thanh hỏi**), the reduplicated syllable has the mid-level tone (**thanh ngang**): **đỏ** "red" → **đo đỏ** "tinged with red," **nhỏ** "small" → **nho nhỏ** "a bit small."

4.2.3.1.3 TONE AND FINAL CONSONANT CHANGE

The whole phonetic resemblance of the syllables may be slightly changed when the reduplicated syllable changes both the tone and the final consonant compared to the base word.

If the base word has the final [p], the reduplicated syllable has the final [m]: **đẹp** "beautiful" → **đèm đẹp** "rather beautiful," **hẹp** "narrow" → **hèm hẹp** "somewhat narrow," **thấp** "low" → **thâm thấp** "somewhat low."

If the base word has the final [t], the reduplicated syllable has the final [n]: **tốt** "good" → **tôn tốt** "pretty good," **mát** "cool" → **man mát** "rather cool," **ngọt** "sweet" → **ngòn ngọt** "a little bit sweet," **ướt** "wet" → **ươn ướt** "somewhat wet."

If the base word has the final [k] denoted by <c> or <ch>, the reduplicated syllable has the final [ŋ] denoted by <ng> or <nh> respectively: **chắc** "firm" → **chăng chắc** "pretty firm," **khác** "different" → **khang khác** "somewhat different," **lệch** "tilted" → **lềnh lệch** "a bit tilted," **nhích** "(to) inch, move slowly," **nhinh nhích** "move very slowly," **sạch** "clean" → **sành sạch** "to some degree clean."

4.2.3.2 Partial resemblance

4.2.3.2.1 RHYME OF REDUPLICATED SYLLABLE CHANGES

The initial consonants of the base word and the reduplicated syllable resemble each other, while the rhyme of the reduplicated syllable changes.

4.2.3.2.1.1. The base word comes first and is followed by the reduplicated syllable:

> **cây** "tree" → **cây cối** "trees"
> **cũ** "old" → **cũ kĩ** "outdated"
> **chen** "jostle" → **chen chúc** "scramble"
> **dựa** "(to) lean" → **dựa dẫm** "depend on"
> **gầy** "thin" → **gầy gò** "skinny"
> **gọn** "neat" → **gọn gàng** "always neat"
> **máy** "machine" → **máy móc** "machinery"

4.2.3.2.1.2. The reduplicated syllable comes first and is followed by the base word:

> **ức** "be irritated" → **ấm ức** "be embittered"
> **bùng** "flare up" → **bập bùng** "burn for a while"
> **lay** "(to) shake" → **lung lay** "be shaken"

4.2.3.2.2 INITIAL CONSONANTS CHANGE

The initial consonants of the base word and the reduplicated syllable differ from each other, while their rhymes are similar.

4.2.3.2.2.1. The base word comes first and is followed by the reduplicated syllable:

> **co** "(to) shrink" → **co ro** "be shriveled"
> **khéo** "skillful" → **khéo léo** "agile"
> **mảnh** "thin" → **mảnh khảnh** "lean"
> **qua** "(to) cross" → **qua loa** "without necessary focus or attention"
> **thiêng** "sacred" → **thiêng liêng** "sacred"
> **thô** "coarse" → **thô lỗ** "rude"

4.2.3.2.2.2. The reduplicated syllable comes first and is followed by the base word:

leo "climb" → **cheo leo** "be perched high"
mò "grope for" → **tò mò** "be nosy"
ngát "be spread out (speaking of fragrance)" → **bát ngát** "immense"
ngần "hesitate" → **tần ngần** "be undecided"
nhắng "ostentatious" → **bắng nhắng** "pretentious"
rối "be tangled" → **bối rối** "be perplexed"
tượng "appearance" → **mường tượng** "imagine"
thầm "whisper" → **âm thầm** "quiet"
vênh "be slanted" → **chênh vênh** "be in an unstable postiton"
vờn "(to) caper" → **chờn vờn** "flutter"

Many reduplicated syllables of this type have the initial consonant [l]:

đảo "turn over" → **lảo đảo** "stagger"
khọm "look old usually with stooped shoulders" → **lọm khọm** "walk with a stoop"
mờ "be blurred" → **lờ mờ** "vague"
nhí "little (slang) → **lí nhí** "(speaking) quietly and unclearly"
quẩn "be confused" → **luẩn quẩn** "not be able to think clearly"
vòng "circle" → **lòng vòng** "move around"

Note 1: Some Chinese bisyllabic loanwords are perceived by Vietnamese as Vietnamese reduplicatives, although each component of those bisyllabic words has its own lexical meaning in Chinese. For example, Vietnamese borrowed the whole word **liên miên** "continuous(ly)" from Chinese, which is 連綿 \ 连绵 [lián mián] meaning "continuous." The first component **liên** means "to join" in modern Vietnamese and is used as a bound component in many words, but the meaning of the second component **miên** is unclear to many Vietnamese. In Chinese, 連\连 means "to connect," and 綿 \ 绵 means "silk floss; continuous." Another word that contains the component **miên** is **triền miên** "lingering." This word was borrowed from Chinese 纏綿 \ 缠绵 [chán mián] as a whole word. The first component of the word 纏 \ 缠 means "wind, coil, twine." Neither component is used in modern Vietnamese as an independent word, and most Vietnamese speakers assume that this is a Vietnamese reduplicative. (See Note 2.) The word **thâm thuý** meaning "deep, profound" came into Vietnamese as a whole word from 深邃 [shēn suì]. Only the first component **thâm** 深 meaning "deep" is still used with a figurative meaning in modern Vietnamese. The meaning of the second component **thuý** 邃, which in Chinese means "remote; profound," is unclear to many Vietnamese, and **thâm thuý** is perceived as a reduplicative.

Note 2: The meanings of the components of some other Chinese loanwords are unclear to Vietnamese at all, and they are perceived as Vietnamese reduplicatives, such as **tận tuỵ** < 盡瘁 \ 尽瘁 "be devoted," **tiều tuỵ** < 憔悴 "thin and pallid," **trù trừ** < 躊躇 \ 踌躇 "hesitate, be undecided." For more on Chinese loanwords, see 4.6.1.

4.2.3.3 Trisyllabic reduplicatives

The number of trisyllabic reduplicatives is rather small. They are chiefly used in colloquial Vietnamese. Most of them contain the whole resemblance with slight phonetic changes (see 4.2.3.1.3.). Many of the trisyllabic reduplicatives are derived from bisyllabic reduplicatives:

mơ "(to) dream" → **lơ mơ** "vague" → **lơ tơ mơ** "vague"
con "small, little" → **cỏn con** "pretty small" → **cỏn còn con** "pretty small"
dưng "distant (speaking of relations)" → **dửng dưng** "be indifferent" → **dửng dừng dưng** "be totally indifferent"
khít "tight" → **khít khịt** "very tight" → **khít khìn khịt** "very tight"
sát "be close to" → **sát sạt** "be very close to" → **sát sàn sạt** "be very close to"

Some of them are trisyllabic reduplicatives which do not have corresponding bisyllabic reduplicatives:

sạch "clean" → **sạch sành sanh** "be all used up"

4.2.3.4 Quadrisyllabic reduplicatives

They are formed from bisyllabic reduplicatives with partial resemblance and, like trisyllabic reduplicatives, are used in colloquial Vietnamese.

4.2.3.4.1. The vowel [a] or the vowel [ơ] is inserted:

[a]: **ấm ớ** "be inarculate" → **ấm a ấm ớ** "be inarculate"
[a]: **nghênh ngang** "be haughty" → **nghênh nga nghênh ngang** "be haughty"
[ơ]: **hớt hải** "be in a rush" → **hớt hơ hớt hải** "be in a rush"

4.2.3.4.2. The tone changes, the syllables remain:

[`] and [?]: **bồi hồi** "feel nervous" → **bổi hổi bồi hồi** "feel nervous"

4.2.3.4.3. Each syllable of the bisyllabic reduplicative is repeated:

vội vàng "(to) hurry" → **vội vội vàng vàng** "(to) hurry"

4.2.3.5 None of the syllables convey any meaning

Reduplicatives none of whose syllables conveys any meaning, but as whole words they convey certain meanings that are clear to native speakers: **bâng khuâng** "be melancholy," **đủng đỉnh** "walk slowly," **linh tinh** "miscellaneous," **mênh mông** "huge, immense," **suôn sẻ** "go well, successfully," **thình lình** "all of a sudden."

4.2.3.6 Reduplicatives containing -iếc

Many nouns form the reduplicatives by maintaining the initial consonant of the base noun which is followed by the reduplicated syllable with the suffix **-iếc**: **bàn** "desk, table" → **bàn biếc** "desks, tables," **ghế** "chair" → **ghế ghiếc** "chairs," **sách** "book" → **sách siếc** "books," **xe** "motorbikes, cars" → **xe xiếc** "motorbikes, cars." The reduplicative nouns of this kind are collective nouns, and in some contexts may convey a belittling description of the objects. They are used mostly in colloquial Vietnamese.

Some verbs can also form the reduplicatives this way: **đọc** "read" → **đọc điếc** "read (in general)," **học** "study" → **học hiếc** "read (in general)," **tập** "practice" → **tập tiếc** "practice (in general)." The reduplicative verbs of this kind refer to the action in a general sense, not to a particular action, and, like the reduplicative nouns containing **-iếc**, are used chiefly in colloquial Vietnamese.

4.2.3.7 Meanings of reduplicatives

4.2.3.7.1 NOUNS

The reduplicative noun conveys the collective meaning compared to the base noun:

máy "(a) machine" → **máy móc** "machinery"
chim "(a) bird" → **chim chóc** "birds"
cây "(a) tree" → **cây cối** "trees"

Thus, the base noun can take a number with a classifier, whereas the reduplicative noun cannot: **một cái máy** "one machine," but not *****một máy móc**; **hai con chim** "two birds," but not *****hai chim chóc**. The reduplicative nouns, however, can be used after the words **nhiều** "many" and **ít** "few": **nhiều máy móc** "many machines," **ít chim chóc** "few birds."

Main processes of forming new words in Vietnamese

4.2.3.7.2 ADJECTIVES

The reduplicative adjectives with the whole resemblance (4.5.1.) refer to a lower degree of the quality denoted by the base adjectives:

đỏ "red" → **đỏ đỏ / đo đỏ** "reddish"
nặng "heavy" → **nằng nặng** "a bit heavy"

The reduplicative adjectives with the partial resemblance (4.2.3.2.) usually denote figurative meanings while the base adjectives from which they are derived convey the literal meanings. Some examples:

> **nặng** vs. **nặng nề**: **cái bàn nặng** "a heavy desk," **cái túi nặng** "a heavy bag" vs. **cuộc sống nặng nề** "a hard life," **những bước chân nặng nề** "heavy footsteps," **dáng đi nặng nề** "a heavy tread;"
> **nhẹ** vs. **nhẹ nhàng** and **nhẹ nhõm**: **cái bàn nhẹ** "a light desk," **cái túi nhẹ** "a light bag" vs. **công việc nhẹ nhàng** "an easy job," **những bước chân nhẹ nhàng** "light footsteps," **dáng đi nhẹ nhàng** "a light tread," **khuôn mặt nhẹ nhõm** "delicate features (of one's face)," **thấy trong lòng nhẹ nhõm** "feel such a sense of relief."

Note: In some cases, a reduplicative is used just for phonetic symmetry between the parts of a phrase or a sentence. For instance, in the sentence **Trời mát** "The weather is cool", the word **trời** meaning "weather" is monosyllabic, therefore the monosyllabic adjective **mát** meaning "cool" is used as the predicate. In the sentence **Thời tiết mát mẻ** "The weather is cool", the word **thời tiết** meaning "weather" is bisyllabic and is followed by the reduplicative adjective **mát mẻ**, although the reduplicative does not add any nuance to the sentence. The sentence **thời tiết mát** is not incorrect, but the quadrisyllabic phonetic symmetry disappears. See 4.2.4.1.6. for further details about quadrisyllabic template.

4.2.3.7.3 VERBS

A reduplicative verb usually refers to a repeated action characteristic of a person, whereas the base verb from which it is derived denotes a particular action in a particular situation. Compare **vội** and **vội vàng**:

> **Anh ấy đang vội ra sân bay.** He is in a rush to get to the airport. (a particular action in a particular situation)
> **Anh ấy lúc nào cũng vội vàng.** He is always in a big hurry. (perhaps being in a hurry is a trait of his nature)

4.2.3.7.4 ONOMATOPOEIC WORDS

A large number of words which are formed by imitation of sounds are reduplicatives. Some examples: **ào ào** (sounds made by a powerful water flow), **ầm ầm** (noisy sounds), **đùng đùng** (explosions), **gầm gừ** (dog growling), **ha hả** (sound made by loud laughing), **lạo xạo** (sounds made by gravel under shoes), **leng keng** (sounds made by a bell), **oang oang** (sounds made by a very loud and unpleasant voice), **quang quác** (chickens' loud sounds), **sột soạt** (sounds made by paper or pages when they are turned over), **xôn xao** (sounds made by many voices), **xủng xoảng** or **loảng xoảng** (sounds made by metal instruments or utensils).

4.2.4 *Borrowing*

Vietnamese, like most languages, has borrowed and continues borrowing words from several languages to denote new objects and concepts. Those borrowed words are called *loanwords*. The main external sources from which Vietnamese has borrowed words are Chinese, French and English. We are discussing loanwords from each of these languages.

4.2.4.1 Loanwords from Chinese

Vietnamese came into contact with Chinese in the second century BC, when Vietnam for the first time was invaded by China. After Vietnam regained independence in the tenth century, Chinese remained the administrative written language of the Vietnamese royal court. Due to a large number of similarities between the Vietnamese and Chinese phonetic systems and also to the fact that both languages are isolating languages, a set of rules for transcribing Chinese characters into Vietnamese, called **cách đọc Hán-Việt** "the method of transcribing Chinese words," was probably created in the eighth or ninth century. Those rules incorporated Chinese loanwords into Vietnamese and made them a part of the Vietnamese vocabulary. Chinese words were borrowed into Vietnamese at different points in time. This section focuses on three of them: before the seventh century, between the seventh and seventeenth centuries, and after the seventeenth century.

4.2.4.1.1 FROM SECOND CENTURY BC TO SEVENTH CENTURY AD

From the second century BC to the seventh century AD, Chinese was a foreign language in the territory of present-day northern Vietnam and the northern part of central Vietnam. Chinese vocabulary was borrowed by the Vietnamese to indicate new cultural items and ideas. Most of them were monosyllabic words. Because

4 Word-formation

they came into Vietnamese before the set of rules for the transcription of Chinese words into Vietnamese was created, they were pronounced by the Vietnamese as they were heard in everyday speech. Nowadays, most Vietnamese without knowledge of Chinese do not recognize the Chinese origin of those words, such as **bàn** "table, desk" < 盤 \ 盘 [pán];[1] **beo** "leopard" < 豹 [bào]; **buồng** "room" < 房 \ 房 [fáng]; **chè** "tea" < 茶 [chá]; **chúng** "they" < 眾 \ 众 [zhòng]; **chuông** "bell" < 鐘 \ 钟 [zhōng]; **gấp** "urgent" < 急 [jí]; **hè** "summer" < 夏 [xià]; **kim / ghim** "needle" < 針 \ 针 [zhēn]; **làn** "basket" < 籃 \ 篮 [lán]; **lìa** "(to) leave" < 離 \ 离 [lí]; **mả** "grave" < 墓 [mù]; **múa** "(to) dance" < 舞 [wǔ]; **ngan** "bird in the duck family" < 雁 [yàn]; **ngược** "contrary" < 逆 [nì]; **qua** "(to) cross" < 過 \ 过 [guò]; **quen** "be acquainted with" < 慣 \ 惯 [guàn]; **ta** "we" < 咱 [zán]; **thêu** "embroider" < 繡 \ 绣 [xiù]; **thước** "ruler" < 尺 [chǐ]; **xe** "vehicle" < 車 \ 车 [chē], etc. These loanwords are used independently as full words in modern Vietnamese.

4.2.4.1.2 FROM SEVENTH TO SEVENTEENTH CENTURIES

Chinese culture and literature of the Tang Dynasty (618–907) had a significant influence on East Asian nations and Vietnam. The previously mentioned set of rules for transcribing Chinese characters was devised in this period of time, and Vietnamese systematically adopted many Chinese words. Some words that had previously come into spoken Vietnamese were now borrowed again based on the new rules of transcription. Compare the new loanwords and the loanwords discussed in 4.2.4.1.1. The first word of each pair is the version initially adopted into spoken Vietnamese, while the second is the version resulting from a later borrowing of the same word according to the rules of transcription:

> **beo** vs. **báo** "leopard;" **gấp** vs. **cấp** "urgent;" **kim / ghim** vs. **châm** "needle;" **chuông** vs. **chung** "bell;" **hè** vs. **hạ** "summer;" **lìa** vs. **li** "(to) leave;" **mả** vs. **mộ** "grave;" **ngược** vs. **nghịch** "contrary;" **ngan** vs. **nhạn** "bird in the duck family;" **buồng** vs. **phòng** "room;" **qua** vs. **quá** "(to) cross;" **quen** vs. **quán** "be acquainted;" **thêu** vs. **tú** "embroider;" **chè** vs. **trà** "tea;" **múa** vs. **vũ** "dance;" **xe** vs. **xa** "vehicle;" **thước** vs. **xích** "ruler."

Many monosyllabic loanwords that came into Vietnamese in this time period are used as free words in modern Vietnamese. They were borrowed to denote new objects and concepts in different areas. For instance:

Geographical directions and natural events:

> **hướng** "direction" < 向 [xiàng]; **đông** "east" < 東 \ 东 [dōng]; **tây** "west" < 西 [xī]; **nam** "south" < 南 [nán]; **bắc** "north" < 北 [běi]; **tuyết** "snow" < 雪 [xuě]; **băng** "ice" < 冰 [bīng].

Plants and animals:

> **đậu** "bean" < 豆 [dòu]; **liễu** "willow" < 柳 [liǔ]; **lê** "pear" < 梨 [lí]; **tùng** "pine" < 松 [sōng]; **lan** "orchid" < 蘭 \ 兰 [lán]; **huệ** "small white lily" < 蕙 [huì]; **quế** "cinnamon" < 桂 [guì]; **hổ** "tiger" < 虎 [hǔ]; **báo** "leopard" < 豹 [bào]; **nhạn** "wild goose" < 雁 [yàn]; **hạc** "crane" < 鶴 \ 鹤 [hè]; **phượng** "phoenix" < 鳳 \ 凤 [fèng].

Administrative entities and positions:

> **thôn** "village, hamlet" < 村 [cūn]; **xã** "commune" < 社 [shè]; **tổng** "canton" < 總 \ 总 [cǒng]; **huyện** "district" < 縣 \ 县 [xiàn]; **quận** "district" < 郡 [jùn]; **phủ** "prefecture" < 府 [fǔ]; **tỉnh** "province" < 省 [shěng]; **thành [phố]** "city" < 城 [chéng]; **khu** "area, region" < 區 \ 区 [qū]; **châu** "an old administrative division" < 州 [zhōu]; **quan** "official, mandarin" < 官 [guān]; **tướng** "general" < 將 [jiàng]; **chúa** "lord" < 主 [zhǔ]; **thần** "official under a feudal ruler" < 臣 [chén]; **dân** "people" < 民 [mín]; **đinh** "man; member of a family" < 丁 [dīng]; **viên** "person holding a post" < 員 \ 员 [yuán] (see 4.4.2. for **viên**).

Moral and religious concepts:

> **trung** "loyal" < 忠 [zhōng]; **hiếu** "filial piety" < 孝 [xiào]; **trọng** "(to) respect" < 重 [zhòng]; **kính** "(to) esteem" < 敬 [jìng]; **khinh** "think something unimportant" < 輕 \ 轻 [qīng]; **quí** "(to) highly value" < 貴 \ 贵 [guì]; **Phật** "Buddha" < 佛 [fó]; **thánh** "saint" < 聖 \ 圣 [shèng]; **thần** "god, deity, divinity" < 神 [shén]; **tiên** "celestial being" < 仙 [xiān]; **kinh** "Bible" < 經 \ 经 [jīng]; **tu** "practice a religious doctrine" < 修 [xiū]; **tăng** "Buddhist monk" < 僧 [sēng]; **ni** "Buddhist nun" < 尼 [ní]; **ma** "evil spirit" < 魔 [mā], **qui** "demon" < 鬼 [guǐ].

Ten Heavenly stems:

> **giáp** < 甲 [jiǎ]; **ất** < 乙 [yǐ]; **bính** < 丙 [bǐng]; **đinh** < 丁 [dīng]; **mậu** < 戊 [wù]; **kỉ** < 己 [jǐ]; **canh** < 庚 [gēng]; **tân** < 辛 [xīn]; **nhâm** < 壬 [rén]; **quí** < 癸 [guǐ].

Twelve Earthly branches:

> **tí** < 子 [zǐ]; **sửu** < 丑 [chǒu]; **dần** < 寅 [yín]; **mão** < 卯 [mǎo]; **thìn** < 辰 [chén]; **tị** < 巳 [sì]; **ngọ** < 午 [wǔ]; **mùi** < 未 [wèi]; **thân** < 申 [shēn]; **dậu** < 酉 [yǒu]; **tuất** < 戌 [xū]; **hợi** < 亥 [hài].

4 Word-formation

Some of the monosyllabic loanwords that were borrowed in this period of time cannot be used as full words in modern Vietnamese. They must be used together with other Chinese components in loanwords. For instance, the verb **múa**, which had been borrowed in the previous period of time, is freely used as a full word, whereas **vũ** can be only a part of Chinese bisyllabic loanwords such as **khiêu vũ** "to dance" < 跳舞 [tiào wǔ], **vũ đài** "stage" < 舞台 [wǔ tái], **vũ hội** "dance party" < 舞會 \ 舞会 [wǔ huì], **vũ khúc** "dance music" < 舞曲 [wǔ qǔ], **vũ kịch** "ballet" < 舞劇 \ 舞剧 [wǔ jù], **vũ trường** "dance hall" < 舞場 \ 舞场 [wǔ chǎng].

Chinese polysyllabic words, and most of them are bisyllabic, were borrowed as whole words to denote new concepts and ideas in a wide variery of areas. They have become an important part of the modern Vietnamese vocabulary. Some examples.

Royal court, government and administation:

> **triều đình** "royal court" < 朝廷 [cháo tíng]; **hoàng đế** "emperor" < 皇帝 [huáng dì]; **hoàng hậu** "empress" < 皇后 [huáng hòu]; **hoàng cung** "royal palace" < 皇宮 \ 皇宫 [huáng gōng]; **chính phủ** "government" < 政府 [zhèng fǔ]; **hành chính** "administration" < 行政 [xíng zhèng]; **cơ quan** "office" < 機關 \ 机关 [jī guān]; **quốc hội** "national assembly, congress, parliament" < 國會 \ 国会 [guó huì]; **cảnh sát** "police" < 警察 [jǐng chá].

Economics:

> **kinh tế** "economy" < 經濟 \ 经济 [jīng jì]; **thị trường** "market" < 市場 \ 市场 [shì chǎng]; **cạnh tranh** "compete; competition" < 競爭 \ 竞争 [jìng zhēng]; **đầu tư** "invest; investment" < 投資 \ 投资 [tóu zī]; **công ti** "company, firm" < 公司 [gōng sī]; **công nghiệp** "industry" < 工業 [gōng yè]; **nông nghiệp** "agriculture, farming" < 農業 \ 农业 [nóng yè]; **thủ công nghiệp** "handicraft" < 手工業 \ 手工业 [shǒu gōng yè]; **giao thông** "transportation, traffic" < 交通 [jiāo tōng]; **điện thoại** "telephone" < 電話 \ 电话 [diàn huà]; **ngân hàng** "bank" < 銀行 \ 银行 [yín háng]; **phát triển** "develop" < 發展 \ 发展 [fā zhǎn].

History:

> **cổ đại** "ancient" < 古代 [gǔ dài]; **cổ điển** "classical" < 古典 [gǔ diǎn]; **đương đại** "contemporary" < 當代 \ 当代 [dāng dài]; **hiện đại** "modern" < 現代 [xiàn dài]; **lịch sử** "history" < 歷史 \ 历史 [lì shǐ];

phong kiến "feudal" < 封建 [fēng jiàn]; **triều đại** "dynasty" < 朝代 [cháo dài].

Politics and laws:

cách mạng "revolution" < 革命 [gé mìng]; **chiến sĩ** "soldier" < 戰士 \ 战士 [zhàn shì]; **chiến tranh** "war" < 戰爭 \ 战争 [zhàn zhēng]; **chính trị** "politics" < 政治 [zhèng zhì]; **đại sứ** "ambassador" < 大使 [dà shǐ]; **đại sứ quán** "embassy" < 大使館 \ 大使馆 [dà shǐ guǎn]; **độc lập** "independence; independent" < 獨立 \ 独立 [dú lì]; **hiến pháp** "constitution" < 憲法 \ 宪法 [xiàn fǎ]; **hoà bình** "peace" < 和平 [hé píng]; **ngoại giao** "diplomacy" < 外交 [wài jiāo]; **nhân dân** "people" < 人民 [rén mín]; **pháp luật** "law" < 法律 [fǎ lǜ]; **quân đội** "armed forces" < 軍隊 \ 军队 [jūn duì]; **tự chủ** "independent" < 自主 [zì zhǔ]; **tự do** "freedom; free" < 自由 [zì yóu].

Culture and education:

âm nhạc "music" < 音樂 \ 音乐 [yīn yuè]; **đại học** "higher education; college, university" < 大學 \ 大学 [dà xué]; **giáo dục** "education" < 教育 [jiào yù]; **học sinh** "student" < 學生 \ 学生 [xué shēng]; **kiến trúc** "architecture" < 建築 \ 建筑 [jiàn zhù]; **ngoại ngữ** "foreign language" < 外語 \ 外语 [wài yǔ]; **văn hoá** "culture" < 文化 [wén huà]; **văn học** "literature" < 文學 \ 文学 [wén xué].

Geographical names:

Anh "England" < 英[國 \ 国] [yīng guó]; **Ấn Độ** < 印度 [yìn dù]; **Ba Lan** "Poland" < 波蘭 \ 波兰 [bō lán]; **Bồ Đào Nha** "Portugal" < 葡萄牙 [pú táo yá]; **Đức** "Germany" < 德[國 \ 国] [dé guó]; **Hà Lan** "The Netherlands, Holland" < 荷蘭 \ 荷兰 [hé lán]; **Hi Lạp** < 希臘 \ 希腊 [xī là]; **Mĩ** "America, the USA" < 美[國 \ 国] [měi guó]; **Nga** "Russia" < 俄[國 \ 国] [é guó]; **Nhật Bản** < 日本 [rì běn]; **Pháp** "France" <法[國 \国] [fǎ guó]; **Tây Ban Nha** "Spain" < 西班牙 [xī bān yá]; **Thái [Lan]** < 泰[國 \ 国] [tài guó]; **Thuỵ Điển** < 瑞典 [ruì diǎn]; **Thuỵ Sĩ** < 瑞士 [ruì shì]; **Ý** "Italy" < 意[大利] [yì dà lì].

Note 1: Vietnamese changes the sequence of components of some bisyllabic Chinese loanwords. For instance, 語言 \ 语言 [yǔ yán] "language" would be *ngữ ngôn in Vietnamese, but has become ngôn ngữ. More examples: 例外 [lì wài] "exception" *lệ ngoại → ngoại lệ; 疾病 [jí bìng] "disease, illness" *tật bệnh → bệnh tật; 智謀 \ 智谋 [zhì móu] "resourcefulness" *trí mưu → mưu trí; 刺激

[cì jī] "stimulate" ***thích kích** → **kích thích**; 釋放 \ 释放 [shì fàng] "release" ***thích phóng** → **phóng thích**; 潮水 [cháo shuǐ] "tide, tidewater" ***triều thuỷ** → **thuỷ triều**.

<u>Note 2</u>: Vietnamese changes the meanings of some Chinese loanwords. For instance, 緊張 \ 紧张 [jǐn zhāng] in Chinese means "be nervous," while the Vietnamese **khẩn trương** means "be quick, hurry up." Some other examples: 方言 [fāng yán] "dialect" vs. **phương ngôn** "proverb, saying;" 到底 [dào dǐ] "to the end; finally" vs. **đáo để** "contentious, pugnacious;" 渾然 \ 浑然 [hún rán] "complete; integral and indivisible" vs. **hồn nhiên** "sincere, genuine, unfaigned;" 元旦 [yuán dàn] "(Solar) New Year's Day vs. **(Tết) Nguyên Đán** "(Lunar) New Year."[2]

<u>Note 3</u>: Some Chinese loanwords are used in Vietnamese with a narrower meaning than they are used in Chinese, or are used in the formal style in Vietnamese whereas they are neutral in Chinese. For instance, 改正 [gǎi zhèng] in Chinese means "correct, rectify in general" while the Vietnamese **cải chính** conveys only the meaning "rectify information that turned out untrue." The Chinese phrase 改正發音 \ 改正发音 [gǎi zhèng fā yīn] "correct the pronunciation" in Vietnamese would be **sửa phát âm**, not ***cải chính phát âm**. Or, 建議 \ 建议 [jiàn yì] means "suggest, propose" while the Vietnamese **kiến nghị** means "petition" and is used only in formal Vietnamese. The Chinese sentence 我朋友建議去看電影 \ 我朋友建议去看电影 "My friend suggested that we go to watch a movie" would be **Bạn tôi <u>mời</u> / <u>rủ</u> đi xem phim**, not ***kiến nghị đi xem phim**.

<u>Note 4</u>: Vietnamese borrowed some Chinese words which in modern Chinese are obsolete and replaced with other words. However, those old words remain in modern Vietnamese. For instance, "piano" was 洋琴 [yáng qín] in Chinese, which came into Vietnamese as **dương cầm**. **Dương cầm** is still used in Vietnamese along with **piano** or **pi-a-nô** (see 4.2.4.2.), whereas in modern Chinese the musical instrument is called 鋼 \ 钢 琴 [gāng qín] (**cương cầm**). Or, one of the old Chinese words for "student" was 生員 \ 员 [shēng yuán], which was borrowed by Vietnamese as **sinh viên**. **Sinh viên** is still used in Vietnamese with the meaning "college student," while the modern Chinese word for any student is 學 \ 学生 [xué shēng], that is **học sinh** in Vietnamese with a narrower meaning "elementary or high school student".

<u>Note 5</u>: Occasionally, Vietnamese took two Chinese characters and put them together to refer to a new object. For example, **phi** < 飛 \ 飞 [fēi] meaning "(to) fly" and **trường** < 場 \ 场 [chǎng] meaning "place, field" were combined as **phi trường** to denote "airport", whereas the Chinese word for "airport" is 飛機場 \ 飞机场 [fēi jī chǎng], that would be ***phi cơ trường** in Vietnamese. The same way of combining happened to the word **xa lộ** meaning "highway," that came from **xa** "vehicle" < 車 \ 车 [chē] and **lộ** "road, way" < 路 [lù]. The Chinese word

for highways is 高速公路 \ 高速公路 [gāo sù gōng lù], which would be *cao tốc công lộ in Vietnamese. The contemporary Vietnamese took the first part of the Chinese word to form the new word **đường cao tốc** for highways.

| 4.2.4.1.3 | FROM SEVENTEENTH CENTURY ON |

During the second half of the seventeenth century and onwards, a large number of Chinese immigrated to Vietnam for political reasons. Most of them came from the southern coastline provinces of Fujian and Guangdong. Vietnamese obtained many loanwords during that time through contact with the immigrant population. This included some of the words adopted twice, having already entered into spoken Vietnamese or during the Tang period. This wave of Chinese loanwords usually obtained a pronunciation slightly different from the previously borrowed words and became employed by Vietnamese as independent words. For instance, the word **gác** meaning "pavilion; cabinet" came from 閣 \ 阁 [gé]. The other loanword for this Chinese character had already been borrowed, that is **các**. **Gác** can be used freely in modern Vietnamese as a free noun with the meaning "a floor higher than the first floor." For instance, **lên gác** "go upstairs," **trên gác** "be upstairs," **căn hộ ở gác ba** "an apartment on the third floor." The bound syllable **các** is used only as a component of Chinese loanwords, such as **đài các** "snobbish" < 臺閣 \ 台阁 [tái gé], **khuê các** "boudoir" < 閨閣 \ 闺阁 [guī gé], **nội các** "cabinet (of a government)" < 內閣 \ 内阁 [nèi gé]. Some other examples of corresponding bound and free loanwords:

bound	free
ấn "print" < 印 [yìn]	**in**
cẩm "brocade" < 錦 \ 锦 [jǐn]	**gấm**
cận "near" (bound) < 近 [jìn] vs.	**gần**
cấp "urgent; anxious" < 急 [jí]	**gấp**
đại "era, time" < 代 [dài]	**đời**
hoạch "plan" < 劃 \ 划 [huà]	**vạch**
khuyến "advise" < 勸 \ 劝 [quàn]	**khuyên**
long "dragon" < 龍 \ 龙 [lóng]	**rồng**
ngoại "outside; external side" < 外 [wài]	**ngoài**
nhượng "cede, yield" < 讓 \ 让 [ràng]	**nhường**
quả "widowed" < 寡 [guǎ]	**goá**

Main processes of forming new words in Vietnamese

143

4 Word-formation

bound	free
sàng "bed" < 床 [chuáng]	**giường**
thi "poetry" < 詩 \ 诗 [shī]	**thơ**
vị "for the benefit of" < 為 \ 为 [wèi]	**vì**

Some of those loanwords corresponding to the same Chinese characters differentiate their meanings in Vietnamese. For instance, **kính** < 鏡 \ 镜 [jìng] "glass, mirror" came into Vietnamese earlier, **gương** was borrowed later. In modern Vietnamese, **kính** denotes glasses, including glasses for viewing, while **gương** refers to mirrors. Note that the Saigon dialect uses only **kiếng** for both glasses and mirrors.

4.2.4.1.4 LOANWORDS FROM THE DIALECTS OF CHINESE

While communicating with speakers of different dialects of Chinese, Vietnamese borrowed a number of words that they heard in conversations. Most of those loanwords came from the dialects spoken in Fujian and Guangdong Provinces and are used to refer to food items. Some examples:

bó xôi "spinach" < 菠菜[3].
ca la thầu "salted vegetable roots" < Min Nan (Hokkien) 菜頭 \ 菜头, Cantonese 菜脯, Mandarin 醃蘿蔔 \ 腌萝卜.
chí mà phù "sesame paste as a dessert" < 芝麻糊.
há cảo "shrimp fritter" < 蝦餃 \ 虾饺.
lạp xường / lạp xưởng "southern Chinese sausage" < Cantonese 臘腸 \ 腊肠, Mandarin 香腸 \ 香肠.
lẩu "chafing dish, firepot" < Cantonese 盧 \ 卢, Mandarin 火鍋 \ 火锅 (compare **tả pí lù**).
lục tào xá "dessert made from green beans" < 綠豆沙 \ 绿豆沙.
mằn thắn / vằn thắn / hoành thánh "dumplings eaten with noodle soup" < 餛飩 \ 馄饨.
quẩy < **dầu cháo quẩy** < **dầu trá quẩy** "deep-fried twisted dough sticks" < Cantonese 油炸鬼, Mandarin 炸油條 \ 炸油条.
sủi cảo "dumplings" < 水餃 \ 水饺.
tả pí lù "chafing dish, firepot" < Cantonese 打邊盧 \ 打边卢 < 打甌盧 \ 打瓯卢, Mandarin 火鍋 \ 火锅 (compare **lẩu**).
xá xíu "roasted pork" < 叉燒 \ 叉烧.
xì dầu "soy sauce" < 醬油 \ 酱油.
xíu mại "steamed dumplings with dough gathered at the top" < 燒賣 \ 烧卖.

Other words and phrases borrowed from Cantonese refer to different areas, including the name of a popular game **[đánh] mạt chược** "[play] mahjong" < Cantonese [打]麻雀 , Mandarin [打]麻將 ; phrase **xập xí xấp ngầu** "cheat" < 十四十五 , literally "fourteen and fifteen are the same."

4.2.4.1.5 CHINESE MONOSYLLABIC LOANWORDS AS COMPONENTS FOR WORD-FORMATION

Vietnamese uses many Chinese monosyllabic loanwords as components to form new words in Vietnamese. See 4.2.2. for details.

4.2.4.1.6 CHINESE QUADRISYLLABIC TEMPLATE

Vietnamese not only borrowed a large number of vocabulary from Chinese, but also adopted the so-called quadrisyllabic template from Chinese to form fixed expressions in Vietnamese. The concept of *phonetic symmetry* in Vietnamese is based on this template.

Many Chinese quadrisyllabic expressions were translated into Vietnamese. Although some of them have died out of normal usage, a large number of expressions are still common in modern Vietnamese. Just a few examples:

an cư lạc nghiệp "live a peaceful life and enjoy one's work" < 安居樂業 \ 安居乐业.
bác cổ thông kim "be conversant in both ancient and modern affairs" < 博古通今.
bách chiến bách thắng "be invincible" < 百戰百勝 \ 百战百胜.
danh bất hư truyền "be true to one's name" < 名不虛傳 \ 名不虚传.
diễu võ dương oai "throw one's weight around" < 耀武揚威 \ 耀武扬威 (should be ***diệu võ dương oai**;[4] 耀 [yào] = **diệu**).
đồng cam cộng khổ "share joys and sorrows" < 同甘共苦.
hằng hà sa số "countless" < 恒河沙數 \ 恒河沙数.
hậu sinh khả uý "the younger generation will surpass the older" < 後生可畏 \ 后生可畏.
kính nhi viễn chi "stay at a respectful distance" < 敬而遠之 \ 敬而远之.
lực bất tòng tâm "one's ability is not equal to one's ambition" < 力不從心 \ 力不从心.
môn đăng hộ đối "families of similar backgrounds" < 門當戶對 \ 门当户对 (should be ***môn đang / đương hộ đối**; 當 \ 当 = **đang / đương**).
ôn cố tri tân "review the past helps one to understand the present" < 溫故知新 \ 温故知新.

tao nhân mặc khách "men of letters" < 騷人墨客 / 骚人墨客.
tâm phục khẩu phục "be utterly convinced" < 心服口服.
tôn sư trọng đạo "respect the teacher and revere his teaching" < 尊師 \ 师重道.
văn dĩ tải đạo "the function of literature is to convey the truth or moral values" < 文以載道 \ 文以载道.
ý tại ngôn ngoại "meaning is implied" < 意在言外.

Note: In two of the previously mentioned expressions, the correct word **diệu** changes to **diễu** in **diễu võ dương oai**; the correct word **đang** or **đương** changes to **đăng** in **môn đăng hộ đối**. Diễu and diệu, đăng and đang / đương are to some extent phonetically close to each other. In some expressions, Vietnamese has replaced a Chinese word with an entirely different word. For instance, in the expression **bế quan toả cảng** "close a country to external contact" the last word **cảng** "port," which is also a Chinese loanword 港, replaces the Chinese word **quốc** < 國 \ 国 "country" in the original Chinese expression 閉關鎖國 \ 闭关锁国. It should be *bế quan toả quốc. Some other examples: in the expression **nhập gia tuỳ tục** "conform to local practices; when in Rome do as the Romans do" the Chinese word **hương** < 鄉 \ 乡 "native place" in the Chinese original expression 入鄉隨俗 \ 入乡随俗 is replaced by another Chinese word **gia** < 家 "home, family;" it should be *nhập hương tuỳ tục; the expression **trà dư tửu hậu** "at one's leisure" contains the Chinese loanword **tửu** < 酒 meaning "alcoholic drink," that replaces the word **phạn** < 飯 \ 饭 "cooked rice, meal" in the original Chinese expression 茶餘飯後 \ 茶余饭后; it should be *trà dư phạn hậu.

In some cases, Vietnamese has made use of the meaning of a Chinese expression, but replaced most of the words with the Vietnamese ones; for instance, **thả hổ về rừng** "set free a deadly enemy." The Chinese expression is 縱虎歸山 \ 纵虎归山, whose Vietnamese transcription would be *túng hổ qui sơn. Only the word **hổ** < 虎 \ 虎 is kept in the Vietnamese expression. Often, a Vietnamese expression is just the translation of a Chinese expression without any Chinese loanword; for example, **lá rụng về cội** "fallen leaves return to their roots; a person wherever residing will eventually return to his ancestral home," which is the translation of 葉落歸根 \ 叶落归根. The Vietnamese transcription of the Chinese expression would be *diệp lạc qui căn.

Among the quadrisyllabic expressions borrowed from Chinese, there are many expressions containing two numbers. Such expressions are very common in modern Vietnamese; for instance:

độc nhất vô nhị "unparalleled < 獨一無二 \ 独一无二.
lục phủ ngũ tạng "internal ograns of the body" < 五臟六腑 \ 五脏六腑 (the Chinese word order is *ngũ tạng lục phủ).

nhất cử lưỡng tiện "kill two birds with one stone" < 一舉兩得 \ 一举两得 (should be *__nhất cử lưỡng đắc__; 得 = **đắc**).

thất điên bát đảo "be at sixes and sevens" < 七顛八倒 \ 七颠八倒 (lit. "be at sevens and eights").

Based on this template, Vietnamese has created a large number of its own fixed expressions. Some examples of most common Vietnamese quadrisyllabic expressions:

ba hoa chích choè "blow one's own horn"
buôn thúng bán mẹt "peddle, be a peddler, hawker"
chân cứng đá mềm "be strong to overcome any difficulties"
coi trời / giời bằng vung "be contemptuous of all the risks"
con dại cái mang "the child acts wrongly or breaks the law and her / his mother bears the blame"
đầu tắt mặt tối "hoil hard, be extremely busy"
già néo đứt dây "pushing too hard cannot achieve a desirable result or may even lead to a failure"
hao binh tổn tướng "suffer heavy losses in battles"
khóc dở mếu dở "be in a desperate situation"
làm dâu trăm họ "struggle to satisfy needs of too different people"
mặt dạn mày dày "as bold as brass, dead to shame"
mềm nắn rắn buông "treat different people in different ways depending on their nature and reaction to the circumstances"
năng nhặt chặt bị "accomplish much by making small steps, little by little"
ôm rơm rặm bụng "get into trouble by taking someone else's responsibility"
phai hương nhạt phấn "a woman's beauty fades away as she grows older"
qua sông lụy đò "beg someone for help in a hopeless situation"
rán sành ra mỡ "be too stingy, as close as a vise"
sinh sau đẻ muộn "have the disadvantage of being born later than others"
tai bay vạ gió "disaster strikes out of the blue"
vào luồn ra cúi "humiliate oneself to get things done"
xôi hỏng bỏng không "lose everything due to bad planning"
yên giấc ngàn thu "breathe one's last"

Some examples of Vietnamese quadrisyllabic expressions containing two numbers:

ba chân bốn cẳng "take to one's heels"
chín bỏ làm mười "be forbearing; wink at small faults"
một vốn bốn lời "a highly profitable business"

năm thì mười hoạ "once in a blue moon"
trăm công nghìn việc "be extremely busy"

4.2.4.2 Loanwords from French

In the late nineteenth century and in the first half of the twentieth century, French was the dominant language in French Indochina, including Vietnam. Many words were borrowed from French to denote new objects and concepts. Unlike loanwords from Chinese, which belongs to the same structural type of languages as Vietnamese does, French loanwords were generally made to conform to the sound patterns of Vietnamese. Some of them became obsolete and were replaced with Vietnamese words, but many others are still frequently used in modern Vietnamese. Here are some examples.

Technology and transportation:

ắc qui "battery (of a car)" < accumulateur; **bu gi** "spark plug" < bougie; (đinh)⁵ **bù loong** "bolt" < boulon; (xe) **buýt** < autobus, bus; **công tắc** "switch" < contact; **cốp** (xe) "trunk (of a car) < coffre; **cờ lê** "wrench" < clé; (dây) **cu roa** "belt" < courroire; **đi-ê-den** "diesel" < diesel; **ê cu** "nut (which is screwed onto a bolt)" < écrou; **ê tô** "vise" < étau; **ga** "natural gas" < gaz; (nhà) **ga** "railroad station" < gare; **ga ra** "garage" < garage; **lốp** "tire" < enveloppe (pneu); (xe) **mô tô** "motorcycle" < moto, motocyclette; **phanh** "brake; to brake" < frein; freiner; **pin** "battery" < pile; **rông đen / lông đen** "washer" < rondelle; **rơ moóc / moóc** "trailer" < remorque; **tuốc nơ vít** "screwdriver" < tournevis; **van** "valve" < valve; **vít** "screw" < vis; **xăng** "gasoline" < essence; **xi lanh** "cylinder" < cylindre; (xe) **xích lô** "pedicap" < cyclo.

Measurements:

gam "gram" < gramme; **héc ta** "hectare" < hectare; **ki lô [gam]** "kilogram" < kilogramme; **ki lô mét** "kilometer" < kilometre; **lít** "liter" < litre; **mét** "meter" < metre; **oát** "watt" < watt; **vôn** "volt" < volt; **xăng ti mét** "centimeter" < centimetre.

Money:

xu "cent, penny" < sou; **séc** "check" < chèque; **tem** "postage stamp" < timbre.

Culture items:

áp phích "poster" < affiche; **băng rôn** "banner" < banderole; **búp bê** "doll, dolly" < poupée; **búp phê** "kitchen cabinet" < buffet; **cát xê**

"payment, compensation (paid to an artist, actor, singer etc.) < cachet; **căng tin** "canteen" < cantine; **công-xéc-tô** "concerto" < concerto; **ghi-ta** "guitar" < guitare; **phim** "film" < film; **pi-a-nô** "piano" < piano; **tăng-gô** "tango" < tango; **van** "waltz" < valse; **vi-ô-lông** "violin" < violon; **vi-ô-lông-xen** "cello" < violoncelle; **xi nê** "film" < cinéma; **xiếc** "circus" < cirque; **xô-nát** "sonata" < sonate.

Main processes of forming new words in Vietnamese

Garments and other everyday life items:

(áo) **bành tô / măng tô** "coat" < manteau; (áo) **bu dông** "jacket" < blouson; **ca vát / cà vạt** "necktie" < cravate; **các** "card" < carte; **các vi dít** "business card" < carte de visite; (mũ) **cát** "(hard) hat" < casque; (mũ) **cát két** "cap" < casquette; **công lê** "suit" < complet; **đăng ten** "lace" < dentelle; **găng** "glove" < gant; **len** "wool" < laine; (áo) **may ô** "athletic shirt" < maillot; (khăn) **mùi xoa** "handkerchief" < mouchoir; (khăn) **phu la** "scarf" < foulard; (áo) **sơ mi** "shirt" < chemise; (quần) **soóc** "shorts" < short < English shorts; **va li** "suitcase" < valise; **ve** (áo) "lapel" < revers; (áo) **vét** "jacket" < veste; (áo) **vét tông** "jacket" < veston; **xà phòng / xà bông** "soap" < savon; (dép) **xăng đan** "sandals" < sandales; **xô** "bucket" < seau.

Food items:

ba tê "liverwurst" < pâté; **bia** "beer" < bière; (bánh) **bích qui / qui** "cookie, cracker" < biscuit; **bít tết** "steak" < beef steak; **bơ** "butter" < beurre; **cà phê** "coffee" < café; **cà rốt** "carrot" < carotte; **cải xoong** "watercress" < cresson; **giăm bông** "ham" < jambon; **kem** "ice cream" < crème; **mù tạc** "mustard" < moutarde; (trứng) **ôm lét** "omelette" < omelette; (trứng) **ốp lét** "sunny-side up" < œuf au plat, œuf sur le plat; **phó mát / phô mai** "cheese" < fromage; **sô cô la** "chocolate" < chocolat; **su su** "chayote" < chouchou / chouchoute; (rượu) **vang** "wine" < vin; (rượu) **xâm banh** "champagne" < champagne; **xi rô** "syrup" < sirop; **xốt vang** "wine sauce" < sauce au vin; **xu hào** "kohlrabi" < chou-rave; **xúc xích** "sausage" < saucisse, saucisson; **xúp lơ** "cauliflower" < chou-fleur.

Note 1: In contemporary Vietnamese, most French loanwords are spelled with separate syllables. However, some are still hyphenated along with the versions of separate syllables; for example, **ba tê / ba-tê, xi rô / xi-rô**.

Note 2: Vietnamese borrowed a number of English words via French, but they are used with the new meanings different from the original meanings in English.

Bồi was derived from *boy* with the meaning "waiter in a restaurant." **Bồi** is a bit old-fashioned and is replaced with **người phục vụ** (formal) or **người chạy bàn** (colloquial).

Cao bồi came from *cowboy* and is used chiefly as an adjective meaning "reckless and ridiculous."

Mít tinh means "a political rally." The Vietnamese word for the English *meeting* is **cuộc họp** or **buổi họp**, and *to have a meeting* is **họp**.

4.2.4.3 Loanwords from English

Over the last few decades, Vietnamese has borrowed a relatively large number of vocabulary from English. Unlike the French loanwords, which were changed to fit into the phonetic patterns of Vietnamese, English loanwords usually retain the English spelling. How they are pronounced is a different story. Those Vietnamese who know English try to pronounce these words in the British or American way. Those who do not know English pronounce them in the Vietnamese way. Some examples of English loanwords.

Technology and computer science: account, blog, blogger, camcorder, camera, cell phone, chat, check, check mail, click, copy, download, email, file, format, game, internet, laptop, mail, mobile phone, offline, online, password, paste, reboot, type, upload, username, webcam, website.

Business and banking: account, manager, marketing, on sale, shopping, shopping mall, supermarket.

Showbiz and sports: bowling, cup, diva, Euro Cup, fair play, fan, golf, hat trick, hockey, playoff, show, showbiz, tennis, World Cup. Only one commonly used English loanword in this area is spelled in the Vietnamese way: (chạy) sô < (put on a) show.

Note: Some English loanwords have recently been replaced by the Vietnamese translations. For instance, T-shirt → **áo phông**, part time (job) → **bán thời gian**, girl friend → **bạn gái**, boy friend → **bạn trai**, update → **cập nhật**, mouse (of a computer) → **chuột**, deadline → **hạn chót**, brand name → **hàng hiệu**, password → **mật khẩu**, supermarket → **siêu thị** (Chinese: 超市), market share → **thị phần** (Chinese: 市場份額 \ 市场份额), VAT (value added tax) → **thuế giá trị gia tăng**.

In some instances, Vietnamese translated the components of an English word into equivalent Vietnamese components item by item, which in linguistic works is called *loan translation* or *calque*. The previously mentioned words **bạn gái**, **bạn trai**, **siêu thị** and **thị phần** are examples. The calque of the English *weekend* is **cuối tuần** (**cuối** = end; **tuần** = week), which would not make sense in Vietnamese because Sunday (**chủ nhật**) is considered to be the first day of the week. Monday is called **thứ hai**, which lit. means "the second day of the week." Nevertheless, **cuối tuần** is accepted as the term for *weekend* in contemporary Vietnamese.

Notes

1 [ ] square brackets in this part of the chapter enclose the Chinese Mandarin pinyin of the character for comparrison of the pronunciation in the two languages.
2 Befor 1949, in China 元旦 was used to refer to the Lunar New Year. Vietnamese maintains the old meaning of the term.
3 Since these words came into Vietnamese from some dialects of Chinese rather than Mandarin, they are not accompanied by pinyin.
4 *asterisk in this part of the chapter denotes a word-for-word translation from Chinese that is not used in Vietnamese. A slightly paraphrased quadrisyllabic expression is used instead.
5 ( ) parentheses in this part of the chapter enclose the Vietnamese word which is used together with the French loanword. The Vietnamese word may precede or follow the loanword. In comtemporary Vietnamese, the loanwords in these cases rarely appear alone.

Chapter 5

Sentences

5.1 Introduction to the Vietnamese sentences

5.1.1 The constituents of a sentence

5.1.1.1 Subject and predicate

The basic constituents of a standard sentence are the subject and the predicate. The sequence of the basic constituents of a Vietnamese sentence is similar to the sequence in an English sentence, that is, the subject comes first, and the predicate follows the subject.

(1) **Trời mưa.** It's raining. (lit. "sky rain").
(2) **Tuần này lạnh.** It's cold this week. (lit. "this week cold").
(3) **Tuần này lạnh hơn tuần trước nhiều.** It's much colder this week than last week.
(4) **Họ là sinh viên.** They are students.
(5) **Họ là sinh viên năm thứ nhất.** They are freshmen.
(6) **Sinh viên trường này đang chuẩn bị thi.** This college's / university's students are studying for the final exams.
(7) **Tham quan cũng là học.** Visiting (a place) is also studying.
(8) **Tham quan bảo tàng lịch sử là một cách học lịch sử rất có kết quả.** Visiting the museum of history is a very effective way of studying history.
(9) **Ngày mai có bão.** There will be a storm tomorrow.
(10) **Trong bảo tàng có tranh của một số hoạ sĩ theo trường phái ấn tượng.** There are in the museum paintings by several impressionists.

The subject can be expressed by a noun: **trời** (1), or a noun phrase: **tuần này** (2) and (3), **sinh viên trường này** (6), by a pronoun: **họ** (4) and (5), by a verb: **tham quan** (7), or a verb phrase: **tham quan bảo tàng lịch sử** (8).

The predicate can be expressed by a verb: **mưa** (1), verb phrase: **đang chuẩn bị thi** (6), by a noun after the verb **là**: **sinh viên** (4), a noun phrase after the verb **là**:

sinh viên năm thứ nhất (5), by a verb after the verb là: học (7), by an adjective: lạnh (2), an adjective phrase: lạnh hơn tuần trước nhiều (3). Sentences (9) and (10) are specific constructions, where the adverbial of time ngày mai "tomorrow" and the adverbial of place trong bảo tàng "in the museum" function as the subject, and the verb có is the predicate. This type of sentences is called existence sentences, which are discussed in 5.1.1.3.2. and 5.1.1.3.3.

5.1.1.2 Object and object predicative

The object is another constituent of a sentence, which is exemplified in the sentences that follow.

(1) **Sinh viên học tiếng Việt.** The students are studying Vietnamese.
(2) **Tôi tặng anh ấy sách.** I gave him books (as a gift).
(3) **Tôi tặng anh ấy một quyển sách mới của tôi.** I gave him my new book (as a gift).
(4) **Tôi tặng các bạn tôi sách.** I gave my friends books (as a gift).
(5) **Cháu bé giỏi nhạc.** The child is good at music.
(6) **Chúng tôi rất kính trọng bà ấy.** We have a great respect for her.
(7) **Chúng tôi coi bà ấy như một người bạn lớn.** We regard her as a great friend.
(8) **Buổi khiêu vũ làm cho chúng tôi rất mệt nhưng cũng rất vui.** The dance made us exhausted, but very happy as well.

The direct object of a transitive verb is expressed by a noun: **tiếng Việt** (1), **sách** (2) and (4), by a noun phrase: **một quyển sách mới của tôi** (3), by a pronoun: **bà ấy** (6). An adjective may take a direct object: **nhạc** (5).

The indirect object of a transitive verb is expressed by a pronoun: **anh ấy** (2) and (3), by a noun or a noun phrase: **các bạn tôi** (4).

A transitive verb, in addition to the direct object, may take an object predicative, which is expressed by a noun or a noun phrase: **một người bạn lớn** (7), and by an adjective or an adjective phrase: **rất mệt** and **rất vui** (8). For more on this construction, see 2.4.5.

Note: The so-called subject predicative in English that characterizes the person or thing referred to by the subject corresponds to either the adjective serving as the predicate without the verb là, as in (2) and (3) in 5.1.1.1., or the noun following the verb là, as in (4) and (5) in 5.1.1.1.

5.1.1.3 Adverbials

The basic structure of a sentence does not include a group of items whose frequent function is to modify an action denoted by a verb. Those items called adverbials. Adverbials are optional in the sense of the basic structure of a sentence, but in many instances they are informationally crucial in a situation or context. For that reason, the sentence may be communicatively insufficient if an adverbial is left out. Semantically, adverbials refer to the following aspects of a sentence.

5.1.1.3.1 ADVERBIAL OF MANNER

An adjective can modify a verb in a verb phrase (see 2.5.) and serves as an adverbial of manner in a sentence to indicate the mode of an action:

Cô ấy hát <u>thật là hay</u>. She sang so beautifully.
Ông ấy đang thuyết trình <u>say sưa</u> về đề tài ấy. He is talking enthusiastically on that topic.

<u>Note</u>: If the adjective is a monosyllabic word, it follows the verb, as in the first sentence. If the adjective is a bisyllabic word and the verb is also a bisyllabic word, it may either follow the verb, as in the second sentence, or precede it:

Ông ấy đang <u>say sưa</u> thuyết trình về đề tài ấy.

For more on this construction see 2.5.3.

5.1.1.3.2 ADVERBIAL OF PLACE

Ông ấy đang làm vườn <u>ở ngoài kia</u>. He is working in the garden out there.
Họ đã từng sống <u>ở nhiều nước châu Âu</u>. They have lived in a number of European countries in the past.

The demonstrative pronouns **đây**, **đấy**, **đó** and **kia** can function as adverbials of place. Each of them refers to either a location or a movement, as their English counterparts *here* and *there* do. Compare:

Location

Ông ấy làm việc ở <u>đây</u> hai mươi năm rồi. He has been working *here* for twenty years.
Họ đang tập bóng chuyền ở <u>đấy / đó</u>. They are practicing volleyball *there*.

Movement

Lại <u>đây</u> xem cái này. Come *here* and look at this.
Đừng đi đến <u>đấy / đó</u> vào ban đêm. Nguy hiểm lắm. Do not go *there* at night. It is very unsafe.

The demonstrative pronoun **kia** is rarely placed immediately after a verb. A preposition of location is inserted between the verb and **kia**:

> **Người ta đang làm gì <u>dưới</u> <u>kia</u> mà ồn ào thế?** What is going on down there? It's so noisy. (location)
> **Anh xuống <u>dưới</u> <u>kia</u> xem có chuyện gì thế.** Go down there and find out what is going on. (movement)

The adverbial of place in Vietnamese can perform the function of the subject in the so-called existence sentences. Usually, the verbs **có** and **là** are used as the predicate. However, some other verbs can function as the predicate as well. This construction has a specific word order:

place + verb + [classifier] + noun

and is equivalent to the English construction

there is / there are + noun + place

Note the opposite word order in Vietnamese and English. Some examples:

(1) **Trong công viên có một cái hồ lớn.** There is a big lake inside the part.
(2) **Giữa hồ là một hòn đảo.** There is an island in the middle of the lake.
(3) **Trên hòn đảo trồng rất nhiều hoa.** There are a lot of flowers [grown] on the island.
(4) **Gần đây có bưu điện không bác?** Ma'am / Sir, is there a post office in the vicinity / in this neighborhood?
(5) **Trên tường treo một bức tranh thời kì Phục hưng.** There is a Renaissance painting [hanging] on the wall.

In (1) and (4) the verb **có** is the predicate; in (2) **là** is the predicate; in (3) **trồng** "(to) plant, grow" is the predicate; in (5) **treo** "(to) hang" is the predicate.

These types of sentences may be regarded as topic – comment sentences (see 5.5.18. for more about topic – comment sentences).

5.1.1.3.3 ADVERBIAL OF TIME

> **<u>Đêm qua</u> nóng quá.** It was so hot last night.
> **<u>Tuần sau</u> anh ấy đi công tác.** He is leaving on a business trip next week.

<u>Note 1</u>: When the adverbial of time is not a long phrase, it is usually fronted in Vietnamese, whereas it comes last in English.

Note 2: A short adverbial of time can be placed at the end of a sentence for more emphasis on the time an action occurs. In that case, a preposition should be used before the word referring to time. For instance, the second sentence can have the time expression **tuần sau** at the end with the preposition **vào** in front of it:

Anh ấy đi công tác <u>vào tuần sau</u>.

Note 3: There is a distinction between the adverbial of time in (1) and the phrase indicating an amount of time which an action requires to be done in (2):

(1) **<u>Đầu tháng hai</u> các lớp bắt đầu học lại.** Class meetings resume in early February.
(2) **Lớp hè này học <u>hai tháng</u>.** This summer course lasts for two months.

The adverbial of time in Vietnamese can perform the function of the subject in existence sentences. Usually, the verbs **có** serves as the predicate. This construction has a specific word order:

time + verb + [classifier] + noun

and is equivalent to the English construction

there is / there are + noun + time

Note the opposite word order in Vietnamese and English. Some examples:

Đêm qua có mưa đá. Hoa màu bị thiệt hại nặng. There was hail last night. The crops were severely damaged.
Tuần sau có đá bóng. There will be a soccer game next week.

If both time and place are indicated in an existence sentence, time comes first and is followed by place. Again, Vietnamese and English have different word order:

Hôm qua ở ngã tư này xảy ra tai nạn giao thông nghiêm trọng. There was a serious traffic accident [that happened] at this intersection yesterday.
Tối mai trong công viên có xiếc. There will be circus in the park tomorrow night.

These types of sentences may be regarded as topic – comment sentences (see 5.5.18 for more about topic – comment sentences).

5.1.1.3.4 ADVERBIAL OF FREQUENCY

Adverbial of frequency: see 2.6.2.

5.1.1.3.5 ADVERBIAL OF DEGREE

In addition to the adverbs of degree, which are discussed in 1.3.3.2. and 2.6.1., Vietnamese also uses some other adverbs of degree such as **hoàn toàn** "completely," **thiếu** "not enough," **hơi** "a bit," **tuyệt đối** "absolutely," **gần như** "nearly, almost," **hầu như** "almost," **suýt** "nearly, almost," **suýt nữa thì** "nearly, almost," **tí nữa thì** "nearly, almost," **tương đối** "relatively, pretty," **quá** "really, excessively, too". As the adverbials of degree, most of them come before the predicate:

> Chị <u>hoàn toàn</u> đúng. You're absolutely right.
> Ông ấy <u>thiếu</u> may mắn. He's unlucky. (lit. He's not lucky enough.)
> Hôm nay <u>hơi</u> lạnh. Today is a bit cold.
> Chúng ta phải <u>tuyệt đối</u> giữ bí mật chuyện này. We should absolutely keep this story secret.
> Tuần vừa rồi <u>gần như</u> / <u>hầu như</u> tất cả mọi người đều bị ốm. Nearly everybody got sick last week.
> Nó <u>hầu như</u> không có tiền. He has almost no money.
> Họ <u>suýt</u> / <u>suýt nữa thì</u> / <u>tí nữa thì</u> nhỡ máy bay. They nearly / almost missed their flight.
> Dạo này tôi <u>tương đối</u> bận. I'm pretty busy these days.
> Quyển tiểu thuyết hay <u>quá</u>! The novel is really good!
> Chiếc xe <u>quá</u> nhỏ đối với gia đình tôi. The car is too small for my family.

<u>Note 1</u>: **Hơi** can be used only before the words that imply something unpleasant or unfavorable. Such a sentence is impossible: *Trời hôm nay <u>hơi</u> ấm. "It's pretty warm today." Because **ấm** refers to something pleasantly warm, **hơi** should be replaced with **khá** or **tương đối**: Trời hôm nay <u>khá</u> / <u>tương đối</u> ấm. For more on **hơi**, see 1.3.3.2.

<u>Note 2</u>: **Suýt** always precedes the predicate, whereas **suýt nữa thì** and **tí nữa thì** may come first in a statement:

> <u>Suýt nữa thì</u> / <u>tí nữa thì</u> họ nhỡ máy bay. They nearly / almost missed their flight.

<u>Note 3</u>: When **quá** follows the predicate or comes at the end of a statement, it expresses the speaker's strong emotion and is often used in exclamatory sentences:

> Nó làm chậm <u>quá</u>! He works really slowly!

5 Sentences

When **quá** precedes the word it modifies, it means "more than what is wanted, needed, acceptable or possible" and is equivalent to the English adverb *too*:

Nó làm quá chậm. He works *too* slowly.

5.1.1.3.6   ADVERBIAL OF CAUSE

They are preposition phrases whose head words are the prepositions of cause such as **vì, tại, nhờ** and **do**. **Nhờ** refers to a positive cause (corresponding to the English *thanks to*), while **tại** and **do** denote a negative cause (compare with the English *because of*, *due to* and *owing to*). The phrases usually come after the predicate:

(1) **Chuyến đi cắm trại phải huỷ bỏ vì thời tiết xấu.** Our trip for camping has been canceled *due to* bad weather.
(2) **Chúng tôi nhỡ chuyến xe buýt tại anh.** We missed the bus *because of* you.
(3) **Chúng ta ngay lập tức có thể liên lạc với bất cứ nơi nào trên trái đất nhờ mạng Internet.** We are able to get in touch instantly with any place on the earth *thanks to* Internet.
(4) **Khu phố này xe không qua lại được do nước ngập.** This area is closed for traffic *owing to* flash flooding.

However, these phrases may be fronted to emphasize the cause. In this case, the conjunction **mà** is placed after the phrase of cause and before the subject:

(1a) **Vì thời tiết xấu mà chuyến đi cắm trại bị huỷ bỏ.**
(2a) **Tại anh mà chúng tôi nhỡ chuyến xe buýt.**
(3a) **Nhờ mạng Internet mà chúng ta ngay lập tức có thể liên lạc với bất cứ nơi nào trên trái đất.**
(4a) **Do nước ngập mà khu phố này xe không qua lại được.**

Vì is used for a wide variety of causes that are indicated by different prepositions in English. Some examples of **vì**:

Anh ta hỏi chỉ vì tính tò mò. He asked just *out of* curiosity.
Chúng tôi ủng hộ ông ấy vì lòng trung thành. We supported him *from* a sense of loyalty.
Huế nổi tiếng vì các di tích lịch sử. Huế is famous *for* its historic sites.
Bà ấy chết vì bệnh ung thư. She died *of* cancer.

5.1.1.3.7 ADVERBIAL OF PURPOSE

They are preposition phrases whose head words are the prepositions of purpose such as **cho** and **vì**. The phrase with **cho** always follows the predicate, while the phrase with **vì** either follows the predicate or along with **mà** at the end of the phrase precedes the predicate for more emphasis on the purpose:

> **Họ đã chiến đấu <u>cho</u> nền độc lập của đất nước.** They fought for independence of the country.
> **Tôi làm việc ấy <u>vì</u> lợi ích chung.** I did that for the good of everybody.

Or:

> **<u>Vì</u> lợi ích chung <u>mà</u> tôi làm việc ấy.**

5.1.1.3.8 ADVERBIAL OF MEANS

They are preposition phrases whose head words are the prepositions of means such as **bằng** and **với**. The phrase with **bằng** follows the predicate; the phrase with **với** either comes after the predicate or is fronted:

> **Chúng tôi đi đến các thác nước trên Đà Lạt <u>bằng</u> xe máy.** We traveled to the waterfalls in Đà Lạt by motorbike.
> **Ông ấy đã chữa xong chiếc máy <u>với</u> một số dụng cụ đơn giản.** Or:
> **<u>Với</u> một số dụng cụ đơn giản, ông ấy đã chữa xong chiếc máy.**
> He has already finished fixing the machine with some basic tools.

Note: The preposition **bằng** is used with the names of languages to indicate a language in which something is done. **Bằng** is equivalent to the English *in*:

> **Nhà văn ấy viết <u>bằng</u> hai thứ tiếng là tiếng Pháp và tiếng Anh.** The author wrote his books *in* two languages, which are French and English.

5.1.1.3.9 INDEFINITE PRONOUNS AND ADVERBS

They are formed by placing a question word before the demonstrative **đấy** or **đó**: **ai đấy / đó** "someone," **cái gì đấy / đó** "something," **ở đâu đấy / đó** "somewhere," **khi nào đấy / đó** "sometime," **nơi nào đấy / đó** "somewhere, someplace, in some place," **người nào đấy / đó** "someone." In a sentence, indefinite pronouns and adverbs serve as subject (1), attributive of a noun (2), adverbial of time (3) and adverbial of place (4) as in the following examples:

(1) **Có <u>ai đấy / đó</u> ngoài kia muốn gặp chị.** Or: **Có người nào đấy / đó ngoài kia ...** There is someone outside who wants to talk to you.

(2) **Tôi muốn ăn một món <u>gì đấy / đó</u> nóng**. I would like to eat something hot.
(3) **<u>Khi nào đấy / đó</u> tôi sẽ trở lại nơi này**. I will be back here sometime.
(4) **Chúng mình đến một <u>nơi nào đấy / đó</u> yên tĩnh hơn đi**. Let's go someplace quieter.

| 5.1.1.3.10 | SENTENCE ADVERBIALS |

Sentence adverbials expressing the speaker's or narrator's standpoint or opinion. Some examples.

<u>**Rõ ràng là**</u> **cậu sai rồi**. You're obviously wrong.
<u>**Thực ra,**</u> **việc này không dễ như các anh tưởng đâu**. Actually / In fact, this job is not as easy as you think.
<u>**Chắc chắn là**</u> **tôi sẽ hỏi ý kiến chị về vấn đề này**. I will certainly / definitely consult you on this matter.
<u>**Đương nhiên là**</u> **/ <u>Tất nhiên là</u> chúng tôi đã đọc kĩ bài báo ấy rồi**. Of course, we have carefully read the newspaper article.
<u>**Nói thật là**</u> **tôi rất muốn từ chối lời mời của họ**. Frankly / Honestly, I wanted to decline their invitation.
<u>**Thật không may là**</u> **đang trên đường đến hội thảo thì xe tôi bị hỏng**. Unfortunately, my car broke down when I was on the way to the conference.

| 5.1.2 | *Classification of sentences* |

| 5.1.2.1 | Based on major purposes of communication |

Sentences are classified as declarative, interrogative, imperative and exclamatory according to their major purposes in communication. The declarative sentences chiefly serve for statements, interrogative – for questions, imperative – for directives and exclamatory – for exclamations. Here are four examples for the four types of sentences:

Declarative: **Chị ấy làm việc rất giỏi**. She works very well.
Interrogative: **Chị ấy làm việc có giỏi không?** Does she work well?
Imperative: **Cứ làm việc đi. Đừng mất tập trung**. Keep working. Don' be distracted.
Exclamatory: **Chị ấy làm việc giỏi thật là giỏi!** How well she works!

| 5.1.2.2 | Based on internal construction |

We also can distinguish three types of sentences with respect to their internal construction, which are simple, compound and complex sentences. A simple sentence contains only one clause. A clause is a minimal construction typically consisting of a subject and a predicate. A compound sentence is composed of two or more clauses at the same grammatical level, each of which is a main clause and basically can function as an independent sentence. A complex sentence minimally consists of one main clause and one subordinate clause. Here are three examples for the three types of sentences:

Declarative sentences

Simple: **Chị ấy làm việc giỏi.** She works well.
Compound: **Chị ấy làm việc giỏi và sống rất cởi mở với mọi người.** She works well and has a hectic social life.
Complex: **Chị ấy làm việc tại một viện nghiên cứu nơi có một số nhà khoa học được giải thưởng Nobel.** She works at a research institute, where a number of scientists have been awarded Nobel prizes.

5.1.2.3 Positive and negative sentences

Sentences are either positive or negative.

Positive: **Chị ấy đang làm việc.** She is working now.
Negative: **Hiện giờ chị ấy không làm việc.** She is currently not working.

5.1.2.4 Active and passive sentences

In European languages, sentences are active and passive based on the forms of the verbs which are opposed as active voice and passive voice. Vietnamese uses some constructions to convey the passive voice. They are introduced in 2.12.

We will discuss the sentences from the previously mentioned perspectives, except for the imperative sentences, that are discussed in depth in 2.11.

5.2 Declarative sentences

5.2.1 *Positive declarative sentences*

The major types of the predicates in declarative sentences are verbal predicate, adjectival predicate and nominal predicate.

5.2.1.1 Verbal predicate

All the verbs and verb phrases but **là** can serve as the verbal predicate. The word order in Vietnamese is similar to the word order in English.

Các bạn tôi thích đi du lịch. My friends like traveling.
Các bạn tôi có nhiều thời gian rỗi. My friends have a lot of free time.

5.2.1.2 Adjectival predicate

An adjective or adjective phrase functions as the adjectival predicate *without* the verb **là**:

Ngôi nhà ấy lớn. That house *is* big.

Note: The sentence *Ngôi nhà ấy là lớn. is incorrect.

5.2.1.3 Nominal predicate

A noun or noun phrase following the verb **là** functions as the nominal predicate:

Các bạn tôi là sinh viên. My friends are students.

The demonstrative pronouns **đây**, **kia**, **đấy** and **đó** can serve as the subject of the sentence containing the nominal predicate:

Đây / kia / đấy / đó là bạn tôi. This / That is my friend.

For more on the demonstrative pronouns and demonstrative adjectives see 1.3.3.4.

Note: The possessive preposition **của** "of" as part of a noun phrase is introduced in 1.3.3.5.2. **Của** can function as a verbal predicate meaning "belong to":

Chiếc máy vi tính này của bạn tôi. This computer belongs to my friend.

Là can be added in front of **của** to emphasize the possession:

Chiếc máy vi tính này là của bạn tôi.

5.2.2 Negative declarative sentences

5.2.2.1 Negative sentences with verbal predicate

The negation **không** is placed in front of the verb or verb phrase to negate the predicate:

(1) **Các bạn tôi không thích đi du lịch.** My friends do not like traveling.
(2) **Các bạn tôi không có nhiều thời gian rỗi.** My friends do not have much free time.

Note: In the Saigon dialect, especially in colloquial speech, there is a tendency to use the negation **không** together with **có** before the verbal predicate, except for the verbal predicate expressed by **có**, as in (2). That being said, (1) in the Saigon dialect would be:

(1a) **Các bạn tôi <u>không có</u> thích đi du lịch.**

When the predicate is indicated by a verb phrase that contains an adjective modifying the verb, the negation can be placed either before the verb, or is inserted between the verb and the adjective to put more emphasis on the modifier. Compare:

Positive: **Anh ấy hiểu đúng câu hỏi.** He understood the question correctly.
Negative 1: **Anh ấy <u>không</u> hiểu đúng câu hỏi.** He did not understand the question correctly (with no emphasis).
Negative 2: **Anh ấy hiểu <u>không</u> đúng câu hỏi.** He did not understand the question correctly (with emphasis on **đúng** "correctly").

When a verb of feelings serves as the predicate and is modified by an adverb of degree (see 2.6.1.1.), the negation **không** is used in a sentence with **lắm** and cannot be placed right before the adverb **rất** or in a sentence containing the adverb **quá**.

Positive

Các bạn tôi <u>rất</u> thích loại nhạc này. My friends like this kind of music very much.
Các bạn tôi thích loại nhạc này <u>lắm</u>. My friends like this kind of music very much.
Các bạn tôi thích loại nhạc này <u>quá</u>! How much my friends like this kind of music!

<u>Note</u> that the adverbs of degree **lắm** and **quá** come at the end of a statement.

Negative

Các bạn tôi <u>không</u> thích loại nhạc này <u>lắm</u>. My friends do not like this kind of music very much.
But not: *****Các bạn tôi <u>không</u> <u>rất</u> thích loại nhạc này.**
And not: *****Các bạn tôi <u>không</u> thích loại nhạc này <u>quá</u>!**

However, **không** can be placed right after **rất** to emphasize the negation:

Các bạn tôi <u>rất</u> <u>không</u> thích loại nhạc này. My friends do not like this kind of music at all (they hate it).

See 2.3.2.3. for the use of the negation **chưa** meaning "not yet."

5.2.2.2   Negative sentences with adjectival predicate

The negation **không** is placed in front of the adjective or adjective phrase:

> **Ngôi nhà ấy <u>không</u> lớn.** That house is not big.

If the adjective is modified by the adverbs of degree **rất**, **lắm** and **quá**, their positions follow the rule introduced in 5.2.2.1.

Positive

> **Ngôi nhà ấy <u>rất</u> lớn.** That house is very big.
> **Ngôi nhà ấy lớn <u>lắm</u>.** That house is very big.
> **Ngôi nhà ấy lớn <u>quá</u>!** How big that house is!

Negative

> **Ngôi nhà ấy <u>không</u> lớn <u>lắm</u>.** That house is not very big.

5.2.2.3   Negative sentences with nominal predicate

The negation contains **không phải** placed before the verb **là**.

> **Các bạn tôi <u>không phải là</u> sinh viên.** My friends are not students.

<u>Note 1</u>: When **của** functions as the predicate, in the negative sentences, it is treated as a nominal predicate. For instance:

> **Chiếc máy vi tính này <u>không phải</u> [là] của bạn tôi.** This computer does not belong to my friend.

<u>Note 2</u>: In colloquial Vietnamese, **chẳng** and **chả** are used instead of **không**. For instance:

> **Các bạn tôi <u>chẳng</u> có nhiều thời gian rỗi.** My friends don't have much free time.
> **Ngôi nhà ấy <u>chả</u> lớn.** That house isn't big.

5.2.2.4   Double negative with meaning of affirmation

There are several double negative constructions in Vietnamese. All of them refer to the <u>affirmation</u> of an action or fact.

I **subject + không + modal verb thể + không + verb phrase**

  (1) **Anh ấy <u>không</u> thể <u>không</u> biết chuyện ấy.** He should be aware of that.

2 **subject + không phải là + không + verb phrase**

or:

không phải là + subject + không + verb phrase

Sentence (1) may be paraphrased as follows; the meaning remains unchanged:

(1a) **Anh ấy <u>không phải là</u> <u>không</u> biết chuyện ấy. / <u>Không phải là</u> anh ấy <u>không</u> biết chuyện ấy.** He should be aware of that. (lit.: It is not the case that he is not aware of that.)

3 **không ai không + verb phrase**

or:

không + (classifier) + noun + nào + không + verb phrase

(2) **<u>Không</u> <u>ai</u> <u>không</u> biết chuyện ấy.** Everybody is aware of that.
(3) **<u>Không</u> <u>tờ báo nào</u> <u>không</u> nói về chuyện ấy.** Every newspaper is writing about that.

Là can be added to sentences (2) and (3) to put more emphasis on the affirmation; **là** precedes the second negation:

(2a) **<u>Không</u> <u>ai</u> <u>là</u> <u>không</u> biết chuyện ấy.**
(3a) **<u>Không</u> <u>tờ báo nào</u> <u>là</u> <u>không</u> nói về chuyện ấy.**

<u>Note</u>: The verb **khỏi** meaning "avoid, cannot help doing something" is often used with double negative:

(4) **Nghe bài hát này, chúng tôi <u>không</u> <u>khỏi</u> <u>không</u> nhớ đến những ngày vui đã qua.** When listening to this song, we cannot help recalling memories of the good old days.

In modern Vietnamese, however, the second negation **không** is usually left out:

(4a) **Nghe bài hát này, chúng tôi <u>không</u> <u>khỏi</u> nhớ đến những ngày vui đã qua.**

The sentences (4) and (4a) convey the same meaning. See 2.7.2. for the use of **khỏi** as a preposition.

Declarative sentences

5.3 Interrogative sentences

5.3.1 Interrogative sentences that do not contain questions word

5.3.1.1 Construction có . . . không

The interrogative expression **có . . . không** encircles the verbal and adjectival predicate, that is, **có** is placed in front of the verb or adjective, and **không** comes last.

> Positive declarative: **Các bạn tôi thích đi du lịch.** My friends like traveling.
> Question: **Các bạn anh có thích đi du lịch không?** Do your friends like traveling?

Note: When the verb **có** meaning "have" functions as the verbal predicate, only one **có** is used.

> Positive declarative: **Các bạn tôi có nhiều thời gian rỗi.** My friends have a lot of free time.
> Question: **Các bạn anh có nhiều thời gian rỗi không?** Do your friends have a lot of free time?

The question *****Các bạn anh có có nhiều thời gian rỗi không?** is incorrect.

5.3.1.2 Construction có phải . . . không

The interrogative expression **có phải . . . không** encircles the nominal predicate and the predicate expressed by **của**.

> Positive declarative: **Các bạn tôi là sinh viên.** My friends are students.
> Question: **Các bạn anh có phải là sinh viên không?** Are your friends students?
> Positive declarative: **Đấy là bạn tôi.** That is my friend.
> Question: **Đấy có phải là bạn anh không?** Is that your friend?
> Positive declarative: **Chiếc máy vi tính này [là] của bạn tôi.** This computer belongs to my friend.
> Question: **Chiếc máy vi tính này có phải [là] của bạn anh không?** Does this computer belong to your friend?

5.3.1.3 Replies that begin with *Yes, Yeah* or *No*

Vâng is the formal positive reply, which is equivalent to the English *Yes*. In the southern dialect, **Dạ** is used instead of **Vâng**. **Không** is the negative reply, which is equivalent to the English *No*.

> Question: **Chiếc máy vi tính này có phải [là] của bạn anh không?**
> Positive reply: **Vâng, chiếc máy vi tính này [là] của bạn tôi.** Yes, this computer belongs to my friend.
> Negative reply (1): **Không, chiếc máy vi tính này không phải [là] của bạn tôi.** No, this computer does not belong to my friend.
> Negative reply (2): **Không phải, chiếc máy vi tính này không phải [là] của bạn tôi.**

The negative reply to a question containing ... **có phải [là]** ... **không** may begin with either **không**, as in (1), or **không phải**, as in (2). One more example:

Q: **Đấy có phải là bạn anh không?** Is that your friend?

A: **Không / Không phải, đấy không phải là bạn tôi.** *No, that is not my friend.*

5.3.1.4 Construction đã ... chưa

When the sentence or the context refers to the past tense, the question words should be **đã ... chưa**.

> Positive declarative: **Họ [đã] làm xong việc ấy rồi.** They have finished that work.
> Question: **Họ đã làm xong việc ấy chưa?** Have they finished that work?
> Positive reply: **Vâng, họ đã làm xong việc ấy rồi.** Yes, they have finished that work. (formal)
> **Ừ, họ đã làm xong việc ấy rồi.** Yeah, they've finished that work. (informal)
> Negative reply: **Chưa, họ chưa làm xong việc ấy.** No, they have not yet finished that work.

Note: English uses only *No* for a negation which refers to any tense, whereas Vietnamese differentiates **không** for the present or future tense and **chưa** for the past tense. **Không** would be incorrect in such a reply: ****Không, họ chưa làm xong việc ấy.**

5.3.1.5 Construction ..., phải không

The interrogative expression **phải không** is added to the end of a positive statement to form a question, which is similar to the English tag questions. A comma precedes **phải không**:

(1) **Chị ấy là người Mĩ, phải không?** She is American, isn't she?
(2) **Chị ấy thích đi du lịch, phải không?** She likes traveling, doesn't she?
(3) **Trời hôm nay nóng, phải không?** It's hot today, isn't it?

The distinction between this construction and the construction **có ... không** or **có ... phải không** is that **..., phải không** conveys the speaker's strong belief that the hearer would agree with the statement in question.

Positive reply

(1a) **Vâng, chị ấy là người Mĩ.** Yes, she is (American).
(2a) **Vâng, chị ấy thích đi du lịch.** Yes, she does (likes traveling).
(3a) **Vâng, hôm nay trời nóng.** Yes, it is (hot today).

Negative reply

(1b) **Không / Không phải, chị ấy không phải là người Mĩ.** No, she isn't (American).
(2b) **Không / Không phải, chị ấy không thích đi du lịch.** No, she doesn't (like traveling).
(3b) **Không / Không phải, hôm nay trời không nóng.** No, it isn't (hot today).

Note: The negative reply to the question with **phải không** at the end begins either with **Không** or **Không phải**, no matter whether the predicate is verbal, adjectival or nominal.

5.3.1.6 Construction có phải ... không

The interrogative expression **có phải ... không** encircles a positive statement to form a question that conveys the same meaning as the question with **..., phải không** at the end:

(1c) **Có phải chị ấy là người Mĩ không?** She is American, isn't she?
(2c) **Có phải chị ấy thích đi du lịch không?** She likes traveling, doesn't she?
(3c) **Có phải hôm nay trời nóng không?** It's hot today, isn't it?

The positive and negative replies to this type of questions are similar to the replies to the questions with **..., phải không** at the end.

A negative reply can have **không phải** placed at the beginning and followed by the positive statement with no comma. This type of negative replies imply the negation of the subject, whereas the reply with **không / không phải** at the beginning before the comma and negation **không** placed before the predicate negates an action or event. Note that **Không phải** begins the reply without **Không / Không phải** meaning "No." Compare the negative replies to (1c), (2c), and (3c):

(1d) **Không phải** chị ấy là người Mĩ. Anh ấy là người Mĩ. She is not American. He is.

vs. (1b) **Không / Không phải, chị ấy không phải là người Mĩ.** No, she isn't American.

(2d) **Không phải** chị ấy thích đi du lịch. Bạn chị ấy thích đi du lịch. It is not her who likes traveling. Her friends like traveling.

vs. (2b) **Không / Không phải, chị ấy không thích đi du lịch.** No, she doesn't like traveling.

(3d) **Không phải** hôm nay trời nóng. Ngày mai mới bắt đầu đợt nóng. Today is not hot. The heat wave will not begin until tomorrow.

vs. (3b) **Không / Không phải, hôm nay trời không nóng.** No, it isn't hot today.

5.3.1.7 Construction ... à

The interrogative particle **à** is added to the end of a positive statement to form a question that is asked to invite the hearer to agree with the speaker. The speaker's belief that the hearer would agree with her / him is even stronger that the question with **phải không** at the end and with **có phải ... không** encircling a positive statement. No comma precedes **à**.

(1e) **Chị ấy là người Mĩ à?** She is American, right?
(2e) **Chị ấy thích đi du lịch à?** She likes traveling, right?
(3e) **Hôm nay trời nóng à?** It is hot today, right?

The positive replies to these questions are similar to the replies to the questions with **phải không** at the end. The negative replies can start with **Không phải** meaning "No" only to the questions with nominal predicate. Compare:

(1b) **Không / Không phải, chị ấy không phải là người Mĩ.** No, she isn't (American).
(2b) **Không, chị ấy không thích đi du lịch.** No, she doesn't (like traveling).
(3b) **Không, hôm nay trời không nóng.** No, it isn't (hot today).

5.3.1.8 Construction . . . chứ

The interrogative particle **chứ** is added to the end of a positive statement to form a question which invites the hearer to agree with the speaker. That is, the speaker is fairly certain that the hearer would agree with her / him, and the belief is even stronger than the question with **. . . à**. **Chứ** is chiefly placed at the end of a statement with the verbal predicate and is similar to an English tag question containing such adverbs as *certainly, definitely, surely*:

> **Anh ấy viết xong luận án rồi chứ?** He has certainly finished his dissertation, hasn't he?
> Positive reply: **Vâng, anh ấy viết xong luận án rồi.** Yes, he has.
> Negative reply: **Chưa, anh ấy chưa viết xong luận án.** No, he hasn't.

One more example:

> **Cậu đi đá bóng với chúng mình chứ?** You're going to play soccer with us, aren't you?
> Positive reply: **Ừ, mình đi với các cậu.** Yeah, I'm.
> Negative reply: **Không, mình không đi được.** No, I'm unable to / I can't.

5.3.1.9 Construction . . . được không

The interrogative expression **được không** is added to the end of a positive statement to form a question which denotes a polite request. **Được không** follows a comma and is similar to the English *OK?* For example:

> **Sáng mai anh chở tôi ra sân bay, được không?** Please drive me to the airport tomorrow morning, OK?

The positive reply to such a question begins with **Vâng**, or **Được**, or **Vâng, được** together:

> **Vâng / Được / Vâng, được, sáng mai tôi chở anh ra sân bay.** OK, I will.

The negative reyly begins with either **Không** or **Không được**:

> **Không / Không được, sáng mai tôi bận rồi.** No, I have already a commitment tomorrow morning.

One more example:

> Q: **Chị mua cho chúng tôi năm vé hoà nhạc ở Nhà hát Lớn vào tối thứ bảy này, được không?** Please purchase five tickets for us for the concert at Opera House this Saturday night, OK?

A *(POSITIVE)*: **Vâng / Được / Vâng, được, tôi sẽ mua.** *OK, I will.*
A *(NEGATIVE)*: **Không / Không được, tối thứ bẩy này hết vé rồi.** *No, unfortunately, tickets for Saturday night have been sold out.*

5.3.1.10 Construction ... hay ... meaning "or"

Vietnamese has two conjunctions **hoặc [là]** and **hay [là]** that convey the meanings of the English *or*, but they perform different functions in a sentence.

Hoặc [là] is used to connect two parts of a declarative positive sentence only:

> **Hè này họ định đi du lịch sang Pháp hoặc [là] sang Đức.** They are planning to travel to France or Germany this summer.

Hoặc [là] can be replaced with **hay [là]** in this sentence with no change in the meaning:

> **Hè này họ định đi du lịch sang Pháp hay [là] sang Đức.**

Only **hay [là]** is used to form a question:

> **Hè này họ định đi du lịch sang Pháp hay [là] sang Đức?** Is they planning to travel to France or Germany this summer?

Hoặc [là] cannot be used to form this type of questions. Since the structure of the positive statement and the question containing **hay [là]** is identical, the intonation is the only means to distinguish between a statement and a question.

5.3.1.11 Construction *either . . . or . . .* in Vietnamese

The English construction refers to two choices or possibilities (sometimes more than two), which is conveyed by **hoặc là ... hoặc là ...** in Vietnamese.

(1) **Hè này chúng ta đi du lịch hoặc là sang châu Âu hoặc là sang châu Á.** We will travel either to Europe or Asia this summer.
(2) **Trước đây tôi có gặp anh ấy nhưng không nhớ ra tên anh ấy. Hoặc là Dũng hoặc là Hùng.** I met him some time ago, but his name escapes me. It is either Dũng or Hùng.
(3) **Hoặc là chị sai, hoặc là tôi sai.** Either you or I am wrong.

Note 1: Unlike **[là]** in 5.3.1.10, which is optional, **là** in this construction is mandatory.

Note 2: As in English, the construction should be balanced, that is, the same kind of structures follow **hoặc là ... hoặc là ...** In (1) they are prepositional phrases; in (2) they are nominal predicates; in (3) they are subjects.

Note 3: In (3), the predicate **sai** should be repeated, unlike the English adjective *wrong*, which is used only once, and the verb *to be* is also used only once and agrees with the subject closer to it. In this case, that subject is *I (I am)*.

5.3.2 Interrogative sentences containing question words

The important distinction between the Vietnamese question words and their English counterparts is that an English question word always comes first in a question, whereas Vietnamese question words come at different positions in a question depending on their meaning and syntactical function they perform in the question. In some instances, different positions of a question word convey different meanings. See 5.3.2.3.

5.3.2.1 Location

Ở đâu meaning "at what place?" or "in what place" is the questiton word for a location and corresponds to the English question word *where*. The English *where* actually refers either to location or to motion. The question word for motion is introduced in 5.3.2.2.

In Vietnamese, the question word **ở đâu** is placed at the end of the question. The reply contains the location with the preposition **ở** (neutral) or **tại** (formal) meaning "at" or "in":

Q: **Chị làm việc ở đâu?** Where do you work?
A: **Tôi làm việc ở / tại Viện Văn học.** *I work at the Institute of Literature.*

Q: **Anh làm quen với anh ấy ở đâu?** Where did you meet him?
A: **Tôi làm quen với anh ấy tại một cuộc Hội thảo quốc tế về Việt Nam học.** *I met him at an international conference on Vietnamese studies.*

Q: **Họ sống ở đâu?** Where do they live?
A: **Họ sống ở trong Sài Gòn.** *They live in Sài Gòn.*

5.3.2.2 Motion

Đâu meaning "to what place" is the question word for a motion and corresponds to the English question word *where*. **Đâu** is placed at the end of the question:

Q: **Họ đang đi đâu?** Where're they going [to]?
A: **Họ đang đi ra sân bay.** *They're going to the airport.*

Q: **Chị ấy đưa chúng ta đi đâu?** *Wher's she taking us?*
A: **Chị ấy đưa chúng ta đi Bảo tàng Mĩ thuật.** *She's taking us to the Museum of Fine Arts.*

Q: **Nghỉ đông này các bạn định đi đâu?** *Where're you planning to travel during the winter break?*
A: **Chúng mình định đi thăm Huế.** *We're planning to visit Huế.*

Interrogative sentences

Note: In colloquial Vietnamese, the question word for a location **ở đâu** can be shortened to **đâu**. The meaning of location is clear from the context:

Chìa khoá tôi <u>đâu</u>? *Where're my keys?*

5.3.2.3 Time

The most general question words equivalent to the English *when* are **bao giờ** and **khi nào**. In addition to them, Vietnamese uses other question words to refer to a particular period of time when something happens. They are **ngày nào** or **hôm nào** "what day," **thứ mấy** "what day of the week," **ngày mùng mấy** or **ngày bao nhiêu** "what date of the month," **tháng mấy** "what month."

The question word is placed at the end of a question to refer to the past tense:

(1) Q: **Chị ở Hà Nội về <u>khi nào</u>?** *When did you return from Hà Nội?*
(1A) A: **Tôi ở Hà Nội về tuần trước.** *I returned from Hà Nội last week.*

The question word is fronted to refer to the future tense:

(2) Q: **<u>Bao giờ</u> chị đi Hà Nội?** *When will you go to Hà Nội?*
(2A) A: **Tuần sau tôi đi.** *Next week.*

Some further examples of the questions about time.

(3) Q: **Chị ấy bảo vệ luận án <u>hôm nào</u>?** *When (on what day) did she defend her dissertation?*
(3A) A: **Chị ấy bảo vệ luận án hôm kia.** *She defended her dissertation the day before yesterday.*

(4) Q: **<u>Bao giờ</u> anh tốt nghiệp?** *When will you graduate?*
(4A) A: **Sang năm.** *Next year.*

Note 1: In the reply, the time expression comes in the position of the question word in the question, as in (1a), (2a) and (3a). In colloquial speech, the reply can contain only the time expression, as in (4a).

Note 2: The emphatic particle **thì** can follow the question word of time referring to the future tense to place more emphasis on the speaker's expectation of an event that should take place soon:

Bao giờ thì anh ấy đến? When indeed will he come?

In some instances, **thì** may show the speaker's impatience with the delays of an event:

Khi nào thì người ta làm xong đoạn đường này? When indeed will they finish constructing this section of the road? (People are waiting impatiently for the delays to end so that the traffic will not have to take the detour.)

5.3.2.4 Cause

The common question words for cause which are equivalent to the English *why* are **vì sao**, **tại sao** and **sao**. They are placed at the beginning of a question. **Vì sao** is formal, **tại sao** is neutral and **sao** is informal:

Vì sao hôm nay học sinh nghỉ học? Why are students not going to school today?
Tại sao anh không hẹn trước với bác sĩ? Why didn't you make an appointment (ahead of time) to see your doctor?
Sao cậu lại cười? Why are you laughing?

Note 1: The word **lại** is inserted between the subject and the predicate to express the speaker's surprise, as in the third question. Occasionally, the question may suggest a mild reprimand that the person who is asked the question shouldn't do or shouldn't have done something. For instance:

Tại sao anh lại trêu nó? Why are you teasing him? (You shouldn't be teasing him.)
Sao cậu lại vượt đèn đỏ? Why did you run the red light? (You shouldn't have run the red light.)

The speaker may show more emphasis on the reprimand by using the following constructions:

tại làm sao mà + subject + lại + verb phrase

or:

subject + verb phrase + là tại làm sao

In English, this kind of emphasis in questions is expressed by the phrases *on earth* or *in the world*. For example:

Tại làm sao mà anh **lại** làm một việc dại dột như thế? / **Anh làm một việc dại dột như thế là tại làm sao?** Why *on earth / in the world* did you do such a stupid thing?

Note 2: The English *why* conveys two meanings: *for what reason* and *for what purpose*. Vietnamese uses different question words to distinguish between the reason (**vì sao**, **tại sao** and **sao**) and the purpose (**[để] làm gì**), which is introduced in 5.3.2.5.

5.3.2.5 Purpose

The question word *for what purpose* is **[để] làm gì**, which is placed at the end of the question:

Q: **Chị học tiếng Việt [để] làm gì?** Why (for what purpose) do you study Vietnamese?
A: **Tôi học tiếng Việt để đi Việt Nam làm việc.** *I study Vietnamese to go to work in Vietnam.*

For more on the use of **để** in a subordinate clause of purpose, see 5.8.3.7.

The meaning of the question changes if the question word for the reason **vì sao**, **tại sao** or **sao** is used instead of the question for the purpose **[để] làm gì**:

Vì sao chị học tiếng Việt? Why (for what reason) do you study Vietnamese?

The meaning of the question is that the speaker is surprised when learning about the person's intention to study Vietnamese, perhaps because (s)he is supposed to study Japanese or Spanish but has decided to take Vietnamese instead. Some further examples of questions about the purpose.

Q: **Anh đi thư viện Quốc gia làm gì?** Why (for what purpose) are you going to the National Library?
A: **Tôi cần đọc một số bài trong hai tạp chí Đông Dương tạp chí và Nam Phong xuất bản đầu thế kỉ 20.** *I need to look at some articles published in magazines Đông Dương tạp chí and Nam Phong in the early twentieth century.*

Q: **Người ta xây dựng khu nhà để làm gì?** Why (for what purpose) are they building this house?

A: **Để làm viện nghiên cứu về bệnh ung thư.** *To establish a cancer research center.*

5.3.2.6 Quantity

For countable nouns, Vietnamese has two question words **mấy** and **bao nhiêu**, that are equivalent to the English *how many*. **Mấy** is used when the speaker presumes a quantity from one to ten, and **bao nhiêu** is used for a quantity of more than ten. The English *how many* is always fronted in a question, whereas the position of the Vietnamese **mấy** and **bao nhiêu** that precede a noun depends on the function the noun phrase performs in the question. Compare:

> **<u>Mấy</u> người đến họp tối qua?** How many people attended last night's meeting? (presumably fewer than eleven)
> Or: **<u>Bao nhiêu</u> người đến họp tối qua?** How many people attended last night's meeting? (presumably eleven or more)

The noun phrases **mấy người** and **bao nhiêu người** function as the subjects of the questions, therefore they come first.

> **Cậu định mời <u>mấy</u> người đến ăn sinh nhật?** How many peope do you plan to invite to your birthday party? (presumably fewer than eleven)
> Or: **Cậu định mời <u>bao nhiêu</u> người đến ăn sinh nhật?** How many peope do you plan to invite to your birthday party? (presumably eleven or more)

The noun phrases **mấy người** and **bao nhiêu người** function as the direct objects of the verb **mời**, therefore they come after the verb.

The question words **mấy** and **bao nhiêu** are treated as numbers. If the nouns which follow them usually take a classifier, the classifier should be used:

> **Chị cần mua mấy <u>quyển</u> từ điển?** How many dictionaries do you need to buy?
> **Lớp này cần bao nhiêu <u>quyển</u> từ điển?** How many dictionaries does this class need?

For uncountable nouns, only **bao nhiêu** is used. It is equivalent to the English *how much*:

> **<u>Bao nhiêu</u> gạo được xuất khẩu trong năm vừa qua?** How much rice was exported last year? (phrase **bao nhiêu gạo** functions as the subject of the question)
> **Làm việc này mất <u>bao nhiêu</u> thời gian?** How much time would it take to do this job? (phrase **bao nhiêu thời gian** functions as the object of the verb **mất**)

5.3.2.7 Who and whom in Vietnamese

Who and *whom* as question words in Vietnamese

Ai is equivalent to the English *who* or *whom* (in formal English). The English *who* or *whom* always come first in a question (for *who* and *whom* as relative pronouns in relative subordinate clauses, see 5.8.2.), whereas the position of the Vietnamese **ai** depends on the function it performs in a question. Compare:

<u>Ai</u> nói cho chị biết chuyện ấy? Who told you that story?

Ai serves as the subject of the question and is fronted.

Các anh các chị định mời <u>ai</u> đến họp? Who are you planning to invite to attend the meeting? or: Whom are you planning to invite to attend the meeting? (very formal English)

Ai is the direct object of the verb **mời**, therefore, it is placed right after the verb.

Chị đã nói với <u>ai</u> chuyện ấy rồi? Who did you tell that story to? or: To whom did you tell that story? (very formal English)

Ai is the indirect object of the verb **nói**, which takes the preposition **với**, therefore **ai** is placed after the preposition **với**, that in turn follows the verb **nói**.

When the verb of the question is **là**, the meaning of the question depends on the position of **ai**. Compare:

<u>Ai</u> là Thanh? Who is Thanh?

The speaker assumes that Thanh is among the people (s)he is talking with, thus, the question implies *Who of you is Thanh who(m) I am looking for*.

Thanh là <u>ai</u>? Who is Thanh?

The speaker is looking for more information about the person named Thanh, probably about her / his occupation, background or the position (s)he holds.

5.3.2.8 What and which as question words in Vietnamese

Vietnamese has two question words corresponding to the English *what* and *which*. They convey different meanings, perform different functions in questions and are not interchangeable.

Gì serves as the subject of a question meaning "what." In order to be placed at the beginning of a question, **gì** should follow the word **cái**:

<u>Cái gì</u> làm cho bà ấy vui thế? What made her so happy?

However, the question sounds colloquial. In more formal speech, the question with the same meaning would be **Chuyện gì làm cho bà ấy vui thế?** Or: **Điều gì làm cho bà ấy vui thế?** In this case, **gì** follows the noun **chuyện** "story" or the noun **điều** "thing" as the attributive of the noun phrases, whose function is introduced later.

Gì serves as the object of a verb and is placed after the verb:

Tối nay cậu định làm gì? What are you planning to do tonight?

Gì following **là** is part of a nominal predicate:

Tên anh là gì? What is your name?

Gì following **là** can function as the object predicative (see 2.4.5.):

Cái này tiếng Việt gọi là gì? What is this called in Vietnamese?

Gì follows a noun as the attributive of a noun phrase and refers to a general kind of things which are indicated by the noun:

Chị thích đọc sách gì? What kind of books would you like to read?

Nào, that is equivalent to the English *which*, always follows a noun as its attributive; **nào** alone cannot function as the subject or object. For instance:

Chị muốn đọc quyển sách nào? Which book would you like to read?

The speaker seems to have mentioned several books before, and the question now is about choosing one of them.

Nào is treated as a demonstrative adjective; thus, a noun should take a classifier if applicable. Some further examples of using **gì** and **nào**:

Anh hay xem phim gì? What kind of movies do you usually watch?
Chúng ta phải xem bộ phim nào để viết bài? Which film should we see to write the paper?
Chị cần áo gì? Để mặc mùa đông hay mùa hè? What kind of clothes do you need? For winter or summer?
Chị định lấy chiếc áo nào? Which shirt (blouse, sweater, etc.) are you going to buy?

5.3.2.9 Plural marker những preceding question words ai, đâu, gì

When the speaker implies the plurality of people, places or things (s)he is asking about, the plural marker **những** precedes the question words **ai**, **đâu** or **gì**:

Những ai sẽ đọc báo cáo tham luận tại hội thảo? Who will deliver papers at the conference?
Hè vừa rồi các bạn đi **những đâu**? Where did you travel in the summer?
Nghỉ lễ sắp tới chúng ta sẽ làm **những gì**? What are we going to do on the holiday?

5.3.3 *Rhetorical questions*

A rhetorical question is a question that expects no answer. It is asked only in order to make a point stand out. Very often, the answer is evident from the speaker's point of view. The initial particles **phải chăng, chẳng nhẽ / chẳng lẽ** and **lẽ nào**, and the final particle **chăng** are the most common words for rhetorical questions. **Phải chăng** is chiefly used in formal speech, while **chẳng nhẽ / chẳng lẽ** and **lẽ nào** are used in any kind of speech and are interchangeable in most cases. Some examples:

Phải chăng nguyên nhân thất bại của công ti là điều hành quá yếu? The reason for the company's failure is the bad management, isn't it?
Chẳng nhẽ / chẳng lẽ / lẽ nào họ lại không đến? Are they not coming?
Sắp mưa **chăng**? It's going to rain, isn't it?

The question words **làm sao** and **thế nào** placed in front of **được** can be used to express the speaker's belief that something is not going to happen. Often, the reason is indicated or clear from the context. For examples:

Học ít thế thì thi đỗ **làm sao được / thế nào được**? If you study so little, how would you pass the exam?
Tôi no rồi, ăn **làm sao được / thế nào được** nữa? I am already full, how could I eat more?

5.4 Exclamatory sentences

5.4.1 Quá, ôi

The adverb of degree **quá** placed at the end of a statement is the most common way to form exclamations, whose counterparts in English usually begin with *how* and *what*. As in the case of the *how*- and *what*-phrases in English, **quá** is stressed in Vietnamese:

Cháu bé thông minh 'quá! How smart the kid is!
Nóng 'quá! How hot it is!
Chị ấy hát hay 'quá! How beautifully she sings!
Nó bừa bộn 'quá! What a mess he made!
Ảnh đẹp 'quá! What lovely photos!
Anh ta mất lịch sự 'quá! What a rude man!

The interjection **ôi**, which to some extent corresponds to the English *wow*, can be added to the beginning of these exclamations to make them stronger:

Ôi! Cháu bé thông minh 'quá! Wow, how smart the kid is!
Ôi! Ảnh đẹp 'quá! Wow, what lovely photos!

5.4.2 Thật

The adverb of degree **thật** can be used instead of **quá** in the given examples to express an exclamation along with the additional meaning of affirmation. **Thật** is stressed:

Ảnh đẹp 'thật! The photos are truly lovely!
Anh ta mất lịch sự 'thật! He's really rude!

5.4.3 Thật là

The adverb of degree **thật là** placed before the adjective may be used instead of **quá** in less formal speech. **Thật** is stressed:

Cháu bé 'thật là thông minh! How smart the kid is!
Ảnh 'thật là đẹp! What lovely photos!

If the adjective is a one-syllable word, it can be repeated, and **thật là** is inserted between them:

Ảnh đẹp 'thật là đẹp! What lovely photos!

5.4.4 Ơi là

In colloquial Vietnamese, a monosyllabic adjective is repeated and the repeated adjective encircles the adverb of degree **ơi là**. **Ơi** is stressed:

Món này ngon 'ơi là ngon! How delicious this dish is!
Xa 'ơi là xa! How far away!

5.5 Emphatic constructions

5.5.1 Emphatic positive declarative sentences with cũng

Cũng is used together with a question word to place emphasis on a part of a sentence with the meaning "all," "every" or "any." The word order is crucial. The question word is always stressed. If a question word consists of two components, the second component is stressed.

5.5.1.1
Emphasized subject is denoted by the question word **ai** or the noun phrase **noun + nào**; the word order is as follows:

ai / noun + nào + cũng + predicate

'Ai cũng đi tham quan đồng bằng sông Cửu Long. Everybody will travel to the Mekong River Delta.
Bộ phim 'nào cũng hay. All the movies are good.

5.5.1.2
Emphasized object is expressed by the question word **ai** or the noun phrase **noun + gì / nào**; the word order is as follows:

ai + subject + cũng + predicate
noun + gì / nào + subject + cũng + predicate

'Ai cô ấy cũng sẵn sàng giúp đỡ. She is always ready to help everybody.
Phim 'gì cháu bé cũng thích xem. The child likes to watch any (kind of) movies.
Quyển từ điển 'nào tôi cũng cần. I need all of those dictionaries.

5.1.1.3
Emphasized adverbials of place and time that are indicated by **ở đâu, bao giờ** or the noun phrase **noun + nào**; the word order is as follows:

ở đâu + subject + cũng + predicate
bao giờ + subject + cũng + predicate
noun + nào + subject + cũng + predicate

Ở **'đâu** ông ấy cũng là một người lãnh đạo giỏi. He is a fine leader everywhere.
Bao **'giờ** chị ấy cũng đúng giờ. She is always on time.
Chủ nhật **'nào** gia đình tôi cũng đi nghỉ. My family is away to relax every single Sunday.

5.5.2 Emphatic positive declarative sentences with chẳng and chả following a question word

This emphatic construction conveys the meaning which is close to the meaning of the contruction discussed in the previous section. However, this kind of emphatic statements is characteristic of conversational or colloquial speech due to the conversational negation **chẳng** and colloquial **chả**. The question words commonly used in this construction are **ai**, **bao giờ**, **ở đâu**, **gì** and **nào**. Very often, **mà** is inserted between the question word and **chẳng** / **chả** to show more emphasis. As in the previous construction, the question word is stressed:

'Ai [mà] chẳng / chả biết chuyện ấy. Everybody knows the story.
Đi bao **'giờ [mà] chẳng / chả** được. We / You can leave anytime.
Thành phố này ở **'đâu [mà] chẳng / chả** có cây xanh. There are green trees everywhere in this town.
Ông ấy nói **'gì [mà] chẳng / chả** đúng. Whatever he says is correct.
Chị ấy nấu món **'nào [mà] chẳng / chả** ngon. Whatever dish she cooks is delicious.

Occasionally, such a statement can be made in a sarcastic way:

Nó ăn **'gì mà chẳng / chả** thấy ngon. Whatever he eats is delicious in his opinion. (He has no (sense of) taste.)

Note that the negation **không** is not used in this construction.

5.5.3 Emphatic positive declarative sentences with bất cứ / bất kì

Emphatic positive declarative sentences with **bất cứ** / **bất kì** meaning "any".

As in the previous construction, a question word is also used in this construction. The question word or question word phrase follows **bất cứ** / **bất kì**:

Chị hãy hỏi thêm <u>bất cứ</u> / <u>bất kì</u> ai trong công ti về việc này. You should talk more on this matter with anybody in our company.

Anh ấy có thể làm <u>bất cứ</u> / <u>bất kì</u> việc gì cho chúng ta. He can do any job for us.

Emphatic constructions

The phrase with **bất cứ** / **bất kì** can be fronted to show more emphasis on it. In this case, **cũng** is added after the subject and in front of the predicate:

<u>Bất cứ</u> việc gì anh ấy <u>cũng</u> có thể làm cho chúng ta.

5.5.4 Emphatic positive declarative sentences with có

The verb **có** is placed before a verb or verb phrase functioning as the predicate to stress the fact that an action actually took place or will take place. **Có** with this usage is similar to the English verb *do* used before a bare infinitive and is pronounced with strong stress:

Tối qua anh ấy '<u>có</u> gọi điện nói chuyện với tôi về việc ấy. He *did* call me to talk on that matter last night.
Ngày mai tôi '<u>có</u> đi Đà Lạt với các anh. I *do* go with you to Đà Lạt tomorrow.

5.5.5 Emphatic positive declarative sentences with có . . . mới . . .

This construction is used to express emphasis on the fulfillment of a requirement in order to perform an action. The fulfillment follows the word **có**, and the action is placed after **mới**. This construction is similar to the English *[if and] only if*. Note the different word order in Vietnamese and English:

Cậu <u>có</u> chuẩn bị tốt <u>mới</u> thi đỗ. You'll pass the exam *[if and] only if* you well prepare for it.
Anh <u>có</u> đi với tôi, tôi <u>mới</u> đi. I'll go *[if and] only if* you come with me.
Trời <u>có</u> mưa <u>mới</u> đỡ hạn hán. The drought will be less severe *[if and] only if* it rains.

5.5.6 Emphatic positive declarative sentences with mới showing emphasis on the adverbial of time

Emphatic positive declarative sentences with **mới** showing emphasis on the adverbial of time. This construction is similar to the English *not until*, but, again, the word order is different in the two languages. The word order in Vietnamese is as follows:

time expression + subject + mới + predicate

Hôm qua chị ấy <u>mới</u> ở Việt Nam về. She *didn't* return from Vietnam *until* yesterday. / *Not until* yesterday *did* she return from Vietnam. (formal English).

Tuần sau sinh viên <u>mới</u> nghỉ đông. Students *will not* have winter break *until* next week. / *Not until* next week *will* students have winter break. (formal English).

5.5.7 Emphatic positive declarative sentences with vừa / mới / vừa mới ... đã ...

Emphatic positive declarative sentences with **vừa / mới / vừa mới ... đã ...** and **chưa ... đã ...**

This construction shows emphasis on the fact that one action took place very soon after another and usually refers to the past tense. **Chưa** puts more emphasis on the quickness of the second action. The construction is equivalent to the English constructions *hardly / scarcely ... when ...* or *no sooner ... than ...*

(1) **Tôi <u>vừa mới / chưa</u> ngồi xuống ăn <u>đã</u> nghe thấy tiếng chuông điện thoại.** I had *hardly / scarcely* sat down to eat *when* the phone rang. / *Hardly / Scarcely* had I sat down to eat *when* ... (formal English). Or: I had *no sooner* sat down to eat *than* the phone rang. / *No sooner* had I sat down to eat *than* ... (formal English).

(2) **Chúng tôi <u>vừa mới / chưa</u> bước vào đến cổng, chủ nhà <u>đã</u> chạy ra mời chúng tôi vào phòng khách.** We had *hardly / scarcely* walked in through the gate *when* the host ran out to invite us to the living room. / *Hardly / Scarcely* had we walked in through the gate *when* ... (formal English). Or: We had *no sooner* walked in through the gate *than* the host ran out to invite us to the living room. / *No sooner* had we walked in through the gate *than* ... (formal English).

Note that if the subject of the two actions is the same person(s), there is no comma, as in (1). If the subjects are different, a comma should be used to separate the two parts of the sentence, as in (2).

5.5.8 Not only ... but also ... in Vietnamese

They are **không những / không chỉ ... mà còn ...** and **không chỉ ... mà cả ...** The parts that follow these words are more complicated than in English depending on what word class they belong to.

không những / không chỉ ... mà còn ... is used before two verbs or adjectives which serve as the predicate of a sentence:

Đường phố trong khu phố cổ <u>không những / không chỉ</u> chật hẹp <u>mà còn</u> quanh co nữa. The streets in the Old Quarter of the city are *not only* narrow *but also* winding.

If **không những / không chỉ ... mà còn ...** is followed by two verb phrases, the word **cả** may be placed before the object of the second verb, and **nữa** comes at the end of the sentence to show more emphasis on the addition:

Khách du lịch <u>không những / không chỉ</u> đi thăm Đồng bằng sông Cửu Long <u>mà còn</u> ra [<u>cả</u>] đảo Phú Quốc [<u>nữa</u>]. Tourists *not only* visited the Mekong River Delta *but also* went out to Phú Quốc Island.

không chỉ ... mà cả ... is used with two nouns or noun phrases. If the nouns or noun phrases function as the subjects of a sentence, **cũng** is placed in front of the verb to emphasize the addition:

<u>Không chỉ</u> người nước ngoài <u>mà cả</u> nhiều người Việt <u>cũng</u> thích phơi nắng trên bãi biển cát trắng ở Nha Trang. *Not only* foreigners *but also* many Vietnamese like to sunbathe on the white sand beaches in Nha Trang.

If the nouns function as the objects, **nữa** can be placed at the end of the sentence to put more emphasis on the addition:

Các nghệ sĩ trình diễn <u>không chỉ</u> chèo <u>mà cả</u> dân ca quan họ Bắc Ninh [nữa]. The artists performed *not only* chèo plays *but also* folksongs of Bắc Ninh Province.

This construction with two nouns as the objects can place **không chỉ** in front of the verb, and the meaning remains the same:

Các nghệ sĩ <u>không chỉ</u> trình diễn chèo <u>mà cả</u> dân ca quan họ Bắc Ninh [nữa].

5.5.9 Emphatic *có and những*

These two words precede a number or an amount for emphasis, but they convey opposite meanings. **Có** is used to emphasize the number or amount which is fewer or less that the speaker expected. **Thôi** can be placed at the end of the sentence to show more emphasis on a small number or amount. **Có** is equivalent to the English *only*:

Hôm nay tôi đọc được <u>có</u> mười trang sách [<u>thôi</u>]. I read *only* ten pages of the book today.

Những refers to a number or amount which is more than the speaker expected. There is no English equivalent of **những** with this meaning:

Hôm nay anh ấy đọc được <u>những</u> năm mươi trang sách. He read fifty pages of the book today.

5.5.10 Emphatic chính

This word is used before a part of a sentence to put emphasis on that part and corresponds to different constructions in English.

5.5.10.1 Subject

<u>Chính</u> viện nghiên cứu này đã tìm ra giải pháp cho vấn đề ách tắc giao thông của thành phố. It was this research institute that found a solution to the city's traffic congestion.

5.5.10.2 Predicate with là

Quảng trường này <u>chính</u> là nơi diễn ra sự kiện lịch sử ấy cách đây 75 năm. This square is the very place where that historic event occured 75 years ago.

5.5.10.3 Object

Chúng tôi cần gặp <u>chính</u> giám đốc điều hành công ti. We need to talk just to the company's CEO.

5.5.10.4

Adverbials of cause and purpose. **Là** may be added after **chính** to put more emphasis on the cause or purpose.

Những khu phố mới này hay bị ngập lụt khi mưa to <u>chính</u> [<u>là</u>] vì qui hoạch kém. Precisely because of the poor design, these areas of the city are often flooded when it rains hard.

Chúng tôi lên Sapa <u>chính</u> [<u>là</u>] để tìm hiểu văn hoá và phong tục của các dân tộc ít người trên ấy. We traveled to Sapa just to learn about culture and customes of the ethnic minorities up there.

5.5.11 Emphatic *ngay*

This word is placed before the adverbials of place and time to put emphasis on the place or time. It is similar to the English *right* or *just*:

Tai nạn xẩy ra ở <u>ngay</u> ngã tư này. The traffic accident happened *right / just* at this intersection.
Chúng tôi đi <u>ngay</u> đêm nay. We are leaving *right / just* tonigh.

5.5.12 Emphatic *ngay cả*

In 1.3.2.2.1. we discussed **cả** with the meaning "even." **Ngay** can be added in front of **cả** to put more emphasis:

[<u>Ngay</u>] <u>cả</u> tôi cũng không biết chuyện ấy. Even I didn't know that.
[<u>Ngay</u>] <u>cả</u> một việc đơn giản thế nó làm cũng không xong. He was unable to complete even such an easy work.

5.5.13 Emphatic *chỉ . . . là . . .*

Each of them is placed before a verb in two parts of a sentence to suggest that an amount of something needed for an action to take place is smaller than expected:

(1) **Từ đây đến khu phố cổ <u>chỉ</u> đi bộ mươi phút <u>là</u> đến.** It would take just about ten minutes to walk from here to the Old quarter of the city.
(2) **Việc ấy <u>chỉ</u> làm năm phút <u>là</u> xong.** It would take five minutes to do that job.

Chỉ may be inserted between the first verb and the amount to show more emphasis on the small amount:

(1a) **Từ đây đến khu phố cổ đi bộ <u>chỉ</u> mươi phút <u>là</u> đến.**
(2a) **Việc ấy làm <u>chỉ</u> năm phút <u>là</u> xong.**

5.5.14 Emphatic *mãi*

Mãi meaning "interminable, uninterrupted; interminably, uninterruptedly" performs two functions.

1 As an adverb of manner, **mãi** modifies a verb or a verb phrase with the implication that an action continues for too long and therefore becomes annoying:

Mưa <u>mãi</u>. It's raining interminably (for too long).
Chúng tôi đợi họ <u>mãi</u>. We waited for them for too long.
Ông ấy nói <u>mãi</u>, một số người phát chán đã bắt đầu bỏ về. He spoke uninterrupted. Some people got bored and began to walk out of the room.

When used for the past tense, **mãi** can modify an action that continued for too long and succeeded in getting what was expected (1) or did not succeed (2). Different constructions are used for the positive results (1), (3) and negative results (2), (4):

(1) **Chúng tôi đợi <u>mãi</u> họ <u>mới</u> đến**. We waited for them for too long, and they finally showd up.
(2) **Chúng tôi đợi <u>mãi</u> mà họ <u>không</u> đến**. We waited for them for too long, but they didn't show up.
(3) **Tôi nghĩ <u>mãi</u> <u>mới</u> nhớ ra tên anh ấy**. It took me too long to recall his name.
(4) **Tôi nghĩ <u>mãi</u> mà <u>không</u> nhớ ra tên anh ấy**. I tried very hard to recall his name but was unable to recall it.

2   As an adverb of degree, **mãi** shows emphasis on time (5), (6) or place (7), (8):

(5) **Chúng tôi ngồi nói chuyện <u>mãi</u> đến khuya**. We kept sitting and talking until late at night.
(6) **<u>Mãi</u> hôm qua anh ấy <u>mới</u> đến**. He didn't arrive until yesterday. (Compare with 5.5.6.).

When used with a time expression, **mãi** implies an action that went on or goes on longer than was / is expected, as in (5), or an action that took place much later than it was expected, as in (6).

(7) **Nhà họ xa lắm, ở <u>mãi</u> ngoại thành**. Their place is really far away, on the outskirts of the city.
(8) **Tôi phải tha cái túi nặng này lên <u>mãi</u> tầng năm vì khu nhà không có thang máy**. I had to drag this heavy bag up to the fifth floor because the building did not have an elevator.

5.5.15   Emphatic tận

Tận meaning "end; finish, reach the limit" was borrowed from Chinese (盡 \ 尽) and performs two functions:

1   As an adjective in some idiomatic expressions:

năm cùng tháng <u>tận</u> "last days of a lunar year"
thế cùng lực <u>tận</u> "to be in a desparate situation"
khổ <u>tận</u> cam lai "after the bitter comes the sweet; after suffering comes happiness" (Chinese: 苦盡甘來 \ 苦尽甘来)

2 As an adverb of degree which means "as far as," "all the way to," "as long as" and expresses the emphasis on the destination that is farther that usual, or the time that is longer that expected:

Chủ nhà ra <u>tận</u> cửa đón khách. The hosts went out all the way to the gate to greet their guests.
Chị làm ơn chuyển bức thư này đến <u>tận</u> tay bác sĩ Loan. Please hand this letter to Doctor Loan in person.
Kỉ niệm dễ chịu về chuyến đi tôi nhớ đến <u>tận</u> bây giờ. Even now I still have pleasant memories of the trip.

Note: The difference between the adverbs of degree **mãi** and **tận** is that **mãi** refers to the length of the action, whereas **tận** emphasizes the end of the destination or the action. Compare:

(7a) **Nhà họ xa lắm, ở <u>tận</u> ngoại thành.** Their place is really far away, on the outskirts of the city.
(8a) **Tôi phải tha cái túi nặng này lên <u>tận</u> tầng năm vì khu nhà không có thang máy.** I had to drag this heavy bag up all the way to the fifth floor because the building did not have an elevator.

Tận in (7a) and (8a) shows the emphasis on the destination, while **mãi** in (7) implies that it would take very long to get to their place, and **mãi** in (8) indicates the length of the action.

Mãi and **tận** can be used together to show more emphasis:

(7b) **Nhà họ xa lắm, ở <u>mãi tận</u> ngoại thành.**
(8b) **Tôi phải tha cái túi nặng này lên <u>mãi tận</u> tầng năm vì khu nhà không có thang máy.**

5.5.16 Emphatic quantity bao nhiêu là and toàn là

When the quantity of something is stressed, **bao nhiêu là** and **toàn là** are placed in front of a noun:

Trong phòng làm việc của bà ấy <u>bao nhiêu là</u> sách. Or: **Trong phòng làm việc của bà ấy <u>toàn là</u> sách.** Her office is full of books.

In the construction **toàn là**, the same noun can be repeated, the first one inserted between **toàn** and **là**, the second one follows **là** to show more emphasis on the large quantity:

> **Trong phòng làm việc của bà ấy <u>toàn sách là sách</u>**.

This construction may also convey the additional meaning that there are only one kind of things in a particular place. **Trong phòng làm việc của bà ấy <u>toàn sách là sách</u>**. implies that one can see a lot of books and only books in her office. Another example:

> **Trong vườn <u>toàn hoa hồng là hoa hồng</u>**. There are a lot of roses and only roses in the garden.

5.5.17 Emphatic negative declarative sentences

5.5.17.1 Hề

Hề is placed after **không** or **chưa** to express more emphasis on the negation:

> **Ông ấy không <u>hề</u> quên chuyện gì**. He does not forget anything.
> **Tôi chưa <u>hề</u> gặp anh ấy**. I have never met him.

5.5.17.2 Specific construction "negation + verb + question word"

Specific construction **subject + negation + verb + question word [cả]**

(1) **Ở công ti này tôi không quen ai [cả]**. I don't know anybody at this company.
(2) **Tôi không nhìn thấy gì [cả]**. I don't see anything.
(3) **Nghỉ hè vừa rồi chúng tôi không đi du lịch ở đâu [cả]**. We didn't travel anywhere on this past summer vacation.
(4) **Anh ấy chưa sang châu Âu bao giờ [cả]**. He has never traveled to Europe.
(5) **Tôi chưa xem phim ấy lần nào [cả]**. I haven't seen that movie yet.

Note 1: The word **cả** is optional. It puts more emphasis on the negation. In the Saigon dialect, **hết** is used instead of **cả**.

Note 2: The time question word **bao giờ** may be placed in front of the verb. Example (4) can be **Anh ấy chưa bao giờ sang châu Âu [cả]**.

Note 3: There is a big difference between **chưa** and **không** with this construction. The sentence **Anh ấy không bao giờ sang châu Âu [cả]** may convey the meaning "He will never ever go to Europe."

Note 4: The question for this construction is: **subject + có + verb + question word + không** or **subject + đã + verb + question word + chưa**. For instance:

(1a) **Anh có quen ai ở công ti này không?** Do you know anybody at this company?
(2a) **Chị có nhìn thấy gì không?** Do you see anything?
(3a) **Nghỉ hè vừa rồi các anh các chị có đi du lịch ở đâu không?** Did you travel anywhere on this past summer vacation?
(4a) **Anh ấy đã sang châu Âu bao giờ chưa?** Or: **Anh ấy đã bao giờ sang châu Âu chưa?** Has he ever traveled to Europe?
(5a) **Anh đã xem phim ấy lần nào chưa?** Have you ever seen that movie?

Actually, two questions are combined in one. For example, in (1a), they are: **Anh có quen không?** and **Anh quen ai?** In (2a), they are: **Chị có nhìn thấy không?** and **Chị nhìn thấy gì?** The first questions do not contain question words, the second ones do: **ai** and **gì**.

Note 5: In conversational Vietnamese, the adverb of degree **tí nào** (**chút nào** in the Saigon dialect) serving as the question word is used with the meaning "any" and is equivalent to the English constructions *any + comparative adjective* in the question and *not . . . at all* in the negative statement:

A: **Hôm nay trời có ấm lên tí nào không?** Is it getting any warmer today?
B: **Không, không ấm lên tí nào [cả]**. No, it's not getting warmer at all.
A (talking to someone who has gotten sick): **Anh có thấy đỡ tí nào không?** Are you feeling any better?
B: **Không, tôi không thấy đỡ tí nào [cả]**. No, I'm not feeling better at all.

Note 6: One emphatic negative sentence may contain more than one question word. For example:

Chưa có ai nói gì với tôi về chuyện ấy bao giờ cả. Nobody has ever told me anything about that.

5.5.17.3 English negative pronouns *none, no one, nobody, nothing, neither, nor* and negative adverbs *never, nowhere* in Vietnamese

Here we discuss these pronouns and adverbs functioning as the subject of a sentence only. See 5.5.17.2. for these pronouns and adverbs functioning as the object and adverbials.

None with the meaning "not any of a group of people or things" corresponds to **không [có] ai, không [có] ... gì / nào**:

> *None* of them can speak Vietnamese. **Không [có] ai trong số họ nói được tiếng Việt.**
> Of all the tests in this semester, *none* is / are more important than this one. **Trong số các bài kiểm tra trong học kì này, không [có] bài nào quan trọng như bài này.**

No one and *nobody* are also expressed by **không [có] ai**:

> I waited for them about half an hour, but *no one / nobody* came. **Tôi chờ họ khoảng nửa tiếng, nhưng không [có] ai đến.**

When functioning as the real subject of a sentence, *nothing* is placed after the preparatory *there is*, which is expressed by **không có gì**. Note that **có** is mandatory in this phrase:

> There is *nothing* wrong with the idea. **Không có gì sai khi nghĩ như thế.**

Neither with the meaning "not one or the other of two people or things" corresponds to **không [có] ai** or **không [có] ... nào**:

> *Neither* of the parents attended the meeting at their children's school. **Không [có] ai trong số bố mẹ các cháu đến họp phụ huynh ở trường các cháu.**

This sentence may be structured in the way of topic – comment that sounds more normal:

> **Bố mẹ các cháu không [có] ai đến họp phụ huynh ở trường các cháu.**

In this sentence, **bố mẹ các cháu** is the topic, the rest of the sentence is the comment.

See 5.5.18.1. for the subject as topic.

> We discussed those two options, but *neither* would work for us. **Chúng tôi đã bàn đến hai phương án ấy nhưng không [có] phương án nào khả thi.**

Neither with the meaning "also not" is similar to *not either*, but they come with different word orders and correspond to the Vietnamese **cũng**:

A: I have never traveled to Đà Lạt. **Tôi chưa bao giờ đi Đà Lạt cả.**
B: *Neither* have I. / I have *not either*. **Tôi cũng thế.**

For the use of **cũng** in negative statements, see 6.2.

Nor performs the same function as *neither* in the previous negative reply by B: *Nor* have I.

The meaning of *nor* used in a pair with *neither* is expressed by the construction **cả ... và ... đều không ...** :

Neither she *nor* I am aware of what happened. **Cả chị ấy và tôi đều không biết chuyện gì đã xẩy ra.**

The negative adverb *never* is expressed by **không bao giờ** or **chưa bao giờ**. See 5.5.17.2. for more detail.

The English negative adverb *nowhere* usually functions as an adverbial of place and corresponds to **không [ở] đâu**. See 5.5.17.2. (3) for detail. The Vietnamese **không [ở] đâu**, however, can serve as the subject of a sentence. In this case, English places *nowhere* in front of the preparatory *there is / there are*:

Nowhere there are more tornadoes than in this region. **Không [ở] đâu có nhiều bão bằng / như vùng này.**

5.5.18 Emphatic constructions "topic – comment"

Until now we have discussed the ways of showing emphasis by using special words or grammatical constructions. The word order together with some particles is another way of emphasizing a part of a sentence. The part of a sentence which contains the information known to the addressee is called *topic* and is fronted. The part of a sentence which provides new information to the addressee follows the topic and is called *comment*.

5.5.18.1 Subject as topic

Since the subject of a sentence comes before the predicate, there is no inversion. In order to be emphasized, the subject precedes the word **thì**, that is equivalent to the English *as for*. If the subject is a monosyllabic word, it may be repeated, and **thì** is inserted between them. The rest of the sentence is the comment. The vertical line separates topic and comment. Compare:

Tôi không thích bộ phim ấy lắm. I don't like that movie very much.

Tôi thì [tôi] | không thích bộ phim ấy lắm. As for me, I don't like that movie very much.

The part **tôi thì [tôi]** is the topic, and **không thích bộ phim ấy lắm** serves as the comment. Some further examples:

Nó thì [nó] | chẳng bao giờ muốn giúp ai cả. As for him, he is never willing to help anyone.
Ngôi nhà này thì | đắt quá! As for this house, it is too expensive.

5.5.18.2 Subject as topic followed by a sentence

This type of the topic – comment sentence has the subject as the topic and the sentence that serves as a comment has its own grammatical subject. For instance:

Bà ấy | con mới được nhận vào một trường đại học nổi tiếng. She | her daughter has just been admitted to a prestigious university.

In this sentence, the subject **bà ấy** "she" is the topic, and **con** "daughter" is the grammatical subject of the comment sentence. Some other examples:

Việt Nam | kinh tế phát triển với nhịp độ cao. Vietnam | its economy has a high growth rate.
Bạn tôi | nhà bị ngập lụt trong đợt mưa lũ vừa rồi. My friend | his house was flooded during the recent torrential rains.

5.5.18.3 Predicate as topic

The whole predicate or a part of the predicate is fronted and followed by **thì**. Very often, the comment gives some additional information. Compare:

Anh ấy không làm xong được việc này trong ba ngày. He won't be able to finish this job in three days. (a normal subject – predicate construction)
Làm xong việt này trong ba ngày thì | anh ấy không làm được. As for finishing this job in three days, he won't be able to do so. (a topic – comment sentence: the part **làm xong việc này trong ba ngày** is the topic, **anh ấy không làm được** is the comment)

Some other examples:

Dịch văn học tiếng Anh ra tiếng Việt thì | chị ấy dịch rất giỏi. As for translating literary works from English into Vietnamese, she's really good at it.

Tốt thì | quyển từ điển này có tốt, nhưng hơi đắt. As for the quality, this dictionary is good, but it's a little bit expensive.

When the superlative of adjective functions as the predicate, it may be placed at the beginning of a sentence as the topic, which is followed by **là** preceding a noun or noun phrase as the comment. For example:

Trẻ nhất lớp này là Dũng. Dũng is the youngest in this class.
Chăm tập thể thao nhất là bạn tôi. My friend works out most regularly.

See 3.3.2. for more about this construction of adjectives.

5.5.18.4 Object as topic

The object as topic is fronted, and **thì** is optional. Compare (1) and (2) as normal subject – predicate sentences with (1a) and (2a) as topic – comment sentences:

(1) **Sinh viên thi xong môn ấy rồi.** Students have already taken the final exam for that course.
(1a) **Môn ấy [thì] | sinh viên thi xong rồi.** As for the final exam on that course, students have already taken it.
(2) **Chúng tôi đã đi thăm các thành phố lớn ở Đồng bằng sông Cửu Long.** We have visited the large cities in the Mekong River Delta.
(2a) **Các thành phố lớn ở Đồng bằng sông Cửu Long [thì] | chúng tôi đã đi thăm.** As for the large cities in the Mekong River Delta, we have already visited them.

In 1.3.2.3. we discussed **đều** as the emphatic word for the plurality. **Đều** is placed in front of the verb to show more emphasis on the object in the plural. For example, **đều** is added to (2a):

Các thành phố lớn ở Đồng bằng sông Cửu Long [thì] | chúng tôi đều đã đi thăm.

5.5.18.5 Place and time as topic

See 5.1.1.3.3. and 5.1.1.3.4.

5.6 Sentence particles

Until now we have discussed a number of sentence particles, which are not components of particular parts of a sentence, but their presense in a sentence

5 Sentences

is important as they convey a broad range of information related to the speaker's attitude, mood or opinion. For instance, some particles are used as imperatives (see 2.11.), others serve as question words in interrogative sentences (see 5.3.1.7. for **à** and 5.3.1.8. for **chứ**). Here are some other commonly used sentence particles.

In addition to **à** as a final particle to turn a statement into a question and **à** as an initial particle (5.6.1.1.), **ấy**, **mà** and **này** can be used either as an initial particle or as a final particle as well. They convey different meanings in each position and should not be mixed up. For the demonstrative **ấy**, see 1.3.3.4.

5.6.1 Initial particles

5.6.1.1 À

À comes at the beginning of a statement to say that the speaker suddenly recalls something (s)he has nearly forgotten. Often, it is separated from the rest of a sentence by a comma:

> **À, tối nay mấy giờ bắt đầu chiếu phim?** Oh, what time will the movie begin tonight?
> **À, nhớ nhắc nó mang theo vợt. Chiều nay họp xong mình đánh bóng bàn một lúc.** Oh, remind him to bring his racket. This afternoon, we'll play ping-pong for a while after the meeting.

5.6.1.2 Ấy

Ấy is placed in front of a statement and separated from it by a comma to tell someone not to do something. It is similar to the English *No*:

> **Ấy, đừng ngồi vào chỗ ấy.** No, please don't take that seat.
> **Ấy, đừng làm thế.** No, don't do that.

See 5.6.2.2. for **ấy** as a final particle.

5.6.1.3 Dạ

Dạ is used as a reply when the speaker is addressed by someone older. The particle expresses respect for the older person. There is no English equivalent to **dạ**. Some examples:

> Father: **Thắng ơi, con đang làm gì đấy?** Thắng, what are you doing?
> Son: **Dạ, con đang làm bài tập về nhà.** I'm doing my homework.

Elder sister: **Hiền ơi, em đang ở đâu thế?** Hiền, where are you?
Younger sister: **Dạ, em đang ở trên gác.** I'm upstairs.

In the Saigon dialect, **dạ** is also used instead of **vâng** with the meaning "Yes."

5.6.1.4 Mà

Mà is a complicated word due to a variety of functions it performs. See 5.6.2.7. for **mà** as an emphatic final particle, 5.7.2. and 5.7.4. for **mà** as a conjunction of contrast, 5.8.2. for **mà** as a relative pronoun and adverb, 5.8.3.3.4. for **mà** as a conjunction of condition, and 5.8.3.7.2. for **mà** as a conjunction of purpose. With this emphatic function, **mà** is fronted in a second statement with the meaning "moreover, besides" to introduce something new that is added to the idea conveyed in the previous statement:

> **Chiếc áo này mầu hơi sặc sỡ. Mà giá đắt quá.** The pattern of this shirt is a bit gaudy. *Besides*, the price is too high.
> **Chúng tôi biết ai là tác giả bài báo này. Mà chúng tôi biết cụ thể bài báo được viết trong hoàn cảnh nào.** We know who the author of the article is. *Moreover*, we know exactly under what circumstances it was written.

5.6.1.5 Nào

Nào comes first and is separated from the rest of the sentence by a comma to encourage someone to start doing something. It may denote the speaker's impatience. Often, it is used together with **đi** that comes last (for **đi** as an imperative particle, see 2.11.3.).

> **Nào, bắt đầu đi.** Go ahead and start.
> **Nào, kể đi. Có chuyện gì thế?** Go ahead and tell what happened.

5.6.1.6 Ơi

Although **ơi** follows a second personal noun or a name, the phrase is fronted and separated from the rest of a sentence by an exclamation mark and is considered an initial particle. It is used to attract somebody's attention who is some distance away from the calling person. It does not have an equivalent in English.

> **Mẹ ơi! Mẹ cho con đi với mẹ.** Mom, take me with you.
> **Hiền ơi! Hiền có nhớ tên bài hát là gì không?** Hiền, do you remember the title of the song?

When two people are at a very short distance from each other, for instance, they are sitting next to each other, **này** is used instead of **ơi**:

Hiền này! . . .

See 5.6.2.8. for **này** as a final particle.

Note: Unlike an English name that can be used alone to attract someone's attention, a Vietnamese name cannot be used this way. Without the particle **ơi** or **này** or something like that, using the person's name alone to address her / him or attract her / his attention may sound rude.

5.6.1.7 Thảo nào

Thảo nào is used in conversational Vietnamese to connect two statements made by two people. It is fronted in the statement of a second person to refer to the reason for what has been spoken of in the first person's statement. **Thảo nào** is similar to the English phrases *no wonder*, *small wonder*, *little wonder*:

> A: **Chị ấy tốt nghiệp đại học ở Tokyo rồi làm việc ở bên ấy lâu lắm.** She graduated from a university in Tokyo and then worked there for a long time.
> B: **Thảo nào chị ấy nói tiếng Nhật như người Nhật.** *No wonder she speaks Japanese as a native speaker.*

Another example:

> A: **Ông ấy chuyển sang công ti khác rồi.** He's left to work for another company.
> B: **Thảo nào lâu rồi không gặp.** *Small wonder I haven't seen him for a while.*

Note: In the Saigon dialect, **hèn chi** is used instead of **thảo nào**.

5.6.1.8 Thế à

Thế à is used in the form of a question. It is the reply to a statement to denote the speaker's surprise at what (s)he has just heard. It corresponds to the English *Oh really?* and is placed before a statement to explain what the speaker is surprised at, or it may be used alone as a reply:

> A: **Chị ấy ở Việt Nam về rồi.** She has already returned from Vietnam.
> B: **Thế à? [Về bao giờ?]** *Oh really? When [did she return]?*

A: **Bờ biển miền Trung lại sắp bị bão.** The coastline of central Vietnam is going to be hit by a storm again.
B: **Thế à?** [**Bão có lớn lắm không?**] *Oh really?* [Will the storm be powerful?]

Note: In the Saigon dialect, **vậy hả** is used instead of **thế à**.

5.6.1.9 Thế thì

Thế thì is fronted in a reply to someone's statement to continue the conversation with the meaning "then, well then, in that case." Some examples:

A: **7 giờ sớm quá.** 7 o'clock is too early.
B: **Thế thì 7 rưỡi, được không?** *Well then*, is 7:30 OK?

A: **Nhà hàng này đóng cửa rồi.** This restaurant is already closed.
B: **Thế thì mình đi nhà hàng khác.** *Then* let's go to another restaurant.

Note: In the Saigon dialect, **vậy thì** is used instead of **thế thì**.

5.6.1.10 Thì

Thì is fronted in a statement to put emphasis on the fact that something did happen. To some extent, **thì** with this meaning is similar to the English *as a matter of fact*:

Thì tất cả mọi người đều quyết định như thế. *As a matter of fact*, everybody came to this decision.
Thì ai cũng hiểu là điều đó sẽ không bao giờ xẩy đến. *As a matter of fact*, everybody realized that it will never happen.

5.6.1.11 Thưa

Thưa precedes a personal pronoun to show respect for the person the speaker is talking to. A statement or question follows the phrase with **thưa**. In some cases, it is used in a similar way as the English *ma'am, sir*:

Thưa chị, chúng tôi không thể làm xong việc này trong ngày hôm nay được. *We can't finish this work today.* (speaking with a young woman).
Thưa bác, bác có phải là bác sĩ Loan không ạ? *Ma'am*, you're Doctor Loan, aren't you? (speaking with an older woman).

Very often, **thưa** is used together with the final particle **ạ** as in the second sentence (see 5.6.2.1. for **ạ**). In this sentence, the second personal pronoun **bác** is used twice. The first time, it follows **thưa** so that the speaker attracts attention of the person whom (s)he addresses as **bác** in a polite and respectful way. The second **bác** which comes after the comma functions as the subject of the question. *Thưa bác có phải là bác sĩ Loan không ạ? is incorrect.

5.6.2 Final particles

5.6.2.1 Ạ

Ạ is placed at the end of a sentence to express respect for the person the speaker is talking with. The addressed person is usually older than the speaker. Ạ can be used in combination with the initial particle **thưa**, as in the second example of 5.6.1.8. Some further examples of using **thưa** and **ạ** together:

> **Thưa bác, bác muốn ngồi chỗ nào ạ?** *Sir / Ma'am,* which seat would you like to take?

> Q: **Thưa bà, bà có quen anh ấy không ạ?** *Ma'am,* do you know him?
> A: **Thưa ông, không ạ.** *I don't, sir.*

Note: Although both particles **ạ** and **à** (see 5.3.1.7.) are unstressed, they should not be mixed up with each other. First, the constructions and contexts distinguish them clearly. Second, the glottal stop in the pronunciation of the low-falling-broken tone of **ạ** makes it different from the low-falling tone without the glottal stop of **à**.

5.6.2.2 Ấy

Ấy is placed at the end of a statement to refer to a particular feature of an action that has just been spoken of:

> **Anh cứ làm đúng như nó vừa mới chỉ cho anh ấy.** Do it precisely like what he has just shown you.
> **Ông ấy đang chăm chú chữa cái máy gì ấy.** He's focusing on fixing a machine.

In the second sentence, **ấy** shows emphasis on the attention the person pays to fixing a machine. It should not be mixed up with the indefinite pronoun **gì đấy** (for indefinite pronouns and adverbs, see 5.1.1.3.9.).

> **Ông ấy đang chăm chú chữa cái gì đấy.** He's focusing on fixing something. (**gì đấy** functions as indefinite pronoun)

5.6.2.3 Chứ

Chứ comes at the end of a short response to a question to emphasize the certainty of a fact or an action. In the response to a question containing **có ... không**, **chứ** follows either the main verb or **có**:

Q: **Anh có quen chị ấy không?** Do you know her?
A: **Quen chứ / Có chứ. Chúng tôi cùng học đại học với nhau.** *Of course, I do. We were in the same class at college.*

Q: **Chị có biết bơi không?** Do you know how to swim?
A: **Biết chứ / Có chứ. Bố tôi dạy tôi bơi khi tôi còn bé.** *Of course, I do. My dad taught me how to swim when I was little.*

5.6.2.4 Đây

Đây is used at the end of a statement to point out a place or an event the speaker wants to stress. The place or the event can be seen at the moment of speaking. The semantic relationship between **đây** and **này** remains (see 1.3.3.4.). There is no English equivalent of **đây** with this meaning. Some examples:

Máy bay gặp tai nạn ở chỗ này đây. *The airplane crashed right in this place.*
Chúng mình đi đây. Cậu có đi với chúng mình không? *We're leaving now. Are you coming with us?*

Đây also refers to the speaker's idea or feeling of existence or presence of something without certain proof. It may be translated into English as *I believe ...* or *I have the feeling that ...*:

Chị ấy chắc có chuyện gì không vui đây. *I believe she is unhappy with something.*

5.6.2.5 Đấy

Đấy performs two functions. When placed at the end of a question, it makes the question more polite. **Thế** can be in the same position with the same meaning:

Anh đang chờ ai đấy / thế? *Who are you waiting for?*
Cậu đang đọc gì đấy / thế? *What are you reading?*

In the Saigon dialect, **đó** is used instead of **đấy**, **vậy** instead of **thế**.

Đấy comes at the end of an affirmative statement to refer to a real fact and is similar to the English *actually, in fact*:

> **Ông ấy hỏi thăm cậu đấy.** He *actually* said "hi" to you.
> **Máy bay của họ hạ cánh rồi đấy.** Their airplane has *in fact* landed.

In the Saigon dialect, **đó** is used instead of **đấy**.

5.6.2.6 Hở

Hở is placed in front of a personal pronoun, and the phrase comes at the end of a question to make it more polite. It is similar to the English *ma'am*, *sir* or *excuse me*, that are fronted:

> **Bác có biết đến Nhà hát Lớn đi đường nào không, hở bác?** *Ma'am / Sir / Excuse me*, do you know how to get to the Opera House?
> **Bây giờ mấy giờ rồi, hở chị?** *Ma'am / Excuse me*, what time is it?

Very often, **hở** is used in combination with **ơi**:

> **Bác ơi, bác có biết đến Nhà hát Lớn đi đường nào không, hở bác?**
> **Chị ơi, bây giờ mấy giờ rồi, hở chị?**

5.6.2.7 Mà

Mà is placed at the end of a statement to convey two meanings depending on the context.

1. It puts emphasis on the fact that has already happened or is going on:

   > **Chúng tôi đã nói với các anh rồi mà.** We told you. (implying that you didn't listen to us; it's why that happened)
   > **Trời còn đang mưa mà. Chờ cho tạnh đã.** It's still raining. You / We should wait it out.

2. It explains the reason why something happened or is happening:

   > **Nó đi nhanh quá mà. Bị phạt là phải.** He drove so fast. No wonder why he got a speeding ticket.
   >
   > A: **Trời tối nhanh quá.** It's getting dark so quickly.
   > B: **Mùa đông mà.** It's winter now.

5.6.2.8 Này

Này is used to call another person's attention to what the speaker is saying or showing, or to give a caution:

Anh xem tôi làm này. Look at how I'm doing this.
Ngã này! You're going to fall down!

5.6.2.9 Nhỉ

Nhỉ is placed at the end of a statement to invite the hearer to agree with the speaker about what is spoken of:

Sân vận động lớn quá nhỉ. The stadium is huge, isn't it?
Nước biển ở đây ấm nhỉ. The water in this place of the ocean is so pleasantly warm, right?

5.6.2.10 Rồi

Rồi comes at the end of a short state to confirm a true fact:

Phải rồi! That's right!
Đương nhiên rồi! Of course! There's no question about that!
Đẹp rồi! You look great now! (the other person has just put on some make-up or a new piece of clothing)

The use of **rồi** shows emphasis on what has been spoken of in the statement about an action already completed or a thing already done as a *fait accompli*, and the result is evident at the moment of speaking. Note that **rồi** in this case maintains the meaning "already":

A: **Tôi thấy mệt rã rời.** I'm feeling exhausted.
B: **Hình như anh bị ốm rồi.** You seem to have got sick.

A: **Hôm nay trông ông ấy vui lắm.** He looks very happy today.
B: **Chắc là công ti của ông ấy mới kí được hợp đồng rồi.** Probably, his company has signed a lucrative contract.

5.6.2.11 Thật

Thật is placed at the end of a statement to emphasize the fact that something has happened is true and usually unexpected. It is similar to the English *indeed*:

Ông ấy nổi giận <u>thật</u>. He got angry *indeed*.
Cô ấy làm thế <u>thật</u>. She did so *indeed*.

See 5.4.2. for the exclamatory **thật** used after an adjective.

5.6.2.12 Vậy

Vậy is placed at the end of a statement to emphasize that the action is not what the speaker would like to do but (s)he has no choice but to act that way:

Anh ấy không đến, mình đi <u>vậy</u>. He didn't come, so we have no choice but to leave.
Nhờ họ giúp <u>vậy</u>. You / We have no choice but to ask them for help.

5.7 Compound sentences

The sentences we have discussed so far are simple sentences that consist of one clause. A clause is a construction that minimally consists of a subject and a predicate. However, a clause, in addition to the subject and predicate, may be composed of an object, an adverbial, etc. In this section and in 5.8, we are discussing compound sentences and complex sentences.

A compound sentence consists of two or more clauses at the same grammatical level. These clauses are main clauses and are co-ordinated by a co-ordinating conjunction. Each clause can stand alone as an independent sentence.

The main semantic types of co-ordination are as follows.

5.7.1 Listing of two or more events with co-ordinating conjunction và meaning "and"

Ngoài đường rất đông người, <u>và</u> cửa hàng cửa hiệu cũng đông người. There are a lot of people in the streets, and the stores and shops are also crowded.
Ông ấy bước vào phòng hội nghị, <u>và</u> tất cả mọi người trong phòng đứng dậy. He walked into the conference room, and all the people in the room stood up.

Note 1: The Vietnamese **và** is chiefly used for listing items or events, while the English *and* performs more functions, which correspond to different words and grammatical constructions in Vietnamese. Compare:

(1) We walked for three blocks *and* stopped to ask for directions.
Chúng tôi đi ba ngã tư <u>rồi</u> dừng lại hỏi đường.

(2) This semester I am taking German, *and* my roommate is taking French. **Học kì này tôi học tiếng Đức, <u>còn</u> bạn cùng phòng với tôi học tiếng Pháp.**

(3) They worked *and* talked. **Họ <u>vừa</u> làm việc <u>vừa</u> nói chuyện.**

For more about the use of **vừa . . . vừa . . .** , see 5.7.6.

(4) He told us to go *and* we went. **Ông ấy bảo chúng tôi đi, <u>thế là</u> chúng tôi đi.**

(5) I went *and* had dinner with my friends last night. **Tối qua tôi đi Ø ăn với mấy người bạn.**

(6) The course is getting more *and* more difficult. **Môn học này <u>ngày càng</u> trở nên khó hơn.**

In (1), *and* is used to describe two action that occur after one another. **Rồi** is used with this function. In (2), *and* is used to change the subject in the second sentence, which is equivalent to **còn** in Vietnamese. In (3), *and* describes two or more actions that occur at the same time, which corresponds to **vừa . . . vừa . . .** placed in front of each verb. In (4), *and* is used to indicate an action that occurs after another action and is caused by the other action. **Thế là** is used with this function. In (5), *and* refers to the purpose of the action *went*. Vietnamese does not use anything between the two verbs. In (6), *and* denotes the increasing degree of quality, that corresponds to the Vietnamese **ngày càng**. For more about **ngày càng**, see 2.6.1.2.

Note 2: In English, a serial (or Oxford) comma may be placed in front of *and* in a series or list of items, although it is controversial and is not recognized by some grammarians. In Vietnamese, such a comma is not used:

We are going to visit England, France [,] *and* Germany. **Chúng tôi sắp đi thăm Anh, Pháp Ø và Đức.**

If the last item that follows **và** is a long phrase, a serial comma is likely to be used but not mandatory:

We stopped to have a drink, to relax, *and* to share our thoughts of what has just happened. **Chúng tôi dừng lại uống nước, nghỉ ngơi[,] và trao đổi về những gì vừa mới xảy ra.**

5.7.2 Contrasting two events with conjunctions nhưng or mà

Contrasting two events with co-ordinating conjunctions **nhưng** or **mà** meaning "but." This two conjunctions are not interchangeable in many instances.

Nhưng and **mà** can be used in the same position of a sentence to contrast two items or event. However, **mà** always puts more emphasis on the contrast. Compare:

(1) **Tôi đã khuyên anh ấy nhiều lần là đừng làm thế <u>nhưng</u> anh ấy không nghe.** I have advised him not to do so many times, but he didn't listen to me.

(2) **Tôi đã khuyên anh ấy nhiều lần là đừng làm thế <u>mà</u> anh ấy không nghe (nên sự việc mới xẩy ra như thế).** I have advised him not to do so many times, but he didn't listen to me. (It is why such a thing happened.)

In (1), **nhưng** introduces the second statement to add some contrast with the previous one. In (2), **mà** shows more emphasis on the contrast, which is the cause of what happened. **Mà** also suggests the speaker's regret that the other person did not take his advice.

When there is no emphasis on the contrast, **mà** cannot be used. Compare:

(3) **Chiếc xe này đắt <u>nhưng</u> tốt.** This car (or motorbike) is expensive but of high quality.

(4) **Chiếc xe này đắt <u>mà</u> không tốt.** This car is expensive but of poor quality.

In (3), **nhưng** just adds some contrast, while in (4) **mà** emphasizes the contrast between the high cost of the vehicle and its poor quality.

5.7.3 Introducing a choice with conjunctions hoặc [là] or hay [là]

Introducing a choice with conjunctions **hoặc [là]** or **hay [là]** meaning "or":

Tôi có thể đến nhà chị đón chị, <u>hoặc [là]</u> / <u>hay [là]</u> chị chờ tôi ở trước cửa nhà hát. I can pick you up at your place, or you will wait for me in front of the theater.

See 5.3.1.10. for **hay [là]** as a question word.

Hoặc [là] is used twice at the beginning of each clause to convey the meaning of the English *either . . . or . . .* **Hay [là]** cannot perform this function:

<u>Hoặc [là]</u> chúng ta đi lên núi, <u>hoặc [là]</u> chúng ta đi ra biển nghỉ hè. We'll go either to the mountains or to the ocean for summer vacation.

<u>Hoặc [là]</u> anh ra khỏi nơi này ngay lập tức, <u>hoặc [là]</u> chúng tôi sẽ gọi công an đến. Either you leave this place immediately or we'll call the police.

5.7.4 Contrasting two events by confirming one and negating another with không ... mà ... or ... chứ không ...

If the first event is confirmed, while the second one is negated, **không** is placed in front of the first event, **mà** precedes the second one:

(1) **Chị ấy không còn đi học nữa mà đã ra làm việc rồi.** She is no longer a student but is currently working.

If the main verb is **là** followed by a noun, **phải** is added after **không**:

(2) **Ông ấy không phải là kĩ sư điện mà là kĩ sư cơ khí.** He is not an electrical engineer, but a mechanical engineer.

The confirmed event may be fronted, and the negated event follows. In that case, **chứ không** is used instead. The same meanings of (1) and (2) are expressed by **chứ không** with different sequence of the events:

(1a) **Chị ấy đã ra làm việc rồi chứ không còn đi học nữa.** She is currently working and is no longer a student.
(2a) **Ông ấy là kĩ sư cơ khí chứ không phải [là] kĩ sư điện.** He is a mechanical engineer but not an electrical engineer.

Note that the second **là** is optional.

5.7.5 Expressing parallel increase or decrease with càng ... càng ...

Expressing parallel increase or decrease with **càng ... càng ...** This construction is equivalent to the English *the ... the ...* :

Anh lái xe càng nhanh càng dễ bị tai nạn. The faster you drive, the more likely you are to get involved in an accident.
Càng ra đến gần biển, thời tiết càng trở nên dễ chịu. The closer we come out to the ocean, the more pleasant the weather becomes.

5.7.6 Emphasizing a combination of two or more actions, events or features with vừa ... vừa ...

This construction is equivalent to the English *both ... and ...* or *while / at the same time*. **Vừa ... vừa ...** are placed in front of the similar parts of a sentence, which may be:

1 Verbs functioning as the predicates and referring to two actions that occur at the same time:

Chúng tôi vừa xem ti vi vừa nói chuyện với nhau. We're watching TV *while / at the same time* talking to each other.

2 Adjectives functioning as the predicates referring to two features of a subject:

Căn phòng này vừa rộng vừa sáng. This room is *both* large *and* light.

Note: This construction is "balanced" in the sense that both features should be either "favorable" or "unfavorable." An "unfavorable" feature cannot be combined with a "favorable" one and vice versa.

3 Verb **là**:

Cô ấy vừa là nhạc sĩ vừa là ca sĩ. She is *both* a composer *and* a singer.

4 Adjectives modifying verbs (see Note 1 in 3.3.3.):

Ông ấy giải thích vừa ngắn gọn vừa rõ ràng. He explained *both* concisely *and* clearly.

5.7.7 Emphasizing two items denoted by nouns with cả . . . và . . .

This construction is similar to the previous one but the items each of which is included are indicated by nouns or pronouns:

Nhà hát múa rối nước biểu diễn cả ở Hà Nội và Sài Gòn. The shows of the Water Puppet Theater were in *both* Hà Nội *and* Sài Gòn.

When **cả . . . và . . .** are placed in front of two subjects of a sentence, **đều** precedes the predicate:

Cả bạn cùng phòng với tôi và tôi đều thích chơi bóng rổ. *Both* my roommate *and* I like playing basketball.

5.7.8 Emphasizing an added feature with đã . . . lại [còn] . . . [nữa]

This construction is used to emphasize a feature added to another one of the subject. In English, the added feature usually follows the adverb *and moreover*. Note that if the first feature is "favorable" from the speaker's standpoint, the added feature shoud be "favorable." Accordingly, if the first feature is "unfavorable," the second one should be "unfavorable" as well:

(1) **Trời hôm nay đã nóng lại [còn] ẩm [nữa]**. The weather today is hot, and moreover, it's humid.
(2) **Nhà hàng ấy đã xa lại [còn] không ngon [nữa]**. The restaurant is far, and moreover, (the food) is not good.

The subjects may be different in two clauses. For instance, these two sentences may be paraphrased to contain different subjects. Note that **lại [còn]** precedes the predicate in the second part of the sentence:

(1a) **Trời hôm nay đã nóng, độ ẩm lại [còn] cao [nữa]**. The weather today is hot, *and moreover*, the humidity is high.
(2a) **Nhà hàng ấy đã xa, các món ăn lại [còn] không ngon [nữa]**. The restaurant is far, *and moreover*, its food is not good.

One more example with two different subjects:

Khí hậu Nha Trang đã tốt, phong cảnh ở đấy lại [còn] đẹp [nữa]. The climate in Nha Trang is mild, *and moreover / at the same time*, the scenery there is beautiful.

5.8 Complex sentences

A complex sentence consists of a main clause and one or more subordinate clauses. A subordinate clause is grammatically dependent on the main clause or on a word or phrase in the main clause. Our discussion of complex sentences will focus on nominal clauses, relative clauses and adverbial clauses.

5.8.1 *Nominal clauses*

One of the grammatical functions a noun or noun phrase performs is the object of a verb. When a clause serves as the object of a verb, we have a nominal (or noun) subordinate clause. A nominal subordinate clause in Vietnamese is chiefly declarative or interrogative.

5.8.1.1 Subordinate declarative clauses

Subordinate declarative clauses are introduced by the subordinating conjunctions **rằng** or **là** following a verb. **Rằng** is more formal than **là**. They are equivalent to the English *that*:

Anh ấy gọi điện cho tôi nói rằng / là sáng sớm mai anh ấy sẽ ra sân bay đón tôi. He called me and said *that* he will pick me up at the airport in the early morning tomorrow.
Chúng tôi tiếc rằng / là bà ấy không đến tham dự hội thảo được. We regret *that* she will be unable to attend the conference.
Tôi tin rằng / là anh ấy sẽ giữ lời hứa. I am certain *that* he will keep his promise.

Like the English conjunction *that*, the conjunctions **rằng** and **là** are omissible:

Tôi tin Ø anh ấy sẽ giữ lời hứa. I am certain Ø he will keep his promise.

Note: When negative ideas are introduced with the verbs of thinking, Vietnamese makes the verbs in the subordinate clause after **rằng / là** negative, whereas English makes the verbs in the main clause negative. Compare:

Họ tin rằng sẽ không có chuyện gì nghiêm trọng xảy ra. They *didn't* believe that anything serious would happen.
Tôi nghĩ là chị ấy không đến họp. I *don't* think that she will come to the meeting.

5.8.1.2 Subordinate interrogative clauses and the position of the question word in Vietnamese and English

Subordinate interrogative clauses are introduced by the question words and by the question construction **có ... không** or **đã ... chưa**. In English, a question in direct speech and a subordinate interrogative clause differ in word order:

Why didn't he come to class yesterday? vs. *I have no idea why he din't come to class yesterday.*

In Vietnamese, the word order of the two types of questions is identical:

Vì sao hôm qua anh ấy không đi học? vs. **Tôi không biết vì sao hôm qua anh ấy không đi học.**

Some further examples of the subordinate interrogative clauses that correspond to the English clauses with *wh*-words, with *how* or with *if* or *whether ... [or not]*:

Họ không cho chúng tôi biết mùa hè vừa rồi họ đi nghỉ ở đâu. They didn't let us know *where* they went for vacation this past summer.

Tôi không nhớ <u>ai</u> đã kể cho tôi nghe chuyện này. I don't remember *who* told me this.

Chúng tôi không biết anh ấy đã kể cho những <u>ai</u> nghe chuyện này. We don't know *who(m)* he has already told this.

Không ai rõ <u>khi nào</u> anh ấy ở Việt Nam về. Nobody knows for sure *when* he will return from Vietnam.

Chúng tôi hỏi chị ấy cần phải mua <u>gì</u> để chuẩn bị liên hoan. We asked her *what* we should buy for the party.

Bạn cô ấy muốn biết ở chỗ làm mới cô ấy được đối xử <u>như thế nào</u>. Her friends wonder *how* she is treated at her new workplace.

Người bán hàng chỉ cho tôi quyển từ điển <u>nào</u> mới nhất. The salesperson showed me *which* dictionary is the newest.

Complex sentences

The English *if* or *whether . . . [or not]* corresponds (1) to the Vietnamese interrogative construction of the subordinate clause, or (2) to the question word **hay [là]** if *whether* is followed by a *to*-infinitive in English:

(1) **Chúng tôi chưa nghe thấy ông ấy nói <u>có</u> thời gian gặp chúng tôi <u>không</u>.** We haven't heard from him *if* he'll have time to meet with us. Or: We haven't heard from him *whether* he'll have time to meet with us *[or not]*.

(2) **Cô ấy phân vân không biết nên đi <u>hay</u> [<u>là</u>] ở lại.** She was uncertain *whether* to go *or* stay.

For details of using **nếu** as the subordinating conjunction of conditional clauses, see 5.8.3.3.

If the main clause is a question with the construction **có . . . không**, **có** precedes the verb of the main clause, **không** comes at the very end of the subordinate clause:

Chị <u>có</u> biết chuyến đi này kéo dài <u>bao lâu</u> <u>không</u>? Do you know *how long* this trip will last?

5.8.2 Relative clauses

Another grammatical function a noun or noun phrase performs is modifying a noun as its attributive. When a clause serves as the modifier of a noun, we have a relative subordinate clause. In general, Vietnamese relative subordinate clauses are the result of contact between Vietnamese and European languages. They are more common in formal Vietnamese rather than conversational Vietnamese.

The subordinating conjunction **mà** corresponds to the English relative prounouns *who*, *whom*, *whose*, *which*, *that*, *where* and *when*. The subordinating conjunctions **nơi**, **khi** and **vì sao** correspond to the English relative adverbs *where*, *when* and *why*.

5.8.2.1   Conjunction **mà**

(1) **Đấy là những quyển sách mà tôi cần đọc để viết luận án.** Those are the books *which / that* I need to read to write my dissertation.

(2) **Người mà tôi giới thiệu với chị hôm qua là một chuyên gia về di truyền học.** The person *who(m) / that* I introduced to you yesterday is an expert on genetics.

(3) **Huế là thành phố mà tôi sinh ra và lớn lên trong những năm chiến tranh.** Huế is the city *where* I was born and grew up during the war.

(4) **Công ti du lịch này có các chuyến đi lên Sa Pa vào mùa đông mà nhiều người Hà Nội lên đấy xem tuyết rơi trên núi.** This travel agency has tours to Sa Pa in the winter *when* people from Hà Nội go up there to watch snow falling in the mountains.

In (1) and (2), **mà** serves as the object of the verbs in the subordinate clauses, which are **đọc** and **giới thiệu**. **Mà** in (3) functions as the adverbial of place, and in (4) as the adverbial of time of the subordinate clause.

When *who*, *which* and *that* function as the subject of the subordinate clause, **mà** cannot be used in Vietnamese. Compare:

The man *who* caused the accident was driving under influence. **Người đàn ông Ø gây ra tai nạn lái xe khi say rượu.**

The river *which / that* flows across the city of Huế is called the Parfume River. **Con sông Ø chảy qua thành phố Huế tên là sông Hương.**

5.8.2.2   Nơi, khi and vì sao

Conjunctions **nơi**, **khi** and **vì sao / tại sao**

When **mà** connects a relative clause to a noun that refers to a place, it may be replaced by the conjunction **nơi**, which lit. means "place, location." For instance, sentence (3) can have **nơi** instead of **mà**:

(3a) **Huế là thành phố nơi tôi sinh ra và lớn lên trong những năm chiến tranh.** Huế is the city *where* I was born and grew up during the war.

One more example:

Khách sạn nơi chúng tôi ở trong chuyến đi thăm thành phố Cần Thơ nằm ngay trên bờ sông Hậu. The hotel *where* we stayed during our trip to Cần Thơ City lies right on the Hậu River.

When **mà** connects a relative clause to a noun that refers to a time, it may be replaced by the conjunction **khi**, which lit. means "time, moment." For instance, sentence (4) in the previous section can have **khi** instead of **mà**:

Complex sentences

(4a) **Công ti du lịch này có các chuyến đi lên Sa Pa vào mùa đông <u>khi</u> nhiều người Hà Nội lên đấy xem tuyết rơi trên núi.** This travel agency has tours to Sa Pa in the winter *when* people from Hà Nội go up there to watch snow falling in the mountains.

One more example:

(5) **Chúng tôi đến Việt Nam vào cuối tháng giêng <u>khi</u> người Việt Nam đang chuẩn bị đón Tết.** We arrived in Vietnam in late January, *when* Vietnamese were preparing for the Lunar New Year.

Nơi and **khi** are commonly used in combination with **mà**, which follows them:

(3b) **Huế là thành phố <u>nơi</u> <u>mà</u> tôi sinh ra và lớn lên trong những năm chiến tranh.**
(5a) **Chúng tôi đến Việt Nam vào cuối tháng giêng <u>khi</u> <u>mà</u> người Việt Nam đang chuẩn bị đón Tết.**

The conjunction **vì sao / tại sao** is used in most cases after the nouns **nguyên nhân** "cause, reason" or **lí do** "reason." The nouns follow a statement that is the reason for what is spoken of in the subordinate clause. The construction was created under the influence of European languages and is equivalent to the English *the reason why*. It is used only in formal Vietnamese:

Bạn cùng phòng với tôi bận viết luận văn tốt nghiệp. Đấy là nguyên nhân <u>vì sao</u> / <u>tại sao</u> anh ấy không đi với chúng ta. My roommate was busy writing his senior thesis. That was *the reason why* he didn't come with us.
Một số nhà máy lọc dầu bị ngập lụt trong cơn bão vừa qua. Đấy là <u>lí do</u> <u>vì sao</u> / <u>tại sao</u> giá xăng tăng vọt. Several oil refineries were flooded during the hurricane. It is *the reason why* the gas price has skyrocketed.

5.8.3 Adverbial clauses

5.8.3.1 Place clauses

A place clause refers to the location or direction of the action in the main clause and is connected to it by the conjunction **nơi**, that is equivalent to the English *where*:

Chị cứ chờ tôi ở nơi chị đang đứng nhé. Tôi đến ngay. Please wait for me *where* you're standing now. I'll be right there.

Chúng tôi muốn đi đến nơi các dân tộc ít người sinh sống để tìm hiểu về văn hoá của họ. We'd like to travel to *where* ethnic minorities live in order to learn about their cultures.

5.8.3.2 Temporal (or time) clauses

The situations in the main clause and subordinate clause may occur before one another, after one another or at the same time. The main difference between the Vietnamese and English subordinating conjunctions is that the English *before* and *after* serve either as prepositions or as conjunctions, while the Vietnamese **trước** and **sau** are the prepositions only. **Khi** is added to form conjunctions. For instance:

(1) *Before* my trip to Vietnam, I studied Vietnamese for one year. **Trước chuyến đi Việt Nam tôi học tiếng Việt một năm.**

Before is a preposition used in front of the noun phrase *my trip to Vietnam*. **Trước** is the preposition.

(1a) *Before* I went to Vietnam, I studied Vietnamese for one year. **Trước khi đi Việt Nam, tôi học tiếng Việt một năm.**

Before is a conjunction connecting the subordinate clause *I went to Vietnam* to the main clause *I studied Vietnamese for one year*. **Trước khi** is the conjunction.

(2) *After* my trip to Vietnam, I'd like to have another opportunity to go to work there. **Sau chuyến đi Việt Nam, tôi muốn lại có cơ hội sang đấy làm việc.**

After is a preposition used in front of the noun phrase *my trip to Vietnam*. **Sau** is the preposition.

(2a) *After* I worked in Vietnam for one year, I'd like to have another opportunity to return there to work. **Sau khi làm việc ở Việt Nam một năm, tôi muốn có cơ hội trở lại đấy làm việc.**

After is a conjunction connecting the subordinate clause *I worked in Vietnam for one year* to the main clause *I'd like to have another opportunity to return there to work*. **Sau khi** is the conjunction.

Từ khi meaning "since" is often used with the prepositional phrases **đến giờ** or **đến nay** "until now." This construction corresponds to the English present perfect or perfect progressive tense in the main clause with *since* in the subordinate clause:

(1) **Từ khi tốt nghiệp đại học đến giờ, chị ấy vẫn làm cho công ti phần mềm này.** *Since she graduated from university, she has been working for this software company.*

The subordinate and main clauses may switch their positions:

(1a) **Chị ấy vẫn làm cho công ti phần mềm này từ khi tốt nghiệp đại học đến giờ.** *She has been working for this software company since she graduated from university.*

Khi is placed at the beginning of the subordinate clause of time to convey three different situations occurring in the main and subordinate clauses:

1. The actions in the subordinate clause and main clause occur at the same time. Both actions are of long duration. Conjunctions **khi** or **trong khi** are used. They are equivalent to the English *when* or *while*. **Trong khi** is more emphatic than **khi**:

    Khi / Trong khi tôi làm việc ở Việt Nam, tôi đi du lịch rất nhiều nơi ở cả miền Bắc, miền Trung và miền Nam. *When / while [I was] working in Vietnam, I traveled to many places in both northern, central and southern Vietnam.*

2. The action in the subordinate clause is right away followed by the action in the main clause. Both actions are momentary. **Khi** is equivalent to the English *when*. **Thì** can be added to the beginning of the main clause if it follows the subordinate clause:

    (1) **Khi tôi ra khỏi nhà [thì] trời bắt đầu mưa.** *When I left my house, it began to rain.*

If the main clause precedes the subordinate clause, **thì** cannot be used:

(1a) **Trời bắt đầu mưa khi tôi ra khỏi nhà.**

However, if the subordinate clause precedes the main clause, as in (1), the conjunction **khi** may be omitted, **thì** is mandatory, and the meaning of the sentence remains unchanged. This type of clauses is characteristic of conversational speech:

(1b) **Tôi ra khỏi nhà thì trời bắt đầu mưa.**

3   The momentary action in the main clause took place when the action of long duration in the subordinate clause was in progress. **Khi** or **trong khi** is used as the conjunction. The conjunctions are equivalent to the English *when* or *while*:

(1) **Anh ấy đến hội thảo <u>khi</u> / <u>trong khi</u> diễn giả chính đọc tham luận.** He arrived at the conference *when / while* the keynote speaker was making his presentation.

The aspect marker **đang** can be added to show emphasis on the long duration of the action in the subordinate clause:

(1a) **Anh ấy đến hội thảo <u>khi</u> / <u>trong khi</u> diễn giả chính <u>đang</u> đọc tham luận.**

This type of subordinate clause commonly refers to the past tense. It may, however, refer to the future tense:

(2) **Đầu tháng sau, chị ở Việt Nam về <u>khi</u> / <u>trong khi</u> vẫn còn là học kì hai. Năm học chưa kết thúc.** You will be back from Vietnam early next month *when / while* the spring semester is still going on. The academic year will not have finished yet.

The aspect marker **đang** can be added to put more emphasis on the duration:

(2a) **Đầu tháng sau, chị ở Việt Nam về <u>khi</u> / <u>trong khi</u> vẫn <u>đang</u> còn là học kì hai. Năm học chưa kết thúc.**

The conjunction **một khi** combines the meanings of time and condition. It is similar to the English conjunction *once* with the meaning "after, as soon as":

<u>**Một khi**</u> **chúng ta đã bắt đầu làm việc này, chúng ta phải làm cho xong.** *Once we started this project, we should finish it.*
<u>**Một khi**</u> **mệt thì không thể tập trung làm bất cứ việc gì được.** *Once exhausted, you are unable to focus on anything.*

5.8.3.3 Conditional clauses

5.8.3.3.1 NẾU

Nếu is the most common conjunction in a subordinate clause of condition. It corresponds to the English *if* and conveys different meanings.

1 Probability: the action in the **nếu**-clause is quite probable. As in English, the verb in the main clause may refer to the future, and the verb in the **nếu**-clause does not have any tense marker:

> (1) **Ngày mai chúng ta sẽ đi ra ngoại thành chơi <u>nếu</u> trời đẹp.** We'll go to the suburbs of the town to relax tomorrow *if* weather permits.
>
> (2) **Anh sẽ bị muộn <u>nếu</u> anh không đi ngay bây giờ.** You'll be late *if* you don't leave right now.

If the subordinate clause precedes the main clause, **thì**, which is similar to the English *then*, can be added to the beginning of the main clause:

> (1a) **<u>Nếu</u> ngày mai trời đẹp <u>thì</u> chúng ta sẽ đi ra ngoại thành chơi.** *If* the weather permits tomorrow, *then* we'll go to the suburbs of the town to relax.
>
> (2a) **<u>Nếu</u> anh không đi ngay bây giờ <u>thì</u> anh sẽ bị muộn.** *If* you don't leave right now, *then* you'll be late.

If the main clause precedes the subordinate clause as in (1) and (2), **thì** cannot be used.

Mà can be used after **nếu** to emphasize the probability:

> (1b) **<u>Nếu</u> <u>mà</u> ngày mai trời đẹp <u>thì</u> chúng ta sẽ đi ra ngoại thành chơi.**
>
> (2b) **<u>Nếu</u> <u>mà</u> anh không đi ngay bây giờ <u>thì</u> anh sẽ bị muộn.**

2 Unreality: the action in the **nếu**-clause did not happen, or the fact was not true in the past. **Đã** is commonly used before the verb in the main clause:

> (3) **Vụ mùa ở đồng bằng sông Cửu Long đã bội thu <u>nếu</u> không bị hạn hán.** The harvest in the Mekong River Delta would have been bountiful *if* there had not been drought.
>
> (4) **<u>Nếu</u> nó học chăm hơn <u>thì</u> nó <u>đã</u> thi đỗ.** *If* he had studied harder, he would have passed the exam.

Như can be added after **nếu** to put more emphasis on the unreality:

> (3a) **Vụ mùa ở đồng bằng sông Cửu Long <u>đã</u> bội thu <u>nếu</u> <u>như</u> không bị hạn hán.**
>
> (4a) **<u>Nếu</u> <u>như</u> nó học chăm hơn <u>thì</u> nó <u>đã</u> thi đỗ.**

<u>Note</u>: The English *if* performs two functions, which are 1) to form a subordinate clause of condition; and 2) to introduce a statement, a question or a noun clause

about something that is not certain. With the second function *if* is equivalent to *whether [or not]*. **Nếu** in Vietnamese only refers to the conditionality. In order to form a noun clause with the meaning *whether [or not]*, Vietnamese uses the construction **có . . . không** for the present or future tense and **đã . . . chưa** for the past tense:

> We don't know *if* he is coming with us tomorrow. **Chúng tôi không biết ngày mai anh ấy có đi với chúng tôi không**.
> She asked *if* he had graduated from college. **Bà ấy hỏi nó đã tốt nghiệp đại học chưa**.

The sentence ***Chúng tôi không biết nếu ngày mai anh ấy đi với chúng tôi**. is incorrect.

5.8.3.3.2   GIẢ SỬ

Giả sử is another way to denote the unreality or a hypothesis, but the conjunction is more formal. The **giả sử**-clause is always fronted and the main clause contains **thì** and **đã**:

- (3b) **Giả sử không bị hạn hán thì vụ mùa ở đồng bằng sông Cửu Long đã bội thu**. *If* there had not been drought, the harvest in the Mekong River Delta would have been bountiful.
- (4b) **Giả sử nó học chăm hơn thì nó đã thi đỗ**. *If* he had studied harder, he would have passed the exam.

5.8.3.3.3   GIÁ [NHƯ]

Giá [như] introduces a subordinate clause that expresses regret about a present or past situation.

Present situation

- (1) **Giá [như] hôm nay anh ấy đi được với chúng mình thì hay quá**. If he could come with us today, it would be great.
- (2) **Giá [như] biết được số điện thoại của chị ấy thì có thể gọi điện ngay cho chị ấy**. If we / I knew her phone number, we / I could call her right away.

Giá [như] is used in the similar way as the English *wish* or *if only*. The two sentences shown can be translated into English as follows:

(1) We *wish* he could come with us today. (It would be great.) / *If only* he came with us today. (It would be great).

(2) We / I *wish* we / I knew her phone number. (We / I could call her right away.) / *If only* we / I knew her phone number. (We / I could call her right away.)

Past situation

The **giá [như]**-clause always precedes the main clause that contains **thì** and **đã**:

Giá [như] ông ấy bỏ được thuốc lá **thì** ông ấy **đã** khoẻ mạnh hơn nhiều. If he had quitted smoking, he would have been much healthier.
Giá [như] cháu bé biết bơi **thì đã** không bị chết đuối. If the child had been able to swim, he would not have drowned.

5.8.3.3.4   MÀ

Mà introduces a subordinate clause that conveys a hypothesis or the speaker's regret. It is always used together with **thì** and in some instances is similar to the English subjunctive:

(1) **Bạn tôi mà ở đây bây giờ thì chị ấy biết chúng ta phải làm gì.** If my friend were here now / Were my friend here now, she would know what we should do. (regret about the present situation)
(2) **Tôi mà là anh ấy thì tôi đã đối xử với họ tử tế hơn.** If I were in his shoes / Were I in his shoes, I would have treated them in a nicer way. (regret about the past situation)

In this construction, the same subject should be repeated in both parts of the sentence: **bạn tôi** and **chị ấy** in (1), **tôi** in (2). It cannot be omitted as in some other types of compound and complex sentences.

5.8.3.3.5   HỄ CỨ ... LÀ / THÌ

Hễ cứ ... là / thì introduces a subordinate clause that indicates automatic or habitual results. The **hễ cứ**-clause always comes first. **Là** or **thì** is placed at the beginning of the main clause. The construction is similar to the English *whenever*-clause:

Hễ cứ có gió mùa đông bắc **là** bà ấy bị cảm lạnh. Whenever there is northeastern monsoon, she catches a cold.
Hễ cứ có dịp về Hà Nội **thì** chị ấy đến thăm chúng tôi. Whenever she has a chance to be back in Hà Nội, she comes by to see us.

5.8.3.3.6   TRỪ PHI

Trừ phi, which was borrowed from Chinese 除非, introduces a subordinate clause to suggest that something will happen or will be true if something else

Complex sentences

does not happen or is not true. The **trừ phi**-clause either precedes or follows the main clause. If it comes first, a comma is usually placed to separate the subordinate clause from the main one. It is equivalent to the English *unless*:

(1) **Ngày mai các anh không phải đến văn phòng trừ phi có việc gì thật gấp phải giải quyết.** You don't have to come to the office tomorrow *unless* you have someting urgent to do.
(1a) **Trừ phi có việc gì thật gấp phải giải quyết, ngày mai các anh không phải đến văn phòng.**
(2) **Năm nay sẽ được mùa trừ phi có thiên tai.** This year's crop will be good *unless* there is a natural disaster.
(2a) **Trừ phi có thiên tai, năm nay sẽ được mùa.**

5.8.3.3.7 KẺO

Kẻo introduces a clause that expresses an unfavorable event if the action or event in the previous clause does not happen. The speaker wants the hearer to avoid that. The subject is the same in both clauses. **Kẻo** is similar to the English *otherwise*, *or else* or *if not*:

Chúng ta phải đi nhanh hơn kẻo muộn. We should hurry up, *otherwise / or else / if not* we'll be late.
Cậu nên ăn cái gì đó kẻo tí nữa đói. You should eat something now, *otherwise / or else / if not* you'll be hungry later.

Note: In the Saigon dialect, **không thôi** is used instead of **kẻo**.

5.8.3.3.8 MUỐN ... PHẢI

Muốn ... phải ... connect two clauses, the first of which expresses the goal that needs to be achieved, and the second one refers to the condition that should be fulfilled to achieve the goal. The **muốn**-clause always comes first, and **thì** may be added to the beginning of the second clause:

Muốn tiếp xúc với người dân sống ở đấy [thì] phải học tiếng của họ. In order to / If you want to interact with the people living there, you should learn their language.
Muốn tự đi chơi phố cổ ở Hà Nội [thì] phải có bản đồ Hà Nội. In order to / If you want to walk around in the Old Quarter of Hà Nội on your own, you should have a map of Hà Nội.

5.8.3.3.9 NHỠ

Nhỡ is used in the subordinate clause to convey the meaning "for fear that the action or event may happen." **Nhỡ** is similar to the English *in case*:

Chị ấy nấu nhiều đồ ăn hơn <u>nhỡ</u> có người đưa cả bạn đến. She will cook more food *in case* someone also brings friends (to the party).
Lúc nào tôi cũng có đèn pin trong nhà <u>nhỡ</u> mất điện. I always keep a flashlight at home *in case* there is a power outage.

<u>Note</u>: In the Saigon dialect, **lỡ** is used instead of **nhỡ**.

5.8.3.4 Concessive clauses

The conjunctions **mặc dù** and **tuy** join a subordinate clause of concession and a main clause. Either the main clause or the subordinate clause can come first. However, when the subordinate clause is fronted, the adverb **vẫn** (1a and 1b) or **cũng** (2a and 2b) is necessary before the predicate in the subordinate clause (compare with **vẫn** introduced in 2.3.2.6.). When the clause with **tuy** comes first, **nhưng** (1b and 2b) should also be added to the beginning of the main clause. These conjunctions are similar to the English *though* and *although*:

(1) **Cô ấy vừa nói vừa cười <u>mặc dù</u> / <u>tuy</u> cô ấy giận chúng tôi lắm.** She was smiling when talking to us *though / although* she was very angry with us.

(2) **Bà ấy phải đi làm <u>mặc dù</u> / <u>tuy</u> bị ốm vì không có ai thay.** She had to go to work *though / although* she was sick because there was no substitution for her.

(1a) **<u>Mặc dù</u> cô ấy giận chúng tôi lắm, cô ấy <u>vẫn</u> vừa nói vừa cười.**

(2a) **<u>Mặc dù</u> bị ốm, bà ấy <u>cũng</u> phải đi làm vì không có ai thay.**

(1b) **<u>Tuy</u> cô ấy giận chúng tôi lắm <u>nhưng</u> cô ấy <u>vẫn</u> vừa nói vừa cười.**

(2b) **<u>Tuy</u> bị ốm <u>nhưng</u> bà ấy <u>cũng</u> phải đi làm vì không có ai thay.**

<u>Note 1</u>: The English *even though* and *even if* correspond to the Vietnamese **ngay cả khi**. The conjunctions of concession are not used in this case. For instance:

Even though / Even if you don't like him, you should still be polite to him.
<u>Ngay cả khi</u> chị không ưa ông ấy, chị <u>vẫn</u> nên lịch sự với ông ấy.
Even though / Even if it rained really hard, he didn't miss any outdoor work-out. **<u>Ngay cả khi</u> trời mưa rất to, anh ấy <u>cũng</u> không bỏ một buổi tập ngoài trời nào.**

Note 2: The English conjunction *however* is used to join two statements and convey the meaning of concession "although something is, was or may be true in the previous statement." It corresponds to **tuy nhiên** and **song** in Vietnamese. Both of them are formal. **Song** is used in written Vietnamese only:

> He just returned from an overseas business trip and was still tired. *However*, he went to work right away because his company has a lot of work. **Ông ấy mới đi công tác nước ngoài về còn rất mệt. Tuy nhiên / Song, ông ấy đi làm ngay vì công ti đang rất nhiều việc.**

The English *however* can be placed in the middle of a sentence, whereas the Vietnamese **tuy nhiên** and **song** are always fronted:

> At first he decided not to participate in the conference. Later, *however*, he changed his mind. **Lúc đầu ông ấy định không tham dự hội nghị. Tuy nhiên / Song, sau đó ông ấy thay đổi ý kiến.**
>
> He made a lot of efforts. The results, *however*, were not as good as expected. **Anh ấy cố gắng rất nhiều. Tuy nhiên / Song, kết quả không như mong muốn.**

5.8.3.5 Reason clauses

The conjunctions **vì**, **bởi vì** and **tại vì** introduce subordinate clauses of cause that contain the reason for what happens in the main clause. **Vì** can be used in all styles, **bởi vì** is rather formal, whereas **tại vì** is informal. The subordinate clause can either be fronted or follow the main clause. The conjunctions are similar to the English *because*, *as* and *since*:

(1) **Vì / Bởi vì / Tại vì thiếu anh ấy, đội chúng tôi bị thua trận đấu hôm nay.** *Because / As / Since he didn't play today, our team lost the game.*

(2) **Vì / Bởi vì / Tại vì sương mù quá dầy đặc, chúng tôi quyết định không đi thăm một số di tích lịch sử trên vùng núi nữa.** *Because / As / Since the fog was so thick, we decided not to go to visit some historic sites in the mountains.*

Or:

(1a) **Đội chúng tôi bị thua trận đấu hôm nay vì / bởi vì / tại vì thiếu anh ấy.**

(2a) **Chúng tôi quyết định không đi thăm một số di tích lịch sử trên vùng núi nữa vì / bởi vì / tại vì sương mù quá dầy đặc.**

The clause of reason can be followed by a clause of result which is introduced by **cho nên** or **nên**, which are similar to the English *so* or *therefore*. The clause of reason always precedes the clause of result:

(1b) **Vì** / **Bởi vì** / **Tại vì** thiếu anh ấy <u>cho nên</u> / <u>nên</u> đội chúng tôi bị thua trận đấu hôm nay. *Because* / *As* / *Since* he didn't play today, (*so* / *therefore*) our team lost the game.

(2b) **Vì** / **Bởi vì** / **Tại vì** sương mù quá dầy đặc <u>cho nên</u> / <u>nên</u> chúng tôi quyết định không đi thăm một số di tích lịch sử trên vùng núi nữa. *Because* / *As* / *Since* the fog was so thick, (*so* / *therefore*) we decided not to go to visit some historic sites in the mountains.

For result clauses, see 5.8.3.6.

5.8.3.6 Result clauses

A subordinate clause of result is connected to the main clause by conjunctions **vì vậy**, **vì thế**, **cho nên** or **nên**, which are used in any style. The conjunction **thành thử** is commonly used in colloquial speech. The result clause always follows the main clause. Thus, the reason clauses in the previous section can be paraphrased with the same meaning as follows; a comma is usually placed after the main clause:

(1c) **Thiếu anh ấy,** <u>vì vậy</u> / <u>vì thế</u> / <u>cho nên</u> / <u>nên</u> **đội chúng tôi bị thua trận đấu hôm nay.** He didn't play today, *so* / *therefore* our team lost the game.

(2c) **Sương mù quá dầy đặc,** <u>vì vậy</u> / <u>vì thế</u> / <u>cho nên</u> / <u>nên</u> **chúng tôi quyết định không đi thăm một số di tích lịch sử trên vùng núi nữa.** The fog was so thick, *so* / *therefore* we decided not to go to visit some historic sites in the mountains.

An example with **thành thử**:

Hôm qua bận quá <u>thành thử</u> **không đến được.** I was busy yesterday so I was unable to come.

<u>Note</u>: The English clause of result with *such . . . that* and *so . . . that* corresponds to the Vietnamese clause with **đến nỗi**. For example:

She delivered *such* a wonderful speech *that* the audience gave her a standing ovation. **Bà ấy nói hay** <u>đến nỗi</u> **tất cả hội trường đứng lên vỗ tay.**

The streets in the Old Quarter of Hà Nội are *so* confusing *that* even natives of Hà Nội may easily get lost there. **Đường phố trong khu phố cổ phức tạp** <u>đến nỗi</u> **ngay cả người Hà Nội cũng dễ bị lạc.**

5.8.3.7 Purpose clauses

5.8.3.7.1 ĐỂ

A subordinate clause of purpose is introduced by the conjunction **để** meaning "in order to" or "so that":

> **Lớp chúng tôi xem bộ phim *Người Mĩ trầm lặng* rồi thảo luận để viết bài về việc Mĩ bắt đầu can thiệp vào Việt Nam như thế nào.** Our class watched film *The Quiet American* and discussed it *in order to* write a paper on how the USA started getting involved in Vietnam.
> **Tôi mang máy vi tính xách tay về nhà để bạn tôi đến chữa giúp tôi.** I brought my laptop home *so that* my friend came by and fixed it for me.

If the subject in the main and subordinate clauses is the same, **để** is omitted in informal Vietnamese:

> **Tôi mang máy vi tính xách tay về nhà Ø làm việc thứ bẩy và chủ nhật.** I brought my laptop home to work on the weekend.

5.8.3.7.2 MÀ

In conversational Vietnamese, a clause of purpose can be introduced by the conjunction **mà**, which suggests that the two actions in the main clause and subordinate clause occur right after one another, and the second action is the purpose of the first one. The subject of the main and subordinate clauses should be the same person:

> **Chị lấy xe tôi mà đi đến đấy.** Please take my car to (drive to) go there.
> **Nếu anh cần gặp ông ấy ngay thì ngồi đây mà chờ.** If you need to see him right now, you can sit down here to wait for him.

5.8.3.7.3 NHẰM

In written Vietnamese, a clause of purpose can be introduced by the conjunction **nhằm** with the meaning "with the aim of":

> **Công trình nghiên cứu đang được thực hiện nhằm nâng cao năng suất lao động.** The research is being conducted with the aim of increasing the productivity.

5.8.3.8 Manner clauses

Như connects a subordinate clause of manner that refers to the manner of the action in the main clause. **Như** is similar to the English *as*, *as if* or *as though*:

> **Anh cứ làm <u>như</u> ông ấy đã hướng dẫn anh.** You should do that *as* he has already instructed you.
>
> **Anh ấy ứng xử <u>như</u> anh ấy là giám đốc điều hành công ti.** He is acting *as if / as though* he is the CEO of the company.

5.8.3.9 Proportion clauses

Càng ... càng ... are used to join two clauses to suggest that things in the two clauses change together, or two qualities are systematically related. **Càng ... càng ...** are placed before the predicate of each clause and are equivalent to the English *the ... the ...*:

> **Cô ấy <u>càng</u> lớn <u>càng</u> hiểu ra rằng những gì bố mẹ đã dậy cô ấy là đúng.** *The* older she got, *the* better she understood that those things which her parents had taught her were right.
>
> **Chúng tôi <u>càng</u> nhận được nhiều thông tin, tình hình <u>càng</u> trở nên rối ren.** *The* more information we get, *the* more confused the situation becomes.
>
> **Ông ấy <u>càng</u> giải thích, tôi <u>càng</u> không hiểu ông ấy định nói gì.** *The* more he explained to me, *the* less I understood what he wanted to say.

5.8.3.10 Similarity clauses with correlative words ai – người ấy, nào – ấy, đâu – đấy, thế nào – thế ấy / sao – vậy

These words form semantically related pairs in Vietnamese sentences. They perform different syntactic functions.

(1) **<u>Ai</u> xong, <u>người ấy</u> có thể về được.** *Whoever* is done can go home.
(2) **Anh thấy quyển <u>nào</u>, mua cho tôi quyển <u>ấy</u>.** *Whichever* book you see, purchase it for me.
(3) **Chị đi <u>đâu</u>, tôi đi đến <u>đấy</u> với chị.** *Wherever* you go, I will come with you.
(4) **Pháp luật qui định <u>thế nào</u>, chúng ta làm <u>thế ấy</u>. / Pháp luật qui định <u>sao</u>, chúng ta làm <u>vậy</u>.** We will do *however* the laws require.

In (1) **ai** and **người ấy** are the subjects of the clauses; in (2) **nào** and **ấy** are the attributives modifyiing the same noun; in (3) **đâu** and **đấy** are the adverbials of place; in (4) **thế nào** and **thế ấy**, **sao** and **vậy** are the adverbials of manner.

In colloquial Vietnamese, "n" can be added in front of **ấy** in (1), (2) and (4) and the sentences read as follows:

(1a) <u>Ai</u> xong, <u>người nấy</u> có thể về được.
(2a) Anh thấy quyển <u>nào</u>, mua cho tôi quyển <u>nấy</u>.
(4a) Pháp luật qui định <u>thế nào</u>, chúng ta làm <u>thế nấy</u>.

Thì can be added at the beginning of the second statement. The comma is not used before **thì**:

(1b) <u>Ai</u> xong <u>thì</u> <u>người ấy</u> có thể về được.
(2b) Anh thấy quyển <u>nào</u> <u>thì</u> mua cho tôi quyển <u>ấy</u>.
(3b) Chị đi <u>đâu</u> <u>thì</u> tôi đi đến <u>đấy</u> với chị.
(4b) Pháp luật qui định <u>thế nào</u> <u>thì</u> chúng ta làm <u>thế ấy</u>. / Pháp luật qui định <u>sao</u> <u>thì</u> chúng ta làm <u>vậy</u>.

5.8.3.11 W-CONDITIONAL CLAUSES AND *NO MATTER* IN VIETNAMESE

English has a number of words beginning with *W* and containing *ever* such as *whoever*, *whatever*, *whichever*, *wherever* and *whenever*, as well as *however*. They convey different meanings and introduce different types of clauses. The main idea of these words is that does not matter who, what etc. is. Vietnamese uses different constructions.

5.8.3.11.1 BẤT CỨ / BẤT KÌ ... CŨNG ...

Bất cứ or **bất kì** is used before a question word in the first clause, **cũng** is used before the predicate in the second clause when the **bất cứ** / **bất kì**-clause comes first. A comma should be used to separate two clauses:

<u>Bất cứ</u> / <u>bất kì</u> <u>ai</u> gọi điện cho tôi, chị <u>cũng</u> nói là tôi đi vắng.
Whoever calls me, tell them I'm not available.
Thấy <u>bất cứ</u> / <u>bất kì</u> tờ báo <u>nào</u> có bài về vấn đề ấy, anh <u>cũng</u> mua cho tôi. You see *whatever* newspaper that has an article on that story, please purchase it for me.
<u>Bất cứ</u> / <u>bất kì</u> chuyện gì xảy đến, anh <u>cũng</u> phải bình tĩnh. Stay calm, *whatever* happens.
<u>Bất cứ</u> / <u>bất kì</u> <u>khi nào</u> chúng tôi vào Sài Gòn, chúng tôi <u>cũng</u> ở chỗ họ. *Whenever* we come down to Sài Gòn, we stay with them.

See 5.8.3.3.5. for **hễ cứ ... là / thì** that corresponds to the English *whenever*.

Chúng ta đang được nghỉ hè, có thể đi <u>bất cứ</u> / <u>bất kì</u> đâu chúng ta muốn. We're on summer vacation, we can go *wherever* we'd like to.

5.8.3.11.2 DÙ ... THÌ ... CŨNG ...

Dù is used before a question word in the first clause, **thì** joins it to the second clause which contains **cũng** before the predicate. Note that, unlike English, the comma is not used in this construction:

(1) **<u>Dù</u> anh quyết định <u>thế nào</u> <u>thì</u> tôi <u>cũng</u> chấp nhận.** *Whatever* decision you make, I will accept it.
(2) **<u>Dù</u> chị ấy ăn nhiều đến <u>thế nào</u> <u>thì</u> chị ấy <u>cũng</u> không bao giờ lên cân.** *However* much she eats, she never gains weight.
(3) **<u>Dù</u> tôi làm việc cần cù đến <u>thế nào</u> <u>thì</u> xếp tôi <u>cũng</u> không vừa lòng nên tôi thôi không làm ở đấy nữa.** *However* hard I worked, my boss was never happy with me, so I quit.

Đi chăng nữa can be added after the question word to put more emphasis:

(1a) **<u>Dù</u> anh quyết định <u>thế nào</u> <u>đi chăng nữa</u> <u>thì</u> tôi <u>cũng</u> chấp nhận.**
(2a) **<u>Dù</u> chị ấy ăn nhiều đến <u>thế nào</u> <u>đi chăng nữa</u> <u>thì</u> chị ấy <u>cũng</u> không bao giờ lên cân.**
(3a) **<u>Dù</u> tôi làm việc cần cù đến <u>thế nào</u> <u>đi chăng nữa</u> <u>thì</u> xếp tôi <u>cũng</u> không vừa lòng nên tôi thôi việc ở đấy.**

Vẫn can be used instead of **cũng** with no difference in meaning:

(1b) **<u>Dù</u> anh quyết định <u>thế nào</u> <u>đi chăng nữa</u> <u>thì</u> tôi <u>vẫn</u> chấp nhận.**
(2b) **<u>Dù</u> chị ấy ăn nhiều đến <u>thế nào</u> <u>đi chăng nữa</u> <u>thì</u> chị ấy <u>vẫn</u> không bao giờ lên cân.**
(3b) **<u>Dù</u> tôi làm việc cần cù đến <u>thế nào</u> <u>đi chăng nữa</u> <u>thì</u> xếp tôi <u>vẫn</u> không vừa lòng nên tôi thôi việc ở đấy.**

5.8.3.11.3 NO MATTER IN VIETNAMESE

The English *no matter* is used before question words *who*, *what*, *which*, *where*, *when* and *how* and conveys the meaning of concession that is to some degree similar to the *W*-clauses. *No matter* suggests that something does not affect something else, and the explanations are not necessary because they make no difference to the speaker. Vietnamese uses the construction **dù** as in 5.8.3.11.2.:

5 Sentences

No matter what you say, I'll do it that way. **Dù anh nói gì <u>đi chăng nữa</u> <u>thì</u> tôi <u>cũng</u> cứ làm như thế.**

No matter where you go, you'll find a phở eatery. **Dù các bạn đi đến <u>đâu</u> <u>đi chăng nữa</u> <u>thì</u> các bạn <u>cũng</u> sẽ tìm thấy hàng phở.**

No matter who comes with you, we'll be very pleased to meet the person. **<u>Dù</u> <u>ai</u> đi cùng với chị đến đây <u>đi chăng nữa</u> <u>thì</u> chúng tôi <u>cũng</u> rất vui được làm quen.**

Chapter 6

Problem words, phrases and constructions

This chapter singles out the Vietnamese words, phrases and grammatical constructions that are most difficult for English speakers to use. The difficulties are caused by the complexity of the functions a word or phrase performs, and by the negative transfer of English. The explanations and comparison of the two languages help learners of Vietnamese overcome these linguistic difficulties.

6.1 Còn

6.1.1 As a full verb meaning "have something left; there is / are left":

Tôi không còn đồng nào cả. I don't have any money left.
Chúng ta còn bao nhiêu thời gian nữa thì phải ra sân bay? How much time do we have left before we should leave for the airport?
Chỉ còn vài người ở trong hội trường sau buổi khiêu vũ. There are only a few people left in the hall after the dance.

6.1.2 As an aspect marker denoting a continuing action or state. **Còn** is equivalent to the English *still*:

(1) **Trời còn mưa.** It's *still* raining.
(2) **Ông ấy còn ngủ.** He's *still* asleep.
(3) **Cô ấy còn rất trẻ.** She's *still* very young.

Very often, **còn** follows the aspect markers **vẫn**, **đang** and **vẫn đang** to express more emphasis on the continuation:

(1a) **Trời vẫn đang còn mưa.**
(2a) **Ông ấy vẫn đang còn ngủ.**
(3a) **Cô ấy vẫn đang còn rất trẻ.**

229

6.1.3 As an adverb of degree placed before an adjective in the comparative to refer to a greater extent or degree. **Còn** is similar to the English *even* or *still*:

> **Mùa đông năm ngoái <u>còn</u> rét hơn mùa đông năm nay.** Last winter was *even* colder than this one.
> **Họ gặp phải một vấn đề <u>còn</u> phức tạp hơn nhiều.** They have encountered a *still* more difficult problem.

6.1.4 As a conjunction that serves to switch from one subject to another one. **Còn** is similar to the English *and*:

> **Bố anh ấy là chuyên gia về tin học, <u>còn</u> mẹ anh ấy là bác sĩ.** His father is an expert on computer science, *and* his mother is a physician.
> **Chúng tôi không định đi. <u>Còn</u> chị? Chị có đi không?** We're not planning to go. *And* you? Are you going?

See 2.3.2.4. for **còn** as an aspect marker.

6.2 Cũng and English *also, too, as well* and *either* (in a negative statement)

The main difference between **cũng** and *also, too* and *as well* is that the Vietnamese **cũng** always goes between the subject and predicate, whereas the English words can be placed in different positions:

> **Họ đã thi xong. Chúng tôi <u>cũng</u> thi xong rồi.** They have already taken the finals. We have *also* taken them. Or: We have, *too*. Or: We, *too*, have taken them. Or: We have taken them *as well*.

In informal speech *too* is used after the object pronoun in a short reply. In Vietnamese, **cũng** is used after the subject and before **thế** or **vậy**:

> A: **Mình xem phim ấy rồi.** I have already watched the movie.
> B: **Mình <u>cũng</u> thế / vậy.** Me *too*.

In a negative statement **cũng** is also used, while in English *also, too* or *as well* is replaced by *either*:

> A: **Mình không định đi gặp ông ấy.** I am not going to go to meet with him.
> B: **Mình <u>cũng</u> không định đi gặp ông ấy.** I am not [going to go to meet with him] *either*.

If the predicate is a verb phrase, **cũng** is placed in front of the entire verb phrase. In the following sentences, **hay đi tập thể thao** "often go to work out" is the verb **phrase**:

A: **Mình hay đi tập thể thao vào chủ nhật. Trong tuần bận quá, không có thì giờ.** I often go to work out on Sundays. Too busy on the weekdays, don't have time [for working out].

B: **Mình cũng hay đi tập thể thao vào thứ bảy chủ nhật.** I *also* often go to work out on Satudays and Sundays.

6.3 Được

6.3.1
As a full verb meaning "receive, get." The object should be something favorable:

Bà ấy mới được tin vui là các con sắp về thăm nhà. She just received the good news that her children are coming home to visit her soon.

Năm ngoái ông ấy được một giải thưởng lớn về qui hoạch đô thị. He won a prestigious award in urban designing last year.

6.3.2
As a full verb meaning "gain something necessary for further movement or development":

Xe được đà lao xuống chân đồi. The car gathered momentum and rolled down the hill.

Thuyền buồm được gió lướt nhanh về phía trước. Wind filled the sails and the boat in full sail moved forward.

6.3.3
As a full verb meaning "win a lawsuit; win a card game and get money":

Họ kiện công ti và được kiện. They sued the company and won the lawsuit.

Bà ấy đánh bài được cuộc với một số tiền lớn. She played a card game and won it with a lot of money.

6.3.4
As a full verb used before a number to suggest that a number or an amount has been reched:

Họ đi được một lúc rồi. They left a while ago.
Hôm qua cháu bé được sáu tháng. The baby turned six months old yesterday.

6.3.5 As a verb placed in front of another verb to convey the meaning "have the right or permission to do something":

Tuần này tất cả mọi người <u>được</u> nghỉ ba ngày liền vì thứ hai là ngày lễ. Everybody has three consecutive days off this weekend because Monday is a holiday.
Cháu bé <u>được</u> đi đá bóng với bạn hai tiếng. The child was allowed to go to play soccer with his friends for two hours.

6.3.6 As a verb placed in front of another verb to denote an opportunity or a chance to do something:

Hôm qua chúng tôi <u>được</u> nói chuyện với nhà vật lí được Giải thưởng Nobel năm ngoái. Yesterday we had an opportunity of speaking to the physicist who had won the Nobel Prize last year.
Vận động viên này đã từng <u>được</u> tranh tài tại Thế vận hội. This athlete had a chance to compete in the Olympic Games.

6.3.7 As a verb inserted between another verb and the object or placed at the end of a statement with the meaning "be able to do something":

(1) **Họ chữa <u>được</u> chiếc máy vi tính này. / Họ chữa chiếc máy vi tính này <u>được</u>.** They were / will be able to fix this computer.
(2) **Tôi không dịch <u>được</u> câu này. / Tôi không dịch câu này <u>được</u>.** I was / am unable to translate this sentence.

Often, **có thể** or **không thể** can be added before the first verb to show more emphasis on the ability:

(1a) **Họ <u>có thể</u> chữa <u>được</u> chiếc máy vi tính này. / Họ <u>có thể</u> chữa chiếc máy vi tính này <u>được</u>.**
(2a) **Tôi <u>không thể</u> dịch <u>được</u> câu này. / Tôi <u>không thể</u> dịch câu này <u>được</u>.**

If the verb phrase is long, **được** should be placed between the verb and the object, not at the end of the statement:

Tôi <u>không thể</u> dịch <u>được</u> một câu trong bài về phố cổ Hà Nội đăng trên báo Hà Nội mới. I was unable to translate a sentence in the article about the Old quarter published in *Hà Nội mới* newspaper.

Được

6.3.8 As a verb placed before a transitive verb to refer to an action that is expressed by the passive voice in English:

Bài tham luận đã <u>được</u> trình bầy tại hội thảo vào tháng 12 vừa rồi. The paper was delivered at the conference this past December.

When the performer of the action is mentioned, it is inserted between **được** and the verb:

Bài tham luận đã <u>được</u> <u>cô ấy</u> trình bầy tại hội thảo vào tháng 12 vừa rồi. The paper was delivered by her at the conference this past December.

See 2.12. for more about the passive voice.

6.3.9 As an adjective meaning "good, suitable":

Nó <u>được</u> đấy. (S)he is good. (suitable for a job or position)
Chỗ ấy <u>được</u>. Thứ bẩy chủ nhật này mình ra đấy nghỉ. That place is OK. We will be going there to relax for this weekend.

With this meaning, **được** can be used as a reply:

<u>Được</u>. **Tôi sẽ chờ anh.** OK / All right. I will wait for you.

6.3.10 As an adverb used after a verb to emphasize the favorable feature of an event or action. The event or action itself is favorable from the speaker's perspective:

Tỉ lệ thất nghiệp năm vừa qua đã giảm <u>được</u> đáng kể. The unemployment rate has significantly decreased over the last year.

If the verb takes a direct object, **được** is inserted between the verb and the object:

Cô ấy may mắn gặp <u>được</u> người chồng tốt. She is fortunate to be married to a decent man.

6.3.11 As an adverb used after a negation and in front of an adjective to reduce the unfavorable feature of an event. The event itself is unfavorable from the speaker's point of view:

Dạo này bà ấy không <u>được</u> khoẻ. She's not feeling very well these days.
Việc này anh ấy làm chưa <u>được</u> tốt lắm. He didn't do this job in a perfect way.

6.4 Lại

6.4.1 As a full verb, **lại** conveys the meaning "come or go over, usually within a short distance" and is used chiefly in conversational Vietnamese:

Chủ nhật này lại chỗ tôi nhé. Please come over to my place this Sunday.
Hình như chị Thuỷ ở đằng kia thì phải. Mình lại chào chị ấy một tiếng đi. I believe I see Thuỷ over there. Let's go over and say "hi" to her.

6.4.2 **Lại** follows a verb

6.4.2.1 To convey the sense of redoing something or performing an action again. In some cases, **lại** is similar to the English prefix *re-*:

Anh ấy thi trượt một môn, hai tuần nữa thi lại. He failed a final exam, will retake it in two weeks.
Họ xây lại ngôi nhà sau khi nhà bị cháy. They rebuilt their house after it was destroyed by a fire.
Chúng ta không thể viết lại lịch sử. We cannot rewrite history.

6.4.2.2 To convey the sense of an action opposite of another action that was done before:

Anh ấy cho tôi mượn quyển sách này với điều kiện tuần sau tôi phải trả lại anh ấy. He lent me this book on the condition that I return it to him next week.
Chúng tôi mời bà ấy đọc tham luận tại hội thảo. Bà ấy đã đáp lại lời mời của chúng tôi. We invited her to give a speech at the conference, and she accepted our invitation.
Nó không bao giờ cãi lại bố mẹ. He never talks back to his parents.

Lại is part of a number of verbs, which without **lại** convey a different meaning. Compare:

giữ lại "preserve" vs. **giữ** "hold"

Mặc dù bị chiến tranh tàn phá, thành phố cổ này vẫn còn giữ lại được một số di tích lịch sử. Although this old town was destroyed during the war, it has preserved some historic buildings.
Anh làm ơn giữ cửa cho tôi. Please hold the door open for me.

gửi lại "leave something with someone for someone" vs. **gửi** "send, mail"

Chị làm ơn cho tôi gửi lại tờ tạp chí này cho anh Cường. Could I leave with you this journal for Cường, please?

Tôi gửi cho anh Cường tờ tạp chí qua đường bưu điện. I sent Cường the journal through the mail.

nhắc lại "repeat" vs. **nhắc** "remind"

Chị làm ơn nhắc lại câu hỏi, được không? Would you mind repeating the question, please?

Anh nhắc tôi sáng sớm mai gọi điện cho ông ấy nhé. Please remind me to call him tomorrow in the early morning.

nhớ lại "recall, recollect one's memory" vs. **nhớ** "remember"

Tôi đang nhớ lại xem chuyện gì đã xảy ra. I'm trying to recall / recollect what happened.

Tôi không nhớ chuyện gì đã xảy ra. I don't remember what happened.

6.4.2.3 To convey the sense of an action directed towards one point:

Mọi người xúm lại chỗ ấy xem chuyện gì đã xảy ra. People crowded around that spot to find out what happened.

Lá rụng trong vườn được quét dồn lại thành một đống. Leaves in the garden were raked up into a pile.

6.4.2.4 To convey the sense of keeping something closed, locked or stopped; if the verb takes an object, the object is inserted between the verb and **lại**:

Xe phải dừng lại khi có đèn đỏ hay biển dừng. A car should stop on the red light or at a stop sign.

Anh làm ơn đóng cửa sổ lại. Ngoài đường ồn quá. Please close the window(s). There is a lot of noise from the street.

Khi ra khỏi nhà nhớ khoá cửa lại nhé. When leaving remember to lock the door.

6.4.3 **Lại** follows some adjectives to convey the meaning of reduction in size or amount:

Căn phòng nhiều đồ đạc quá nên trông như nhỏ lại. The room is full of stuff and looks smaller.

Trên đường đi, chúng tôi nói chuyện rất vui nên cảm thấy quãng đường ngắn lại rất nhiều. We had such a lovely conversation on the way that the distance seemed much shorter.

6.4.4 **Lại** serves as a conjuction to join two parts or a sentence to suggest that something is added to what has been spoken of before. Both parts should be either "favorable" or "unfavorable." **Đã** can be used before the first part to show emphasis on the addition. It is similar to the English *and moreover*:

Nhà hàng ấy [đã] ngon lại rẻ. The restaurant is good, *and moreover*, is inexpensive.

Sáng nay tôi [đã] vội, đường lại tắc nên đi làm muộn. I was in hurry this morning, *and moreover*, the road was congested so I came late to wok.

6.4.5 **Lại** is an adverb placed before a verb to imply that what happened or is happening is unfavorable. It is similar to the English *again*:

Mấy bang miền Đông Nam lại bị bão. Đây là cơn bão thứ ba trong vòng một tháng. The southeast states were hit by a hurricane *again*. This is the third hurricane in a month.

Chị ấy lại ốm à? Has she gotten sick *again*?

6.4.6 **Lại** is an adverb placed after the question words of cause **tại sao** and **sao** to refer to the speaker's surprise:

Tại sao / Sao anh lại làm thế? Why did you do so?

See Note 1 in 5.3.2.4. for more details about the use of **lại** after the question words of cause.

6.5 Mà

6.5.1 Mà serves as a conjunction

6.5.1.1 To contrast two events, the second one of which is unexpected because of the first one:

Bây giờ là tháng mười rồi mà trời vẫn nóng. This is October now, *but* it is still so hot. (October is expected to be cool.)

Hiệu sách này lớn nhất ở đây mà không có quyển sách ấy. This bookstore is the largest one here, *but* does not have that book. (The largest bookstore is supposed to have the book.)

See 5.7.2. for more details.

6.5.1.2 To contrast two events. The first one is negated and the second one is confirmed:

Tôi không lái xe đi làm mà đi xe buýt. I don't drive to work. I take the bus instead.

Họ không phải là người Trung Quốc mà là người Hàn Quốc. They are not Chinese. They are South Korean.

See 5.7.4. for more details.

6.5.1.3 To refer to a condition:

Tôi mà có nhiều thời gian hơn thì tôi đã học thêm một thứ tiếng. If I had more time, I would have learned one more language.

See 5.8.3.3.4. for more details.

6.5.1.4 To refer to a purpose:

Anh ghé vào một hàng phở mà ăn cho đỡ đói. You may want to stop by a *phở* stall to eat to reduce your hunger.

See 5.8.3.7.2. for more details.

6.5.1.5 To show emphasis on the reason:

Do hạn hán mà vụ mùa năm nay rất kém. Due to the drought this year's harvest is really bad.

See 5.1.1.3.6. for more details.

6.5.1.6 To be part of correlative conjunction **không những / không chỉ ... mà còn ...** and **không chỉ ... mà cả ...** :

Anh ấy không những / không chỉ bỏ thuốc lá mà còn bắt đầu tập thể thao. Not only has he quit smoking, but he has also started working out.

Không chỉ sinh viên mà cả giảng viên cũng tham gia khiêu vũ. Not only students but also faculty participated in dancing.

See 5.5.8. for more details.

6.5.1.7 To connect a subornative relative clause to the main clause as

6.5.1.7.1 Relative pronoun:

Người mà tôi gặp hôm qua là một nhà thơ nổi tiếng. The person who(m) I met yesterday is a well-known poet.

6
Problem words, phrases and constructions

6.5.1.7.2 Relative adverb of place:

Quảng trường Nhà hát Lớn là nơi mà nhiều sự kiện quan trọng đã diễn ra. The Opera House Square is the place where many significant events took place.

6.5.1.7.3 Relative adverb of time:

Chúng tôi đến Việt Nam vào cuối tháng giêng là thời gian mà các gia đình Việt Nam chuẩn bị đón Tết. We arrived in Vietnam in late January, which was the time when Vietnamese families prepared for the celebration of the Lunar New Year.

See 5.8.2. for more details.

6.5.1.8 To join two phrases of a sentence to convey the speaker's surprise or warning that something is unusual or bad may happen:

Anh chạy đi đâu mà vội thế? You're in such a rush. Where're you running?
Tám giờ sáng rồi mà chưa đi là đến muộn đấy. It's already eitght o'clock, and we / you haven't left. We / You would be late.

6.5.2 Mà serves as an emphatic particle

6.5.2.1 As an initial particle, **mà** is fronted in a second statement with the meaning "moreover, besides" to introduce something new that is added to the idea conveyed in the previous statement:

Khu phố cổ còn giữ lại được một số nét kiến trúc của Hà Nội thời xa xưa. Mà nhiều nhà hàng trong khu phố cổ cũng giới thiệu về văn hoá ẩm thực của Việt Nam. The Old Quarter preserves some features of Hanoi's ancient architecture. *Besides*, many restaurants in the Old Quarter introduce to you Vietnamese food culture.

See 5.6.1.4. for more details.

6.5.2.2 As a final particle, **mà** is placed at the end of a statement to show emphasis on the fact that has already happened or is going on. The statement explains the reason for what has been mentioned:

A: **Sao chị lại gọi anh của mẹ là cậu?** Why do you call your mother's elder brother **cậu?**
B: **Tôi là người Nam mà.** I'm a southerner. (It's why.)

See 5.6.2.7. for more details.

6.6 Mới

6.6.1 As an adjective meaning "new":

Thiết bị trong phòng thí nghiệm rất <u>mới</u>. The equipment in the lab is quite new.
Cô ấy là một người đồng nghiệp <u>mới</u> của tôi. She is a new colleague of mine.

6.6.2 As an aspect marker meaning "just":

Chị ấy <u>mới</u> về lúc sáu giờ. She just came back at six o'clock.

See 2.3.2.1. for more details on the use of the aspect marker **mới**.

6.6.3 As an aspect marker to put emphasis on the adverbial of time:

Tuần trước người ta <u>mới</u> sửa xong đoạn đường cao tốc này. They didn't finish fixing this section of the highway until last week.
Tháng sau sinh viên trường này <u>mới</u> thi. Students at this school will not take the final exams until next month.

See 5.5.5. for more details on the use of the emphatic aspect marker **mới**.

6.6.4 As a corellative aspect marker used with **đã**, **mới** shows emphasis on the quickness of the second action that took place right after the first action:

<u>Mới</u> bắt đầu làm việc <u>đã</u> thấy mệt rồi. I had hardly started working when I felt tired.

See 5.5.7. for more details on the use of the correlative words **mới** and **đã**.

6.6.5 As a correlative word used with **có**, **mới** emphasizes the fulfillment of a requirement in order to perform an action:

Các anh <u>có</u> mời, chúng tôi <u>mới</u> đến. We'll come [if and] only if you invite us.

See 5.5.5. for more details on the use of the correlative words **có** and **mới**.

6.6.6 As a correlative word used with **thôi** which is placed at the end of a statement, **mới** means "just, only" and refers to the past tense:

Sân vận động này <u>mới</u> được xây dựng cách đây vài năm <u>thôi</u>. This stadium was built just / only a few years ago.

Máy bay mới hạ cánh cách đây năm phút thôi. The airplane landed just / only five minutes ago.

6.6.7 As an emphatic word placed before a number or a time to suggest that the number is too small or the time is too early; the word **có** can follow **mới** and precede the number for more emphasis:

Tôi nói chuyện với ông ấy mới [có] một lần. I had a chance to talk with him just once.
Họ đi làm lúc mới tờ mờ sáng. They left to work when dawn broke.

With this meaning, **mới** is used for someone's age:

Cô ấy mới ngoài hai mươi. She is only in her early twenties.

6.7 Phải

6.7.1 As an adjective meaning "right": **tay phải** "right hand / arm;" **chân phải** "right leg / foot;" **phía bên [tay] phải** "on the right side;" **rẽ [tay] phải** "turn right;" etc.

Họ không thể đối xử với anh như thế. Thật là không phải. They can't treat you like this. It's not right.

6.7.2 As a modal verb placed in front of another verb to express advice or an obligation:

Chị phải nói chuyện với họ về vấn đề này. You should talk to them on this matter.
Tôi bị nhỡ chuyến xe buýt cuối cùng nên phải đi tắc-xi về nhà. I missed the last bus so I had to take the taxi to go home.

See 2.10.7. for **phải** as a modal verb.

6.7.3 As an adverb inserted between the main verb and the object to suggest that the subject runs into something unpleasant:

Sáng nay đi làm tôi đi phải chuyến xe buýt đông quá. The bus I took this morning to go to work was so crowded.
Anh ấy vấp phải hòn gạch tí nữa ngã. He stumbled on a brick and almost fell.
Nó vô ý dẫm phải cái đinh, bây giờ chân đau lắm. He accidentally stepped on a nail. His foot hurts badly now.

6.8 Rồi

6.8.1 As an aspect marker that refers to the completion of an action that began in the past. With this function, **rồi** is similar to the English *already*:

Sinh viên thi tất cả các môn rồi. The students have *already* taken all the finals.
Lâu rồi không gặp! Long time no see!

See 2.3.2.7. for **rồi** as an aspect marker.

6.8.2 As an aspect marker that suggests that an event will be arriving in the future earlier than expected:

Mấy tuần nữa đến Tết rồi. The Lunar New Year is arriving in a few weeks.
Nguy đến nơi rồi. We're going to get into trouble. (lit. The danger is arriving.)

6.8.3 As a conjunction which denotes two actions occurring after one another. **Rồi** is similar to the English *and* or *and then*:

Họ nghỉ mấy phút rồi lại làm tiếp. They took a break for a few minutes *and* [*then*] continued working.
Chị ấy đến rồi chúng ta đi cũng vẫn còn kịp. She'll come here, *and* [*then*] we'll leave. It wouldn't be too late.

See Note 1 in 5.7.1. for more about **rồi** with this function.

6.8.4 As a conjunction to join two parts of a sentence, the first of which serves as the reason or condition leading to the result in the second one. There is no equivalent in English:

Làm việc tốt đi rồi sẽ được thưởng. You should work well and will receive a bonus.
Bây giờ không nghe rồi sẽ hối tiếc. If you don't listen (to someone's advice) now, you will regret.

6.8.5 As a final particle:

Đúng rồi! That's right!
Tất nhiên rồi! Of course!

A: **Hôm nay anh ấy đến muộn quá.** He is so late today.
B: **Chắc là bị tắc đường rồi.** He might have got stuck in a traffic jam.

See 5.6.2.10. for more about **rồi** with this function.

6.9 Thì

6.9.1 As a correlative conjunction, **thì** is used together with **nếu**, **giá**, **mà** and **hễ** in a complex sentence with a subordinate clause of condition. The subordinate clause precedes the main clause, and **thì** comes at the beginning of the main clause. In some instances, **thì** is equivalent to the English *then*:

Nếu anh ấy lại đến muộn thì chúng ta đừng chờ anh ấy nữa. If he is late again, *then* we shouldn't wait for him.

Giá không phải đi làm gia sư kiếm tiền thì cô ấy đã học xong cao học từ lâu rồi. If she hadn't have to work as a private tutor to make money, she would have completed her master's degree a long time ago.

Ông ấy mà biết chuyện này thì anh chết. If he learns about it, you would be in big trouble.

Hễ thấy quyển này ở đâu thì mua ngay cho tôi nhé. If you happen to see this book anywhere, please buy a copy for me right away.

6.9.2 As a correlative conjunction, **thì** is used together with **khi** or **trong khi** in a complex sentence with a subordinate clause of time. The subordinate clause precedes the main clause, and **thì** comes at the beginning of the main clause. With this function, **thì** does not have the English equivalent. The action is long-lasting in the subordinate clause and short in the main clause:

[Trong] khi tôi học đại học thì chị tôi lấy chồng. When I was a college student, my elder sister got married.

The actions in both subordinate and main clauses are long-lasting:

[Trong] khi tôi học năm thứ tư đại học thì em tôi học lớp mười hai trung học. When I was a fourth-year student in college, my younger sister / brother was a twelfth grader in high school.

6.9.3 As an emphatic word used before the second action that took place right after the first one. This use of **thì** refers to the past tense:

Ông ấy đi được mấy phút thì anh đến. He just left a few minutes ago and you came.

Often, **thì** is used together with **vừa** to place more emphasis on the quickness of the second action:

Ông ấy vừa đi thì anh đến. He had scarcely left when you came.

6.9.4 As an emphatic word used after the question word of time that denotes the future tense. **Thì** shows emphasis on the speaker's expectation of an event that, in her / his opinion, should happen soon. **Thì** may also express the speaker's impatience. A parent may say to the child:

Bao giờ thì con tắt ti vi đi ngủ? When will you turn off the TV and go to sleep?

See Note 2 in 5.3.2.3. for more details on the use of the emphatic **thì** with this meaning.

6.9.5 As an emphatic word used after the subject or the topic to introduce a comment on the subject or topic:

Mùa đông ngày thì ngắn mà đêm thì dài. In the winter, daytime is short and nighttime is long.
Thời gian chẳng còn bao nhiêu trong khi công việc thì nhiều quá. We don't have much time left while there's still a lot of work to be done.

6.10 English *and* and Vietnamese *và*

see Note 1 in 5.7.1.

6.11 English *good* and Vietnamese *tốt*

The English adjective *good* conveys a much broader range of meanings than the Vietnamese **tốt**. **Tốt** corresponds only to some of the meanings of *good*. The other meanings of *good* are expressed by other words in Vietnamese. Here are the main meanings of *good* and their Vietnamese equivalents.

6.11.1 of high quality. Vietnamese uses **tốt** only in in some phrases:

a good car **một chiếc xe tốt**; a good computer **một chiếc máy vi tính tốt.**

When speaking of something that has good content, Vietnamese uses **hay** instead of **tốt**:

a good movie **một bộ phim hay**; a good novel **một quyển tiểu thuyết hay**; a good poem **một bài thơ hay**; a good game **một trận đấu hay**, a good song **một bài hát hay** a good presentation at the conference **một bài tham luận hay tại hội thảo.**

6.11.2 having or showing talent or skill. Vietnamese uses **giỏi**, not **tốt**:

a god tennis player **một đấu thủ quần vợt giỏi**; a good doctor **một bác sĩ giỏi**; a good teacher **một giáo viên giỏi**; a good cook **một đầu bếp giỏi.**

6 Problem words, phrases and constructions

In some cases, **giỏi** and **tốt** can modify the same noun but convey different meanings:

> **một bác sĩ giỏi** a good doctor / physician
> **một bác sĩ tốt** a nice / kind doctor, a morally correct doctor

Vietnamese uses **giỏi** to convey the idea of being good at something:

> good at math **giỏi toán**; good at music **giỏi âm nhạc**; good at languages **giỏi ngoại ngữ**.

When speaking of someone's good command of a language, Vietnamese also uses **giỏi** instead of **tốt**:

> He has a good command of German. **Anh ấy biết tiếng Đức giỏi**.
> She speaks very good Japanese. **Cô ấy nói tiếng Nhật rất giỏi**.

Hay can be used in the second sentence implying beautiful pronunciation and correct grammar:

> **Cô ấy nói tiếng Nhật rất hay**.

6.11.3 pleasant, enjoyable. Vietnamese uses different words depending on the nouns:

Tốt or **đẹp** for weather:

> good weather **trời tốt** or **trời đẹp**;

but Vietnamese uses only **tốt** for climate:

> good climate for farming **khí hậu tốt đối với nông nghiệp**.

Ngon for food:

> good food **thức ăn ngon** or **cơm ngon**; a good restaurant **một nhà hàng ngon**; a good dish **món ăn ngon**.

Đẹp for appearances:

> You look really good in this dress. **Chị mặc chiếc váy này trông rất đẹp**.

But if someone looks good or does not look good in the sense of being or not being healthy, Vietnamese uses **khoẻ mạnh** or **không được khoẻ**:

> You look very good. **Trông chị / anh khoẻ mạnh lắm**.
> You don't look so good. **Trông chị / anh không được khoẻ**.
> I will take tomorrow off because I'm not feeling very good. **Ngày mai tôi nghỉ vì tôi không được khoẻ lắm**.

tốt đẹp or **dễ chịu** for some abstract nouns:

> a good impression **một ấn tượng <u>tốt đẹp</u>**; a good feeling **một cảm giác <u>dễ chịu</u>**.
> I have heard a lot of good things about you. **Tôi được nghe nhiều điều <u>tốt đẹp</u> về chị / anh.**

6.11.4   convenient, suitable. Vietnamese used different words depending on the nouns:

> It's a good day for camping. **Hôm nay đi cắm trại thì <u>tuyệt</u>.**
> Is tomorrow good for you to have the meeting? **Ngày mai họp có <u>tiện</u> cho chị / anh không?**
> It's a good time to invest in the stock market. **Bây giờ là thời điểm <u>thích hợp</u> để đầu tư vào thị trường chứng khoán.**
> Hot tea and honey are good for a cold. **Bị cảm lạnh mà uống trà nóng với mật ong rất <u>tốt</u>.**

6.11.5   producing or promising to produce a favorable result

Tốt is used with some nouns:

> good results **kết quả <u>tốt</u>**; good grades **điểm <u>tốt</u>**; good advice **lời khuyên <u>tốt</u>**; a good idea **ý tưởng <u>tốt</u>**.

Hay can be used with some nouns that imply content:

> a good project **dự án <u>hay</u>**; a good program **chương trình <u>hay</u>**;

hay may be used with **ý tưởng** "idea":

> **ý tưởng <u>hay</u>.**

6.11.6   used to say how long something will continue or be valid, or something is still suitable to eat or drink. Vietnamese uses different expressions:

> My entry visa is good for ninety days. **Thị thực nhập cảnh của tôi <u>có giá trị</u> trong chín mươi ngày.**
> This old car is good for a few more years. **Chiếc xe cũ này <u>còn chạy được</u> vài năm nữa.**
> Is the dip sauce still good or has it gone bad? **Nước chấm <u>còn ăn được</u> không hay hỏng rồi?**

Note: Vietnamese does not have equivalents of the English greetings *Good morning! Good afternoon! Good evening!* Vietnamese people just use the transitive verb **chào** before a second personal pronoun without a specified time of the day. Such a greeting as **Chào buổi sáng* is incorrect. The English *Good night!* is **Chúc** + second personal pronoun + **ngủ ngon**, which lit. means "I wish you a sound sleep." Vietnamese does not have an equivalent of the English *Have a good day!* or *Have a good one!* either.

6 Problem words, phrases and constructions

6.12 English *for* and Vietnamese cho

Like the English adjective *good*, the English *for* conveys a wider variety of meanings than the Vietnamese **cho**. Learners of Vietnamese often mechanically use **cho** whenever *for* is used in English. On the other hand, the Vietnamese **cho** functions not only as a preposition, but also as a verb (see 2.4.1.), whereas the English *for* cannot function as a verb. Here are the main functions and meanings of the English *for* and how they are expressed in Vietnamese.

6.12.1
For as a conjunction meaning "because" is used in formal speech. *For* is fronted in a subordinate clause to refer to the reason why the preceding statement is true. It does not suggest why an action was performed, but just gives a piece of additional information which explains it. Vietnamese uses **vì** for this function:

We have to work on the weekends this month, *for* the project deadline is tight. **Tháng này chúng tôi phải làm việc cả thứ bảy chủ nhật vì sắp đến thời hạn phải hoàn thành dự án rồi.**

She was obviously overwhelmed by grief, *for* I saw her crying. **Bà ấy rõ ràng là rất buồn vì tôi trông thấy bà ấy khóc.**

It gets colder and colder, *for* it's now December. **Trời mỗi ngày một lạnh hơn vì bây giờ là tháng mười hai.**

6.12.2
For as a preposition conveys many meanings. Only some of them correspond to the Vietnamese **cho**. The other ones are expressed by different words or phrases in Vietnamese.

6.12.2.1
indicating that something is intended to be given to someone or to belong to someone. Vietnamese uses **cho**:

She cooked a delicious dinner *for* us. **Chị ấy nấu cho chúng tôi một bữa cơm rất ngon.**

We have a gift *for* you. **Chúng tôi có món quà cho anh.**

It also denotes an action that is carried out for someone:

Please translate this article into English *for* me. **Chị làm ơn dịch bài này ra tiếng Anh cho tôi.**

Let me carry this bag *for* you. **Để tôi xách cái túi này cho chị.**

6.12.2.2
referring to an employee working for a company or a player of a particular team. Vietnamese uses **cho**:

His father worked *for* a large computer company for more than thirty years, just retired last year. **Ông cụ anh ấy làm việc cho một công**

ti máy tính lớn trong hơn ba mươi năm, mới về hưu năm ngoái.
He happened to play *for* the national team. **Anh ấy đã từng chơi <u>cho</u> đội tuyển quốc gia.**

English *for* and Vietnamese cho

| 6.12.2.3 | indicating that someone votes for someone. Vietnamese uses **cho**:

I will definitely not vote *for* him. **Tôi chắc chắn là sẽ không bầu <u>cho</u> ông ấy.**

Vietnamese also uses **cho** when someone represents someone else. English uses the transitive verb *represent*:

She *represented* the National University at the conference. **Bà ấy đại diện <u>cho</u> Đại học Quốc gia tại hội thảo.**

| 6.12.2.4 | referring to a place someone or something is going to or towards. Vietnamese uses different verbs of motion as prepositions or just the verb **đi**:

We're heading *for* the classroom. **Chúng tôi đang đi <u>đến</u> lớp.**
He left *for* the office at 6 AM. **Anh ấy <u>đi làm</u> lúc sáu giờ sáng.**
When's the next train *for* New York? **Khi nào có chuyến tàu sắp tới <u>đi</u> New York?**

| 6.12.2.5 | indicating an amount of time or space. Vietnamese expresses this meaning in different ways:

She stayed with us *for* the entire summer. **Bà ấy ở với chúng tôi suốt cả mùa hè.**
I won't be here *for* long, just stopped by to say "hi" to you. **Tôi không ở lại đây lâu đâu, chỉ ghé qua chào anh thôi.**
He felt totally exhausted after having walked *for* ten kilometers. **Ông ấy cảm thấy hoàn toàn kiệt sức sau khi đi bộ mười cây số.**

| 6.12.2.6 | indicating the time an event is scheduled for. Vietnamese uses the preposition **vào** for a date and **vào lúc** for a clock time:

I have an appointment with my dentist *for* this Friday. **Tôi có hẹn với nha sĩ <u>vào</u> thứ sáu này.**
The meeting is scheduled *for* the 10th of November. **Cuộc họp sẽ diễn ra <u>vào</u> ngày mùng mười tháng mười một.**
We invited our guests *for* 7:30 PM. **Chúng tôi mời khách đến <u>vào lúc</u> bảy rưỡi tối.**

6
Problem words, phrases and constructions

6.12.2.7 indicating the price or rate at which one pays. Vietnamese does not use any preposition:

He bought the dictionary *for* two million Vietnamese dong. **Anh ấy mua quyển từ điển hai triệu đồng.**
I paid three million Vietnamese dong *for* the airticket from Hanoi to Saigon. **Tôi trả ba triệu đồng tiền vé máy bay từ Hà Nội vào Sài Gòn.**

6.12.2.8 showing the purpose of an object or action. Vietnamese uses **để**:

dry-erase markers *for* writing on a white board **bút dạ xoá được dùng để viết bảng trắng**; a knife *for* cutting cheese **dao dùng để cắt phó-mát**.
What did you do that *for*? **Anh làm thế để làm gì?**

6.12.2.9 used to say what someone is (un)able to do. Vietnamese uses **đối với**:

This job is too hard *for* him. **Việc này quá khó đối với anh ấy. / Đối với anh ấy, việc này quá khó.**
It's easy *for* him to forget what he promised to do. **Đối với anh ta, thật dễ dàng có thể quên đi những gì anh ta đã hứa.**

6.12.2.10 used as a preposition of reason. Vietnamese chiefly uses **vì**:

The child shouted *for* joy. **Cháu bé hét lên vì mừng rỡ.**
She wept *for* sorrow. **Cô ấy ứa nước mắt vì đau buồn.**

For is also used after a number of verbs denoting that someone has done something good and is rewarded for it. Vietnamese uses **vì** as well:

He was decorated *for* courage during the war. **Anh ấy được tặng thưởng huân chương vì lòng dũng cảm trong chiến đấu.**

A different construction without **vì** can also be used:

She was rewarded *for* her effort. **Nỗ lực của chị ấy được đền bù.**

6.12.2.11 There are several frequently used English phrases or constructions containing *for*, whose ideas Vietnamese conveys (1) with **cho** and (2) without **cho**:

(1) *for* rent **cho thuê**

We just played ping-pong *for* fun. **Chúng tôi chỉ chơi bóng bàn cho vui thôi.**

I am feeling sorry *for* him. **Tôi rất lấy làm tiếc <u>cho</u> anh ấy.**
This store sells clothes *for* children. **Hiệu này bán quần áo [dành] <u>cho</u> trẻ em.**

(2) books *for* sale **sách bán**
for now **vào lúc này**
for the time being **[chỉ] vào lúc này [thôi]**
if not *for* **nếu không có**:
If it were not *for* this new medicine, more people would die of the disease. **Nếu không có loại thuốc mới này, nhiều người đã chết vì căn bệnh ấy.**
If it hadn't been *for* your help, we wouldn't have been able to meet the deadline. **Nếu không có sự giúp đỡ của các bạn, chúng tôi đã không thể hoàn thành công việc đúng thời hạn.**
to long *for* home **mong muốn được trở về nhà**
to look *for* a job **tìm việc làm**
to study *for* the final exams **học thi**
to wait *for* someone **chờ ai đó**
For more information, call our main office at ... **Xin liên hệ với văn phòng chính của chúng tôi theo số ... để biết thêm thông tin.**
Can I borrow your pen *for* a while? **Tôi mượn chị cái bút một lúc, được không?**
He didn't work here *for* long. **Ông ấy làm việc ở đây không lâu.**
We haven't seen him *for* a long time. **Đã lâu chúng tôi không gặp anh ấy.**
She looks young *for* her age. **Chị ấy trông trẻ hơn [so với] tuổi.**
I was there *for* the first time two years ago. **Lần đầu tiên tôi đến đấy cách đây hai năm.**
We're warning you *for* the last time. **Đây là lần cuối cùng chúng tôi cảnh cáo anh.**
Our children will be coming home *for* the Lunar New Year. **Các cháu sẽ về ăn Tết.**

6.13 English *if* and Vietnamese nếu

If is used at the beginning of a subordinate clause to perform the following main functions:

6.13.1
indicating the condition on which an action can or cannot be done. Vietnamese uses **nếu**:

If she calls, please tell her that I will be back in an hour. **<u>Nếu</u> chị ấy gọi điện đến, anh làm ơn nói với chị ấy là một tiếng nữa tôi sẽ về.**

If he told you that, he was lying. **Nếu anh ta nói với chị như thế là anh ta nói dối.**

The condition may be untrue because the action did not happen in the past. Vietnamese uses **giá như**:

If you had listened to us, you wouldn't be in such trouble now. **Giá như anh nghe chúng tôi thì bây giờ anh đã không gặp chuyện phiền phức như thế.**

6.13.2 indicating the concession, meaning "althogh, in spite of the fact that." *If* is often used with *even*. Vietnamese uses the construction **dù [cho] ... thì ... cũng [vẫn]**:

We'll go camping *even if* it rains. **Dù [cho] trời mưa thì chúng ta cũng [vẫn] đi cắm trại.**
Even if you don't like oyster sauce, you should try this dish. **Dù [cho] anh không thích dầu hào thì anh cũng nên ăn thử món này.**

6.13.3 making a polite request or suggestion. Vietnamese does not have the equivalent construction and uses **được không** at the end of the question instead:

Would you mind *if* I sat here? **Tôi ngồi xuống chỗ này, được không?**
If I could make a suggestion, why don't we take the subway instead of driving there? **Tôi có thể đề nghị chúng ta đi tầu điện ngầm chứ đừng lái xe đến đấy, được không?**

6.13.4 used in reported questions meaning "whether." Vietnamese uses the construction **có ... không** for the present or future tense and **đã ... chưa** for the past tense that encirles the predicate:

I have no idea *if* it will be cold tomorrow. **Tôi không rõ ngày mai trời có lạnh không.**
Please ask the mechanic *if* he has already finished fixing your car. **Chị hỏi ông thợ đã chữa xong xe cho chị chưa.**

6.14 English *so*

6.14.1 Adverb *so* means:

6.14.1.1 to a degree that is suggested or stated. *So* is used before an adjective. Vietnamese uses **như thế** or **như vậy** after the adjective:

I have never seen him *so* angry. **Tôi chưa bao giờ thấy ông ấy giận dữ <u>như thế</u>.**

No one could believe that he would complete his thesis in *so* short a time. **Không ai nghĩ rằng anh ấy có thể hoàn thành luận văn trong một thời gian ngắn <u>như vậy</u>.**

With this meaning, *so* can be used with *that* as correlatives. Vietnamese uses **đến nỗi**:

He is *so* hard to please *that* no one would like to work with him. **Ông ấy khó tính <u>đến nỗi</u> không ai muốn làm việc với ông ấy.**

See Note in 5.8.3.6. for more details about **đến nỗi**.

6.14.1.2 to a great degree; extremely. Vietnamese uses **rất, lắm, thật** or **vô cùng**:

Our children are *so* excited about the trip. **Các cháu <u>rất</u> nóng lòng chờ đợi chuyến đi.**

Thank you *so* much for your help. **Cám ơn chị <u>thật</u> nhiều đã giúp đỡ chúng tôi.**

She was *so* touched by their story. **Bà ấy <u>vô cùng</u> xúc động sau khi nghe câu chuyện của họ.**

6.14.1.3 in the same way. Vietnamese uses **cũng thế** or **cũng vậy**:

I enjoyed the movie and *so* did my friend. **Tôi rất thích bộ phim ấy. Bạn tôi <u>cũng thế</u>.**

A: I am going to leave. **Tôi sắp đi đây.**
B: *So* am I. **Tôi <u>cũng thế</u>.**

A: I don't smoke. **Tôi không hút thuốc.**
B: *So* don't I. **Tôi <u>cũng vậy</u>.**

6.14.2 Pronoun *so* refers to something that has just been stated or suggested. Vietnamese uses **như thế** or **như vậy**:

A: It is true? **Có đúng thế không?**
B: I believe *so*. **Chắc là <u>như thế</u>.**

A: Has he fully recovered from the flu? **Ông ấy khỏi hẳn cúm rồi chứ?**
B: I hope *so*. **Tôi mong là <u>như vậy</u>.**

A: I heard you're going to be promoted. **Tôi nghe nói anh sắp được đề bạt.**
B: Who told you *so*? **Ai nói với chị <u>như thế</u>?**

6 Problem words, phrases and constructions

6.14.3 Conjunction *so*

6.14.3.1 meaning "therefore, for that reason." Vietnamese uses **vì vậy, vì thế, nên** or **cho nên**:

The traffic was very heavy at rush hour, *so* we were late. **Vào giờ cao điểm, đường đông xe quá, <u>vì thế</u> chúng tôi đến muộn.**

He failed the final, *so* he will have to retake the course. **Anh ấy thi trượt <u>nên</u> sẽ phải học lại môn ấy.**

See 5.8.3.6. for more about the conjunctions of result.

6.14.3.2 used to state the purpose of the action mentioned in the previous statement. Vietnamese uses **để**:

Please speak a bit more slowly *so* I can write down all of it. **Chị làm ơn nói chậm hơn một tí <u>để</u> tôi kịp ghi lại tất cả những gì chị nói.**

So may be used together with *that* conveying the same meaning:

We should leave right now *so that* we can get good seats. **Chúng ta phải đi ngay bây giờ <u>để</u> kiếm được chỗ tốt.**

See 5.8.3.7.1. for more about the conjunction of purpose **để**.

6.14.3.3 placed in front of a statement or a question to introduce them. Vietnamese uses **thế là** for the statement and **thế nào** for the question. **Thế là** is not followed by a comma, but **thế nào** is:

So here we are. **<u>Thế là</u> chúng ta đã đến nơi.**
So, how was your trip to the central plateaux? **<u>Thế nào</u>, chuyến đi Tây Nguyên của các bạn ra sao?**

6.14.3.4 used as an unpolite reply to a statement which is unimportant in the speaker's opinion. Vietnamese uses **thì đã sao [nào]**:

A: You're crying again. **Chị lại khóc rồi.**
B: *So?* **<u>Thì đã sao</u> [nào]?**

With this meaning, *so* can precede *what* with the same meaning:

A: You're speaking so loudly again. **Anh lại to tiếng rồi.**
B: *So what?* **<u>Thì đã sao</u> [nào]?**

6.14.4 Adjective *so* functioning as the predicate with the meaning "true." Vietnamese uses different expressions:

He thinks he's the best player of the team, but that just isn't *so*. **Anh ta tưởng rằng anh ta chơi giỏi nhất đội, nhưng <u>không phải như thế</u>.**
I was told you're angry with me. Is that *so*? **Tôi nghe nói anh giận tôi. Có <u>đúng thế</u> không?**

6.15 English *that*

This word performs different functions in English that correspond to different words and constructions in Vietnamese.

6.15.1 Demonstrative adjective *that, those*

6.15.1.1 used before a noun to indicate which person, thing or idea is being shown, pointed to or mentioned. Vietnamese uses **ấy** or **đó**, that are interchangeable, and **kia**. For the difference between **ấy / đó** and **kia**, please see 1.3.3.3.

Those dictionaries are the newest Vietnamese-English dictionaries. **Mấy quyển từ điển <u>ấy</u> / <u>đó</u> là những quyển từ điển Việt-Anh mới nhất.**
Do you see *that* tall building? **Anh có thấy ngôi nhà cao <u>kia</u> không?**

6.15.1.2 used before *one* or *ones* to refer to the one that is far away or less familiar, compared to the one denoted by *this*. Vietnamese uses **kia** for *that* and **này** for *this*:

A: Which dictionary are you taking? *This* one or *that* one? **Chị lấy cuốn từ điển nào? Cuốn <u>này</u> hay cuốn <u>kia</u>?**
B: I'm taking *that* one. **Tôi lấy cuốn <u>kia</u>.**

A: Do you like *these* pants or *those* pants over there? **Anh thích cái quần <u>này</u> hay cái quần <u>kia</u>?**
B: I like *those* ones. **Tôi thích cái <u>kia</u>.**

6.15.2 Demonstrative pronoun *that*

6.15.2.1 used before the verb *to be* with the same meaning as in 6.14.1.1

Vietnamese used **đấy / đó** and **kia**. The difference between **đấy / đó** and **kia** remains:

That's my computer. **<u>Đấy</u> / <u>đó</u> / <u>kia</u> là máy vi tính của tôi.**
That's the athletic center where I work out every day. **<u>Đấy</u> / <u>đó</u> / <u>kia</u> là khu thể thao nơi tôi tập luyện hằng ngày.**

6 Problem words, phrases and constructions

6.15.2.2 used after a verb or a preposition to refer to an action or event that has just been mentioned. Vietnamese uses **điều ấy / đó, việc ấy / đó, chuyện ấy / đó** or just **thế / vậy** after a verb and **đó / đấy** after a preposition:

Why did you do *that*? **Sao anh lại làm <u>việc ấy</u>? / Sao anh lại làm <u>thế</u>?**
I did my master's degree in Vietnamese studies, and before *that* as an undergraduate I majored in Southeast Asian studies. **Tôi học cao học về Việt Nam học. Trước <u>đó</u> / <u>đấy</u> ở bậc đại học tôi chuyên về Đông Nam Á học.**

In some instances, Vietnamese uses set expressions containing **kìa**:

Look at *that*! **Trông <u>kìa</u>! / Xem <u>kìa</u>!**

6.15.3 Conjunction *that* connects a nominal declarative subordinate clause to the main clause. Vietnamese uses **rằng** or **là**:

He never said *that* he would agree to be your advisor. **Ông ấy chưa bao giờ nói <u>rằng</u> / <u>là</u> ông ấy đồng ý hướng dẫn luận văn của anh cả.**

See 5.8.1. for more details about nominal clauses.

That can be fronted as the subject. Vietnamese uses **chuyện**:

That he was upset is not surprising at all. **<u>Chuyện</u> anh ấy thất vọng không có gì là lạ cả.**

When *that* connects a clause to a noun in the main clause, only **là** is used; **rằng** cannot be used in this construction:

You can drive my car on the *condition that* you will not drive too fast. **Anh có thể lái xe của tôi với điều kiện <u>là</u> anh không lái quá nhanh.**
There's no *proof that* he was at the scene of assault at that time. **Không hề có bằng chứng <u>là</u> anh ta có mặt ở hiện trường nơi xảy ra vụ tấn công vào thời điểm ấy.**

6.15.4 Relative pronoun *that* connects a relative subordinate clause to the main clause. Vietnamese uses **mà** if *that* is not the subject of the subordinate clause:

The movie *that* we watched last night was about the last days of World War 2 in Europe. **Bộ phim <u>mà</u> chúng tôi xem tối qua nói về những ngày cuối cùng của cuộc Chiến tranh Thế giới thứ hai ở châu Âu.**

If *that* functions as the subject of the subordinate clause, Vietnamese does not use anything in that position:

English *that*

> The producer *that* made the movie passed away last year. **Đạo diễn Ø dựng bộ phim ấy mất năm ngoái.**

See 5.8.2. for more about relative clauses.

6.15.5 Adverb of degree *that* placed in front of an adjective or another adverb, which is usually a quantifier, refers to the degree that is stated or suggested. Vietnamese uses **[đến] như thế**:

> We didn't realize that he lives *that* far away from the town. **Chúng tôi không ngờ ông ấy sống cách xa thành phố [đến] như thế.**
>
> She won a lottery and now doesn't know what she would do with *that* much money. **Bà ấy trúng số số rồi bây giờ không biết phải làm gì với số tiền lớn [đến] như thế.**

That with this meaning can be used in a negative statement. Vietnamese uses the negation **không** or **chưa** with **lắm** placed at the end of the statement:

> She didn't take her study *that* seriously. **Cô ấy học hành không nghiêm túc lắm.**
>
> A: When did he leave? **Ông ấy ra về lúc nào?**
> B: Not *that* long ago. **Cách đây chưa lâu lắm.**

Glossary of grammatical terms

ACTIVE VOICE see **voice**

ADJECTIVAL PREDICATE see **predicate**

ADJECTIVE An adjective in Vietnamese is a word which typically can 1) follow a noun to modify it as in the noun phrase **một ngôi nhà lớn** "a big house," **lớn** "big" is the adjective which modifies the noun **nhà** and functions as its attributive; 2) function as the predicate of a sentence, as in the sentence **Ngôi nhà ấy lớn.** "That house is big." The adjective **lớn** is the predicate; 3) follow a verb to modify it as an adverb, as in the verb phrase **làm việc giỏi** "work well," **giỏi** "good" is the adjective that modifies the verb **làm việc**; 4) be intensified by adverbs of degree, as in the phrase **rất lớn** "very big," **lớn lắm** "very big;" 5) permit comparison, as in **lớn hơn** "bigger" (comparative) and **lớn nhất** "biggest" (superlative).

ADJECTIVE PHRASE An adjective phrase is a phrase that has an adjective as its head word. **Rất lớn, lớn lắm, lớn hơn** and **lớn nhất** are adjective phrases whose head word is the adjective **lớn**.

ADVERB Adverbs are a word class whose typical function is to specify the mode of action. In European languages, an adverb can refer to the manner of an action. The verb phrase *to drive slowly* contains the adverb of manner *slowly* that modifies the action of driving. In Vietnamese, this function is performed by adjectives, as in the verb phrase **lái xe chậm** "drive slowly" the adjective **chậm** modifies the action of driving. Vietnamese adverbs chiefly refer to 1) the place where an action occurs, as in the verb phrase **làm việc ở đây** "work here," **ở đây** is the adverb of location; 2) the time when an action occurs, as in the verb phrase **làm việc ban đêm** "work at night," **ban đêm** is the adverb of time; 3) the degree of a quality or an action, as in the adjective phrase **rất lớn** "very big," **rất** is the adverb of degreee intensifying the quality of **lớn**, or as in the verb phrase **rất thích nhạc cổ điển** "like classical music very much," **rất** is the adverb of degree modifying the verb of feelings **thích**; 4) frequency with which an action occurs, as in the verb phrase **thường xuyên tập luyện** "exercise regularly," the adverb of frequency **thường xuyên** modifies the verb **tập luyện**.

ADVERBIAL When an adverb functions as a component of a clause or a sentence, it is called adverbial. In the sentence **Bạn tôi thường xuyên tập luyện nên rất khoẻ** mạnh "My friend regularly exercises, therefore (s)he is very healthy," the adverb of frequency **thường xuyên** is the adverbial of frequency in the main clause and the adverb of degree **rất** is the adverbial of degree in the subordinate clause.

ADVERBIAL CLAUSE An adverbial subordinate clause functions as the adverbial of the main clause. In the complex sentence **Hẹn gặp các bạn ở Hà Nội khi chúng tôi sang tham dự hội thảo** "We'll see you in Hà Nội when we come to participate in the conference," the subordinate clause **khi chúng tôi sang tham dự hội thảo** functions as the adverbial of time for the main clause **hẹn gặp các bạn ở Hà Nội**.

AFFIXATION Affixation is the process of making new words in which a derivational component called *affix* is added to a word. There are two types of affixation in Vietnamese: 1) prefixation, when a derivational component called *prefix* is placed in front of a word. The component **nhà** in the words such as **nhà báo** "journalist," **nhà khoa học** "scientist," **nhà kinh tế** "economist" is a prefix; 2) suffixation, when a derivational component called *suffix* follows a word. The component **trưởng** in the words such as **bộ trưởng** "minister, secretary of a department," **cửa hàng trưởng** "manager of a department store," **hiệu trưởng** "principal, chancellor, president (of a university)" is a suffix.

ANIMATE NOUN An animate noun refers to people and animals as opposed to an inanimate noun.

ASPECT Aspect is a grammatical category of verbs in European languages which typically indicates the duration, repetition, beginning or completion of the action denoted by the verb. Vietnamese has a number of words which are used together with the main verb of a sentence to indicate the notions of the recent past (**vừa mới**), immediate future (**sắp**), duration (**đang**), persistence (**vẫn còn**) or completion (**rồi**) of an action. The aspect markers are placed in different positions of verb phrases.

ATTRIBUTIVE An attributive is a word or a phrase which modifies a noun as the head of a noun phrase. In the following noun phrases (1) **từ điển mới** "new dictionary," (2) **từ điển tiếng Việt** "Vietnamese dictionary," and (3) **từ điển giải thích** "explanatory dictionary" the adjective **mới** "new" in (1), the noun phrase **tiếng Việt** "Vietnamese language" in (2) and the verb **giải thích** "explain" in (3) are attributives which modify the same noun **từ điển** "dictionary."

BORROWING Introducing into a language a word, grammatical construction or morphological element from another language is called borrowing. In this work, borrowing refers to the introduction of words from other languages into Vietnamese. See **loanword**.

CLASSIFIER Classifiers come before some nouns in particular grammatical constructions. Classifiers themselves are nouns, some of which convey abstract meanings and are used in front of other nouns, while the others have their own lexical meanings and can be used either in front of other nouns or as independent nouns. When a numeral appears in front of a noun, a classifier is inserted between the numeral and the noun: **một ngôi nhà** "a house;" or

Glossary of grammatical terms

when a demonstrative adjective follows a noun, the classifier for houses comes in front of the noun: **ngôi** nhà kia "that house."

CLAUSE A clause is a grammatical unit that is smaller than a sentence, but larger than a phrase. This term is used for 1) compound sentences that are composed of two or more main clauses; and 2) complex sentences that are composed of a main clause and a subordinate clause. A main clause is an independent clause that can stand alone as a sentence. A subordinate clause is dependent on the main clause and gives additional information to one word or phrase of the main clause (see nominal clauses and relative clauses) or to the entire main clause (see adverbial clauses).

COLLECTIVE NOUN It is a noun that refers to individuals as a group. Such nouns as *family*, *police*, *team* are collective nouns in English. In Vietnamese, some nouns can refer either to individuals or to individuals as a group. For instance, the noun **sinh viên** "student" in the noun phrase **ba sinh viên ấy** "those three students" refers to the three students as individuals, whereas in the sentence **Sinh viên trường này đang nghỉ hè** "Students at this school are currently on summer vacation" the noun **sinh viên** as a collective noun refers to all the students at a particular school.

COMMENT A comment is the part of a sentence which says something about the topic. "Topic – comment" is another binary characterization of sentence structure that is an alternative to the traditional characterization "subject – predicate." In the sentence **Anh ấy thì tôi quen lâu rồi** "[As for him], I've known him for a long time," the comment **tôi quen lâu rồi** gives some additional informartion to the topic **anh ấy**. See *topic* as the opposite term of *comment*.

COMMON NOUN Common nouns are a subclass of nouns that refer to general concepts and are contrasted with proper nouns that are names of individuals.

COMPLEMENT OF A PREPOSITION A complement of a preposition is a noun or noun phrase that is "completing" a preposition. For instance, in the sentence **Tôi đang đọc một quyển sách về lịch sử** "I'm reading a book on history," the noun **lịch sử** is the complement of the preposition **về** "on, about." In the sentence **Tôi đang đọc một quyển sách về lịch sử Việt Nam thế kỉ 17** "I'm reading a book on Vietnamese history of the 17th century," the noun phrase **lịch sử Việt Nam thế kỉ 17** "Vietnamese history of the 17th century" is the complement of the preposition **về**.

COMPLEX SENTENCE A complex sentence is a sentence that consists of one main clause and at least one subordinate clause. (See **main clause** and **subordinate clause.**)

COMPOUND SENTENCE A compound sentence is a sentence that consists of two or more main clauses. They are connected to each other by a conjunction. For example, the sentence **Chúng tôi đi, còn chị ấy ở lại** "We left, and she remained" consists of two main clauses **chúng tôi đi** and **chị ấy ở lại**. The conjunction **còn** "and" connects the two sentences to one another. The two sentences can function independently as complete sentences: **Chúng tôi đi. Chị ấy ở lại.**

COMPOUNDING Compounding is one of the processes of making new words in which a new word is created by putting together two or more base words. The new word is called a *compound*. **Nhà cửa** "houses" and **nhà ăn** "dining hall" are compounds. The first word is created by putting together the word **nhà** "house" and the word **cửa** "door." The second one – by putting together the word **nhà** and the word **ăn** "eat."

There are two types of compounds: co-ordinate compounds and subordinate compounds. The components of a co-ordinate compound have the same grammatical status and belong to the same word class. In the co-ordinate compound **nhà cửa**, both **nhà** and **cửa** are nouns and grammatically equal to each other. In a subordinate compound, one component depends on the other one grammatically and modifies it. They may be the same word class, but may belong to different word classes as well. In the subordinate compound **nhà ăn**, the verb **ăn** is added to the noun **nhà** and modifies it.

CONJUNCTION A conjunction is a word whose primary function is to connect words or clauses. Conjunctions may be co-ordinating or subordinating. In the phrase **Hà Nội và Sài Gòn**, **và** is the co-ordinating conjunction that connects the two geographical names to each other. In the sentence **Hà Nội và Sài Gòn, nơi sẽ diễn ra SEA Games, đã bắt đầu chuẩn bị đón vận động viên các nước đến tham dự** "Hà Nội and Sài Gòn, where the SEA Games will take place, have already started preparations to welcome athletes from the other countries," **nơi** is a subordinating conjunction which functions as the relative adverb to connect the relative clause **sẽ diễn ra SEA Games** to the proper nouns **Hà Nội** and **Sài Gòn**.

CO-ORDINATE COMPOUND see **compounding**

COUNTABLE NOUN A countable noun denotes individuals which can be counted. In most European languages, a countable noun can distinguish singular and plural: English *table* vs. *tables*, German *Tisch* vs. *Tische*, French *table* vs. *tables*, Russian *стол* vs. *столы*; take a numeral: English *two tables*, German *zwei Tische*, French *deux tables*, Russian *два стола*; or take the indefinite article: English *a table*, German *ein Tisch*, French *une table*. In Vietnamese, a countable noun can take a classifier: **cái bàn**, and the classifier should be used when the noun takes a numeral: **hai cái bàn** "two tables," or a demonstrative adjective: **cái bàn này** "this table."

DECLARATIVE SENTENCE A declarative sentence serves to express a statement, as opposed to interrogative, imperative and exclamatory sentences. **Họ đang họp** "They're having a meeting now" is a declarative sentence.

DEMONSTRATIVE ADJECTIVE Vietnamese has four demonstrative adjectives **này, kia, ấy** and **đó**, that serve as attributives for nouns and correspond to the English demonstrative adjectives *this / these* and *that / those*. In Vietnamese,

Glossary of grammatical terms

Glossary of grammatical terms

a demonstrative adjective follows a noun, whereas in English it precedes a noun: **tháng này** "this month."

DEMONSTRATIVE PRONOUN Vietnamese has four demonstrative pronouns **đây**, **kia**, **đấy** and **đó**. They function as the subject of a sentence and correspond to the English *this* and *that*. For instance, in the sentence **Đây là quyển sách mới về Tây Nguyên** "This is a new book about the central plateaux," **đây** is the demonstrative pronoun.

DETERMINER A determiner is a word which is placed before a noun to refer to the number or quantity. In the noun phrase **tất cả những quyển sách này** "all these books," **tất cả** and **những** are determiners expressing the quantity and plurality respectively.

DIRECT OBJECT see **object**

EXCLAMATORY SENTENCE An exclamatory sentence serves to convey an exclamation, as opposed to declarative, imperative and interrogative sentences. **Họ họp lâu quá!** "What a long meeting they're having!" is an exclamatory sentence.

GENDER Gender is a grammatical category in a number of European languages, which have morphological means to express both the grammatical and natural gender (see 1.1.3). Vietnamese does not have the grammatical category of gender. The natural gender is expressed by the lexical meanings of nouns themselves. For instance, **ông** "grandfather" vs. **bà** "grandmother," or by some lexical means, for instance, the words **nam** "male" and **nữ** "female" in **học sinh nam** "male students" and **học sinh nữ** "female students."

GRAMMATICAL CATEGORY A grammatical category is a category of elements which convey certain grammatical meanings, as opposed to a lexical category. For instance, in Russian the inflection **-a** usually conveys the meaning of the feminine grammatical gender for many word classes. In the sentence **Та хорошая книга была издана** "That good book was published," the inflection **-a** indicates the grammatical feminine gender and the singular of the demonstrative adjective (та), adjective (хорошая), noun (книга), the auxiliary verb (была) and the past participle (издана). Vietnamese does not have the grammatical category of gender. The gender is a lexical category that may be denoted by an animate noun itself. For example, **sinh viên** "student(s)" → **sinh viên nữ / nữ sinh viên** "female student(s)" vs. **sinh viên nam / nam sinh viên** "male student(s)."

HOMONYM Homonyms are words whose forms are the same but whose meanings are different and cannot be connected. They are treated as different lexical units in dictionaries. For instance, the English nouns *ear* "organ of hearing" and *ear* "fruiting spike of a cereal;" or *left* "the opposite of right" and *left* "the past tense and past participle of *to leave*" are homonyms. The Vietnamese adjective **hay** "interesting," conjunction **hay** "or" and adverb of frequency **hay** "often" are homonyms.

IMPERATIVE This term is used in the grammatical classification of sentence types as opposed to declarative, interrogative and exclamatory.

IMPERATIVE SENTENCE An imperative sentence serves to express a command. **Kết thúc cuộc họp đi** "(It's time to) wrap up the meeting" is an imperative sentence.

INANIMATE NOUN An inanimate noun refers to things, not to people, as opposed to an animate noun.

INDIRECT OBJECT see **object**

INFLECTING LANGUAGES An inflecting language is a language whose words change their forms to express different grammatical categories. For instance, Russian is an inflecting language in which the noun книга "book" contains the inflection -а that refers to 1) the feminine gender, 2) the singular, as opposed to the plural книги "books" and 3) the nominative case, as opposed to genitive книги, dative книге, accusative книгу, instrumental книгой and prepositional в книге.

INTERROGATIVE SENTENCE An interrogative sentence serves to express a question, as opposed to declarative, exclamatory and imperative sentences. **Họ vẫn còn họp à?** "Are they still at the meeting?" is an interrogative sentence.

INTRANSITIVE VERB An intransitive verb does not take a direct object. For example, the English verb *to leave* is intransitive in the sentence *He left an hour ago*. However, the same verb *to leave* can be transitive in the sentence *He has left a message for you*, in which the verb *to leave* takes the direct object *message*. See **transitive verb**.

ISOLATING LANGUAGES An isolating language is a language in which all the words are invariable, a grammatical category is represented by a separate word and the syntactic relationships are in many cases shown by the word order. Vietnamese, Chinese and many Southeast Asian languages are isolating languages. For instance, in the Vietnamese sentence **Chị ấy sắp đi** "She is about to leave," the grammatical caterogy of aspect is represented by the word **sắp**. In the question **Chị ấy đi khi nào?** "When did she leave?" the question word **khi nào** is placed at the end of the question to refer to the past tense. In the question **Khi nào chị ấy đi?** "When will she leave?" the question word **khi nào** is fronted to refer to the future tense.

LOANWORD A loanword is a word which is borrowed from another language. Vietnamese has borrowed a considerable number of words from Chinese. They are Chinese loanwords. Vietnamese also has French and English loanwords.

NEGATIVE TRANSFER OF ENGLISH Negative transfer, also called interference, is the influence that knowledge of one language has on the way a person uses another language. In this case, the knowledge of English influences the way English speakers use Vietnamese. Contrastive analysis of Vietnamese and English grammatical constructions, usage and sounds conducted in this work helps English speakers overcome the negative transfer when learning Vietnamese.

NOMINAL CLAUSES A nominal clause is a subordinate clause which functions as the object of the main clause. In the complex sentence **Chúng tôi hiểu rằng chúng tôi không có sự lựa chọn nào khác** "We understand that we don't have any other choice," the subordinate clause **rằng chúng tôi không có sự**

Glossary of grammatical terms

lựa chọn nào khác is a nominal clause which functions as the object of the verb **hiểu** "understand" in the main clause.

NOMINAL PREDICATE see **predicate**

NOUN Nouns are a word class that denotes names of persons, places or things. In most languages, they perform syntactic functions of subject and object. In Vietnamese, in addition to the subject and object, a noun can function as the attributive of another noun as well. For instance, in the phrase **sinh viên đại học** "undergraduate students" the noun **đại học** "college, university" functions as the attributive of the noun **sinh viên**. See also **common nouns, proper nouns, countable nouns, uncountable nouns, collective nouns.**

NOUN PHRASE A noun phrase is a phrase whose head word is a noun. **Ngôi nhà đẹp kia** "that beautiful house" is a noun phrase, in which the noun **nhà** is the head word of the phrase. The English noun phrase *that beautiful house* has the noun *house* as the head.

OBJECT The object is one of the major components of the basic sentence or clause structure. Traditional grammatical analysis distinguishes direct object, which identifies someone or something directly involved in an action or process, and indirect object, whose semantic role is typically that of a recipient. Thus, in the following Vietnamese and English sentences **Chúng tôi tặng cô ấy hoa** "We gave her flowers" and **Chúng tôi tặng hoa cho cô ấy** "We gave flowers to her", **hoa** and *flowers* are the direct object, **cô ấy** and *her* are the indirect object.

OBJECT PREDICATIVE see **predicative**

ONOMATOPOEIC WORDS They are words whose phonetic form is perceived as imitating a sound. The English words *boom, bubble, hiss, splash* are onomatopoeic words. In Vietnamese, many onomatopoeic words are reduplicatives. For instance, **gầm gừ** (dog growling), **leng keng** (sounds made by a bell), **xủng xoảng** (sounds made by metal instruments or utensils) are onomatopoeic reduplicative words.

PARTICLE In European languages, particles are usually short words that perform some grammatical functions but do not easily fall under any of the word classes. In English, the infinitive marker *to* is regarded as a particle; or the postpositional components of verbal phrases such as *against, around, in, into, off, on* in *turn against, turn around, turn in, turn into, turn off, turn on* are particles. Vietnamese is rich in particles that perform different grammatical functions or add different meanings to sentences. For instance, the final particle **à** turns a statement into a question: **Chị ấy không đến** "She didn't come" vs. **Chị ấy không đến à?** "Didn't she come?" The final particle **ạ** makes a statement polite: **Chị ấy không đến ạ** "She didn't come, sir / ma'am."

PASSIVE VOICE see **voice**

PERSONAL PRONOUN This is a subclass of pronouns that distinguishes persons. In English, *I, we, you, she, he, it* and *they* are personal pronouns. Vietnamese has few words which function only as personal pronouns. They are **tôi** "I," **mình** "I," **chúng tôi** "we (exclusive)," **chúng ta** "we (inclusive)," **ta** "we (inclusive)," **chúng mình** "we (exclusive or inclusive), **nó** "she, he, it," **họ** "they," **chúng nó** "they." On the other hand, most kinship terms can function as personal pronouns in Vietnamese.

PHRASE A phrase is a grammatical unit that comes between a word and a clause in the hierachy of grammatical units. A phrase has a word of a specific word class as its head. There are noun phrase, verb phrase, adjective phrase, adverb phrase and prepositional phrase.

PLURAL This is a semantic feature that refers to more than one individuals. In European languages, a noun, for example, uses different inflections to refer to the plurality vs. singularity: English *houses* vs. *house*, German *Häuser* vs. *Haus*, French *maisons* vs. *maison*, Russian *дома* vs. *дом*. Vietnamese uses the plural markers **các** and **những** that come before the noun. These plural markers convey different meanings of the plurality and are not interchangeable in most instances.

POSSESSIVE PRONOUN A possessive pronoun denotes a person who "possesses" something. In the English noun phrase *his car*, *his* is the possessive pronoun that refers to him who possesses the car. Vietnamese uses **của** in front of a personal pronoun to form a possessive pronoun as in the noun phrase **xe của anh ấy** "his car."

PREDICATE The ppredicate is one of two major constituents of a clause or sentence that represents what is said of the subject. The subject is the other major constituent. In Vietnamese, the predicate can be 1) verbal, when it is expressed by a verb or verb phrase. In the sentence **Họ vừa mới đến** "They have just arrived," the verb phrase **vừa mới đến** serves as the verbal predicate; 2) adjectival, when it is expressed by an adjective or adjective phrase. In the sentence **Thành phố này nổi tiếng về các di tích lịch sử** "This city is famous for its historic sites," the adjective phrase **nổi tiếng về các di tích lịch sử** serves as the adjectival predicate; 3) nominal, when it is expressed by the verb **là** followed by a noun or noun phrase. In the sentence **Thành phố này là một trung tâm công nghiệp quan trọng** "This city is an important industrial center," the verb **là** together with the noun phrase **một trung tâm công nghiệp quan trọng** serve as the nominal predicate.

PREDICATIVE A predicative forms a part of the predicate and has a direct relation to the subject or object. In the sentence **Quyển sách này hay** "This book is good," the adjective **hay** is the subject predicative, as opposed to its attributive function in the noun phrase **quyển sách hay này** "this good book," where the adjective **hay** serves as the attributive of the noun **sách**. In the sentence **Tuyết trắng làm cho khu rừng trở nên thơ mộng** "The white snow turned the forest into a picturesque scene," the phrase **trở nên thơ mộng** "become picturesque" is the object predicative, which is the predicate of the object **khu rừng**.

PREFIX see **affixation**

PREFIXATION see **affixation**

PREPOSITION A preposition come before a noun or noun phrase to form a prepositional phrase. Prepositional phrases convey different meanings, including location:

Glossary of grammatical terms

Glossary of grammatical terms

ngoài Hà Nội "in Hà Nội," **trong Sài Gòn** "in Sài Gòn;" time: **vào năm 2017** "in the year of 2017;" cause: **do ngập lụt** "owing to flooding;" purpose: **vì lợi ích của xã hội** "for the good of society;" means: **bằng máy bay** "by airplane."

PRONOUN A pronoun is used to substitute for a noun or noun phrase. The word class of pronouns in Vietnamese includes personal pronouns (**tôi, nó,** etc.), possessive pronouns (**của tôi, của nó,** etc.), demonstrative pronouns (**đây, đấy,** etc.), interrogative pronouns (**ai, gì,** etc.) and relative pronoun (**mà**).

PROPER NOUN Proper nouns are a subclass of nouns that are names of individual persons or places. Proper nouns are opposed to common nouns that refer to general concepts.

QUANTIFIER A quantifier refers to how much or how many we are talking about: **nhiều** "much, many," **ít** "little, few," **mấy** "several," **vài** "a few" are examples of quantifiers in Vietnamese.

REDUPLICATION Reduplication is the process of making new words in which two or more syllables of a new word contain phonetic resemblance to each other.

REDUPLICATIVES A new word formed by means of reduplication is called a reduplicative.

RELATIVE CLAUSE A relative clause is a subordinate clause that modifies the noun or noun phrase in the main clause. In the sentence **Thành phố mà chúng ta sắp đến thăm có nhiều di tích lịch sử thời nhà Nguyễn** "The city that we are going to visit has many historic sites built during the Nguyễn dynasty," the subordinate clause **mà chúng ta sắp đến thăm** modifies the noun **thành phố** "city" in the main clause.

SEMANTICS Semantics is a branch of linguistics which focuses on the study of meaning.

SEMANTIC GROUPS OF WORDS Words of the same word class may be organized in different groups based on their lexical meanings. For instance, the word class of verbs may be divided into semantic groups of verbs of motion, verbs of feelings, verbs of speaking, etc.

SIMPLE SENTENCE A simple sentence is a sentence that does not include another sentence or clause, as opposed to a compound sentence and a complex sentence.

SUBJECT The subject is one of two major constituents of a clause or sentence that represents the "doer" of an action, as opposed to the predicate.

SUBJECT PREDICATIVE see **predicative**

SUBORDINATE COMPOUND see **compounding**

SUFFIX see **affixation**

SUFFIXATION see **affixation**

SYLLABLE A syllable consists of a vowel that can be produced in isolation, either alone or accompanied by one or more units that are not vowels. In European languages, the syllable is a unit of pronunciation. In isolating languages, including Vietnamese, most syllables have their own lexical meanings, therefore the syllable is not only a unit of pronunciation but also a unit of semantics and grammar.

Glossary of grammatical terms

Syntactic function This is a function which a word performs in a sentence.

Syntax Syntax is the study of the rules governing the way words are combined to form sentences. In Vietnamese, as well as in other isolating languages, one of the ways of indicating the syntactic relations between words in a sentence is word order.

Tense Tense is a grammatical category of the verb in European languages which refers to the time of situation. Tense is not a grammatical category of the Vietnamese verb. The time of situation in Vietnamese is indicated by separate words such as **đã** or **sẽ**, by the time expression(s) in a sentence, including the adverbial of time, and by the context.

Topic A topic is the part of a sentence about which something is said. The topic is usually a person, a thing or an event. In the sentence **Những hôm trời rất lạnh anh ấy cũng đi bơi** "He's going swimming even on very chilly days," **những hôm trời rất lạnh** is the event which is the topic of the sentence, and the remainder is the comment. See *comment* as the opposite term of *topic*.

Transitive verb A transitive verb takes a direct object. For instance, the English verb *to leave* is transitive in the sentence *He left a message for you*. In this sentence, the verb *to leave* takes the direct object message. The same verb *to leave* can be intransitive in the sentence *He left an hour ago*. See **intransitive verb**.

Uncountable noun An uncountable noun does not denote individuals that can be counted. In English, such nouns as *information, luggage, music* are uncountable. In Vietnamese, **tin tức** "information," **hành lí** "luggage," **âm nhạc** "music" are uncountable as well. Uncountable nouns cannot take a numeral. Usually, another noun should be inserted between the number and the uncountable noun: *a piece of information, two pieces of luggage, some pieces of music*. In Vietnamese, either another noun is inserted between the number and the uncountable noun: **ba kiện hành lí** "three pieces of luggage," **một nền âm nhạc** "the music of . . ."; or a different word conveying the same meaning is used instead: **một tin** "a piece of information, **hai tin** "two pieces of information." **Tin** is used instead of **tin tức**.

Verb The word class of verbs refers to the words denoting actions or processes. In a Vietnamese sentence, a verb can perform the functions of the predicate, subject, object and modifier of a noun as its attributive.

Verb phrase A verb phrase is a phrase whose head is a verb.

Verbal predicate see **predicate**

Voice Voice is a grammatical category of the verb in European languages by which forms of the verb are opposed as active and passive. Although voice is not a grammatical category of the Vietnamese verb, the language uses certain constructions containing the voice markers **được, bị** and **do** to denote the passive voice.

Word class A word class (or part of speech) is a class of words that share similar grammatical and syntactic characteristics.

Word-formation Word-formation is the process of forming new words from existing words or segments of words. In Vietnamese, there are four major processes of word-formation: compounding, affixation, reduplication and borrowing.

Grammar index

Items in roman type refer to general grammatical concepts. Items in boldface type indicate the Vietnamese words and phrases. Items in italic type denote the English words and phrases whose Vietnamese equivalents are introduced in the entry. Numbers with dots, for example 1.1.1, refer to the entry in a chapter. Numbers in the parentheses () show the page where the item is introduced.

a bit and Vietnamese equivalents 3.2.1 (109)
a little and Vietnamese equivalents 3.2.1 (109)
a little bit and Vietnamese equivalents 3.2.1 (109)
à 5.3.1.7 (169), 5.6.1.1 (196)
ạ 5.6.2.1 (200)
abstract nouns 1.2.2 (4)
addition 1.3.1.1.4 (9)
adjectives (107–118)
adjective + aspect / tense marker 3.2.4 (113)
adjective + comparison marker 3.2.3 (111–113)
adjective + number + weight / length / height / temperature measures 3.2.6 (115)
adjective + object 3.2.5 (114)
adjective + preposition + object 3.2.5 (114)
adjective + verb of motion 3.2.7 (116)
adverb + verb 2.6 (75–81)
adverb of degree + adjective 3.2.1 (108–111)
adverbial clauses 5.8.3 (213–228)
adverbials 5.1.1.3 (153–160)
adverbial of cause 5.1.1.3.6 (158)
adverbial of degree 5.1.1.3.5 (157–158)
adverbial of manner 5.1.1.3.1 (154)
adverbial of means 5.1.1.3.8 (159)
adverbial of place 5.1.1.3.2 (154–155)
adverbial of purpose 5.1.1.3.7 (159)
adverbial of time 5.1.1.3.3 (155–156)
adverbs of degree 1.3.3.2 (34–35), 2.6.1 (75–78)
adverbs of frequency 2.6.2 (79–81)
affixation 4.2.2 (124–129)
after 5.8.3.2 (214)
ai 5.3.2.7 (177)
ai – người ấy 5.8.3.10 (225–226)
all 1.3.2.2 (27–31)
also 6.2 (230–231)
and with different functions 5.7.1 (204–205), 6.1.4 (230)

approximation 1.3.1.1.8 (16)
as a matter of fact 5.6.1.10 (199)
as if 5.8.3.8 (225)
as though 5.8.3.8 (225)
as well 6.2 (230–231)
aspect 2.3.2 (53–61)
aspect / tense marker + adjective 3.2.4 (113)
attributive 1.3.3 (32)
âm lịch lunar calendar **dương lịch** solar calendar 1.3.1.1.7.3 (11–12)
ấy 1.3.3.3 (35), 5.6.1.2 (196), 5.6.2.2 (200), 6.15.1.1 (253)
bản 1.3.1.2 (21)
bạn as personal pronoun 1.3.3.5.6 (46)
bao giờ 5.3.2.3 (173–174)
bao nhiêu 5.3.2.6 (176)
bao nhiêu là 5.5.16 (189–190)
bảo 2.4.3 (66, 68)
bằng 1.3.1.1.4 (9), 3.2.3.4 (112), 5.1.1.3.8 (159)
bắt 2.4.3 (66)
bất cứ 5.5.3 (182–183), 5.8.3.11.1 (226–227)
bất kì 5.5.3 (182–183), 5.8.3.11.1 (226–227)
before 5.8.3.2 (214)
biến mất 2.8.7 (93)
biến thành 2.9 (93)
biến ... thành 2.9 (93–94)
borrowing 4.2.4 (137–151)
both ... and ... 5.7.6 (207–208), 5.7.7 (208)
bộ 1.3.1.2 (21)
bởi vì 5.8.3.5 (222–223)
bức 1.3.1.2 (21)
cả 1.3.2.2.1 (27–28)
cả ... và ... 5.7.7 (208)
các 1.1.2 (2), 1.3.2 (26–27), 1.3.2.2.2 (28), 1.3.3.5.5 (45), 1.3.3.5.6 (46)
cái 1.3.1.2 (20–21)
cái gì 5.3.2.8 (177–178)
cảm thấy 2.4.4 (68–69)

Grammar index

can 2.10.2 (95)
càng ... càng ... 5.7.5 (207), 5.8.3.9 (225)
cardinal numbers 1.3.1.1.1 (5–8)
causative verbs 2.4.3 (65–68)
căn 1.3.1.2 (21)
cặp 1.3.1.2 (21)
cầm 2.4.3 (66)
cần 2.10.1 (94–95)
cây 1.3.1.2 (21)
chả 5.2.2.3 (164)
chắc chắn là 5.1.1.3.10 (160)
chăng 5.3.3 (179)
chẳng 5.2.2.3 (164)
chẳng lẽ 5.3.3 (179)
chẳng nhẽ 5.3.3 (179)
chỉ 2.6.1.4 (78–79)
chỉ ... là ... 5.5.13 (187)
chia 1.3.1.1.4 (9)
chiếc 1.3.1.2 (20–21)
chính (emphatic) 5.5.10 (186)
cho 2.4.3 (66), 6.12 (246–249)
cho nên 5.8.3.6 (223), 6.14.3.1 (252)
cho phép 2.4.3 (66)
cho rằng / là 2.4.4 (68)
chục 1.3.1.1.1 (7)
chuyển 2.7.4 (88)
chuyện 6.15.3 (254)
chớ 2.11.9 (103–104)
chứ 5.3.1.8 (170), 5.6.2.3 (201)
chứ không ... 5.7.4 (207)
chưa 2.3.2.3 (56)
chưa bao giờ 2.6.2 (79)
chưa ... đã ... 5.5.7 (184)
classification of sentences 5.1.2 (160–161)
classifiers 1.3.1.2 (20–24)
clock time 1.3.1.1.7 (14–16)
có 2.2.2 (52–53), 2.8.1 (89), 2.11.7 (102–103), 2.11.9 (103), 5.5.4 (183), 5.5.9 (185–186)
có ... không 5.3.1.1 (166)
có ... mới ... 5.5.5 (183)
có phải ... không 5.3.1.2 (166), 5.3.1.6 (168–169)
có thể 2.10.2 (95)
coi 2.4.5 (73)
collective noun 1.2.3.3 (5)
common noun 1.2.1 (2–4)
comparative of the adjectives 1.3.3.1.1.2 (34)
comparison 3.2.3 (112–113)
complex sentences 5.8 (209–228)
compound sentences 5.7 (204–209)
compounding 4.2.1 (120–124)
con 1.3.1.2 (22)
còn 2.3.2.4 (56–57), 2.8.2 (90), 6.1 (229–230)
concessive clauses 5.8.3.4 (221–222)
concrete nouns 1.2.2 (4)
conditional clauses 5.8.3.3 (216–221)
constituents of a sentence 5.1.1 (152–160)
co-ordinate compounds 4.2.1.1 (120–121)
countable noun 1.2.3 (4–5)

couple 1.3.1.1.10 (19)
cộng 1.3.1.1.4 (9)
con 1.3.1.2 (22)
củ 1.3.1.2 (22)
của 1.3.3.5.2 (39–40), 5.2.1.3 (162)
cũng 1.3.2.2.1 (28), 5.5.1 (181–182), 5.5.12 (187), 5.8.3.4 (221), 5.8.3.11.1 (226), 5.8.3.11.2 (227), 6.2 (230–231)
cuộc 1.3.1.2 (22)
cuốn 1.3.1.2 (22)
cứ 2.11.2 (99–100)
dạ 5.3.1.3 (167), 5.6.1.3 (196–197)
dám 2.10.3 (96)
dare and Vietnamese equivalents 2.10.3 (96)
dates 1.3.1.1.7 (7–14)
dates of a month and a year 1.3.1.1.7.7 (13)
dạy / dậy 2.4.3 (66)
days 1.3.1.1.7.5 (12)
days of the week 1.3.1.1.7.6 (12–13)
dăm 1.3.1.1.8 (17)
dăm ba 1.3.1.1.8 (17)
decimals 1.3.1.1.3 (8–9)
declarative sentences 5.2 (161–165)
demonstrative adjectives 1.3.3.3 (35–36)
demonstrative pronouns 5.1.1.3.2 (154–155), 5.2.1.3 (162)
determiners 1.3.2.2 (27–31)
diễn ra 2.8.6 (92–93)
division 1.3.1.1.4 (9)
division of the day time 1.3.1.1.7.8 (13)
double negative with meaning of affirmation 5.2.2.4 (164–165)
dozens of, hundreds of, thousands of, millions of in Vietnamese 1.3.1.1.1 (8)
dù 5.8.3.11.2 (227), 5.8.3.11.3 (228)
đã 2.3.1 (54), 2.11.6 (102)
đã ... lại [còn] ... [nữa] 5.7.8 (208–209)
đám 1.3.1.2 (22)
đang 2.3.1 (54–55), 2.3.2.5 (57), 5.8.3.2 (216)
đằng ấy as personal pronoun 1.3.3.5.6 (46)
đâu 5.3.2.2 (172–173)
đâu – đấy 5.8.3.10 (225–226)
đây 1.3.3.3 (35), 5.1.1.3.2 (154–155), 5.2.1.3 (162) 5.6.2.4 (201)
đấy 1.3.3.3 (35), 5.1.1.3.2 (154–155), 5.2.1.3 (162), 5.6.2.5 (201–202), 6.15.2.1 (253)
đem 2.7.4 (88)
đẹp 6.11.3 (244–245)
đề nghị 2.4.3 (66)
để 2.4.3 (66), 5.8.3.7.1 (224), 6.12.2.8 (248), 6.14.3.2 (252)
để làm gì 5.3.2.5 (175–176)
đến 2.7.2 (81–82)
đến nỗi 5.8.3.6 (223)
đều 1.3.2.3 (31–32)
đi 2.7.1 (81–82), 2.7.2 (82), 2.11.3 (100), 3.2.7 (116)
đi chăng nữa 5.8.3.11.2 (227)
điều 6.15.2.2 (254)
định 2.10.4 (96)

267

Grammar index

đó 1.3.3.3 (35), 5.1.1.3.2 (154–155), 5.2.1.3 (162), 6.15.1.1 (253), 6.15.2.1 (253)
đôi khi 2.6.2 (80)
đối với 6.12.2.9 (248)
đủ 3.2.1 (108–109)
đưa 2.7.4 (88)
đừng 2.11.7 (102–103)
được 2.12 (104–105), 6.3 (231–233)
được không 5.3.1.9 (170–171)
đương nhiên là 5.1.1.3.10 (160)
either (in a negative statement) 6.2 (230)
either . . . or . . . 5.3.1.11 (171–172), 5.7.3 (206)
emphatic constructions 5.5 (181–195)
emphatic constructions "topic – comment" 5.5.18 (193–195)
emphatic negative declarative sentences 5.5.17 (190–193)
English articles *a* and *the* and Vietnamese classifiers 1.3.1.2.2 (25)
entire 1.3.2.2 (27–31)
even 6.1.3 (230)
even if 5.8.3.4 (221)
even though 5.8.3.4 (221)
every 1.3.2.2 (27–31)
exclamatory sentences 5.4 (180–181)
existence sentence 2.2.2 (52–53), 5.1.1.3.2 (155), 5.1.1.3.3 (156)
fewer than 1.3.1.1.9 (18–19)
final particles 5.6.2 (200–204)
for 6.12 (246–249)
form of a noun 1.1.1 (1)
fractions 1.3.1.1.3 (8–9)
functions of nouns and noun phrases 1.4 (48–49)
gấp 1.3.1.1.5 (10)
gender of a noun 1.1.3 (2)
gì 1.3.3.4 (36–37), 5.3.2.8 (177–178)
giá [như] 5.8.3.3.3 (218–219)
giả sử 5.8.3.3.2 (218)
giải thích 2.4.4 (68, 70)
giỏi 6.11.2 (244)
giúp / giúp đỡ 2.4.3 (66)
gọi 2.4.5 (72)
good 6.11 (243–245)
half and *and a half* 1.3.1.1.6 (10)
hàng chục, hàng trăm, hàng nghìn, hàng vạn, hàng triệu 1.3.1.1.1 (8)
hardly . . . when . . . 5.5.7 (184)
hay 2.6.2 (79, 80–81), 5.3.1.10 (171)
hay as three homonyms 2.6.2 (80–81)
hay [là] 5.3.1.10 (171), 5.7.3 (206)
hãy 2.11.1 (99), 2.11.6 (102)
hãy còn 2.3.2.6 (57–58)
hắn as personal pronoun 1.3.3.5.6 (46)
hẳn 2.3.2.10 (61)
hằng 2.11.6 (102)
here 5.1.1.3.2 (154)
hễ after negations không and chưa 5.5.17.1 (190)
hễ cứ . . . là / thì 5.8.3.3.5 (219)
hết 2.3.2.9 (60–61), 2.8.3 (90)
hết vs. xong 2.3.2.9 (60)
hết sức 3.2.1 (108–109)
hiếm khi 2.6.2 (80)
hiểu 2.4.4 (68)
hoặc [là] 5.3.1.10 (171), 5.7.3 (206)
hỏi 2.4.4 (68)
hòn 1.3.1.2 (22)
hour tiếng vs. giờ 1.3.1.1.7.9 (16)
however 5.8.3.3.7 (220), 5.8.3.4 (222), 5.8.3.11 (226–227)
hôm nào 5.3.2.3 (173–174)
hở 5.6.2.6 (202)
hơi 3.2.1 (108–109)
hơn 3.2.3.3 (112)
hứa 2.4.4 (68, 71)
"idiomatic" adjectives (adjective + noun) 3.2.5 (114–115)
if 5.8.3.3.1 (216–218), 6.13 (249–250)
if not 5.8.3.3.7 (220)
if only 5.8.3.3.3 (218–219)
imperatives 2.11 (98–104)
in case 5.8.3.3.9 (221)
in the world 5.3.2.4 (175)
indeed 5.6.2.11 (203–204)
indefinite adverbs 5.1.1.3.9 (159–160)
indefinite pronouns 5.1.1.3.9 (159–160)
initial particles 5.6.1 (196–200)
interrogative sentences 5.3 (166–179)
ít 1.3.1.1.8 (17–18)
ít khi 2.6.2 (80)
just vs. chỉ 2.6.1.4 (78–79)
kẻo 5.8.3.3.7 (220)
kể 2.4.4 (68, 70)
khá 3.2.1 (108)
khác 3.3.3 (118)
khẩu 1.3.1.2 (22)
khi 5.8.2.2 (212–213), 5.8.3.2 (214–216)
khi nào 5.3.2.3 (173–174)
khỏi as notional verb 5.2.2.4 (165)
khỏi as preposition used with ra 2.7.2 (86)
không . . . mà . . . 5.7.4 (207)
không bao giờ 2.6.2 (79)
không chỉ . . . mà cả . . . 5.5.8 (184–185)
không chỉ . . . mà còn . . . 5.5.8 (184–185)
không những . . . mà còn . . . 5.5.8 (184–185)
khuyên 2.4.3 (67), 2.10.6 (98)
khuyến khích 2.4.3 (66)
kia 1.3.3.3 (36), 5.1.1.3.2 (154–155), 5.2.1.3 (162), 6.15.1.2 (253), 6.15.2.1 (253)
kìa 6.15.2.2 (254)
kiện 1.3.1.2 (22)
kinship terms 1.3.3.5.3 (41–42)
là 2.2.1 (51–52), 5.8.1.1 (209–210), 6.15.3 (254)
là vs. làm before nouns indicating occupations 2.2.1 (52)
lá 1.3.1.2 (22)

Grammar index

lại 2.7.2 (81–82), 3.2.7 (116), 5.3.2.4 (174–175), 6.4 (234–236)
làm gì 5.3.2.5 (175–176)
làm sao được 5.3.3 (179)
lăm 1.3.1.1.1 (6)
lắm 3.2.2.1 (110)
lấy vs. *to take* 2.4.2.2 (65)
lẻ 1.3.1.1.1 (7)
lẽ nào 5.3.3 (179)
lên 2.7.2 (82–84, 86–87), 3.2.7 (116)
lí do 5.8.2.2 (213)
linh 1.3.1.1.1 (7)
little wonder 5.6.1.7 (198)
lo 2.4.4 (68)
loanwords from Chinese 4.2.4.1 (137–148)
loanwords from English 4.2.4.3 (150–151)
loanwords from French 4.2.4.2 (148–150)
lunar calendar **âm lịch** solar calendar **dương lịch** 1.3.1.1.7.3 (11–12)
luôn 2.6.2 (79)
luôn luôn 2.6.2 (79)
mà 2.11.7 (103), 5.6.1.4 (197), 5.6.2.7 (202), 5.7.2 (205–206), 5.8.2.1 (212), 5.8.3.3.1 (217), 5.8.3.3.4 (219), 5.8.3.7.2 (224), 6.5 (236–238), 6.15.4 (254)
mãi 5.5.14 (187–188)
main functions of adjectives and adjective phrases 3.3 (116–118)
main functions of nouns and noun phrases (48–49)
main functions of verbs and verb phrases 2.13 (105–106)
main meanings of reduplicatives 4.2.3.7 (135–136)
mang 2.7.4 (88–89)
manner clauses 5.8.3.8 (225)
mass nouns 1.2.3.2 (5)
may 2.10.2 (95)
mày as personal pronoun 1.3.3.5.6 (46)
mặc dù 5.8.3.4 (221)
mất 2.8.4 (91)
mấy 1.3.1.1.8 (17), 5.3.2.6 (176)
mình 1.3.3.5.3 (40, 43), 2.4.5 (73)
modal verbs 2.10 (94–98)
mọi 1.3.2.2.3 (28–29)
món 1.3.1.2 (22–23)
months 1.3.1.1.7.3 (10–11)
more than 1.3.1.1.9 (18–19)
mỗi 1.3.2.2.4 (29–30)
mồng 1.3.1.1.7.7 (12)
một / hai / ba lần 2.6.2 (79)
một ít 1.3.1.1.8 (17)
một khi 5.8.3.2 (216)
một số 1.3.1.1.8 (17)
một vài 1.3.1.1.8 (17)
mời 2.4.3 (68), 2.11.5 (101–102)
mới 2.3.2.1 (55), 5.5.6 (183–184), 6.6 (239–240)
mới . . . đã . . . 5.5.7 (184)
multiple 1.3.1.1.4 (9)

mùng 1.3.1.1.7.7 (12)
muốn 2.10.5 (97)
muốn . . . phải . . . 5.8.3.3.8 (220)
mươi 1.3.1.1.1 (6–7), 1.3.1.1.8 (17)
mười 1.3.1.1.1 (6)
names and addresses on envelope 1.2.1 (4)
names of languages in Vietnamese 1.3.3.5.1 (38–39)
nào 1.3.3.4 (36–37), 5.3.2.8 (177–178), 5.6.1.5 (197)
nào – ấy 5.8.3.10 (225–226)
nationalities in Vietnamese 1.3.3.5.1 (38–39)
nay 1.3.1.1.7.8 (14)
này 1.3.1.1.7.8 (14), 1.3.3.3 (35), 5.6.2.8 (203), 6.15.1.2 (253)
need 2.10.1 (94–95)
negative declarative sentences 5.2.2 (162–165)
neither 5.5.17.3 (192–193)
neither . . . nor . . . 5.5.17.3 (193)
never 5.5.17.3 (193)
nên 2.10.6 (97–98), 5.8.3.6 (223), 6.14.3.1 (252)
nền 1.3.1.2 (23)
nếu 5.8.3.3.1 (216–218), 6.13 (249–250)
ngàn 1.3.1.1.1 (7–8)
ngay 5.5.11 (187)
ngay cả 5.5.12 (187)
ngay cả khi 5.8.3.4 (221)
ngày bao nhiêu 5.3.2.3 (173–174)
ngày mùng mấy 5.3.2.3 (173–174)
ngày nào 5.3.2.3 (173–174)
nghe 2.4.4 (68, 70–71)
nghĩ 2.4.4 (68)
nghìn 1.3.1.1.1 (7–8)
ngon 6.11.3 (244)
ngôi 1.3.1.2 (23)
nguyên nhân 5.8.2.2 (213)
người 1.3.1.2 (23)
người ta as personal pronoun 1.3.3.5.6 (46)
nhắc 2.4.4 (68, 69)
nhăm 1.3.1.1.1 (6)
nhằm 5.8.3.7.3 (224)
nhân 1.3.1.1.4 (9)
nhé 2.11.4 (100–101)
nhỉ 5.6.2.9 (203)
nhiều 1.3.1.1.8 (17–18)
nhìn 2.4.4 (68, 69)
nhờ 2.4.3 (68)
nhớ 2.4.4 (68, 69)
nhỡ 5.8.3.3.9 (221)
như 3.2.3.4 (112), 5.8.3.8 (225)
như thế 6.14.1.1 (250–251)
như vậy 6.14.1.1 (250–251)
nhưng 5.7.2 (205–206), 5.8.3.4 (221)
những 1.1.2 (2), 1.3.2 (26–27), 5.3.2.9 (179), 5.5.9 (185–186)
No 5.3.1.3 (167)
no matter 5.8.3.11.3 (227–228)
no one 5.5.17.3 (192)

Grammar index

no sooner ... than ... 5.5.7 (184)
no wonder 5.6.1.7 (198)
nobody 5.5.17.3 (192)
nói 2.4.4 (68, 71–72)
nói chuyện 2.4.4 (71)
nói thật là 5.1.1.3.10 (160)
nominal clauses 5.8.1 (209–211)
none 5.5.17.3 (192)
nor 5.5.17.3 (192–193)
not always and Vietnamese equivalents 2.6.2 (80)
not only ... but also ... 5.5.8 (184–185)
nothing 5.5.17.3 (192)
nouns (1–49)
nowhere 5.5.17.3 (193)
nơi 5.8.2.2 (212–213)
numbers 1.3.1.1 (5–8)
nửa 1.3.1.1.6 (10)
ở đâu 5.3.2.1 (172)
object 2.4 (62)
object and object predicative 5.1.1.2 (152–153)
oh really? 5.6.1.8 (198–199)
on earth 5.3.2.4 (175)
once 5.8.3.2 (216)
only vs. **chỉ** 2.6.1.4 (78–79)
only vs. **mới** referring to one's age 2.6.1.4 (79)
onomatopoeic words 4.2.3.7.4 (137)
or else 5.8.3.3.7 (220)
ordinal numbers 1.3.1.1.2 (8)
otherwise 5.8.3.3.7 (220)
over 1.3.1.1.9 (18–19)
Oxford comma 5.7.1 (205)
ôi 5.4.1 (180)
ơi 5.6.1.6 (197–198)
ơi là 5.4.4 (181)
pair 1.3.1.1.10 (19)
passive voice 2.12 (104–105)
people as personal pronoun 1.3.3.5.6 (46)
percentage 1.3.1.1.3 (8–9)
personal pronouns 1.3.3.5.3 (40–46)
personal pronouns in the plural 1.3.3.5.5 (45)
phải 2.10.7 (98), 6.7 (240)
phải chăng 5.3.3 (179)
phải không 5.3.1.5 (168)
pho 1.3.1.2 (23)
phonetic symmetry 2.5.3 (74), 2.5.4 (74–75), 4.2.1.1 (121), 4.2.4.1.6 (145–148)
place clauses 5.8.3.1 (213–214)
plural markers 1.3.2.1 (26–27)
positive declarative sentences 5.2.1 (161–162)
positive of the adjectives 1.3.3.1.1.1 (33)
preference 2.6.1.2 (76–77)
prefixation 4.2.2.1 (125–128)
proper noun 1.2.1 (2–4)
proportion clauses 5.8.3.9 (225)
purpose clauses 5.8.3.7 (224)
qua 2.7.2 (81–83)

quá 1.3.1.1.9 (18), 3.1.3 (108), 3.2.2.1 (110), 5.4.1 (180)
quả 1.3.1.2 (23)
quadrisyllabic template 4.2.3.7.2 (136), 4.2.4.1.6 (145–148)
quantifier 1.3.1.1.8 (17–18)
quên 2.4.4 (68, 69)
quyển 1.3.1.2 (23)
ra 2.7.2 (82, 83, 86–88), 3.2.7 (116)
ra lệnh 2.4.3 (66, 67)
rằng 5.8.1.1 (209–210), 6.15.3 (254)
rất 3.2.1 (108), 3.2.2.1 (110)
reason clauses 5.8.3.5 (222–223)
reciprocal 2.6.2 (79, 106)
reduplication 4.2.3 (130–137)
relative clauses 5.8.2 (211–213)
result clauses 5.8.3.6 (223)
rhetorical questions 5.3.3 (179)
rõ ràng là 5.1.1.3.10 (160)
rồi 2.3.2.7 (58–59), 5.6.2.10 (503), 6.8 (241)
rưởi 1.3.1.1.6 (10)
rưỡi 1.3.1.1.6 (10)
sai 2.4.3 (66)
sang 2.7.2 (81–83)
sao 5.3.2.4 (174–175)
sao – vậy 5.8.3.10 (225–226)
sau 5.8.3.2 (214)
sau khi 5.8.3.2 (214)
sắp 2.3.2.2 (56)
scarcely ... when ... 5.5.7 (184)
sẽ 2.3.1 (54)
seasons 1.3.1.1.7.2 (10)
second + superlative adjective + noun + next to / after + noun 1.3.3.1.1.4 (34)
sentence particles 5.6 (195–204)
sentences (152–228)
serial comma 5.7.1 (205)
similarity clauses 5.8.3.10 (225–226)
small wonder 5.6.1.7 (198)
so 6.14 (250–253)
so ... that ... 5.8.3.6 (223)
so với 3.2.3.5 (113)
song 5.8.3.4 (222)
sợ 2.4.4 (68, 69)
still 6.1.2 (229), 6.1.3 (2300)
subject and predicate 5.1.1.1 (152)
subordinate compounds 4.2.1.2 (121–124)
subtraction 1.3.1.1.4 (9)
such ... that ... 5.8.3.6 (223)
suffixation 4.2.2.2 (128–129)
superlative of the adjectives 1.3.3.1.1.3 (34)
tại sao 5.3.2.4 (174–175), 5.8.2.2 (213)
tại vì 5.8.3.5 (222–223)
tao as personal pronoun 1.3.3.5.6 (46)
tấm 1.3.1.2 (23)
tận 5.5.15 (188–189)
tất cả 1.3.2.2.2 (28)
tất nhiên là 5.1.1.3.10 (160)
tense 2.3.1 (53–55)
tên 1.3.1.2 (23)

Grammar index

thà 2.6.1.2 (77)
tháng mấy 5.3.2.3 (173–174)
thanh 1.3.1.2 (23)
thành thử 5.8.3.6 (223)
thảo nào 5.6.1.7 (198)
that 5.8.1.1 (209–210), 6.15 (253–255)
thật 3.2.2.1 (111), 5.6.2.11 (203–204)
thật không may là 5.1.1.3.10 (160)
thật là 3.2.2.1 (111), 5.4.3 (180)
thấy 2.4.4 (68)
the . . . the . . . 5.7.5 (207), 5.8.3.9 (225)
the reason why 5.8.2.2 (213)
then used after *if* 5.8.3.3.1 (217)
there 5.1.1.3.2 (154)
there is, there are 2.2.2 (52), 5.1.1.3.2 (155), 5.1.1.3.3 (156)
thế 3.2.2.2 (111), 5.6.2.5 (201)
thế à 5.6.1.8 (198–199)
thế là 6.14.3.3 (252)
thế nào 6.14.3.3 (252)
thế nào – thế ấy 5.8.3.10 (225–226)
thế nào được 5.3.3 (179)
thế thì 5.6.1.9 (199)
thì 5.6.1.10 (199), 5.8.3.3.1 (217), 5.8.3.10 (226), 5.8.3.11.2 (227), 6.9 (242–243)
thì giờ vs. thời gian 1.3.1.1.7.10 (16)
thỉnh thoảng 2.6.2 (79, 80)
thời gian vs. thì giờ 1.3.1.1.7.10 (16)
thứ 1.3.1.1.2 (8), 1.3.1.1.7.6 (12–13), 1.3.1.2 (23)
thứ mấy 5.3.2.3 (173–174)
thưa 5.6.1.11 (199–200)
thực ra 5.1.1.3.10 (160)
thường 2.6.2 (79)
thường xuyên 2.6.2 (79)
thuyết phục 2.4.3 (66)
tí nào as question word 5.5.17.2 (191)
tỉ 1.3.1.1.1 (5, 8)
tiếng *hour* and giờ *hour* 1.3.1.1.7.9 (16)
tiếng *hour* and *language* 1.3.1.1.7.9 (16)
time 1.3.1.1.7.10 (16)
time clauses 5.8.3.2 (214–216)
tin 2.4.4 (68, 70)
tớ 1.3.1.2 (23)
tớ as personal pronoun 1.3.3.5.6 (46)
to ask and Vietnamese equivalents 2.4.3 (67–68)
to be able 2.10.2 (95)
to believe vs. tin 2.4.4.3 (70)
to hear and *to listen* vs. nghe 2.4.4.3 (70–71)
to prefer sth to sth 2.6.1.2 (76)
to speak, to talk, to tell and *to say* vs. nói and nói chuyện 2.4.4.3 (71–72)
to want 2.10.5 (97)
to wish 5.8.3.3.3 (218–219)
toà 1.3.1.2 (23)
toàn 1.3.2.2.6 (31)
toàn là 5.5.16 (189–190)
too 6.2 (230–231)
tốt 6.11 (243–245)

tới 2.7.2 (81–82)
trả lời 2.4.4 (68)
trái 1.3.1.2 (24)
trăm 1.3.1.1.1 (5, 7)
triệu 1.3.1.1.1 (5, 8)
trong khi 5.8.3.2 (215–216)
trở nên 2.9 (93–94)
trở thành 2.9 (93)
trừ 1.3.1.1.4 (9)
trừ phi 5.8.3.3.6 (219–220)
trước 5.8.3.2 (214)
trước khi 5.8.3.2 (214)
tuy 5.8.3.4 (221)
tư 1.3.1.1.1 (6–7), 1.3.1.1.7.3 (11–13)
từ khi 5.8.3.2 (214–215)
từng 1.3.2.2.5 (30–31)
tương đối 3.2.1 (108)
tưởng 2.4.4 (68), 2.4.4.4 (72)
twice as much / many 1.3.1.1.5 (10)
uncountable noun 1.2.3 (4–5)
under 1.3.1.1.9 (18–19)
unless 5.8.3.3.6 (219–220)
và 5.7.1 (204–205)
vài 1.3.1.1.8 (17)
vài ba 1.3.1.1.8 (17)
vạn 1.3.1.1.1 (6, 8)
vào 2.7.2 (82, 84, 86–88)
vẫn 2.3.2.4 (56–57), 2.3.2.6 (57–58), 5.8.3.4 (221), 5.8.3.11.2 (227)
vẫn còn 2.3.2.4 (56–57), 2.3.2.6 (57–58)
vâng 5.3.1.3 (167)
vậy 3.2.2.2 (111), 5.6.2.12 (204)
verbs (50–106)
verb + adjective 2.5 (73–75)
verb + adverb 2.6 (75–81)
verb + clause 2.4.4.4 (72)
verb + object 2.4.4.1 (68–69)
verb + preposition + noun / pronoun 2.4.4.3 (69–72)
verbs of appearance, existence and disappearance 2.8 (89–93)
verbs of equating 2.4.5 (72–73)
verbs of feelings and emotions 2.6.1.1 (75–76)
verbs of giving 2.4.1 (62–63)
verbs of motion 2.7 (81–89)
verbs of reaching or bringing to a particular state or condition 2.9 (93–94)
verbs of receiving 2.4.2 (64–65)
verbs of speaking, thinking and perceiving 2.4.4 (68–72)
về 2.7.2 (82, 84–85)
vì 5.8.3.5 (222–223), 6.12.2.10 (248)
vì referring to cause and English equivalents 5.1.1.3.6 (158)
vì sao 5.3.2.4 (174–175), 5.8.2.2 (213)
vì thế 5.8.3.6 (223), 6.14.3.1 (252)
vì vậy 5.8.3.6 (223), 6.14.3.1 (252)
vị 1.3.1.2 (24)
viên 1.3.1.2 (24)

Grammar index

vở 1.3.1.2 (24)
vừa 2.3.2.1 (55)
vừa ... đã ... 5.5.7 (184)
vừa ... vừa ... 5.7.1 (205), 5.7.6 (207–208)
vừa mới 2.3.2.1 (55)
vừa mới ... đã ... 5.5.7 (184)
w-conditional clauses 5.8.3.11 (226–228)
weeks 1.3.1.1.7.4 (12)
what 5.3.2.8 (177–178)
whatever 5.8.3.11 (226–227)
when 5.3.2.3 (173–174), 5.8.2.1 (212–213)
whenever 5.8.3.11 (226)
where 5.3.2.1 (172), 5.3.2.2 (172–173), 5.8.2.1 (213)
wherever 5.8.3.11 (226–227)
which 5.3.2.8 (177–178)
whichever 5.8.3.11 (226)
who 5.3.2.7 (177)
whoever 5.8.3.11 (226)
whole 1.3.2.2 (27–31)
whom 5.3.2.7 (177)
word-formation (119–151)
would like 2.10.5 (97)
would rather ... than ... 2.6.1.2 (76–77)
wow 5.4.1 (180)
xách 2.7.4 (88)
xảy / xảy ra 2.8.6 (92–93)
xem 2.4.4 (68, 69)
xin 2.4.3 (66, 68)
xong 2.3.2.8 (59)
xuất hiện 2.8.5 (92)
xuống 2.7.2 (81–84, 86–88)
y as personal pronoun 1.3.3.5.6 (46)
years 1.3.1.1.7.1 (11)
Yes / Yeah 5.3.1.3 (167)
yêu cầu 2.4.3 (66, 68)

272

Chapter 7

Pronunciation

This chapter gives a brief introduction to the writing systems of the Vietnamese language with focus on the Romanized writing system and discusses the phonetic system of the language in depth. The phonetic system introduced in this work is the ideal system, which is not fully reflected in any of the dialects of Vietnamese. The Hanoi dialect, however, has fewer deviations from the ideal system of the initial consonants and presents the accurate picture of the tones, labialization, nuclear vowels and finals. The difficult sounds and syllables are brought into focus and compared with their English counterparts.

SYMBOLS

In this chapter, a sound is indicated between a pair of square brackets; e.g. [a] refers to the a-sound. Occasionally, a special symbol of the International Phonetic Alphabet (IPA) is used to transcribe a sound, which is also enclosed between square brackets. A sound is represented by an alphabet letter (or character), or by a combination of characters, which are enclosed between a pair of angle brackets; e.g. [ɑ] is represented by <a>; [g] is represented either by <g> or by <gh>. In some cases, the term *phoneme* is used. A phoneme is the minimal unit in the sound system of a language. A phoneme is enclosed between a pair of virgules; e.g. phoneme / a / or phoneme / ɣ / corresponding to the sound [a] and [g] respectively.

7.1 Writing systems

Chinese, which is **chữ Hán** in Vietnamese (**chữ**: a written word or a character; **Hán**: the name of a dynasty in China), was introduced as the official language after the northern part of present-day Vietnam was seized by China in the second century BC. After Vietnam regained independence in the tenth century, Chinese remained the written language of the Vietnamese royal court for administrative purposes, as well as for literary works, education and examinations until the early twentieth century. During that long period of time, Vietnamese borrowed a large number of Chinese vocabulary. See 4.2.4.1 for more on Chinese loanwords.

After the first powerful Vietnamese feudal state was established in the territory of present northern Vietnam in the early eleventh century, the need to create a writing system to transcribe Vietnamese syllables or words arose. A new writing system called **chữ Nôm** (Nôm: south, in this case referring to Vietnam) was developed. The writing system was based on Chinese characters and made use either of separate Chinese characters or of a combination of Chinese characters. In the latter case, one Chinese character represents the sound, the other one denotes the meaning of a Vietnamese syllable or word. A set of rules was created to combine Chinese characters for this Vietnamese writing system. When looking at a text written in **chữ Nôm**, a Chinese person recognizes Chinese characters but is unable to understand it, since it is a text in Vietnamese. The oldest documents written in **chữ Nôm** date back to the twelfth century. In the fifteenth century, Nguyễn Trãi, a Vietnamese national hero, politician, diplomat, military strategist and poet, used **chữ Nôm** to write first poems in Vietnamese, which were collected in **Quốc âm thi tập** (Book of Poems Written in National Language). Literary works created in **chữ Nôm** flourished in the late 18th and early 19th centuries, including **Truyện Kiều** (Story of Kiều), a masterpiece by Nguyễn Du.

The first Jesuit missionaries came to Vietnam to promulgate Christianity in the late 16th and early 17th centuries. Many of them were Portuguese. In order to learn Vietnamese to preach, with assistance of Vietnamese Catholics and Catholics of some other nations,[1] they devised a new phonemic writing system using the Roman script, in which one sound should be represented by one character or one combination of characters. Since then, the Romanized writing system called **quốc ngữ** (quốc: national, ngữ: language) has changed numerous times towards its current form along with its relatively consistent orthographic conventions, i.e. spelling rules. It has become one of the most successful Romanized alphabets based on the principle of sound – character (phoneme – grapheme) correspondence. However, the Vietnamese alphabet and spelling rules still have a number of inconsistencies.

There are three major reasons why the alphabet and spelling rules do not have a consistent one-for-one relation between phoneme and character.

First, the Roman script was used by the missionaries to write down the phonetic system of Vietnamese in the early seventeenth century. As such, some sounds no longer exist in modern Vietnamese. The current alphabet and spelling rules for the most part do not take account of the changes in pronunciation that have affected Vietnamese since the seventeenth century. For example, the missionaries used character <d> to write down a fricative consonant sound which was to some extent similar to the English consonant [ð], i.e. the consonant <th> in *this, that*. In present-day Vietnamese, this consonant has become [z], which is still denoted by character <d>. This way of representing the consonant [z] may be confusing to learners who are speakers of European languages, in which character <d> refers to the stop consonant [d]. Since character <d> is used to denote the previously mentioned fricative consonant [z], the specific character <đ> is used to denote the stop consonant [d].[2]

Second, most of the Catholic missionaries were native speakers of the Romance languages, which have left traces in the present-day Vietnamese alphabet, as well as in the spelling rules. For instance, in the Romance languages, when character <g> precedes the central and back vowels (see 7.2.2. for front, central and back vowels), it represents the consonant [g]; when occuring before one of the front vowels, it denotes a completely different consonant. It is why the missionaries added character <h> to character <g> in those positions to have the combination <gh> that maintains the [g] sound before the front vowels <e>, <ê> and <i>. Compare: **ga** "station" vs. **ghe** "small boat," **ghê** "to feel disgusted," **ghi** "to write down."

A similar situation with pronunciation can be seen in English as well. A large number of English words has character <g> for the initial consonant that occurs before characters <e>, <i> and <y>. The character <g>, however, denotes different sounds depending on the origin of the word. Compare the pronunciation of three English homonyms:

gill[1] [gɪl] (organ of fish) < Old Norse
gill[2] [gɪl] (ravine, stream, brook) < Old Norse
gill[3] [dʒɪl] (unit of liquid measure) < Old French < Latin

The first two words came from Old Norse, which is a Germanic language. In the Germanic languages, character <g> indicates the consonant [g] at all times, no matter what kind of vowel it precedes. The third word was borrowed from Old French, which in turn borrowed it from Latin, a Romance language. This is the reason for the pronunciation of [dʒ] instead of [g].

Third, in certain instances, the European missionaries wrote down the sounds of a regional dialect, which were significantly different from their counterparts in other dialects of Vietnamese; or some of them did not exist in other dialects at all. The missionaries came first to the region which is now the southern part of central Vietnam, interacted with speakers of the local dialect and tried to figure out the phonetic system of that dialect, which differed from the standard Hanoi dialect.

7.2 Vietnamese alphabet

The Romanized Vietnamese alphabet contains twenty-nine letters and five diacritic marks denoting the tones. The mid-level tone is not indicated by any diacritic mark. Here are the Vietnamese names of the letters and tone marks:

a (a), **ă** (á), **â** (ớ), **b** (bê), **c** (xê), **d** (dê), **đ** (đê), **e** (e), **ê** (ê), **g** (giê), **h** (hát), **i** (i), **k** (ca), **l** (e-lờ), **m** (e-mờ), **n** (e-nờ), **o** (o), **ô** (ô), **ơ** (ơ), **p** (pê), **q** (cu), **r** (e-rờ), **s** (ét-xì), **t** (tê), **u** (u), **ư** (ư), **v** (vê), **x** (ích-xì), **y** (i-gờ-rếch).
` (dấu huyền), ´ (dấu sắc), ? (dấu hỏi), ~ (dấu ngã), . (dấu nặng). The mid-level tone, which is not represented by any diacritic mark, is called không dấu.

The Vietnamese alphabet does not contain the letters <f>, <j>, <w> and <z>, which are, however, often used for the transliteration of foreign words. Their Vietnamese names are "e-phờ," "gi," "vê kép" and "dét" respectively.

The circumflex ^ is placed above a vowel to denote a less open vowel than the vowel without the circumflex. For example, ô is less open than o. The hook ' written together with a vowel on the right upper side to indicate an unrounded vowel. For example, o is rounded, ơ is unrounded. The breve ˘ placed above a vowel refers to a vowel shorter than the vowel without the breve. For instance, ă is shorter than a.

The description and discussion of the phonetic system of Vietnamese in this work are based on the Hanoi dialect. Occasionally, some sounds and types of syllable of the Saigon dialect are compared with the Hanoi dialect. When the sounds are described and spelling rules are introduced, the spelling inconsistencies will be referred to as *exceptions*.

7.3 Structure of a Vietnamese syllable

The discussion of each sound of the phonetic system of Vietnamese is based on its function in the syllable structure, which can be presented as follows:

Tone				
Initial consonant	Labialization	Nuclear vowel	Final
	Rhyme		

A syllable consists of five components: tone, initial consonant, labialization, nuclear vowel and final. Two components are mandatory for a syllable: a tone and a nuclear vowel. The other three components may be absent.

The initial consonant is not part of a rhyme that is essential for forming reduplicatives and is a major feature of Vietnamese verse. See 4.2.3. for more on reduplicatives.

Note: In phonological theory, all the five components are present in a syllable at all times. When a component is not represented by a character in writing, a zero phoneme does exist. A zero phoneme is a unit in the system that has no physical realization in speech. In order to make the description of the sound system simple, this work does not discuss the zero phonemes.

We will discuss the mandaroty components of a syllable first, and then the other three components. After all the five components of the syllable are described, we will deal with the phonetic difficulties English-speaking learners encounter.

Structure of a Vietnamese syllable

7.3.1 Tone

Vietnamese is a tone language. Each syllable carries a tone which denotes its particular meaning. A syllable with the same components when carrying different tones refers to different meanings; i.e. they are different words.

A tone is produced at a certain pitch, and some tones can have fluctuating pitches. Vietnamese has six tones, which are fully reflected in the Hanoi dialect: the mid-level tone (**thanh ngang** or **thanh không**; **thanh** is the short form of the word **thanh điệu** meaning "tone"; **ngang**: "horizontal, equal;" **không**: "zero"), the low-falling tone (**thanh huyền**; **huyền**: "grave"), the high-rising tone (**thanh sắc**; **sắc**: "accute, sharp"), the low-falling-rising tone (**thanh hỏi**; **hỏi**: "ask"), the high-rising-broken tone (**thanh ngã**; **ngã**: "fall down") and the low-falling-broken tone (**thanh nặng**; **nặng**: "heavy"). The mid-level tone does not have a diacritic mark, while each of the other five tones is represented by a particular diacritic mark:

ta "we" (mid-level)
tà "evil" (low-falling)
tá "dozen" (high-rising)
tả "describe" (low-falling-rising)
tã "diaper" (high-rising broken)
tạ "weights" (low-falling broken)

The *mid-level* tone has a pitch starting at the mid point of the normal speaking voice range and remaining stable during the pronunciation of a syllable. It is very important to keep the mid-level tone at the same pitch level in the flow of speech, without any fluctuation, when pronouncing the syllables having this tone in a sentence.

The *low-falling* tone starts just slightly lower than the mid point of the normal voice range and trails downwards towards the bottom of the voice range. It is symbolized by the grave accent, which is called in Vietnamese **dấu huyền** (**dấu**: mark).

The *high-rising* tone starts a little higher than the mid-level tone, then approximately in the middle of the syllable the voice sharply rises. It is symbolized by the acute accent, which is called in Vietnamese **dấu sắc**.

The *low-falling-rising* tone starts a little bit lower than the beginning point of the low-falling tone and drops rather abruptly, then is followed by a sweeping rise at the end of the syllable. It is symbolized by an accent made of the top part of a question mark, which is called in Vietnamese **dấu hỏi**.

The *high-rising broken* tone has a high rising pitch starting as high as the high rising tone and is accompanied by a glottal stop. It is symbolized by the tilde, which is called in Vietnamese **dấu ngã**.

The *low-falling broken* tone has a low pitch starting a little bit lower than the beginning of the low-falling tone and then dropping rather sharply. It is almost immediately cut off by a strong glottal stop. This tone is symbolized by a subscript dot, which is called in Vietnamese **dấu nặng**.

<u>Note</u>: The difference between **thanh** and **dấu** is that **thanh** is the sound which can be heard, whereas **dấu** is the diacritic mark which can be seen in writing.

The six Vietnamese tones can be presented as follows:

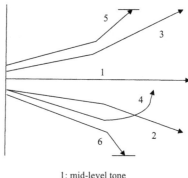

1: mid-level tone
2: low-falling tone
3: high-rising tone
4: low-falling-rising tone
5: high-rising broken tone
6: low-falling broken tone

<u>Note 1</u>: The dash that stops the arrows representing the directions of the high-rising broken tone (5) and low-falling broken tone (6) refers to the glottal stop.

<u>Note 2</u>: The pitch level of the mid-level tone does not change at all when it is produced. The pitch level of the low-falling and high-rising tones does not change significantly either. These three tones are called *register* tones. The pitch patterns of the low-falling-rising, high-rising broken and low-falling broken tones are more complicated. They are called *contour* tones.

7.3.2 Nuclear vowels

The number of nuclear vowels has been under discussion for a long time. This work introduces the traditional number of elevel monophthong vowels [i] <i>/<y>, [e] <ê>, [ɛ] <e>/<a>, [ɯ] <ư>, [ɤ] <ơ>, [ɤ̆] <â>, [ɑ] <a>, [ă] <ă>/<a>, [u] <u>, [o] <ô>, [ɔ] <o>; and three diphthong vowels [ie] <iê>/<ia>, [ɯɤ] <ươ>/<ưa> and [uo] <uô>/<ua>. See 7.3.5.2. for more discussion of nuclear vowels.

The nuclear vowels are represented in a trapezoid as follows:

```
        front      central       back
          i          ɯ            u
          ie         ɯɤ           uo

             e       ɤ  ɤ̆         o

                     ɛ            ɔ
                      ɑ  ă
```

The trapezoid represents the part of the tongue which is raised and the position of the tongue towards the palate.

7.3.2.1 Monophthong nuclear vowels

7.3.2.1.1 FRONT VOWELS

7.3.2.1.1.1 VOWEL [i] <i>/<Y>

This is a high front and unrounded vowel. The lips are spread, the tongue tip is in a low position, and the front of the tongue is rising towards the hard palate. This vowel is almost like the English vowel [i:] as in s**ee**, s**ea**m, s**ee**n. For instance: **đi** "to go," **kí** "to sign," **mì** "noodles made from wheat."

Spelling *exceptions*

1/ The nuclear vowel [i] is in most cases represented by the character <i>.
2/ This vowel may be represented by the character <y>
   a) when [i] is the only sound that forms a syllable, especially for Chinese loanwords, such as **y** "medicine" <醫 \ 医, **y (phục)** "clothes" < 衣服, **ý** "idea, thought" <意, **ỷ (lại)** "be dependent on" < 倚賴 \ 倚赖;
   b) in the diphthong [ie] that does not follow any initial consonant and that precedes a final: **yên** "peaceful," **yêu** "to love." See 7.3.2.2. for more on the diphthongs;

c) in a labialized syllable: **khuy** "button," **luỹ** "wall," **nguy** "dangerous." See 7.3.4. for labialization;
d) in some words containing an initial consonant and the nuclear vowel [i] with no final, either <i> or <y> is used to indicate [i]: **mì / mỳ** "noodles made from wheat," **kí / ký** "to sign," **bác sĩ / bác sỹ** "physician;"
e) in a labialized syllable containing the initial consonant [k] <qu>, either <i> or <y> is possible: **quí / quý** "precious," **quĩ / quỹ** "budget."

 7.3.2.1.1.2 VOWEL [e] <ê>

This is a mid front and unrounded vowel. In the production of this vowel the tip of the tongue is in a low position close to the lower front teeth, the back of the tongue rises slightly towards the hard palate, and the mouth is open wider than in pronouncing [i]: **đê** "dike," **kề** "adjacent," **nể** "respect."

Spelling: The nuclear vowel [e] is always represented by the character <ê>.

 7.3.2.1.1.3 VOWEL [ɛ] <e>/<a>

This is a a low front and unrounded vowel. The tongue has almost the same position as in the production of [e]; however, the place of articulation is deeper than [e], and the mouth is open wider than [e]: **đe** "threaten," **kẻ** "draw a line," **né** "evade." In the front position of the tongue, [i] is the least open vowel, [ɛ] is the most open vowel, and [e] is the half-open (or half-close) vowel.

Spelling *exceptions*

1/ The nuclear vowel [ɛ] is in most cases represented by the character <e>.
2/ This vowel is represented by <a>
   a) when preceding the final consonant [ŋ], which is represented by <nh>, not <ng>: **anh** "elder brother," **cánh** "wing," **mạnh** "strong;"
   b) when preceding the final consonant [k], which is represented by <ch>, not <c>: **ách** "yoke," **cách** "distant," **mạch** "pulse."

See 7.3.5. for more on this nuclear vowel when it is followed by these two final consonants.

7.3.2.1.2 CENTRAL VOWELS

 7.3.2.1.2.1 VOWEL [ɯ] <ư>

This is a high central and unrounded vowel. The tongue blade is moving a little backwards and tense, and the back of the tongue is rising towards the velum. For instance: **ứng** "correspond," **mừng** "glad," **vứt** "throw away."

> Spelling: The nuclear vowel [ɯ] is always represented by the character <ư>.

7.3.2.1.2.2 VOWEL [ɤ] <ơ>

This is a mid central unrounded vowel. The lips keep a neutral position, and the front of the tongue is rising towards the point between the hard palate and the velum. This sound is produced to some degree like the schwa [ə] (the reduced, unstressed vowel characteristic of unstressed syllables) in English, e.g. in alone, system, easily. However, the muffled vowel sound in English occurs only in an unstressed position, while the Vietnamese [ɤ] is always the main vowel of a syllable. For instance: **ở** "in, at," **ơn** "favor," **ớt** "chilly pepper."

> Spelling: The nuclear vowel [ɤ] is always represented by the character <ơ>.

7.3.2.1.2.3 VOWEL [ɤ̆] <â>

This is the short counterpart of the long nuclear vowel [ɤ]. A short vowel should always be followed by a final: **câu** "sentence," **cây** "tree," **cân** "weigh," **mất** "lose," **tập** "practice."

> Spelling: The short nuclear vowel [ɤ̆] is always represented by the character <â>.

7.3.2.1.2.4 VOWEL [ɑ] <a>

This is a a low central and unrounded vowel, which is the openest vowel of the nuclear vowel system. When producing this vowel, the mouth is wide open, and the tongue is in the lowest position. This vowel is almost like the English vowel [ɑ:] as in art, gather, heart, palm. For instance, **an** "peaceful," **bàn** "table," **cát** "sand." In the central position of the tongue, [ɯ] is the least open unrounded vowel, [ɑ] is the most open unrounded vowel, and [ɤ] is the half-open (or half-close) unrounded vowel.

> Spelling: The nuclear vowel [a] is always represented by the character <a>.

Structure of a Vietnamese syllable

7.3.2.1.2.5 | VOWEL [ɑ] <Ă>/<A>

This is the short counterpart of the long nuclear vowel [ɑ]. As in the case of the vowel [ɤ̆], this short vowel should be followed by a final: **căn** "house, apartment," **mắt** "eye," **tắc** "congested."

Spelling exceptions

1/ When preceding a final <u>consonant</u>, this short nuclear vowel is represented by the character <ă>.
2/ When preceding a final <u>semivowel</u>, this short vowel is represented by the character <a>: **cay** "spicy," **máy** "machine," **cau** "betel nut," **màu** "color." The shortness of the vowel is indicated by the characters <y> and <u> denoting the finals. See 7.3.5. for more on the semivowel finals.

7.3.2.1.3 | BACK VOWELS

 7.3.2.1.3.1 | VOWEL [u] <u>

This is a high back and rounded vowel. The tongue tip is in a low position and away from the lower front teeth. The lips are sharply rounded. This vowel is almost like the English vowel [u:] as in cl**u**e, d**o**, f**oo**d, pr**o**ve. For instance, **út** "youngest in the family," **phun** "erupt," **vụn** "to bits."

> Spelling: The nuclear vowel [u] is always represented by the character <u>.

 7.3.2.1.3.2 | VOWEL [o] <ô>

This is a mid back and rounded vowel. The blade of the tongue is moving backwards, and the tip of the tongue is in a very low position. The lips are moving forwards and rounded, and the mouth is open wider than in producing **u**: **ô** "umbrella," **bố** "father," **công** "public."

> Spelling: The nuclear vowel [o] is always represented by the character <ô>.

 7.3.2.1.3.3 | VOWEL [ɔ] <o>

This is is a low back and rounded vowel, which is produced in a deeper position than **ô**. The lips are moving forwards and rounded, and the mouth is open wider than **ô**: **cỏ** "grass," **giòn** "crisp," **ngọn** "sweet." In the back position of the tongue, [u] is the least open rounded vowel, [ɔ] is the most open rounded vowel, and [o] is the half-open (or half-close) rounded vowel.

Structure of a Vietnamese syllable

Spelling: The nuclear vowel [ɔ] is always represented by the character <o>.

7.3.2.2 Diphthong nuclear vowels

A diphthong is a vowel whose quality changes during a syllable. A diphthong vowel can be falling (or descending), when the first element is the main vowel and is pronounced longer and stronger; or rising (or ascending), when the second element is the main vowel and is pronounced longer and stronger. For example, the following English words contain falling diphthongs: *hear* [ɪə], *said* [eɪ], *glow* [əʊ], *my* [ʌɪ], *plow* [aʊ], *tour* [ʊə], *boy* [ɔɪ].

Vietnamese has three falling diphthong vowels: [i̯e], [ɯ̯ɤ] and [u̯o]. In the open syllable which does not have any final, the second element is pronounced as a neutralized mid central vowel between [ɤ] <ơ> and [ɑ] <a>, which is transcribed as [ʌ]: **kìa** [kìʌ] "that," **cưa** [kɯʌ] "saw," **của** [kủʌ] "belong."

In the closed syllable which has a final semivowel or consonant, the second element of the diphthong is pronounced more closed than in an open syllable and is similar to the vowel that is the next lower one in each column of the trapezoid. For example, **kiện** [ki̯en] "sue," **cường** [kɯ̯ɤŋ] "strong," **cuống** [kúoŋ] "hurry."

Spelling *exceptions*

1/ In the open syllalbles, the second element of all the three diphthong vowels is indicated by the character <a> as in **kìa, cưa** and **của**.
2/ In the closed syllables, the second element of the diphthong vowels is indicated by the characters <ê> as in **kiện**, <ơ> as in **cường** and <ô> as in **cuống**.
3/ When the diphthong [i̯e] occurs at the beginning of a syllable with no initial consonant and is followed by a final, it is spelled with <yê>: **yếu** "weak," **yên** "peaceful."
4/ When the diphthong [i̯e] occurs in a labialized syllable containing an initial consonant, the first character is spelled with <y>, and the second character follows the rules of open and closed syllables: **khuya** "late night," **khuyên** "advise."
5/ In the open syllalbles, the tone marks is placed over or underneath the first character of the diphthong: **phía** "side," **phịa** "make up a story;" in the closed syllables the tone mark is written over or underneath the second character: **phiến** "slat of wood," **phiện** "opium."

7 Pronunciation

7.3.3 Initial consonants

Vietnamese has twenty-one initial consonants: [b] <b>, [f] <ph>, [v] <v>, [m] <m>, [t] <t>, [d] <đ>, [tʰ] <th>, [s] <x>, [z] <d>/<gi>, [n] <n>, [l] <l>, [tʃ] <tr>,[3] [ʂ] <s>,[4] [ʐ] <r>,[5] [c] <ch>, [ɲ] <nh>, [k] <c>/<k>/<qu>, [χ] <kh>, [ɣ] <g>/<gh>, [ŋ] <ng>/<ngh>, [h] <h>.

The initial consonants can be represented in the following chart. See Glossary of Phonetic Terms for explanation of the technical terms.

Manner	Place	Labial	Alveolar	Retroflex	Palatal	Velar	Glottal
Stop	Voiceless		t	tʃ	c	k	
Stop	Voiced	b	d				
Stop	Voiceless Aspirated		tʰ				
Fricative	Voiceless	f	s	ʂ		χ	h
Fricative	Voiced	v	z	ʐ		ɣ	
Nasal	Voiced	m	n		ɲ	ŋ	
Lateral	Voiced		l				

This chart shows the ideal system of consonants. None of the dialects of Vietnamese reflects fully this ideal system. The Hanoi dialect does not have three retroflex consonants [tʃ] <tr>, [ʂ] <s> and [ʐ] <r>, that are characteristic of some central dialects. In the Hanoi dialect, these retroflex consonants are pronounced like the consonants [c] <ch>, [s] <x> and [z] <d>/<gi> respectively.

<u>Note 1</u>: Vietnamese does not have the stop voiceless bilabial consonant [p] denoted by the character <p> as an initinal consonant. The character <p> is used for transcribing or transliterating the intial consonant of foreign words, personal and geographical names. For example, **pa** tê "liverwurst, pâté," **P**aris, **P**asteur, **P**eter, **S**ankt-**P**eterburg (Санкт-Петербург), **P**etrograd (Петроград).

<u>Note 2</u>: The rolled (or trill) voiced alveolar consonant [r] denoted by the character <r> do not exist in standard Vietnamese. The character <r> is used for the retroflex initial consonant [ʐ] in some dialects and the initial consonant [z] in the Hanoi dialect. The character <r> is also used for transcribing or transliterating the intial consonant of foreign words. For example, **r**a đi ô "radio," **R**eims, **R**embrandt, **R**hein.

7.3.3.1 Initial consonants similar to English consonants

The Vietnamese consonants [b] <b>, [f] <ph>, [v] <v>, [m] <m>, [d] <đ>, [s] <x> (and <s> in Hanoi dialect), [z] <d>, <gi> (and <r> in Hanoi dialect), [n] <n>, [l] <l> and [h] <h> are pronounced like their English counterparts.

Note that

1/ Consonant [f] is represented by the combination of characters <ph>; the character <f> is used only for transcribing and transliterating foreign words.
2/ Consonant [d] is represented by the specific character <đ> (see 7.1.), that should not be confused with the character <d> denoting the consonant [z].
3/ Both <x> and <s> in the Hanoi dialect refer to the consonant [s]; <x> does not indicate the consonant [z], unlike the English <x> as in *Xerox, xerography, xylography, xylophone*.

Spelling *exception*: the combination of characters <gi> represents the alveolar voiced fricative consonant [z] as in **gieo** "sow," **giếng** "well," **già** "old," **giờ** "hour," **giữ** "maintain," **giỏi** "good," **giống** "similar," **giúp** "help." When occurring before the front vowel [i] <i>, only one <i> is written: **gì** "what" instead of *gìi.

7.3.3.2 Specific initial consonants

7.3.3.2.1 CONSONANT [t] <t>

This voiceless consonant is the counterpart of the voiced consonant [d] <đ>; e.g. **tá** "dozen," **tê** "numb," **tì** "lean," **tiếng** "language," **tơ** "silk," **tử** "dead," **to** "big," **tốt** "good," **tù** "prison." Note that Vietnamese [t] <t> cannot be pronounced as a voiced consonant, unlike <t> and <tt> in American English when this consonant occurs between vowels, as is *wat er, butt er*. On the other hand, it cannot be aspirated because Vietnamese has the aspirated consonant [tʰ] <th>; compare: **ta** "we" vs. **tha** "forgive;" **tu** "become a monk" vs. **thu** "autumn." In English, [t] <t> is aspirated when occurring at the beginning of a word as in *task, toast, top* or at the beginning of the stressed syllable in a polysyllabic word as in *att ack, att endant*.

7.3.3.2.2 CONSONANT [c] <ch>

English does not have a consonant similar to this palatal voiceless stop consonant. The Vietnamese [c] is produced with the tip of the tongue moving downwards near the backs of the lower teeth and the contact being made by the blade of the tongue against the hard palate. For example, **cha** "father," **che** "cover," **chỉ** "only," chờ "wait," cho "give," chỗ "place," chủ "owner." It is to some degree similar to the Russian soft consonant [t'] as in *тень, тётя, тьма, тяга*. This Vietnamese consonant should not be confused with the English consonant [tʃ] <ch>. Compare Vietnamese **chát** "tart," **chê** "criticize," **chú** "uncle" vs. English *chat, cheer, chew*.

   7.3.3.2.3   CONSONANT [ɲ] <nh>

English does not have a consonant similar to this palatal voiced nasal consonant. The Vietnamese [ɲ] is produced with the tip of the tongue being lowered towards the lower teeth and the back of the tongue rising towards the hard palate and contacting it: **nhà** "house," **nhẹ** "light," **nhì** "second," **nhận** "receive," **nhưng** "but," **nhỏ** "small," **nhung** "velvet." Although English does not have this consonant at the beginning of a syllable, it may appear in some words when [n] is pronounced quickly together with the following <i> as in *oni on*. This Vietnamese consonant is similar to the French <gn> as in *Champagn e* ", *sign al* "signal;" to the Spanish <ñ> as in *añ o* "year," *niñ o* "child," *niñ a* "girl;" and to some extent to the soft Russian consonant [n'] <н> as in *нет* "no," *нёс* "carried," *нить* "thread," *нюхать* "smell," *няня* "nursemaid."

   7.3.3.2.4   CONSONANT [k] <c>/<k>/<qu>

This Vietnamese velar voiceless stop consonant is not aspirated, unlike the English [k] that is aspirated when occurring at the beginning of a word, as in *cat, cake*, or at the beginning of the stressed syllable in a polysyllabic word as in *ac ademy, bec ome, sec ure*. Compare: Vietnamese **cát** "sand," **các** "plural marker" vs. English *cat, cake*.

Spelling *exceptions*

1/ This consonant is represented by the character <c> when occurring before the central and back vowels: **cà** "tomato," **cỡ** "size," **cưa** "saw," **cứ** "go ahead," **có** "have," **cổ** "ancient," **cuốn** "roll," **cụ** "great-grandfather;"
2/ When occurring before the front vowels, it is indicated by the character <k>, as in **kẻ** "to draw a lign," **kề** "adjacent," **kiện** "sue," **kí** "to sign;"
3/ When occurring in a labialized syllable (see 7.3.4. for labialization), it is denoted by the combination of characters <qu>, as in **quá** "excessively," **quay** "spin," **quần** "trousers," **que** "stick," **quế** "cinnamon," **quỉ** "devil."

   7.3.3.2.5   CONSONANT [x] <kh>

This Vietnamese velar voiceless fricative consonant is produced by narrowing the passage between the back of the tongue and the roof of the mouth, and the airstream squeezes through with audible turbulence: **khá** "good," **khē** "quiet," **khế**

"star fruit," **khi** "when," **khử** "remove," **khó** "difficult," **không** "not," **khuôn** "mould." This consonant is the voiceless counterpart of the voiced consonant [γ] <g>/<gh> and should not be mixed up with the English stop aspirated [k] when it occurs at the beginning of a word or at the beginning of the stressed syllable of a polysyllabic word (see 7.3.3.2.4.). This Vietnamese consonant is similar to the Russian consonant [χ] <x> as in *хата* "log cabin," *хитрый* "cunning," *хорошо* "well," *худой* "skinny;" to the German [χ] <ch> when it occurs after a central or back vowel, as in *Ba ch* "stream," *Bu ch* "book;" to the Spanish [χ] <j>, as in *traj e* "suit, set of clothes," *viej o* "old;" to the Spanish [χ] <g> when it occurs before a front vowel, as in *ag ente* "agent," *eleg ir* "choose," *Jorg e* "first name equivalent to English *George*."

> Structure of a Vietnamese syllable

7.3.3.2.6 CONSONANT [γ] <g>/<gh>

This Vietnamese velar voiced fricative consonant is produced by narrowing the passage between the back of the tongue and the roof of the mouth, and the air flow squeezes through with audible turbulence. Note that this Vietnamese consonant is fricative, whereas the English consonant [g] <g> is a stop consonant. Compare: Vietnamese **ga** "railroad station," **ghế** "chair," **gỗ** "wood" vs. English *garden, get, go*.

Spelling *exceptions*

1/ When occurring before the central and back vowels, this consonant is represented by the character <g>, as in **ga, gỗ**;
2/ When occurring before the front vowels, it is spelled with <gh>, as in **ghế**;

7.3.3.2.7 CONSONANT [ŋ] <ng>/<ngh>

This Vietnamese velar voiced nasal stop consonant is produced with the tongue blade moving backwards, and the back of the tongue rises to make a contact with the velum, which is lowered to allow airstream to escape through the nasal cavity: **ngã** "fall down," **nghề** "profession," **nghỉ** "rest," **nghiêng** "slanted," **ngờ** "doubt," **ngủ** "sleep."

In English, this consonant appears only at the end of a syllable, as in *ring*, *bring*, *sang*, *fing er*. When this English final consonant is pronounced together with the following article *a*, the initial consonant [ŋ] appears, as in *bring a book*.

Spelling *exceptions*

1/ When occurring before the central and back vowels, this consonant is represented by the combination of characters <ng>, as in **ngà** "ivory," **ngô** "corn," **nguồn** "origin," **ngượng** "be embarrassed;"

2/ When occurring before the front vowels, it is spelled with <ngh>, as in **nghe** "listen," **nghề** "occupation," **nghiền** "grind," **nghỉ** "rest."

Note: Some phoneticians and phonologists consider the glottal stop an initial consonant in such syllables where the initial consonant is not indicated by any character in writing. For instance, the words **an** "peaceful," **ác** "cruel" and **áp** "press" begin with a glottal stop. The symbol [ʔ] is used to refer to the glottal stop. Thus, these Vietnamese words are transcribed as [ʔan], [ʔák] and [ʔáp], i.e. an initial consonant is present in a Vietnamese syllable at all times. Compare with the German *Knacklaut* occurring before the vowel [a] in *arbeiten, die Arbeit, der Arzt, das Auge*. This work introduces only two mandatory components of a Vietnamese syllable, which are the tone and nuclear vowel. We do not consider the glottal stop to be an initial consonant.

7.3.4 Labialization

This term indicates the lip rounding as a secondary articulation. The lips start rounding when an initial consonant begins to be articulated and stop rounding at the beginning of the pronouncing of nuclear vowel. Compare: non-labialized **nhà** "house," **cả** "all," **khi** "when" vs. labialized **nhoà** "blurred," **quả** "fruit," **khuy** "button" respectively. See 7.3.2.1.1.1. c) for the spelling of [i] in labialized syllables.

If a syllable does not contain an initial consonant, the labialization begins with the lip rounding and finishes at the beginning of the nuclear vowel. Compare: non-labialized **à** "particle used in different constructions," **y** "medicine," **ế** "a business having few or no customers" vs. labialized **oà** "burst into tears," **uy** "authority, power," **uế** "dirt" respectively.

Note that labialization never occurs

1/ before the back vowels [u] <u>, [o] <ô>, [ɔ] <o>, [uo] <uô>/<ua>, and before central vowels [ɯ] <ư> and [ɯɤ] <ươ>/<ưa>;
2/ in syllables containing the initial consonants [b], [f] <ph>, [v] <v>, [m] <m>, [n] <n>, [z] <r> and [ɣ] <g>/<gh>;
3/ in syllables with the initial consonant [z] represented by <gi>; when this consonant is spelled with <d>, the labialization is possible: **doạ** "threaten," **doanh** "enterprise," **duy** "but," **duyên** "predestined affinity."

Spelling exceptions

1/ when labialization occurs in syllables with open nuclear vowels [a] <a>, [ɛ] <e> and [ă] <ă>, it is represented by the character <o>, as in **hoà** "peace," **khoẻ** "healthy," **xoăn** "curly;"

2/ when occurring in syllables with nuclear vowels [e] <ê>, [i] <i>/<y>, [ɤ] <o> and [ɤ̆] <â>, it is represented by the character <u>, as in **huệ** "lily," **khuy** "button," **thuở** "time period," **xuân** "spring."

Note that the tone mark should be written over or underneath the nuclear vowel, not over or underneath the character denoting the labialization: **hoà, khoẻ, thuỷ** "water." The spelling **hòa, khỏe, thủy** should be considered nonstandard.

7.3.5 Finals

Vietnamese has two semivowel finals and six consonant finals.

7.3.5.1 Semivowel finals

The semivowel finals [i̯][6] and [u̯] are usually pronounced shorter than the nuclear vowels [i] and [u] respectively. However, their length depends on the type of nuclear vowels they follow. After a long nuclear vowel they are pronounced shorter, whereas after a short nuclear vowel they sound longer. For instance, [i̯] in **cài** "fasten" sounds shorter than in **cày** "plow;" [u̯] in **cáo** "fox" sounds shorter than in **cáu** "angry." See 7.3.2.1.2.5. for the spelling of the short nuclear vowel [ă].

Note that the final [i̯] never follows the front nuclear vowels; the final [u̯] never follows the back nuclear vowels.

Spelling exceptions

1/ final [i̯] is represented by the character <i> after the long nuclear vowels, as in **cài, cởi** "take off," **cửi** "weaving loom," **cói** "sedge," **cối** "mortar," **cúi** "bow" and the two diphthongs [ɯɤ̯] <ươ> and [uo̯] <uô>, as in **cười** "laugh" and **cuối** "last;" it is indicated by the character <y> after the short nuclear vowels [ă] and [ɤ̆], as in **cay** "spicy" and **cây** "tree;"

Note that the shortness of the nuclear vowel [ă] is indicated only once by <y> (**cay**), while the shortness of the nuclear vowel [ɤ̆] is indicated twice by <y> and <â> (**cây**).

2/ final [u̯] is represented by the character <o> after the long nuclear vowels [ɑ] <a> and [ɛ] <e>, as in **cao** "tall," **đeo** "carry;" it is denoted by the character <u> after [i] <i>, [e] <ê>, [i̯e] <iê>, [ă] <a>, [ɤ̆] <â> and [ɯ] <ư>, as in **chịu** "agree," **kêu** "shout," **hiểu** "understand," **sau** "after," **sâu** "deep," **cứu** "rescue."

Note that the shortness of the vowel [ă] is indicated only once by <u> (**sau**), while the shortness of the vowel [ɤ̆] is indicated twice by <u> and <â> (**sâu**).

7.3.5.2 Consonant finals

Vietnamese has six final consonants, which are voiced [m] <m>, [n] <n> and [ŋ] <ng>/<nh>; and voiceless stop [p] <p>, [t] <t> and [k] <c>/<ch>. Final

7 Pronunciation

consonants [m], [n], [ŋ], [t] and [k] are produced like their initial counterparts. Vietnamese does not have [p] as an initial consonant, but does have this stop consonant as a final, which is pronounced like the English final [p] but withouth a plosion.

Note 1: The Vietnamese final voiceless stop consonants [p], [t] and [k] are implosive, i.e. they are made without a strong airstream from inside, unlike their English counterparts, which are plosive and produced with a rapid burst when the closure of the organs of speech is released. Compare: Vietnamese **họp** "have a meeting," **sát** "adjacent" and **mác** "scimitar" vs. English *hop*, *sat* and *make*. (See *plosive* and *implosive consonants* in the Glossary of Phonetic Terms for more on the difference between English plosive consonants and Vietnamese implosive consonants.)

Note 2: The syllables ending in the voiceless stop consonants [p], [t] and [k] can only have either the high-rising tone or the low-falling broken tone, whereas the syllables ending in the voiced consonants [m], [n] and [ŋ] can have all the six tones. Compare: **mang** "carry," **màng** "membrane," **máng** "gutter," **mảng** "piece, chunk," **mãng** "vulgar," **mạng** "web" vs. **mác** "scimitar," **mạc** "desert." The high-rising tone in a syllable with one of the final voiceless stop consonants begins higher and rises more sharply than the high-rising tone in a syllable with one of the final voiced consonants. Compare: **máng** vs. **mác**. The low-falling broken tone in a syllable with one of the final voiceless stop consonants drops abruptly right at the beginning of syllable. Compare: **mạng** vs. **mạc**.

Note 3: In the Saigon dialect, in some positions the final [n] changes to [ŋ], the final [t] changes to [k]. In those positions, the dialect has two fewer final consonants. In other words, the Saigon dialect has more homophones than the Hanoi dialect. For instance:

	Hanoi dialect			Saigon dialect
cáng	[káŋ] "stretcher"	the same		[káŋ]
cán	[kán] "handle"	→		[káŋ]
mắc	[mǎk] "hang"	the same		[mǎk]
mắt	[mǎt] "eye"	→		[mǎk]

Note 4: The quality of some nuclear vowels changes in syllables that end in the final consonants [ŋ] and [k], and the quality of the final consonants changes as

well. In the syllables where these two final consonants occur after the monophthong front nuclear vowels [i] <i>, [e] <ê> and [ɛ] <e>/<a>, they appear as slightly palatalized variants because they fall under the influence of the preceding front vowels, which is called *progressive assimilation*.

Spelling *exceptions* related to the final consonants [ŋ] and [k]:

1/ in this type of syllables, the vowel [ɛ] is spelled with the character <a>; see **banh** and **bạch** next;
2/ the final [ŋ] is spelled with <nh>, and the final [k] is spelled with <ch> to refer to the slight palatalization (progressive assmilation) of the final consonants [ŋ] and [k]:

binh "soldier" = [biŋʲ][7]
bênh "side with" = [beŋʲ]
banh "open wide" = [bɛŋʲ]
bịch "bag" = [bikʲ]
bệch "pale" = [bekʲ]
bạch "white" = [bɛkʲ]

Note that a) this kind of syllable is always relatively short and tense; b) the diphthong front vowel before these final consonants is produced in the regular way, and the spellings <ng> and <c> for the final consonants remain:

biếng "lazy" = [bíeŋ]
biếc "bluish green" = [bíek]

In phonological theory, it would be possible to have one more nuclear vowel phoneme, which is the short front vowel [ɛ̆]. This short vowel is the counterpart of the long vowel [ɛ], as in **sành** [sɛ̆ŋ] "glazed terra-cotta" vs. **xèng** [sɛ̀ŋ] "former Vietnamese currency; computer game;" **cảnh** [kɛ̆ŋ] "view" vs. **kẻng** [kɛ̉ŋ] "bell"; **sảnh** [sɛ̆ŋ] "large auditorium" vs. **xẻng** [sɛ̉ŋ] "shovel"; **cách** [kɛ̆k] "be distant" vs. **kéc** [kɛ́k] "parrot." In that case, the number of the short nuclear vowels would increase to three, which are [ɤ̆], [ă] and [ɛ̆]. Note that the final consonants [ŋ] and [k] after the long [ɛ] are spelled with <ng> and <c>, and after the short [ɛ̆] are spelled with <nh> and <ch>.

Since the number of words containing the long [ɛ] before the final consonants [ŋ] and [k] is small, this work does not introduce the opposition between the short vowel [ɛ̆] and the long vowel [ɛ] in the phonemic system of nuclear vowels; i.e. both are regarded as the nuclear vowel phoneme [ɛ].

Note that in the Saigon dialect, the two final consonants following the three front monophthong vowels are completely palatalized. As a result, they sound more like [ɲ] and [c]; the central vowel [a] sounds like its short counterpart [ă]. Compare the Hanoi and Saigon pronunciation:

Hanoi	Saigon
binh "soldier" = [biŋʲ]	**binh** = [biɲ]
bênh "side with" = [beŋʲ]	**bênh** = [beɲ]
banh "open wide" = [bɛŋʲ]	**banh** = [băɲ]
bịch "bag" = [bikʲ]	**bịch** = [bic]
bệch "pale" = [bekʲ]	**bệch** = [bec]
bạch "white" = [bɛkʲ]	**bạch** = [băc]

 In the syllables where these two final consonants occur after the three back monophthong nuclear vowels [u] <u>, [o] <ô> and [ɔ] <o>, the vowels do not start rounding until the end of their production, as if they are at first articulated like the short central unrounded vowels at the same degree of the openness. This process is denoted by the central vowel with the superscript for the rounded vowels, such as [ɯᵘ], [ɤ̆ᵒ] and [ăᵓ].

On the other hand, the final consonants appear as their labialized variants because they fall under the influence of the preceding rounded vowels (progressive assimilation), which leads to the lips coming together at the end of the production of the syllable. The labialization of the final consonants is indicated by the superscript "ᵐ" after [ŋ] and "ᵖ" after [k]. For instance:

lùng "scour" = [lùɯᵘŋᵐ]
lồng "cage" = [lɤ̆ᵒŋᵐ]
lòng "heart" = [lăᵒŋᵐ]
lục "search" = [lɯᵘkᵖ]
lộc "bud" = [lɤ̆ᵒkᵖ]
lọc "filter" = [lăᵒkᵖ]

Note that a) this kind of syllable is always relatively short and tense; b) the diphthong back vowel before these final consonants is produced in the regular way, and the lips do not come together:

luồng "flow, current" = [lùo̯ŋ]
luộc "boil" = [luo̯k]

 In phonological theory, some phoneticians and phonologists add the opposition between the short [ɔ̆] and the long [ɔ], as in **xong** "complete" vs. **xoong** "sauce pan;" **sóc** "squirrel" vs. **soóc** "shorts." In that case, the number of short vowel phonemes in Vietnamese would increase to four, which are [ɤ̆], [ă], [ɛ̆] and [ɔ̆]. Since the number of words containing the long [ɔ] is small, and all of them are loanwords from European languages, this work is not discussing the opposition between the short vowel [ɔ̆] and the long vowel [ɔ], i.e. the short [ɔ̆] is regarded as the nuclear vowel phoneme [ɔ].

7.4 Difficulties of the Vietnamese sound system

When describing the phonetic system of Vietnamese, we occasionally discussed some sounds which are very different from their English counterparts or do not exist in English (see 7.3.3.2.), as well as some specific types of Vietnamese syllables (see 7.3.5.2.). In addition, English-speaking learners may encounter the following phonetic difficulties.

7.4.1 Tones

7.4.1.1 Mid-level tone

The pitch pattern of the mid-level tone does not change at all. This tone stays at a single pitch level. It seems easiest to produce but is in fact hardest to maintain at the same pitch. Learners' attention should be directed to the importance of keeping the same pitch of voice at all times when they pronounce words with the mid-level tone. In other words, all the words and syllables with the mid-level tone in a sentence should be pronounced at the same pitch, no matter how long the sentence is and how many words carrying other tones are inserted between them. For example:

> **Tôi đi chơi.** "I am traveling".
> **Tôi** mời <u>gia</u> đình <u>anh</u> chủ nhật này <u>đi Tam</u> Đảo <u>chơi</u> với <u>gia</u> đình <u>tôi</u>. "I invite you and your family to travel to Tam Đảo with my family this Sunday."

The first sentence is composed of three words with the mid-level tone only. In the second sentence, other words with different tones are inserted between the three words **tôi**, **đi** and **chơi**, and several other words are added. The first word of the sentence is the same word at the end of the sentence, which is pronounced with the mid-level tone. All the underscored words and syllables which have the mid-level tone should be pronounced at the same pitch.

7.4.1.2 Mid-level tone in front of high-rising tone

Learners very often pronounce the mid-level tone at a lower pitch when it occurs before a word with the high-rising tone. For instance, they would say **Đấy là một** nhà <u>thờ</u> lớn. "That is a big church." when they want to say **Đấy là một nhà <u>thơ</u> lớn**. "That is a famous poet."

 | 7.4.1.3 | Vietnamese tones and English intonation

In English, as in many other European languages, the intonation may function as the only means of distinguishing various types of sentences. For example, intonation turns a statement into a question: English *He is coming.* vs. *He is coming?* Russian *Он придёт.* vs. *Он придёт?*; German *Er kommt.* vs. *Er kommt?*; French *Il vient.* vs. *Il vient?*

In Vietnamese, intonation is rarely used as the only way to form questions (see 5.3.1.10. about the question with **hay**). If an assertive statement ends in a word with the high-rising tone, the voice should be raised at the end of the sentence:

Hôm nay trời nóng <u>lắm</u>. It is really hot today.

On the other hand, if a question ends in a word with the low-falling tone, the voice should be lowered at the end of the question:

Hôm nay trời nóng lắm <u>à</u>? Is it really hot today?

In many European languages the pitch of voice in an assertive statement is usually dropped at the end. In Vietnamese the meanings of the sentences **Ông ấy đi tu**. "He has become a Buddhist monk." and **Ông ấy đi tù**. "He has been sent to prison." are completely different. Learners' attention should be drawn to the fact that Vietnamese uses certain grammatical constructions for assertive, negative and interrogative statements. Intonation is strictly restricted by the tones.

| 7.4.2 | **Sounds**

In addition to the specific initial consonants (see 7.3.3.2.) and types of syllables (see 7.3.5.2.), English-speaking learners should also focus attention on the following sounds.

 | 7.4.2.1 | Rounded and unrounded nuclear vowels

The difference between a rounded vowel and an unrounded vowel, and, accordingly, between a rounded syllable and an unrounded syllable, is critical in Vietnamese. In English a rounded syllable may occasionally be pronounced as unrounded without changing the meaning of the word, e.g. the rounded syllable *on* in the sentence *The computer is <u>on</u>.* may have an element of the unrounded sound [ʌn]. The first name *Bob* may be pronounced either with the rounded [ɔ] like [bɔb] or with the unrounded [ʌ] like [bʌb].

This is impossible in Vietnamese. Some characters denoting the rounded vowels <u>, <ô> and <o> and unrounded vowels <ư>, <ơ> seem to be confusing. If learners do not pay attention to the hook of the characters <ư> and <ơ>, they may perceive these characters as if they represent rounded vowels. Learners should be introduced to the sounds before seeing the characters. Minimal pairs containing the oppositions "unrounded" vs. "rounded" which are <ư> vs. <u>, <ơ> vs. <ô>, <ưa>/<ươ> vs. <ua>/<uô> are very helpful. Compare:

thư "letter" vs. **thu** "autumn"
cớ "reason" vs. **cố** "make efforts"
mưa "rain" vs. **mua** "buy"
mượn "borrow" vs. **muộn** "late"

Difficulties of the Vietnamese sound system

7.4.2.2 Openness of the vowels

The openness degree of the Vietnamese vowels causes some difficulty. Very often, learners do not open the mouth widely enough or do not close the mouth enough to differentiate the vowels that differ from each other in the degree of openness. Groups of the vowels of each column in the trapezoid from the least open vowel to the openest one are helpful. For example:

bì "skin" vs. **bìa** "cover of a book" vs. **bề** "side, edge" vs. **bè** "raft"
cứ "go ahead" vs. **cứa** "to cut" vs. **cớ** "pretext" vs. **cá** "fish"
củ "bulb, edible root" vs. **của** "belong" vs. **cổ** "neck" vs. **cỏ** "grass"

Notes

1 There were Japanese Catholic missionaries among them. See Fukuda Yasuo (福田康男). 2016. *Người Nhật có liên quan sâu sắc tới quá trình thiết lập phiên âm tiếng Việt bằng kí tự La-tinh* (ベトナム語ローマ字表記成立に深く関わった日本人). Hanoi, Vietnam.
2 In Germanic linguistics, character <đ> is used in the opposite way to indicate a *fricative* voiced consonant in Germanic languages, that eventually became the *stop* voiced consonant [d] (<d>) during the first sound shift (die erste Lautverschiebung).
3 This retroflex consonant does not exist in the Hanoi dialect.
4 This retroflex consonant does not exist in the Hanoi dialect.
5 This retroflex consonant does not exist in the Hanoi dialect.
6 The diacritic "̯" in IPA refers to a non-syllabic vowel.
7 The diacritic [ʲ] in IPA indicates the palatalization of a consonant.

Glossary of phonetic terms

ASSIMILATION The modification of a sound that makes it more similar to some other adjacent sound(s) that precede(s) or follow(s) it. **Progressive assimilation** occurs when the articulation of a sound is affected by the preceding sound. For instance, in the English word *hands* the voiceless consonant [s] represented by <s> changes to the voiced consonant [z] because of the influence of the preceding voiced consonant [d]. The word is transcribed as [hændz]. In the Vietnamese word **phòng** "room," the final consonant [ŋ] is rounded under the influence of the preceding rounded nuclear vowel [ɔ] and is transcribed with the superscript [ᵐ]: [fɑ̆ᵒŋᵐ]. **Regressive assimilation** occurs when the articulation of a sound is affected by the following sound. For instance, in the English words *ungovernable*, *unkind* the alveolar consonant [n] represented by <n> in *un-* may change to the velar consonant [ŋ] due to the influence of the following velar consonants [g] and [k], and the words can be transcribed as [ʌŋˈgʌvərnəbəl] and [ʌŋˈkaɪnd].

CONSONANTS The speech sounds in the articulation of which the airstream from inside encounters either a constriction or a complete closure of the speech organs. For example, in English [d] <d> as in *dad*, [t] <t> as in *tad*, [ð] <th> as in *that*, [θ] <th> as in *thank* are initial consonants. In Vietnamese, [d] <đ> as in **đa** "banyan," [t] <t> as in **ta** "we," [tʰ] <th> as in **tha** "forgive" are initial consonants. See also **voiced, voiceless, fricative, stop, plosive, implosive, nasal, roll(ed)** consonants. Compare with **vowels**.

CONTOUR TONE see **tone**

DIPHTHONG A vowel whose quality changes in one direction in a single syllable. A diphthong vowel can be falling (or descending), when the first element is the main vowel and is pronounced longer and stronger; or rising (or ascending), when the second element is the main vowel and is pronounced longer and stronger. Vietnames has three falling diphthong vowels [ie̯] <iê> / <ia>, [ɯɤ̯] <ươ> / <ưa> and [uo̯] <uô> /<ua>.

FINAL CONSONANT In Vietnamese a final consonant is a consonant that appears as a final of a syllable. Some consonants can both begin and end a syllable, i.e. they function as initial and final consonants. For instance, [m] <m> in

mà "but" is an initial consonant, in **ám** "obsess" is a final consonant; in the same way: [n] <n> in **na** "custard apple" and **an** "peaceful;" [ŋ] <ng> in **ngang** "horizontal;" [t] <t> in **ta** "we" and **át** "drown out the noise;" [k] <c> in **cá** "fish" and **ác** "cruel." The consonant [p] <p> appears only as a final consonant, as in **áp** "press," **cáp** "cable" and **táp** "catch in one's mouth." Compare with **initial consonant**.

FRICATIVE CONSONANT The term refers to the manner of articulation of a consonant when two organs of speech come close together, and the airstream from inside moving between them produces audible friction. There is no complete closure between the two organs. [v] <v> and [f] <ph> are fricative consonants in Vietnamese. Compare with **stop**.

GLOTTAL STOP The term refers to a sound whose occlusion and release occur at the glottis. In Vietnamese the high-rising broken tone and low-falling broken tone are accompanied by a glottal stop at the end of their production.

HOMONYMS Words whose forms are identical but whose meanings are different and cannot be connected. For instance, English words *can* "be able" and *can* "container" are homonyms. Vietnamese words **can** "cane," **can** "Heavenly stem," **can** "dissuage" and **can** "container" are homonyms. When two (or more) words are spelled identically but pronounced differently, we have **homographs**. For instance, English words *wind* [wɪnd] and *wind* [waɪnd] are homographs. Vietnamese does not have homographs. When two (or more) words are pronounced identically but spelled differently, we have **homophones**. For example, English words *beat* and *beet* are homophones. In the Hanoi dialect of Vietnamese, **chú** "uncle" and **trú** "take shelter," **dữ** "ferocious" and **giữ** "hold" are homophones.

IMPLOSIVE CONSONANT In this work implosive consonants are referred to as the final consonants which produce an inward flow of lung air when the complete closure of the speech organs is released. In Vietnamese, the final consonants [p] <p> and [t] <t> in the words **bóp** "squeeze with one's hand" and **cắt** "cut" are implosive consonants as opposed to **plosive** consonants. Vietnamese does not have plosive final consonants. The final consonants [p] <p> and [t] <t> in the English words *bop* and *cut* are plosive. See **plosive consonant**.

INITIAL CONSONANT Vietnamese has twenty-one initial consonants (see 7.2.3). Only five of them can appear at the end of a syllable as final consonants, which are [m] <m>, [n] <n>, [ŋ] <ng>, [t] <t> and [k] <c>. Compare with **final consonant**.

LABIALIZATION The term refers to the lips rounding as a secondary articulation. The lips start rounding when an initial consonant begins to be produced and stop rounding at the beginning of the nuclear vowel. The Vietnamese labialized words **qua** "go through," **đoá** "classifier for flowers," **hoạ** "painting and **loà** "blind" contrast with non-labialized **ca** "shift," **đá** "kick," **hạ** "summer" and **là** "be" respectively.

LATERAL CONSONANT When a lateral consonant is articulated, airstream flows past both sides of the tongue. The consonant [l] <l> in most languages is a lateral consonant.

MONOPHTHONG A vowel whose quality does not change at any time in a single syllable. Vietnamese has eleven monophthong vowels, which are [i] <i> / <y>, [e] <ê>, [ɛ] <e> / <a>, [ɯ] <ư>, [ɤ] <ơ>, [ɤ̆] <â>, [ɑ] <a>, [ɑ̆] <ă> / <a>, [u] <u>, [o] <ô>, [ɔ] <o>. Compare with **diphthong**.

NASAL CONSONANT When a nasal consonant is articulated, the soft palate is lowered so that airstream passes through the nose. The consonants [m] <m> and [n] <n> in most languages are nasal consonants. Vietnamese does not have nasal vowels, like the French [ã] in *an, champ, dent*; [ɛ̃] in *cinq, main, simple*; [œ̃] in *un, lundi*; and [ɔ̃] in *bon, mon, son*.

NON-SYLLABIC VOWEL In Vietnamese, a non-syllabic vowel is not used to form a syllable. The two final semivowels in Vietnamese [i̯] and [u̯] are non-syllabic. They follow a nuclear vowel and are pronounced shorter than their nuclear vowel counterparts.

OPPOSITION The difference of sounds based on their distinctive features. For instance, the difference between the initial consonants [d] <d> and [t] <t> in the English words *dab* and *tab*, or [d] <đ> and [t] <t> in the Vietnamese words **đáp** "respond" and **táp** "catch in one's mouth" is the opposition "voiced" vs. "voiceless." The difference between the two Vietnamese nuclear vowels [ɑ] <a> and [ɑ̆] <ă> as in **đáp** "respond" and **đắp** "build" is the opposition "long" vs. "short."

PITCH The highness or lowness of a musical note. Some Vietnamese tones are differentiated only by the pitch. For instance, **Á** "Asia" and **à** "a particle used in a number of grammatical constructions" are contrasted with each other by the high pitch vs. low pitch.

PLOSIVE CONSONANT In this work plosive consonants are referred to as the final consonants which produce an outward flow of lung air when the complete closure of the speech organs is released. In English, the final consonants [p] <p> and [t] <t> in the words *bop* and *cut* are plosive consonants as opposed to **implosive** consonants. Compare with the Vietnamese words **bóp** and **cắt** whose final consonants are implosive. See **implosive consonant**.

This term is also used to refer to stop consonants.

PHONEME An abstract minimum unit in the sound system of a language which is used to distinguish meaningful units. A phoneme is composed of a number of distinctive features. For instance, the phonemes /d/ and /t/ distinguish the English words *down* and *town*, or the Vietnamese words **đổ** "pour" and **tổ** "nest" by the distinctive features "voiced" vs. "voiceless."

> Glossary of phonetic terms

PROGRESSIVE ASSIMILATION see **assimilation**

REGISTER TONE see **tone**

REGRESSIVE ASSIMILATION see **assimilation**

RETROFLEX The term refers to the place of articulation of some consonants. A retroflex consonant is articulated with the tongue tip turned up towards or curled back under the hard palate. Vietnamese has three retroflex [tʃ] <tr>, [ş] <s> and [ʐ] <r>, that exist only in several dialects spoken in central Vietnam. The Hanoi dialect does not have these retroflex consonants.

ROLL(ED) The term refers to the manner of articulation of some consonants. A roll(ed) consonant is articulated by the rapid vibration of one organ of speech against another, as of the tip of the tongue against the teethridge. The consonant [r] is articulated in this way. In modern Vietnamese, this roll(ed) consonant is found only in some dialects spoken in central Vietnam and in the Mekong Delta area. It is also called a *trill*.

SCHWA The neutral vowel [ə] which appears in many unstressed syllables of English, including the syllables where a stressed vowel becomes unstressed. For instance, the initial character <a> in *aback, abide, again, apart*; in the middle of a word: *entra nce*; or <o> in *co nfirm*, <ir> in *confir mation*. The Vietnamese nuclear vowels [ɤ] <ơ> and [ɤ̆] <â> are produced with the tongue in a position that is to some degree similar to the English [ə]; they are, however, the main vowels of a syllable.

STOP CONSONANT The term refers to the manner of articulation of a consonant when the organs of speech come together, then completely cut off the flow of air momentarily (a complete closure of the organs occurs), followed by their abrupt separation. [p] <p> and [t] <t> are stop consonants.

SYLLABLE A unit of speech that is next bigger than a speech sound. In Vietnamese, a syllable consists at least of two components, which are a tone and a nuclear vowel. For instance, Á "Asia" is composed of the nuclear vowel [ɑ] and the high-rising tone. The number of components of a syllable can be increased by adding an initial consonant in front of the vowel to have the pattern CV (C: consonant, V: vowel) as in **cá** "fish;" by adding a final (VC) as in **án** "an action in law;" or by both (CVC), as in **cán** "handle." A syllable may be labialized (C^wVC)[1] as in **quán** "eatery." In the case of **quán**, all five components of a syllable are present.

Syllable is the smallest meaningful unit of the Vietnamese language. In most cases, it is equivalent to a word.

TONE A particular pitch or movement in pitch serving to distinguish syllables and, accordingly, words that are composed of the same sounds in a tone language. In other words, in a tone language each syllable and, accordingly, each word is characterized by a distinct tone. When the pitch pattern of a tone does not significantly change during its production, such a tone is called a **register** tone. When the pitch pattern of a tone changes, such a tone

Glossary of phonetic terms

is called **contour** tone. Vietnamese has six tones. The mid-level, low-falling and high-rising tones are register tones. The low-falling-risng, high-rising broken and low-falling broken tones are contour tones.

TRILL see **roll(ed)**

VOICED CONSONANT A voiced consonants is produced while the vocal cords are vibrating. English [b] <b>, [m] <m>, [v] <v>, [ð] <th>, etc. are voiced consonants. Vietnamese [b] <b>, [m] <m>, [v] <v>, [d] <đ>, etc. are voiced consonants. Compare with **voiceless consonant**.

VOICELESS CONSONANT A voiceless consonant is produced without the vibration of the vocal cords. For instance, English [p] <p>, [f] <f> / <ph>, [θ] <th> are voiceless consonants. Vietnamese [f] <ph>, [t] <t>, [tʰ] <th> are voiceless consonants. Compare with **voiced consonant**.

VOWELS The speech sounds in the articulation of which the airstream from inside does not encounter any occlusion or obstruction caused by the speech organs, as opposed to **consonants**. In Vietnamese the vowel is one of the two mandaroty components of a syllable. The other mandatory component is the tone. Compare with **consonants**.

 Note

1 The symbol "ʷ" in IPA refers to the labialization.

Bibliography

Carr, Philip. 2013. *English Phonetics and Phonology: An Introduction*. 2nd ed. Oxford, UK; Malden, MA: Wiley-Blackwell.

Clark, John and Yallop, Collin. 1995. *An Introduction to Phonetics and Phonology*. 2nd ed. Oxford, UK; Cambridge, MA: Blackwell.

Crystal, David. 1997. *The Cambridge Encyclopedia of Language*. 2nd ed. Cambridge: Cambridge University Press.

Crystal, David. 1997. *Dictionary of Linguistics and Phonetics*. 4th ed. Oxford, UK; Malden, MA: Blackwell.

Deutsche Sprache. Kleine Enzyklopädie. 1983. Leipzig: VEB Bibliographisches Institut.

Đoàn Thiện Thuật. 2016. *Ngữ âm tiếng Việt (Vietnamese Phonetics)*. Hà Nội: Nhà xuất bản Đại học Quốc gia Hà Nội.

Đỗ Hữu Châu. 1981. *Từ vựng – ngữ nghĩa tiếng Việt (Vietnamese Lexicology and Semantics)*. Hà Nội: Nhà xuất bản giáo dục.

Greenbaum, Sidney. 1996. *The Oxford English Grammar*. Oxford: Oxford University Press.

Handbook of the International Phonetic Association. 1999. Cambridge: Cambridge University Press.

Hoàng Phê (chief editor). 2001. *Từ điển tiếng Việt (Vietnamese Dictionary)*. Hà Nội: Viện ngôn ngữ học, Trung tâm từ điển học (Institute of Linguistics, Center for Dictionaries).

Katamba, Francis. 1989. *An Introduction to Phonology*. London and New York: Longman.

Lê Phạm Thuý-Kim, Ngô Như Bình and Kim-Loan Hill. 2004. *Proficiency Guidelines for Vietnamese*. Group of Universities for the Advancement of Vietnamese Abroad (GUAVA). https://guavamerica.wixsite.com/guava/proficiency-guidelines

Leech, Geoffrey and Svartvik, Jan. 1994. *A Communicative Grammar of English*. 2nd ed. London and New York: Longman.

Lexikon Sprachwissenschaftlicher Termini. 1985. Leipzig: VEB Bibliographisches Institut.

Bibliography

Merriam-Webster's Advanced Learner's English Dictionary. 2008. Springfield, MA: Merriam-Webster, Inc.

Ngô Như Bình. 2010. *Continuing Vietnamese.* Tokyo, Japan; Rutland, VT; Singapore: Charles E. Tuttle, Inc.

Ngô Như Bình. 2013. *Elementary Vietnamese.* 3rd ed. Tokyo, Japan; Rutland, VT; Singapore: Charles E. Tuttle, Inc.

Ngô Như Bình. 2016. *Suggestions on How to Improve Vietnamese Alphabet and Spelling Rules.* Paper presented at 3rd International Conference on Vietnamese and Taiwanese Studies, National Cheng Kung University, Taiwan.

Ngô Như Bình and Trần Hoài Bắc. 2005. *Teaching and Learning Framework for Vietnamese.* Council of Teachers of Southeast Asian Languages (COTSEAL).

Nguyễn Đình-Hoà. 1995. *Vietnamese-English Dictionary.* Lincolnwood, IL: NTC Publishing Group.

Nguyễn Đình-Hoà. 1997. *Vietnamese.* Amsterdam and Philadelphia, PA: John Benjamin Publishing Co.

Nguyễn Kim Thản. 1997. *Nghiên cứu ngữ pháp tiếng Việt (A Vietnamese Grammar).* Hà Nội: Nhà xuất bản giáo dục.

Nguyễn Tài Cẩn. 2011. *Nguồn gốc và quá trình hình thành cách đọc Hán-Việt (Chinese-Vietnamese Transliteration).* Hà Nội: Nhà xuất bản giáo dục.

Nguyễn Văn Khang. 2007. *Từ ngoại lai trong tiếng Việt (Loanwords in Vietnamese).* Hà Nội: Nhà xuất bản Giáo dục.

Panfilov, Valery Sergejevich 1993. *Грамматический строй вьетнамского языка (Grammatical Structure of Vietnamese).* Saint Petersburg: Saint Petersburg University Press.

Shiltova Alla Petrovna, Ngô Như Bình and Norova Natalia Viktorovna. 1989. *Учебное пособие по вьетнамскому языку: начальный курс (A Vietnamese Language Textbook: Beginning Course).* Moscow: Moscow University Press.

Swan, Michael. 1997. *Practical English Usage,* 2nd ed. Oxford: Oxford University Press.

Thompson, Laurence C. 1984–1985. *A Vietnamese Reference Grammar.* Edited by Stephen O'Harrow. Honolulu, HI: University of Hawai'i Press.

Thomson, Audrey J. and Martinet, Agnes V. 1993. *A Practical English Grammar.* Oxford: Oxford University Press.